Something Complete and Great

The Fairleigh Dickinson University Press Series on Willa Cather in Memory of Merrill M. Skaggs

Series Editor: Dr. Laura Winters, College of St. Elizabeth

This series is dedicated to publishing outstanding scholarship on the life, writings, influence, and legacy of this acclaimed American writer, whether single-author volumes or essay collections.

On the Web at http://www.fdu.edu/fdupress

Publications

Holly Blackford (editor), *Something Complete and Great: The Centennial Study of* My Ántonia (2017)

Sarah Cheney Watson and Ann Moseley (editors), *Willa Cather and Aestheticism: From Romanticism to Modernism* (2012)

Christine Kephart, *The Catherian Cathedral: Gothic Cathedral Iconography in Willa Cather's Fiction* (2011)

Lucy Marks and David Porter, *Seeking Life Whole: Willa Cather and the Brewsters* (2009)

Wendy K. Perriman (editor), *Willa Cather and the Dance: "A Most Satisfying Elegance"* (2009)

John J. Murphy and Merrill M. Skaggs (editors), *Willa Cather: New Facts, New Glimpses, Revisions* (2008)

Joseph Urgo and Merrill M. Skaggs (editors), *Violence, The Arts, and Willa Cather* (2008)

Merrill M. Skaggs, *Willa Cather's New York: New Essays on Cather in the City* (2000)

Sally Peltier Harvey, *Redefining the American Dream: The Novels of Willa Cather* (1995)

Jo Ann Middleton, *Willa Cather's Modernism: A Study of Style and Technique* (1990)

Something Complete and Great

The Centennial Study of *My Ántonia*

Edited by
Holly Blackford

FAIRLEIGH DICKINSON UNIVERSITY PRESS
Madison • Teaneck

Published by Fairleigh Dickinson University Press
Copublished by The Rowman & Littlefield Publishing Group, Inc.
4501 Forbes Boulevard, Suite 200, Lanham, Maryland 20706
www.rowman.com

Unit A, Whitacre Mews, 26-34 Stannary Street, London SE11 4AB

British Library Cataloguing in Publication Information Available

Library of Congress Cataloging-in-Publication Data

Names: Blackford, Holly editor.
Title: Something complete and great : the centennial study of My Ántonia/
    editor, Holly Blackford.
Description: Madison : Fairleigh Dickinson University Press ; Lanham,
    Maryland : Copublished by The Rowman & Littlefield Publishing Group, Inc.,
    2017. | Series: The Fairleigh Dickinson University Press series on
Willa Cather in memory of Merrill M. Skaggs | Includes bibliographical
    references and index.
Identifiers: LCCN 2017038054 (print) | LCCN 2017044099 (ebook)
Subjects: LCSH: Cather, Willa, 1873-1947. My ?Antonia.
Classification: LCC PS3505.A87 (ebook) | LCC PS3505.A87 M894575 2017
(print)
    | DDC 813/.52—dc23

LC record available at https://lccn.loc.gov/2017038054

ISBN: 978-1-68393-125-6 (cloth)
ISBN: 978-1-68393-127-0 (paper)
ISBN: 978-1-68393-126-3 (Electronic)

Contents

PART III: TRANSGENDER

PART IV: TRANSHUMAN

PART V: TRANSITION

Introduction

Cather's Sod House of Fiction

Introduction to the Centennial Study of My Ántonia

Holly Blackford

In a beautifully crafted meditation on the wonders and limits of human vision, characteristic of the work of Willa Cather, Father Latour in *Death Comes for the Archbishop* explains to his partner Joseph how he understands the emotions of mortal beings in relation to a transcendental force:

> One might almost say that an apparition is human vision corrected by divine love. I do not see you as you really are, Joseph; I see you through my affection for you. The Miracles of the Church seem to me not to rest so much upon faces or voices or healing power coming suddenly near to us from afar off, but upon our perceptions being made finer, so that for a moment our eyes can see and our ears can hear what is there about us always.[1]

These haunting lines, to me, put forth the theory of artistic vision that Cather first perfected in *My Ántonia*, which provides a vision of a subject through affection, so that for a moment our eyes can see and our ears can hear what is there about us always.

My Ántonia situates its subject through human emotions and perceptions, yet achieves a miraculous "more." Jim does not see Nebraska, Ántonia, or any of his cast of characters in his reminiscence as they really are, but he sees them through his affection for them, and this affection bequeaths to us both a momentary vision and a larger apparition, not easily forgotten. Through the lens of *My Ántonia* we see more than a character like Jim can see, not through a healing power "coming suddenly near us from afar off" but through our perceptions of the world being made finer. This volume of essays marks the power and influence *My Ántonia* has held for one hundred years, along with its complexities, ambiguities, and critical conversations. We situate the value of the novel as not only embodying the cusp of the nineteenth- and

1

twentieth-century art of American literature, but also as presenting an intellectual puzzle that is both beautiful and inconclusive, or perhaps beautifully
inconclusive. There will be critical interpretations for another hundred years
because the novel presents more than any one critic can see.

The sense that there *is* a reality glimpsed beyond the novel's vision, a
woman named Ántonia beyond Jim's manuscript and a place called Nebraska
beyond Jim's desire to dissolve into it, is always present in Cather. *My
Ántonia* admits that human vision is always partial and not divine, but that
something more surrounds the eye. There is an immense amount of critical
pleasure in analyzing the glimpses Jim and the narrator of the Introduction
provide and in questioning the apparition suddenly visible with certain tools
of criticism. This volume deploys a variety of methods: biographical and historical criticism; intertextuality and ecological study; childhood studies and
psychoanalytic/queer theory; as well as narrative theory, Marxist theory, and
translation theory to uncover strands of a dexterously woven novel that has
been appreciated for its subject (pastoral literature, immigration, settlement,
feminism); its complex point of view; its intriguing author; and its meticulous
craft, imagery, and prose.

My Ántonia develops elements of Cather's earlier *O Pioneers!*, a pivotal
novel in which Cather reached for an organic American subject, but its perceptions are finer because the art of perception is at the forefront of meaning.
In the feminist *O Pioneers!*, there is "the great fact" of land,[2] but it is unclear
what Alexandra appreciates of it—she seems to register the vivid accounts
of the narrator sometimes, and sometimes her eyes go from the shining pond
to the sorghum patch. Ántonia, who checks on her trees in the middle of
the night, is not Alexandra. The relation between something "complete and
great" and the "great fact" of land bespeaks the stylistic difference between
the two powerful novels. Everyday details of living, great facts, petty feelings, and experiences of human life are always in dialogue with greater vision in Cather; pressing this relationship through time, Cather in *My Ántonia*
determined that the relationship between these matters was essential. While
in a story like "Paul's Case" or a novel like *The Professor's House*, everyday
(often female) details are an annoyance, in the way of the transcendent, in
My Ántonia and *Death Comes for the Archbishop* the finer perceptions are
rooted in the gritty details of how people live, pray, plow, raise children,
design houses, and plant trees. Prosaic reality and moments of sharp clarity
and beauty, as one derives from reading Cather's fiction, are a matter of human perception. It is hard for me not to think of Jim as an early version of
the mature Latour combined with the exuberant Joseph, or of the Professor in
The Professor's House who demonstrates the success of Cather's rendition of
male elegy, but who has Augusta rather than his Ántonia to keep him alive.

The relationship between artistic vision and the reality of life is fleshed out in an experimental and masterful manner in *My Ántonia*. This is why I title my introduction "Cather's Sod House of Fiction," alluding to the novel theory of Henry James on the posted presence of the artist piercing an aperture on the human scene and creating a window onto the house of fiction.[3] It is the perspective that makes *My Ántonia* modern and Jamesian, whereas the core subject of settlement answers a nineteenth-century mythos, even while refusing a romance or bildungsroman. Cather admired and followed the tradition of Henry James early in her career, and in 1908 James explained his technique of putting consciousness at the center of narrative. A complex consciousness (Jim's and the artist's) resides at the heart of *My Ántonia*, much as James's signature modern moment in *A Portrait of a Lady* is Isabel looking into the firelight and reflecting on her entrapment, an internal and backward-moving reflection rather than action or plot. As James writes in his 1908 preface to *Portrait*, many accuse him of not having story enough,[4] precisely the impressionist technique of consciousness we find in the elaborately structured consciousness of Jim in *My Ántonia*, for the novel is careful to frame its books as "his" stream of consciousness. Quite literally, when Jim goes to see the Shimerdas' dugout for the first time, he narrates an aperture that is uniquely his own, partly a result of his appreciation for Ántonia and partly his severe judgment from his grandmother's background. It is this unique and often fluctuating stream of Jim's consciousness that defines the difficulty we have in interpreting *My Ántonia* and what Jim is all about in relation to her. The point of view makes it as complicated as the living subject shining through and beyond its sod house of fiction. A sod house means you have to look a little harder to see it.

For Cather, the settlement project, rather than Jamesian drawing rooms, became the repeated means of pressure for whether reality and dreams would balance; she retold this story from myriad vantage points and in myriad settings, from Plains to Southwest to Quebec. In *My Ántonia* she refused to settle the balance and allowed two narratives to stand—the narrative of the "great fact" of the land, embodied in an earth mother's rise, and the reality of Western dreams, never satisfied and never at rest. Both the female and male stories of American mythography receive their due in this collection. The scholars here feel that Ántonia and Jim are the core couple of the novel and that the "real" subject of the novel is neither Ántonia nor Jim, for they belong to many communities inside and outside the novel.

My Ántonia is a transitional novel in Cather's technique because it fuses her early Jamesian imitation with the organic, vivid voice and natural subject she developed in *O Pioneers!* Sarah Orne Jewett, of course, encouraged Cather to write what she knew, and like Jim Burden she knew what it was like to be dislocated to the plains of Nebraska—to what Jim and Cather see as a radical lack of human boundaries and visions of nothingness, openness, wild grasses, and human dwellings making barely an etch on ancient rock, to borrow metaphors from her other novels—"The record of the plow was insignificant, like the feeble scratches on stone left by prehistoric races."[5] Measuring human perception against ancient rock, which makes humans feel small and insignificant, became a philosophical question of interest throughout Cather's fiction. The slow, steady progress of human civilization was marked by her fiction lovingly and realistically, as a timeless and sometimes futile and hopeless endeavor. In *My Ántonia* these efforts require an eye of affection so that the miracle of human strength and perseverance was indeed marked by fine perception, by art—by Jim and the meaning he derives from his memories of Ántonia. Jim gives divine love to Ántonia, indeed creates her into a divinity and muse, and this one-hundred-year assessment focuses on the complexities and legacies of that act for the communities that have made the novel "their" Ántonia.

  My Ántonia fuses stylistic approaches of Cather's early career, and these fusions give it a peculiar power. Cather's early work featured Jamesian settings and stories; Cather's first novel *Alexander's Bridge* is intensely Jamesian and expresses anxiety about entering the terrain of longer fiction. Revising it while also developing "Alexandra" and "The White Mulberry Tree," Cather began a shift, enhancing work already present in "The Bohemian Girl" and "The Enchanted Bluff," a way to convey less Jamesian, urban dreams and both appreciate the everyday domestic efforts of women yet maintain an outsider perspective, as argued by Sharon O'Brien in *Willa Cather: The Emerging Voice.*[6] While the work of women is distasteful and abject in "Paul's Case," it is admirable and makes Emil dizzy in "The Bohemian Girl." There is also an appreciation of the land in *O Pioneers!* that in *My Ántonia* fuses with appreciation for the arc of a female life adapting to the soil and country. Cather claimed to have found her voice in the Southwest—in what we will understand as ancient rock. Indeed, early on in her career she derided women's writing and failed to appreciate female arts, until she discovered the cliff-dwelling ruins, domestic yet "sculptural" designs nestled in crevices. Jim's participant-observer stance on Ántonia's cultural adaptation and her father's Old World extinction is anthropologically informed, intertwined with a larger American interest in the archeological history of the Anasazi ruins, the contours of landscape in the Southwest, and artistic visions that inflect the red grasses rampant in *My Ántonia*. Understanding the cultural approach early twentieth-century Americans brought to the subject of archeology and native history deepens the stylistic inspirations we find in *My Ántonia*. It is to etchings on ancient rock that we must turn, conceptually, to situate *Ántonia*.

ARCHEOLOGICAL INSPIRATION FOR *MY ÁNTONIA*

Cather shared with her culture interest in the archeological ruins in the South-west, the cliff-dwellings she visited before writing *My Ántonia*. The role of the ruins as artistic inspiration surfaces in her earlier *The Song of the Lark*, a self-reflective narrative of Cather's rise as an artist. Cather's 1912 visit to the ruins of the Anasazi "made her rethink Nebraska, see it against a perspective of native as well as immigrant cultures."[7] In addition to the inspiring land-scape combining crevices and open space, which she used to depict Nebraska, she was inspired by the cliff-dwellings:

> Above all the ancient cliff-dwellings of the vanished Indian tribes, relics of an extraordinary and beautiful civilization, which she saw at Walnut Canyon, Arizona, would haunt her for ever. This was far older history than that of the mid-Western pioneers (though it provided a more ancient version of the interweaving of cultures which so interested her at home), one that had fascinated her since childhood. Seeing it, at last, had a very powerful effect on her.[8]

Just as she rendered the cliff-dwelling ruins and pottery as sources of heal-ing, nourishment, and artistic inspiration for her autobiographical character Thea in *Song of the Lark*, Cather found in them visions of an organic style that fused nature and art and complimented her earlier writing in the style of Henry James. The complex narrative perspective in *My Ántonia* (Jim's) embodies the legacy of Henry James in Cather's work—a study of conscious-ness and its contours—whereas the principle artistic subject (Ántonia, the Plains) embodies what had become in the late nineteenth century a primeval and classical myth of the rise of "early races."

For Jim, whose consciousness revolves around impressionistic perceptions of Ántonia, watching the female immigrant adapt to the tough Nebraska envi-ronment recapitulates myths of the rise of (wo)man and civilization. Cather's own inspiration from pottery of the cliff-dwellers is the unspoken undercur-rent of *My Ántonia*'s power. Echoing the way Thea imagines that Indian women's pottery was an aesthetic mold in which life was captured, Cather imagined Ántonia as an artistic object anchoring perspective:

> Elsie Sergeant famously recalled [Cather], early in 1916, placing an old Sicilian jar filled with scented stock in the middle of a bare, round, antique table, mov-ing the lamp to fall on its glazed colours, and saying (her voice faltering and her eyes filling with tears): "I want my new heroine to be like this—like a rare object in the middle of a table, which one may examine from all sides."[9]

Applying styles of classical pastoral and European painting to her novel,[10] including impressionism, Cather created Ántonia as a fertile muse through whom Jim can create a poetic mythology of idealized American history.

In her biography of Cather, Sharon O'Brien claims that Jim's paradoxical longings for and terror of self-dissolution in the land are rooted in Cather's feelings toward her mother, femininity, and the Nebraska landscape. Her uprooting from gentle, cultivated Virginia to the brutal Plains coincided also with separation from her mother, who was burdened with other children and quite ill. Her early descriptions of Nebraska and small town impressions are neither nourishing nor positive. It was not until Cather experienced the Southwest as an adult that she reconceptualized how to represent the Nebraska plains as expansive space with contours in which traces of human life could be excavated. So many underground and burrowing spaces in the novel correspond to archeological ideas of jars and fragments surfacing to give an artistic but also ambiguous and incomplete vision of culture.

We can trace Cather's ideas about uncluttered prose and sparse landscapes to her feelings about seeing the ruins. Published in *The Denver Times* in 1916, Cather's essay "Mesa Verde Wonderland Is Easy to Reach" describes the cliff-dwelling ruins and her railway journey to them, juxtaposing the difficulty of Nordenskjöld's original journey to reach the inaccessible ruins with today's easy journey and her pleasure in the people of Mancos.[11] The overall purpose of the essay, however, is just the opposite: it is to compare the ugly cluttered residences of modern life with the beautiful, uncluttered cliff-dwellings as they exist in concert with nature as a sort of sculptural design. Excavating fragments of an earlier culture is both a method to defamiliarize one's own culture—the purpose of anthropological fieldwork like Margaret Mead's—and an impossible task of reconstruction because archeological items lack context and history. Cather's 1916 essay itemizes the things found in the ruins and the architecture of the cliff-dwellers to conclude that they are "an affront" to the messy, cluttered lives of modern America. It does not take much effort, however, to understand that one of the uncluttered designs she sought was in her writing itself.

Her description contrasts the "hundreds of ugly little American towns" with the ruins, seeing them as "absolutely harmonious with its site and setting" because the villages are "built back in these gracious natural arches in the cliffs":

The stone villages in the cliff arches are a successful evasion of ugliness—perhaps an indolent evasion. Color, simplicity, space, an absence of clutter, the houses of the Pueblo Indians today and of their ancestors on the Mesa Verde are a reproach to the messiness in which we live.

Everything in the cliff dweller villages points to a tempered, settled, ritualistic life, where generations went on gravely and reverently repeating the past, rather than bathing for anything new. Their lives were so full of ritual and symbolism that all their common actions were ceremonial—planting, harvesting, hunting, feasting, fasting. . . . Their architecture and their religions were their national purpose. . . . They seem not to have struggled to overcome their environment. They accommodated themselves to it, interpreted it and made it personal; lived in a dignified relation with it.[12]

It is easy to see Cather's personal feelings here; known as a little conservative herself and aspiring toward an uncluttered writing linked to the environment and past, for which she was critiqued by contemporary writers especially during the war, Cather locates in the Mesa some of the traits in herself—the desire to leave ugliness and messiness out and to make the everyday ceremonial. Her essay resonates with Jim's final desire to feel in Ántonia "the goodness of planting and tending and harvesting."[13]

O'Brien makes the case that in her discovery of Indian women's pottery, which transcended the practical by being aesthetic and which echoed the shape of the woman's body, Cather found a woman's artistry that hitherto she had devalued.[14] Cather's autobiographical character Thea in *The Song of the Lark* interprets the cliff-dwelling vessels of Panther Canyon as "an effort to make a sheath, a mould in which to imprison for a moment the shining, elusive element which is life itself,"[15] an artistic awakening that Ann Moseley discusses as equally influenced by Henri Bergson's *Creative Evolution*, which Cather read.[16] Cather returned to the Southwest with her partner Edith Lewis in 1915 while writing portions of *My Ántonia*,[17] but Cather had already written about the "enchanted bluffs" as a point of fantasy for pioneer children in 1909.[18] In her story of that name, boys vow they will someday reach the extinct city but they never do because all are fated to grow up into the narrow roles of adulthood. Edith Lewis explained that the cliff-dwellers were a native myth of the American West: "'children knew about them before they were conscious of knowing about them.'"[19] The suggestion of the cliff-dwellers as a regional unconscious distills the point that they could define a mythography of the West even though they had nothing to do with the West: "later Willa Cather viewed the region [of the Southwest] as her artistic birthplace. There, like Thea Kronborg, she thought she had found her voice."[20] If you know this story of the ruins and how they were represented throughout Cather's work, you cannot help seeing Jim's first encounter with Ántonia in the context of this trip. The clay cliffs of Ántonia's dugout at Squaw Creek, edged with "gold and silver trees in fairy tales" and encircled by blue sky and "wine-colored grass,"[21] resemble the idealized Mesa Verde landscapes throughout Cather's writing.

On her 1915 trip Cather was told the story of Richard Wetherill's discovery of the cliff palace from his brother, and in her 1916 essay on Mesa Verde she had begun her reconstruction of Wetherill's discovery, having also at some point read Swedish explorer Nordenskjöld's 1893 archeological book on the

Mesa.[22] While at this point Cather was early in her reading, later her more extensive readings in archeology and anthropology would move her from "the evolutionism of *The Song of the Lark*, in which distinct cultural manifestations are arranged into a singular hierarchical sequence of progressive cultural development," to the "cultural relativism of *The Professor's House*" and the "cultural borderlands of *Death Comes for the Archbishop*," with emphasis on intercultural mediation and negotiation.[23] The Southwest offered Cather the opportunity to reflect on the drama of cultural contact; as David Harrell discusses in the Cather archive, Cather's 1916 story of Wetherill's discovery of the ruins had already shifted in drama and perspective, resembling the rudimentary elements of Tom Outland's journey in her later novel *The Professor's House*.[24] *My Ántonia* falls in the early portion of this journey in understanding archeology and culture. Neither evolution/recapitulation nor cultural relativism, it embodies one white perspective grappling with and vacillating between perspectives on cultural shifts, fractures, and erasures.

As Michael Tavel Clarke discusses in "Lessons from the Past: The Cliff Dwellers and New Historicism," the myriad fantasies about the cliff-dwellers in novels, artwork, and popular conceptions at the turn of the century speak volumes about "old Americans'" cultural anxiety about immigration.[25] Two major World's Fair exhibits in 1893 and 1904, a series of monographs about the ruins (1909, 1911), and myriad novelist representations rework the idea of the ruins as a site of identification for white Americans. The ruins were interpreted as a civilization vanished because it was peaceful and highly advanced, subject to the warlike nomadic tribes at the base, a trope used to reflect on the worry that Old Americans would become extinct given tides of immigrants not idealized by Frederick Turner:

> Jews, Italians, Bohemians, Greeks, and other Eastern and Southern Europeans. In fact, Turner was displeased with the shift in immigration and alarmed by the growing numbers of Eastern and Southern European immigrants (Hofstadter 109). Turner's history of the United States was therefore compatible with and easily assimilated into nativist ideologies. . . . Published in the same year that Turner delivered his speech, Henry B. Fuller's novel *The Cliff-Dwellers* uses a similar preoccupation with Native Americans in order to ruminate on the effects of a growing national pluralism brought about by a recent expansion of immigrations.[26]

As Richard Harris asserts in his comparison of Henry Blake Fuller and Cather, cliff-dweller ruins were commonly used to denote modern skyscrapers, but *The Song of the Lark*, like Fuller's novel, specifically expresses the anxiety that cultural uplift in Chicago leads to extinction.[27] While the cliff-dwellers overturned prior ideas of savage Indians, they were also erroneously described as being white or having blonde, soft hair.[28] Identification with the cliff-dwellers was therefore used to express panic about white Americans facing extinction from "overcivilization." For Jim, displacement is not panic but pleasure. Yet Ántonia is both "other" and "not other," properly socialized and translated, as Diane Prenatt argues in this volume. The real complexity of the novel as a whole, however, derives from how self-conscious Cather is in *My Ántonia* about issues of translation, adaptation, and the rise and fall of cultures and communities.

Susan Rosowski feels that in celebrating the primitive Cather differentiated herself from Turner's frontier thesis:

> Like him Cather described a reversion to primitive conditions. But where Turner wrote of the primitive as an early stage in the evolution of human civilization, Cather wrote of the primitive as an original or archetypal nature. Whereas Turner's primitive is overcome by the progress of western expansion, Cather's primitive is revealed by an awakening of desire.[29]

Jim's awakening desire in the text is a curious desire to feel erased, obliterated, and dissolved, therefore *uncluttered*—to become the silent potter of a vessel that captures life. In doing so he pushes the clutter—violence, murder, sexuality—to the margins of consciousness and sorts the fragments of the archeological site. Archeology in *My Ántonia* becomes a way of seeing and configuring consciousness as assembly of the random fragments unearthed from the past and recalled from the land. Jim's sorting of his memories becomes a reflexive text about the project of nineteenth-century myth making, the theory of recapitulation as it became a national story. Its multifaceted and shifting points of view on its own subject will make it attractive to scholars for years to come.

THE CENTENNIAL STUDY OF *MY ÁNTONIA*

As such, critical appreciation has turned to the complexities of perspective and consciousness, nostalgia and reminiscence, and the problems and artistic visions of Jim, set up by the Introduction as a multilayered manuscript. For *My Ántonia* presents many problems as well as miraculous and beautiful perceptions, problems particularly vexed in a postmodern receptive context in which issues of imperialism, multiculturalism, gender, and sexual normativity fuel critical lenses. This is not unlike when Cather fell out of favor for not being urban and real enough, for returning to old-fashioned subjects with what critics saw as sentiment. There are murders, assaults, poverties, and abjections at the margins of Jim's tale; the unspoken has become as delicious as the spoken—recent scholars focus on Native American policy, imperialism abroad (Spain, etc.), and race (the Southern undercurrent) in Blind d'Arnault.[30] The fact that Jim takes center stage in this volume demonstrates the critical turn from subject to teller. Yet Jim is not the ultimate authority on Ántonia, the community in the novel, and the community of reception, which likewise preoccupy the scholars in this collection as they problematize the novel from myriad theoretical and methodological perspectives.

This volume is organized into five parts, which exemplify a certain flow of thought. I have titled them to indicate this flow. "Translation" (part I) signifies issues of language, loss, expression, legibility, and shifts that occur when language uttered at one moment in time *moves* and becomes something else, something to be received or rejected, altered or stabilized. "Tradition" (part II) measures the genre and structure that Cather deployed to situate herself artistically. "Transgender" (part III) explores boyhood intertexts and legacies through which Cather enters a conversation about proper gender and wrongful discrimination. "Transhuman" (part IV) has an unspoken transhumanist lens by arguing that Cather breaks down boundaries between human and nature/land, male and female, past and present, masculine and feminine desire. And finally "Transition" (part V) demonstrates how modernity and change in the social economy lurks in the text and brings it into crisis with the twentieth century, which is instructive for understanding how *My Ántonia* stands at the forefront of social questions and indeterminate answers.

Part I, "Translation," presents three chapters that explore issues of language and reception in varying ways, but all make the point that the reception of text, even by the author herself, shifts over time, space, and culture. The first chapter by Janis P. Stout, "What Willa Cather's Letters Tell Us about the Reception of *My Ántonia*," capitalizes on her recent editing of Cather's letters newly available to the public and to direct quotation. Cather was sensitive to the comments of her personal contacts about her work. Reflecting on the steady rise of *My Ántonia* in reviews, and reflecting on the type of praise achieved—sometimes for authenticity and sometimes for artistry—Cather in her letters tells a fascinating story of her shifting feelings about her work, especially as she changed publishers and vacillated between desiring praise for being "authentic" versus being a serious artist with a long career ahead. Curiously, she began to devalue and misremember praise for *My Ántonia* even while its status as a classic grew assured. Stout's chapter therefore gives us a vision of how Cather *translated* the success of her novel through time.

What happens when one translates from one language to another, from one context or time to another, is both valuable and problematic. Theorizing translation by looking at the international reception of the novel in the last hundred years, Caterina Bernardini in the next chapter, "'People in countries who read it in the strangest languages': The International Reception of *My Ántonia*," analyzes what is lost and what is altered in European translations, focusing on the role of important intellectual writers who pioneered the projects and instances of passages that shift upon translator interpretation. For example, the passage in which Jim first sees Nebraska as not yet a country but the material from which countries are made depends on the multivalent word "country," which various translators have rendered differently within the confines of their languages, sometimes limiting the word to the land or nation rather than the *idea* of country.

The vexed issue of translation is also at stake in the novel itself. The next chapter by Diane Prenatt, "Ántonia's Mother Tongue: Reading and Translating (in) *My Ántonia*," deploys a close reading of language and translation issues in the novel itself to conclude that so much is lost and untranslatable in the novel that the project of narrative itself is deeply in question, much as critics have intuited issues with Jim's sense that he can render "my" Ántonia. In fact, Prenatt argues, Ántonia herself is a product of translation, receiving lessons in proper femininity, housekeeping, and social languages through her apprenticeships in the novel, all of which separate her from her own mother and mother tongue. Not only is femininity contingent upon the translation of Ántonia, but also masculinity and class are dependent upon Jim's status as a translator as well. These three opening essays demonstrate that *My Ántonia* is a classic partly because it reflects upon the project of language so strongly, so openly, and so rewardingly. The novel dwells on the enterprise of translation and perspective through showing how unstable and interpretive conveying anything in language is. Therefore *My Ántonia* will not only have a postmodern, self-reflective presence as it makes the project of narration self-reflexive, but it will also continue to have relevance to many reception communities for its rendition of multicultural communities and impossibilities.

As most critics are aware, the revisions Cather made to *My Ántonia*'s Introduction likewise foreground issues of translating a subject, writing and editing, perspective and collaboration, and narrative struggle. The two essays in part II, "Tradition," explore the literary traditions and style in which Cather operated but also resisted. Melissa J. Homestead, in "'Live Property': Cather's 1926 Revisions to the Introduction of *My Ántonia* and the Specter of Nineteenth-Century Women's Regionalism," analyzes the 1926 erasure of gender in the speaker of the Introduction alongside Cather's letters of dissatisfaction with her publisher's grouping of her with regionalist writers, concluding that Cather removed the regional female writer from the Introduction as she went forward with her new publisher and asserted her faith in herself as a serious artist (someone about whom a centennial study might be conceived). Analyzing narrative structure as closely as Homestead does the specific changes to the frame, Sarah Young deploys a methodological microscope to show us how *My Ántonia* works narratologically. Her chapter, "Violence in the Pastoral: Darkness in the Narrative Structure of *My Ánto-nia*," demonstrates how the novel uses inset stories and layers of storytellers to fold darkness and violence into larger structures of idyllic frames and therefore embeds realism in a tricky and compelling frame series that render feelings of containment, contentment, and pastoral. These placid frames veil horror and, given one perception of Cather as sentimental, demand reassessment as modernist experimentation in multilayered point of view, which is only simple on the surface. In many ways part III of this volume, titled "Transgender," continues this project of reassessment by focusing on how boyhood traditions and intertexts inform both the construction and legacy of Cather's *My Ántonia*. The two chapters in part II, however, analyze Cather's deployment of framing devices so closely and powerfully that it should give new vigor to Wallace Stevens's comment that Cather "takes such pains to conceal her sophistication that it is easy to miss her quality."[31]

As T. S. Eliot argued in "Tradition and the Individual Talent," when a work enters the canon, all the works that come before and after it are changed:

> No poet, no artist of any art, has his complete meaning alone. His significance, his appreciation is the appreciation of his relation to the dead poets and artists. You cannot value him alone; you must set him, for contrast and comparison, among the dead . . . what happens when a new work of art is created is something that happens simultaneously to all the works of art which preceded it. The existing monuments form an ideal order among themselves, which is modified by the introduction of the new (the really new) work of art among them. The existing order is complete before the new work arrives; for order to persist after the supervention of novelty, the *whole* existing order must be, if ever so slightly, altered; and so the relations, proportions, values of each work of art toward the whole are readjusted; and this is conformity between the old and the new.[32]

If parts I and II on language, translation, and tradition demonstrate that substantial works like *My Ántonia* self-consciously make visible their struggle with entry into the ideal order, reflecting on the costs and benefits of translation and reception, then part III, "Transgender," parses out the strands of literary traditions and purposes woven together in *My Ántonia*'s choice of male perspective and theorizing of boyhood. Martin Woodside, in "Boyhood and the Frontier: Nostalgia and Play in *My Ántonia*," compares the parallel text of Hamlin Garland's *Boy Life on the Prairie*, which likely influenced Cather indirectly, and situates the cultural work of constructing boyhood as a site of outgrown prairie nature according to theories of recapitulation and evolution at the time. Psychologists like G. Stanley Hall articulated the need for white men to exercise their primitive or savage boyhoods as an evolutionary stage, and the frontier thesis of Turner only fueled the sense that prairie boyhoods were proper ways to do so. Understanding the cultural as well as literary context for traditions in which Cather was working demonstrates how Cather both engages with and revises dominant boyhood frontier narratives.

Similarly, in my chapter, "The Nebraskan Neverland: The Archeology of Children's Fantasy Fiction in *My Ántonia*," I explore how the work of J. M. Barrie, whom Cather described as a hero of her youth, influenced the way in which Cather combined boyhood, consciousness, psychology, childhood romance, co-gendered bildungsroman, and space as personal and national history. The Neverland provided a model for how a topographical concept could unify and contain these issues. Understanding the Neverland of Barrie's 1911 novel *Peter and Wendy* allows us to see Jim's circulation around Ántonia and Mrs. Harling as akin to Peter's flights around Wendy and Mrs. Darling, ultimately because the Neverland landscape offers a way to visualize national history as a site of the child mind. In the next chapter, "'Obliterating Strangeness': Willa Cather, Truman Capote, and the Influence of *My Ántonia*," Thomas Fahy continues the intertextual discussion of boyhood by exploring how Truman Capote, who admired Cather, utilized Cather's *My Ántonia* in his work, especially *Other Voices, Other Rooms*, using the insider/outsider status of the narrator for the same purpose of critiquing racism and heteronormativity. Social pressures on the queer youth are equally at issue as discrimination against immigrants in *Ántonia*, and this Capote understood intimately. He rendered certain scenes, such as the snake scene, to reflect his engagement with Cather's novel and its core legacy for him. Cather's Jim lives in Capote's novels, and in Joel, as vividly as Ántonia lives in Jim.

Part IV of the volume moves from transgender to transhumanist issues by focusing on desire and nature, particularly on the way in which *My Ántonia* destabilizes and breaks down boundaries in gender, time, space, and land. The first chapter, by Monroe Street, "Hysterical Resistance: Desire and Narrative in *My Ántonia*," looks closely at the way in which the Freudian view of desire advanced in his writings on hysteria informs a reading of Jim's refusal of closure with Ántonia. Street likewise uses the structure of hysterical desire to understand why the narrator of the Introduction needs Jim to tell his story, why Jim needs to tell him or her the story, and the erasure of gender from the structure of desire that Cather effected when she revised her Introduction in 1926. The detachment of desire from gender and specifically gendered bodies and subjects makes *Ántonia* distinctly theorizing and engaging with contemporary ideas of queer performance, leaving the novel far more open to nongendered identities than earlier queer readings have entertained.

The next chapters provide different points of view on nature in *Ántonia* as it inflects the desire to erase boundaries between human and land/nature, and past and present. In "The Image of Nature in the Past in *My Ántonia*," Fangyuan Xi discusses the function of the train as a vehicle linking past and present as well as a theory of wholeness in self, and the way in which language similarly creates human merging with the land in Cather's writing. Linking this with Cather's appreciation for Native American sensibility, Xi's ecological viewpoint demonstrates a powerful source of healing in Cather's writing, with which Jim Cody agrees in his chapter, "*My Ántonia*: Keatsian Negative Capability and the Dissolution of Boundaries." Cody, however, focuses on the need Jim presents for these healing elements, given his fractured and alienated existence. Cody demonstrates that Jim tries to tell his story of Ántonia but she continually eludes him, and he actually establishes his authenticity as a narrator of landscape, not Ántonia, which, of course, furthers this volume's general consensus that Cather offers glimpses, clues, and hints that are stunningly provocative and require further excavation for discussion.

The last part of this volume, "Transition," showcases two powerful chapters on elements of the novel that distinctly signal social change and a shifting future. The first, by Keiko Arai, "A Portrait of a Self-Made Woman: Lena Lingard in *My Ántonia*," deploys a fascinating methodology to unpack Lena's resonance as a creation of images and the New Woman, which was largely, Arai shows, a construction of magazine culture. A creature of fashion and American perceptions of a modern woman, independent but feminine and sexual, Lena stands as an alternative to Ántonia and, in fact, overturns her earth mother image. The final chapter, by Dana Woodcock and Zachary Tavlin, titled "The Gift Economies of *My Ántonia*," deploys a much-needed structuralist and Marxist reading of the various exchange moments in the novel that dwell in moments of gifts and the return of "*hau*" or spirit embedded in the gift, which it would be dangerous not to return, in a precapitalist trade network. Focusing on the food gifts and object exchanges such as the horse collar that cause a rupture, Woodcock and Tavlin use the work of Marcel Mauss and Lewis Hyde to theorize the gap between how communities regard gifts and relationships, which situates a precapitalist economy undergoing rupture and misunderstanding in a new community and economy. Not only do these two chapters situate *My Ántonia* very precisely at the cusp of an industrializing region and cultural change, but they also gesture to the need for dialogue between the novel and twentieth-century cultural contexts and theories of literature.

A novel inviting such a wide variety of methodologies and approaches gestures to a long academic life not only on university syllabi, but also in focused scholarly projects that treat *My Ántonia* comparatively and theoretically. Of course the novel has interest because it is the cross-dressed product of a lesbian writer and a powerful writer who perfected her disciplined craft, but it also has interest for its engagement with narrative and economic theory, psychoanalytic and ecological theory, posthumanist and feminist theory, translation and intertexuality theory, nationalism, classical/archeological mythography, childhood studies, and postmodern self-reflexive form. Its range is wide indeed. "One might almost say that an apparition is human vision corrected by divine love," articulates one of Cather's most patient characters, albeit with his own imperialist limitations. One might say that each critical approach yields a vision corrected by time and further debate, but it is the placement of perception at the heart of Cather's art that yields our intuition of how classic literature makes perceptions "finer, so that for a moment our eyes can see and our ears can hear what is there about us always."

NOTES

1. Willa Cather, *Death Comes for the Archbishop* (1927; New York: Vintage, 1990), 50.
2. Willa Cather, *O Pioneers!* (New York: Bantam, 1989), 10.
3. Henry James, "Preface to the New York Edition," *The Portrait of a Lady*, second edition, ed. Robert Bamberg (New York: Norton, 1995), 3–15.
4. Ibid., 5.
5. Cather, *O Pioneers!*, 13.
6. Sharon O'Brien, *Willa Cather: The Emerging Voice* (New York: Oxford University Press, 1987).
7. John J. Murphy, *My Ántonia: The Road Home* (Boston: Twayne, 1989), 3.
8. Hermione Lee, *Willa Cather: Double Lives* (New York: Pantheon, 1989), 88.
9. Ibid., 136–37.
10. Murphy, *My Ántonia*, 40–56; Janis P. Stout, "The Observant Eye, the Art of Illustration, and Willa Cather's *My Ántonia*," *Cather Studies* 5, *Willa Cather's Ecological Imagination*, edited by Susan Rosowski (Lincoln: University of Nebraska Press, 2003), 128–52; Jean Schwind, "The Benda Illustrations to *My Ántonia*: Cather's 'Silent' Supplement to Jim Burden's Narrative," *PMLA* 100, no. 1 (1985): 51–67; Edward Piacentino, "A Study in Contrasts: Impressionistic Perspectives of Ántonia and Lena Lingard in Cather's *My Ántonia*," *Studies in the Humanities* 12, no. 1 (1985): 39–44.
11. Willa Cather, "Mesa Verde Wonderland Is Easy to Reach," *The Denver Times*, January 31, 1916, 7, archived at *The Willa Cather Archive*, ed. Andrew Jewell (Center for Digital Research in the Humanities: University of Nebraska–Lincoln, 2004–2016), 1–4, accessed March 7, 2014, http://cather.unl.edu/nf056.html.
12. Ibid., 3–4.
13. Willa Cather, *My Ántonia*, Willa Cather Scholarly Edition, ed. Charles W. Mignon and Kari A. Ronning (Lincoln: University of Nebraska Press, 1994), 342.

14. O'Brien, *Willa Cather*, 416–17.

15. Quoted and analyzed autobiographically in Lee, *Willa Cather*, 124.

16. Ann Moseley, "The Creative Ecology of Walnut Canyon: From the Sinagua to Thea Kronborg," *Cather Studies* 5 (2003): 216–36.

17. Lee, *Willa Cather*, 136.

18. Willa Cather, "The Enchanted Bluff," *Classic Literature*, 1–5, accessed March 6, 2014, http://classiclit.about.com/library/bl-etexts/wcather/bl-wcather-enchant.htm.

19. Quoted in O'Brien, *Willa Cather*, 405.

20. Ibid., 417.

21. Cather, *My Ántonia*, 21.

22. Lee, *Willa Cather*, 232.

23. Christopher Schedler, "Writing Culture: Willa Cather's Southwest," in *Willa Cather and the American Southwest*, ed. John N. Swift and Joseph R. Urgo (Lincoln: University of Nebraska Press, 2002), 122–23.

24. David Harrell, "Willa Cather's Mesa Verde Myth," *Cather Studies* 1, in *The Willa Cather Archive*, ed. Andrew Jewell (Center for Digital Research in the Humanities: University of Nebraska–Lincoln, 2004–2013), accessed March 7, 2014, http://cather.unl.edu/cs001_mesaverde.html.

25. Michael Tavel Clarke, "Lessons from the Past: The Cliff Dwellers and New Historicism," *Western American Literature* 42, no. 4 (2008): 395–425.

26. Ibid., 406–7.

27. Richard C. Harris, "Willa Cather and Henry Blake Fuller: More Building Blocks for *The Professor's House*," in *Willa Cather and Modern Cultures, Cather Studies* 9, ed. by Melissa J. Homestead and Guy J. Reynolds (Lincoln: University of Nebraska Press, 2011), 114–32.

28. Clarke, "Lessons from the Past," 404.

29. Susan J. Rosowski, *Birthing a Nation: Gender, Creativity, and the West in American Literature* (Lincoln: University of Nebraska Press, 1999), 60.

30. See Miles Orvell, "Time, Change, and the Burden of Revision in *My Ántonia*," in *New Essays on My Ántonia*, ed. Sharon O'Brien (Cambridge: Cambridge University Press, 1999), 31–56; Elizabeth Ammons, "*My Ántonia* and African American Art," in *New Essays on My Ántonia*, 57–84; Anne Goodwyn Jones, "Displacing Dixie: The Southern Subtext in Anne Goodwyn," in *New Essays on My Antonia*, 85–110.

31. Quoted in Vivian Gornick, Introduction, *O Pioneers!* by Willa Cather (New York: Bantam, 1989), vii.

32. T. S. Eliot, "Tradition and the Individual Talent," 1920, in *Quotidiana*, ed. Patrick Madden, accessed January 23, 2008, http://essays.quotidiana.org/eliot/tradition_and_the_individual.

Part I

TRANSLATION

Chapter One

What Willa Cather's Letters Tell Us about the Reception of *My Ántonia*

Janis P. Stout

In the one hundred years since Willa Cather's *My Ántonia* was published in 1918, it has become one of the most read and best loved of American novels—a regular in high school English courses, a frequent selection in recent years for Community Reads, and one of those books that people of mature years tend to remember warmly from past encounters. It has become an American classic. To explain precisely how that happened would be a complicated undertaking indeed and certainly one beyond my scope here or indeed my ability. It would entail cultural as well as textual considerations, a deep understanding of the book business and the culture of readership, including how an author's subsequent publications affect the stature of earlier books, and perhaps a study of how celebrity status works, or at any rate worked in Cather's case. At minimum, a consideration of the iconic status of *My Ántonia* would entail an examination of its reviews. Fortunately, resources for such a consideration are readily available. Margaret O'Connor's *Willa Cather: The Contemporary Reviews*, while explicitly disclaiming exhaustiveness, reprints a generous representative sampling for each of Cather's books from the "local, regional, national, and international English-language press," as ever wider readership circles responded to them.[1] The scholarly editions of her various books also provide valuable summaries of the reviews, sometimes supplementing and sometimes compressing O'Connor's sampling.

My purpose here is to examine another layer of the reception and understanding of *My Ántonia* by analyzing Cather's own reactions to both the published reviews and the opinions of her family and friends. Not only did her sense of her level of achievement in the novel and the nature of its impact on its readers shift, but in later years she also altered her early sense of its reception, viewing it through a darker lens that clouded the actual reception of her masterwork. By considering reader reactions alongside Cather's memory of these over time, we glean a deepening sense of her artistic purposes and discontents, which came to cluster around the success of this iconic early novel. For undertaking this project, there is essentially only one resource available: the archival record of Cather's letters. She was, in Ann Moseley's words, "far from indifferent to the reception of her books,"[2] and she often wrote to acquaintances, as well as to her publishers, expressing her appreciation (or not) of what they or others had said, as well as her gratification (or not) at reports of sales figures.

Before 2011, when Cather's last named literary executor, her nephew Charles Edwin Cather, died, it would have been impossible to undertake such a project with the degree of accuracy one wishes. Her last will and testament had forbidden publication of the letters and even partial quotation from them. Under both testamentary and copyright law, her two named executors, first Edith Lewis and then Mr. Cather, enforced this prohibition, at least in theory, making it necessary for scholars to resort to paraphrase. In the wake of Charles Cather's death, however, the situation changed. A trust was set up, with membership composed of the University of Nebraska Foundation, the Willa Cather Foundation, and a member of the Cather family. It was this trust that approved and encouraged the publication of *The Selected Letters of Willa Cather* in 1913, edited by Andrew Jewell and myself. The volume represented only some 28 percent of the known letters, leaving many others not published. But because the Willa Cather Trust operates under fair use doctrine for educational and nonprofit purposes, it is now permissible to quote the letters included in the *Selected Letters* and up to 10 percent of any other particular letter without seeking permission, or more than that if permission is granted. Certainly, as anyone who has ever sought to convey precise meaning by means of paraphrase, quotation of exactly what Cather herself wrote in her letters provides a far better understanding of her meaning than that gleaned through someone else's version of what she meant. Paraphrase requires translation, which is ever imprecise and interpretive.

Even before the publication of *My Ántonia* Cather had a well-established name in leading magazines and had gained a measure of recognition both in the marketplace and among critics with her previously published books: first a volume of poetry, then the volume of short stories *The Troll Garden*, and then three novels. The first of these, *Alexander's Bridge* (1912), attracted some eleven or more reviews,[3] most of them rather perfunctory and of a kind we would call mixed.[4] One reviewer called it "interesting" and "told with some force," and another wrote that there was "some feeling to the story" and "some good writing," but "as a novel, it all seems rather futile." Beginner or not, a writer hopes for better than that! The second, *O Pioneers!* (1913), garnered a larger number of reviews, nearly all of them positive. Recognizing only by faint implication that she had moved to more natural subject matter, reviewers pointed out that she was treating her subject in her own way, free from conventionality. She had produced, they said, "a totally new kind of story" with "a new heroine and a new country."[5] Floyd Dell wrote in the *Chicago Evening Post* that the book had "richness," "charm," and "dignity."[6] Cather's third novel, *The Song of the Lark* (1915), pleased most of its twenty-odd reviewers. Her editor at Houghton Mifflin (his actual title was literary advisor), Ferris Greenslet, called the early reviews "unanimously excellent."[7] H. L. Mencken pronounced in *Smart Set* that with *The Song of the Lark* she had joined "the small class of American novelists who are seriously to be reckoned with."[8] After this, Cather no longer had to doubt whether her work would be published or whether critics would notice it.

For *My Ántonia*, the number of reviews was somewhat down. It was wartime, after all, there were paper shortages, and as James Woodress points out in his "Historical Essay" accompanying the scholarly edition, the country's attention was mainly on other things than books. But the dozen or so reviews (Woodress mentions having seen twelve; O'Connor lists fifteen) were "nearly unanimous in their praise."[9]

What the letters provide with respect to the reviews of *My Ántonia* and Cather's reaction to these published and private responses is a rich lode of reactions and meditations extending from 1918 until the mid-1940s. They show us not only what Cather thought of the reviews as they were coming out, but also what she would come to think of them in retrospect. Curiously enough, only a few years after its publication she would begin to claim that the book's reception by reviewers was almost entirely negative—which was not at all true. The letters also give us considerable insight into the related matter of Cather's decision in 1920 to switch publishers—a redirection of her career that has been extensively studied by, in particular, Susan J. Rosowski, Robert A. Thacker, and Richard C. Harris, but one on which the letters can still shed direct illumination. In addition, the letters are almost our sole resource for learning about the reception of *My Ántonia* among Cather's family and friends and how important their opinions were to her.

Why she came to believe that the reviews of *My* Antonia were negative is a mystery the letters cannot entirely explain. They can, however, reveal the insistence with which she came to believe so, especially in the 1930s after she came under fire from Marxist critics for supposed disregard of social realities, and they can indicate some possible motivations for her perhaps unconscious reconstruction of the reception history. Letters from the early reception period demonstrate her appreciation for authentic personal response as well as increasing recognition that critical respect for her new artistic method was equally desirable and perhaps in tension with her valuation of personal response; this tension was expressed in her increasing dissatisfaction with how Houghton Mifflin regarded and marketed her work.

THE EARLY RECEPTION

My Ántonia was published on September 21, 1918. According to both O'Connor and Woodress, the first two reviews appeared on October 6 in the *New York Times Book Review* and the *New York Sun*. By October 1921, three years later, there had been at least fifteen reviews, almost all of them favorable or even celebratory. This is a point we need to remember when we see how Cather later reconstructed the record of what the reviewers had to say.

At the time the reviews were coming out, she was greatly pleased. On October 26 she wrote to a friend from girlhood, Irene Miner Weisz, enclosing a copy of one of the early ones, probably the review in the *Sun*. Irene seems to have questioned "whether strangers get the little things in a book like this," and Cather was pleased to say that this reviewer "apparently . . . got every least little thing."[10] A person with "an eye trained for literary values," she wrote, was "apt to get the whole picture more *as a whole* than anyone who knew the people from whom the characters were sketched" and would therefore be more likely to be concerned with the accuracy of the portraits. Knowing how Cather always insisted that *My Ántonia* was a different kind of book from the usual novel about the West, we may wonder at her failure to mention the observation by the *Sun* reviewer (probably Grant Overton, who was books editor of the *Sun* from 1910 to 1922) as to her departure from conventionality: "The most extraordinary thing about *My Ántonia* is the author's surrender of the usual methods of fiction in telling her story. Time and again as you read the book it strikes you [that] Miss Cather could have . . . plait[ed] the strands of her story into a regulation plot" but had instead "renounce[d] all that at the beginning."[11]

When Cather's letter to Irene goes on to single out as the main reason she liked the review the fact that it was not so much a "literary appreciation" as an "expression of honest personal enjoyment,"[12] we may wonder whether she was commenting on the review in the *Times* rather than the *Sun*, which was in fact a more literary appreciation. In any event, it is an important comment, because the distinction between a schooled or "literary" appreciation and a forthright expression of "personal enjoyment" was one that would remain in her vocabulary, especially when discussing promotional copy. She was convinced, and would remain convinced, that a personal tone conveying enthusiasm was the most effective recommendation a book could get.

This bias toward sincerity encompassed the reactions of friends and family members as well as those of reviewers and publicists. Cather first mentioned her family's reaction to *My Ántonia* two months after its publication, in a letter dated November 28, 1918, to her brother Roscoe. Roscoe was the sibling closest to her in age, just four years her junior. She, Roscoe, and Douglass, who was two years younger than he, were the threesome who slept in the attic rooms of the home in Red Cloud that the family rented upon moving into town from the ranch where they had first settled after migrating to Nebraska from Virginia. As a threesome, they seem to have retained a much stronger bond among themselves than with the younger four siblings. But it seems to have been Roscoe, of all her family, to whom Cather most confided her plans and progress in her work and whose response mattered most. Indeed, when she was just starting to write *My Ántonia* she wrote Roscoe that its origins derived in part from a trip to Yellowstone he had made several years earlier. She wished he had kept a diary on the trip, she said, because the new novel was "a little that kind of story."[13] She did not give the story a name at that point, just called it "this story" and "a new idea for a novel," so it's possible she may have been referring to "The Blue Mesa," which later became the central section of *The Professor's House* (1925). But probably not. It was probably *My Ántonia* because she went on to explain that "the chief figure" in this "new-old idea . . . must be a boy and a man"—not a boy or man as viewed from within the consciousness of a female "central figure," as she had been careful to do before, but truly a "central," perceiving male figure. And at this point her letter revealed something of far-reaching importance about not only the reception of her novels, plural, but her writing of them: Roscoe's importance in the process. "I'd like to talk it over with you," she said. "You might help me a good deal."

It is startling to see the supposedly resolute, self-directed Willa Cather expressing a wish for consultation on a work not even so much in progress as in conception. But Roscoe's centrality is an important thread running throughout her letters, from this early beginning on through her much later musing to him that the profoundest wellspring of her works was caring ("I have cared too much . . ."), to a late complaint that he was the only member of her family who "care[d] a damn" about her books.[14] Roscoe was central in her assessment of her family's esteem for her writing.

For *My Ántonia*, that esteem seems to have been unanimous. Her letter of November 28, 1918, to Roscoe was a reply to his "nice letter" about the book. Here it is in its entirety:

My Dear Roscoe:

Your nice letter deserved a speedy answer. I am so glad that you and father and mother liked this book. Most of the critics, too, seem to find this the best book I have done. I got quite a wonderful letter about it from France today, and it will be published in France very soon. Personally, I like the book before this one [*The Song of the Lark*] better, because there is more warmth and struggle in it. All the critics find "Antonia" more artistic. A man in the Nation writes that "it exists in an atmosphere of its own—an atmosphere of pure beauty." Nonsense, it's the atmosphere of my grandmother's kitchen, and nothing else. Booth Tarkington writes that it is as "simple as a country prayer meeting or a Greek temple—and as beautiful." There [are] lots of these people who can't write anything true themselves who yet recognize it when they see it. And whatever is really true is true for all people. As long as one says "will people stand this, or that?" one gets nowhere. You either have to be utterly common place or else do the thing people *don't* want, because it has not yet been invented. No really new and original thing is *wanted*: people have to learn to like new things.[15]

Element after element in this letter calls for comment. After the expression of satisfaction that her parents and Roscoe like the book comes an acknowledgment that most of the reviews have been positive "too"—as indeed they had been. By Thanksgiving Day, when she was writing, there had been at least four published reviews, according to O'Connor's compilation, all in major outlets—the *New York Times Book Review*, the *New York Sun*, the *Nation*, and the Socialist publication *New York Call*. Three of the four had mentioned the "fresh" quality of the book, its freedom from conventions of characterization or plot.[16] Cather then introduces what will be a recurring note over the years: translation. Then the contrast with *The Song of the Lark*, revealing that at this point she still preferred it, though she would later come to agree with what Randolph Bourne had said of it (anonymously) in the *New Republic*, that the earlier work was diffuse and did not well represent her gift as a writer. Then her report of reviewers' recognition of the literary quality of Ántonia.

With Cather's putative quotation of the "man in the *Nation*," however, the letter becomes problematic. Although the *Nation* review did find *My Ántonia* "worthy to stand . . . among the best of our recent interpretations of American life," it did *not* include the phrase she quotes or anything similar. As to the Booth Tarkington statement, the words she quotes are more or less the terms he used in praising not *My Ántonia* but *The Autobiography of S. S. McClure* (written, of course, by Cather), not in a review but in a letter to McClure.[17]

How or why she made these misstatements, a stunning reconstruction, is a mystery. Certainly I am not accusing Cather of mendaciousness, but it is not characteristic of her—or not to this point—to be so inaccurate.[18] At any rate, the remainder of the letter is richly interesting. The sentence that follows the nonquotation from Tarkington strongly implies that she places the Indianan in the category of those who "can't write anything true themselves." The succeeding assertion of the universal nature of truth was perhaps an impulse of the moment, a kind of showing off for a brother; she did not always so totally dismiss contingency. But the real highlight comes in the last three sentences, with their indication of her determination to resist "utterly common place" novelistic conventions in favor of the "really new and original things" that readers will "have to learn to like." Here we see Cather the experimentalist— an aspect of her achievement that has at times been insufficiently recognized. This likewise reveals some tension in how she wished to be appreciated and how she defined sincere appreciation.

In what may have been a separate letter to Roscoe, dated December, or perhaps a continuation of the November 28 letter, which remained unsigned and may have lain unmailed on her desk, Cather reported on the October 6 review in the *New York Sun*. Echoing her letter to Irene Miner Weisz in October about the reviewer's "honest expression of enjoyment," she tells Roscoe that the reviewer "surely had a good time with the book" and adds, "It amazes me how many people feel that way."[19] She has received, she says, a letter from a professor who taught their brother Jack at Carnegie Technical School in Pittsburgh, who said that only a "'very great artist'" could "return" to nature or make "the nakedness of nature beautiful in art." "Yet," she adds, "Father likes it 'as well as any book he ever read.'" Having "touched two extremes" this way makes her "well content."[20]

Another letter written before the end of 1918 also provides significant insights into Cather's feelings about early responses to the novel. On December 3 she wrote to her friend Elizabeth Shepley Sergeant, whose response to a complimentary copy sent by Houghton Mifflin had made her, she said, "pleased and happy."[21] What is most interesting about this letter, however, is that it goes on to give the only revelation that I know of that Cather had fallen into a state of depression following her completion of work on the book. She tells Sergeant that when she finished the proofs, "the waters of bitterness simply closed over my head." She felt a sudden conviction that she had achieved "nothing—simply nothing" of what she intended. Even though she had liked the manuscript while she was writing it, she says, "in the proofs it seemed a gray waste of dullness." But then her father said it was "all so exactly the way he remembered it," and between that and "people like you" (Sergeant) liking it, she feels "encouraged."[22] She would express similar postcompletion blues—a pattern that may remind us of Virginia Woolf—after sending *One of Ours* and *Death Comes for the Archbishop* to press, but in those cases more a feeling of missing the company of the central characters than any misgiving that the books themselves were "dull" or otherwise unsuccessful.

In every respect, these letters written between the September 21 publication date and the end of 1918 indicate that Cather was well pleased with the early reception of *My Ántonia.* And well she should have been. As of the end of the year, only the *Booklist* had expressed reservations, finding it to be a falling off from *The Song of the Lark*, and some of the best reviews were yet to come. H. W. Boynton, in the *Bookman*, referred to her as an "accomplished artist" and recognized the minimalism of her approach, with no "superfluous . . . stroke" in the "portrait" of Ántonia that she painted.[23] Randolph Bourne, in the December *Dial*, gave a kind of salute, saying, "Here at last is an American novel, redolent of the Western prairie, that our most irritated and exacting preconceptions can be content with."[24] Bourne also recognized the "artistic simplicity" of the work, with "everything irrelevant . . . scraped away," and noted its "indestructible fragrance of youth."[25]

Cather was especially pleased with Bourne's review. On January 5, 1919, she wrote another letter to Roscoe, which would be a treasure for its amusing language even without the valuable information about her thinking that it provides. Following up on a newspaper notice of Bourne's death (in the influenza epidemic of that year) that she had already sent him, she wrote that Bourne was "the ablest of our critics." He had given her "some sharp knocks" on *The Song of the Lark*, but she was greatly pleased with the distinction he drew between her treatment of the plains in *My Ántonia* and conventional writing about the West as seen in William Allen White's 1918 novel *In the Heart of a Fool*, which Bourne described as "swollen" and "cluttered."[26] "Of course," she continued, she could have told Ántonia's story in "exactly the same jocular, familiar, *grapenutsy* way that Mr. White thinks is so American."[27] "Grapenutsy"! How wonderful![28]

It was praise for technique and unconventionality that elevated *My Ántonia* as art with a new, distinctive edge. In early 1919, H. L. Mencken noticed *My Ántonia* in two successive issues of *Smart Set* (February and March), calling it not only "the best American novel" of the year but "one of the best that any American has ever done."[29] Mencken also, like other critics, praised its method and its avoidance of stale conventionalism, writing that with all the "balderdash" of conventional novels "charmingly absent," the book succeeded "in an altogether different way" from the more typical and certainly wordier method of, say, Theodore Dreiser.[30] The chorus of praise continued, even while, unfortunately for them, Cather's dissatisfaction with her publishing house, Houghton Mifflin, mounted. In retrospect, it is easy to see why.

She found their marketing unimaginative and ineffective and when she tried to offer suggestions even her friend Greenslet seemed impervious. Before turning to her departure from Houghton Mifflin, however, I want to note three particular letters relating to the reception of *My Ántonia* written between 1919 and 1921 because they emphasize Cather's desire for her straitened method and her handling of narrative point of view to be understood.

First, a letter of May 20, 1919, to Will Owen Jones, the editor of the *Nebraska State Journal* and Cather's mentor during her college years and the early years of her career in journalism. Jones had apparently written to her about *My Ántonia*, expressing his liking for the book but questioning her use of Jim Burden as the center of consciousness. In reply, she sent him a review from "a Chicago paper" (almost certainly the *Chicago Daily News* of April 12, 1919), which she said gave a "pretty clear statement of what I have been trying to do from the first."[31] Her endorsement of this review—a strongly positive one that pointed out her avoidance of conventional Western motifs and pronounced the book "real" and "packed with the feel of the country"[32]— is interesting in itself, of course, but her letter about it also provides one of the most cogent of all statements of her aims and methods.

The "device" of the male narrator, Cather told Mr. Jones, was a kind of approach used by various Russian and French authors to establish a desired "mood" or atmosphere. By citing international precedents, of course, she identified herself with their literary status. She wanted, she said, to present "the chief character" of her novel, Ántonia herself, "through a man's memory" because the "most interesting things I knew about the several women of whom she was made, were told me by men."[33] Of course, we know that Ántonia was not made from several models but from just one, Anna Sadilek Pavelka. Cather acknowledged as much in interviews in 1921[34] and in letters of February 2, 1925, to Thomas Masaryk, the president of Czechoslovakia, and February 15, 1926, to Ferris Greenslet.[35] The novel needed to be told in the first person, she insisted to Jones, because it was "so entirely a story of feeling and not of action." And she "felt competent to handle a man's narrative in the first person" from having written S. S. McClure's autobiography.[36] She believed she had succeeded in capturing McClure's voice, the "abruptness and suddenness characteristic of him," and this gave her the confidence to pursue the first-person masculine narrative of *My Ántonia*, even though such an attempt was obviously "dangerous."[37] Providing yet another important insight into her own view of the nature of her work, she went on to say that she believed she had matured beyond the youthful stage of caring about "clever writing" and "fine phrase[s]" to the valuing of "a simple and faithful presentation"[38]—a quality that had already been recognized by several critics. As in her later, frequently noted essay "The Novel Démeublé," she was thinking about her art in terms of deliberate simplification. The need for recognition of both artistic method and authenticity is apparent in these letters preceding her change of publishers.

The second of these three pre-Knopf letters, written to her mother on December 6, 1919, provides an amusing insight into the degree of fame Cather was gaining from *My Ántonia*. Making the heady claim that she was "becoming rather 'famous' lately," but using quotation marks to indicate a degree of hesitancy about making such a claim,[39] she offered an anecdote of having been caught in the kitchen in her apron by a reporter who came to the back door of the apartment seeking an interview. Flustered, she told him Miss Cather was away, presumably leaving him to think he had spoken with the maid. She then went on to report that the reception of *My Ántonia* (now well over a year old) had continued to be positive, with a translation into French and a growing recognition of her work in England. Again, we will want to remember this expression of satisfaction when we come to her later claims that the reviews were mostly negative.

The last of the three pre-Knopf letters that I have singled out was written to Dorothy Canfield Fisher on March 21, 1921, acknowledging the "generous letters" Canfield Fisher, her longtime but sometimes estranged friend, had written about her books (presumably including *My Ántonia*) over the years. Like the letter to Will Jones noted earlier, this letter to Canfield Fisher conveys her satisfaction in being recognized for authenticity, even as she claimed (to Jones and to her mother) a link to the literature of the wider world. Readers in her home town of Red Cloud, she told Dorothy, had "really c[o]me round" after *My Ántonia* and endorsed the accuracy of its vision of the life they knew.[40] Once again we see that Cather was gratified by the reception of *My Ántonia* among friends, as well as among critics, and that she wished to be appreciated for reasons possibly in tension with one another.

THE DEPARTURE FROM HOUGHTON MIFFLIN

Cather's growing tension with her publishing house centered on her desire to be recognized and marketed as a serious artist, and the quality and recognition of *My Ántonia* solidified her claim to such a status. Houghton Mifflin, the publisher of Cather's first three novels as well as *My Ántonia*, was a respected Boston house. Its antecedent, Ticknor and Fields, had published the likes of Nathaniel Hawthorne, Ralph Waldo Emerson, and Harriet Beecher Stowe, and despite shifts in ownership and imprint over the years it retained a solid name that we can assume was at least to some extent an asset among reviewers, and perhaps among buyers as well. Even so, *My Ántonia* would be the last novel Cather published with Houghton Mifflin. Her next book, the short story volume *Youth and the Bright Medusa* (1920), would be published by Alfred A. Knopf, and with the novel that followed, *One of Ours* (1922), her shift to Knopf would become permanent. Rosowski has explained this major redirection of Cather's publishing career by reference to her desire for "a publisher who believed in her as an artist with a long literary life."[41] Clearly, this was true. But the more immediate reason for her shift to Knopf—the "primary reason," in Thacker's judgment[42]—was her disappointment with Houghton Mifflin's "handling" of *My Ántonia*. She became convinced that the book would have enjoyed considerably greater success if her publisher had given it more attention and more effective promotion.

Despite her defiance of readerly expectations, Cather also wanted (and of course, as a self-supporting woman without family wealth, needed) robust sales. As early as September 30 and October 3, 1918, not yet two weeks after the release date, she was complaining to the production manager at Houghton Mifflin, R. L. Scaife, that booksellers in Red Cloud were being shorted on their orders.[43] On October 20, still only a scant month after publication, she lamented to Greenslet the book's insufficient availability in Toronto and a lack of advertising. Thus began a long series of complaints and protests about inadequate promotion.

There was a history at work here. She had expressed dissatisfaction before, in relation to the press' work on *The Song of the Lark*—a cover she did not like, inaccurate text on the dust jacket, and ineffective advertising.[44] Then, as her work on *My Ántonia* was nearing an end, problems arose in relation to the illustrations. Mr. Scaife's idea of artwork for the book leaned toward the customary halftone frontispiece. When Cather instead asked W. T. Benda to do line drawings to be interspersed throughout the text, Scaife was reluctant to pay the artist even a minimally reasonable fee. A testy correspondence ensued. On top of all this came her dissatisfaction over promotional efforts.

Cather had a growing sense that her publisher was not properly investing in her increasing reputation. In a letter to Greenslet dated December 2, 1918, asking how the book was selling, Cather urged him to have a review copy sent to the *New York Globe*.[45] Over a month later she complained that it still had not been sent.[46] In May of that year she learned that Houghton Mifflin was charging her for changes made in proof. The amount was apparently sizable; even Greenslet said it was "fairly expensive."[47] She wrote to him on May 19 going through a long list of complaints. Once again, as in Mencken's review, Dreiser came into the conversation as a comparator. She had seen some of Dreiser's proofs, she said, and knew that his books were "practically re-written" at that stage and he was "never charged a cent for corrections."[48] Houghton Mifflin's unwillingness to underwrite her corrections showed, in her mind, that the press was not willing to invest in her as a repeat author with strong long-term prospects.

The fact that other publishers were approaching her was an indication that "the recognition of the public and reviewers has outstripped that of my publishers."[49] She also offered reasons to believe the company had not made much effort to bring her to the attention of reviewers. One reviewer, in fact, had told her that "nobody had been afraid to come out and say that this book was unique in American fiction, except the publishers!" Even their jacket copy was only a "timid, perfunctory endorsement."[50] We recall her belief that a note of personal enthusiasm made the best promotional copy. But even if Houghton Mifflin was not willing to call her a great writer, why were they "so shy about quoting anything of that sort when other people say it?"[51] She did believe Greenslet liked publishing her books, but was not convinced that anyone else at the firm did. At that point her reference to "publishers" who were approaching her changed from plural to singular: *a* "New York publisher." No doubt she meant Knopf, to whom she then referred by name in saying that he advertised all of Joseph Hergesheimer's books, whereas Houghton Mifflin was no longer advertising even *My Ántonia*. She ended, "I know I can work better for a firm that can give me some of its ingenuity and enthusiasm."[52]

Greenslet had been warned. Even so, after he responded with what she described as a "kind and friendly letter,"[53] she professed herself satisfied on the point of the corrections in proof and content to defer talks about the larger issues until later, though she was still discouraged to note that he did not seem to see a need for change in Houghton Mifflin's promotional efforts. And she continued to press the matter. On December 28, 1919, she mentioned a "controversy in the Tribune about Ántonia," the "impetus" of which would probably carry over to subsequent books, and informed Greenslet that Knopf was going to bring out a new edition of *The Troll Garden*.[54] This became *Youth and the Bright Medusa*.

Even at that point, however, she put off making a decision. Her decision to go forward with Knopf on the volume of short stories, she said, did not mean she was making a change altogether. Yet irritants kept pushing her in that direction. On February 5, 1920, she told Scaife that Brentano's, an important bookstore in New York, seemed to be unable to get copies. Eleven days later she reported that Brentano's now had copies but that people she knew (she may have meant Irene Miner Weisz, for one) had told her copies had not been available in Chicago or Detroit during the several weeks leading up to Christmas.[55] Unfortunately for her relations with the firm, Scaife further offended her in his reply by calling these unnamed people "investigators." In a letter of February 21 she called his reply a "distinct shock" and again complained that supplies of the book were not being kept in stores.[56]

The demand for *My Ántonia* combined with her own dissatisfaction with its marketing by the press to alter the direction of Cather's future publishing career. On January 12, 1921, she informed Greenslet that she was leaving Houghton Mifflin for Knopf.[57] Even after this long history of dissatisfaction, she continued to maintain friendly relations with Greenslet, writing him a personal letter just nine days after announcing her decision, pronouncing herself his "everlasting debtor" for the nice way in which he had responded to her decision.[58]

CONTINUING SUCCESS IN THE KNOPF YEARS

The change of publishers was a sound career move. Alfred A. Knopf's intelligent, innovative approach to both the art and the business of publishing enhanced both Cather's income and her literary reputation. *Youth and the Bright Medusa*, the first book of hers that Knopf published, earned her as much in royalties in its first six months as *My Ántonia* did in its first year,[59] despite the fact that four of its eight stories had previously been collected in *The Troll Garden*. Nevertheless, even though *My Ántonia* was not a major commercial success early on, it continued to sell steadily and to provide her a stable income for the rest of her life. In a sense, however, this would prove to be a not unmixed blessing in that it set a precedent for how subsequent novels would be perceived. It also provided a model for Cather's own thinking about techniques of characterization and the position of a central character in her novels.

As she prepared for the publication of *One of Ours*, she sparred with Alfred Knopf over its title. Her choice for it was "Claude," the name of the central character. To her, the book was all about him, his sense of the narrowness of the world in which he grew up and his perception of the war as an opportunity to experience something broader and grander. But Knopf did not like "Claude" as a title. She insisted, telling him on August 26, 1921, as she was turning in the last sections of manuscript, that "Claude" was what it would have to be.[60] She had "lived with . . . the other title"—apparently a suggestion he had made—"for months," but could not accept anything but "Claude." To justify this she invoked, in a rhetorical move that would prove ironic in both the short and the long term, the precedent of Ántonia, explaining that its title had also seemed "unpromising . . . at first" and she had been asked to change it, but after all "the story has made the title go." By that precedent, she was confident that the title "Claude" would not "offend so many people as you think." In the end, of course—in fact, only five days later—she yielded. Writing from Hastings, Nebraska, on September 1, she informed Knopf that after talking it over with her friend Fanny Butcher, critic and bookstore owner in Chicago, she would be happy with "One of Ours."

The irony of Cather's invoking *My Ántonia* as a precedent on this occasion and again on June 22, 1922, when she wrote to William Allen White that even though he had had good words for *My Ántonia* the new novel was "a much better book," is that she was not pleased when it became a precedent used by reviewers and the general public as they read her subsequent books. So determined were her readers to use *My Ántonia* as a standard of evaluation, she wrote Dorothy Canfield Fisher in the fall of 1922, that Houghton Mifflin had to order another printing for people who wanted to buy it simply in order to prove to friends that it was better than *One of Ours*. Naturally, she was gratified that *My Ántonia* continued to attract praise, but she was troubled when it served as a potentially limiting shaper of expectations and a comparator according to which *One of Ours*, in particular, was devalued. Her recognition of the invidiousness of this elevation of *My Ántonia* was made explicit in a letter to her sister Elsie expressing disappointment in the reviews of *One of Ours* and lamenting that reviewers were "all" saying they "expected it 'would be just like Antonia.'"[61] She put the same idea to writer Lorna Birtwell on November 27, [1922], saying critics "liked 'Antonia' and wanted me to do the same act."[62] She was not strictly accurate in saying that reviewers were "all" disappointed that the new novel was not a repeat of *My Ántonia*, but a number of them did draw a comparison unfavorable to *One of Ours*. H. L. Mencken, for example, began his review in the *Smart Set* of October 1922, "Miss Willa Cather's *One of Ours* divides itself very neatly into two halves, one of which deserves to rank almost with *My Ántonia*."[63] Edwin Edgett in the *Boston Evening Transcript*, Heywood Broun in the *New York World*, Henry Seidel Canby in the *New York Evening Post Literary Review*, Sinclair Lewis in the same publication, and Gilbert Seldes in the *Dial* made similar pronouncements.[64] These "roast[s]" of *One of Ours* by "Heywood Brown & Co." drowned out, for her, its many positive reviews.[65]

Meanwhile, *My Ántonia* only increased in stature. As she wrote to Alfred and Blanche Knopf on May 16, 1923, it was still selling—"3,000 in the last six months."[66] Ferris Greenslet observed that it was increasingly outpacing the sales of her other Houghton Mifflin books.[67] Cather also continued to receive fan letters about Ántonia, and she was pleased with a French review, probably of the translation by Victor Llona published that year, sent to her by Canfield Fisher in 1925.[68]

My Ántonia was ready for a new edition. As Melissa Homestead argues in this volume, in preparing for this edition Cather would revisit her contentious relationship with Houghton Mifflin and reposition herself as an author. In 1926, at Greenslet's suggestion, she revised the Introduction, shortening it and giving it a more economical focus. At that time, according to a letter of Greenslet's on February 17, the book was selling at a rate of about four thousand a year. In the course of their correspondence about the revised edition, Cather made it clear that the Benda illustrations must be retained. "It is one of the few cases," she wrote, "where I think the pictures really help the story, and I would not be willing to leave them out."[69] Nevertheless, retention of the Benda line drawings, avoidance of a proposal by Houghton Mifflin to substitute pictures by Grant Wood, and warding off adaptations for radio or film were among the many struggles she had to go through over the years to defend the integrity of the work.[70]

As a rule, a book is reviewed only on its initial publication. Nevertheless, the 1926 revised edition of *My Ántonia* drew a strong retrospective in the *New York World*, praising the paring down of the Introduction and proclaiming that very few books in the past decade had "surpassed" it in "originality, in truth and in vitality."[71] Greenslet reported on October 23, 1926, and April 24, 1928, that the new edition was selling well. Sales were strong enough that Cather could complain to Alfred Knopf in 1928 (with how much accuracy we do not know) that *Death Comes for the Archbishop*, published the previous year, was less available in Nebraska than *My Ántonia* even then.[72] On November 26, 1931, she wrote Greenslet that she had seen yet another renewal of interest in both *My Ántonia* and *O Pioneers!* since the June 1931 publication of her essay "My First Novel (There Were Two)."[73] On April 30, 1935, Greenslet wrote that sales remained "remarkable and satisfactory," and on October 22, 1941, reported that they had, if anything, increased. On April 30, 1945, he wrote that sales were "steady and even."

Another measure of the stature of a literary work is the interest it attracts abroad, a topic Caterina Bernardini explores in this volume. *My Ántonia* was published in Czech in 1922, in French in 1925, in Danish in 1930, in German in 1928, in Swedish in 1939, and in Finnish in 1934 and again in 1940. Heinemann, in England, which had issued the original version in 1919, published a second British edition in 1930, this time following the 1926 revision.[74] Since 1940 there have been many more translations, including Bengali, Estonian, Korean, and Urdu, among others.[75]

Among various honors for *My Ántonia* that Cather continued to receive was a medal from the Mark Twain Society in 1934, which pleased her,[76] though she declined to travel to St. Louis in order to accept it in person. Certainly she was glad to receive words of praise from Acting Chief Justice Holmes in 1930, relayed to her by Ferris Greenslet[77] and from Sinclair Lewis, in a letter of November 21, 1930, generously telling her that his Nobel Prize should probably have gone to her and saying that his wife supremely treasured *My Ántonia*.[78] She was delighted to learn in 1935 that James M. Barrie, the author of *Peter*

Pan, had written "gracious" praise of the book in a personal letter to editor/ writer Marie Mattingly Meloney.[79] On June 10, 1940, she wrote Greenslet asking for a copy of the "current edition" because it was "still selling" and she was "still perpetually receiving letters about her."[80] The reference to *My Ántonia* as "her" is an example of how Cather tended to personalize her books according to the central character.

All these letters show us what pleasure Cather took in the book's secure place in American letters. She expressed that pleasure at length in a letter of June 9, 1943, to Carrie Miner Sherwood, but then on the last day of that year confessed to Irene in a weepy mood that she had not heard from Carrie in some time and was wondering whether she had boasted too much to her about "the revival of interest in 'Antonia' and the new edition of it in England."[81] Much as Cather cared about books and writing, she also cared about friends. She was greatly moved when, in a Christmas card in 1944, Irene wrote to her about her love for *My Ántonia*.[82] By then she had long since begun to say that only her family and friends had liked the book in its early years, not the critics.

REVISING CRITICAL HISTORY:
THE PUZZLE OF MISREMEMBRANCE

Cather's misremembrance of the early reception of *My Ántonia* began as early as 1922, just four years after its publication. On November 27 of that year she wrote to Lorna Birtwell, thanking her for having published a letter to the editor in the *New York Evening Post* of November 25 in defense of *One of Ours* and adding the jarring note that critics at first ignored *My Ántonia*:

> Aside from war prejudices, the trouble with the critics seems to be that they liked "Antonia" and wanted me to do the same act. But their state of mind does not bother me. "Antonia" had been out for two years before one of these gentlemen were [*sic*] in the least interested. They didn't like it at first because it had no structure etc. etc. . . . and showed a great falling off from its predecessor.

As we have seen, this is not true. One rather tepid and one enthusiastically positive review were published within its first month, three more appeared before the end of 1918, and by the time *My Ántonia* had been out for a year it had had at least thirteen reviews. Many "gentlemen" were interested, and only one (in the *Booklist* of December 1918) drew a negative comparison with *The Song of the Lark*. No one, so far as I have found, complained of a lack of structure. Perhaps Cather was inferring from the references to stylistic "pictures" and "sketches" (for example, in the *New York Times* notice)[83] that reviewers had misgivings about structure. But if anyone stated such a criticism it was by no means the prevailing view. Indeed, Mencken, in the second of his two notices, explicitly praised its "form."[84] Cather also told Birtwell that "all the New York critics except two" said it was "deadly dull." On this point, too, she may have inferred such a criticism from references to the absence of strong plotting or from speculation by one reviewer that the book would have appeal for "those who appreciate style" without compelling action.[85] These were the nearest approaches to a charge of dullness. It is hard to understand how, only four years out, she could so misremember Ántonia's glowing reviews.

But the letter to Birtwell provides a clue. In the fall of 1922, when Cather was writing this letter, she had recently been sorely stung by reviews of *One of Ours*, one of which—by Gilbert Seldes in the *Dial*—had indeed declared *that* novel dull.[86] Perhaps this slight somehow became attached, in her mind, to the previous book as well. By 1922, of course, *My Ántonia*, had proven itself a success. And "this book," Cather wrote, "may go through the same history." She may have been, even if unconsciously, constructing an argument to comfort herself for the reviews of *One of Ours* by revising the reviews of *My Ántonia* in order to project a parallel climb into success.

After the 1922 letter to Birtwell the idea that the reviews of Ántonia were almost all negative, or else it was ignored, continued to echo in Cather's letters. In early September 1927, she went so far as to tell Fanny Butcher that she and Grant Overton had been "the only two reviewers in America who liked 'Antonia' when it first came out."[87] This was, of course, not true. In the context of the rest of this letter, voicing complaints about reviewers' failure to recognize that *Death Comes for the Archbishop* was by no means intended as a conventional novel but rather a "narrative . . . like a folk-song," it might appear that what Cather was lamenting in the reviews of *My Ántonia* was a lack of recognition that she was not trying to work within conventional expectations. But in fact it was precisely that avoidance of convention that several of Ántonia's reviewers singled out for praise.

By September 2, 1931, in a letter to Alfred Knopf, the reviews of *My Ántonia* had deteriorated, in Cather's mind, to "the worst I ever got."[88] Perhaps her motivation for making this patently false claim (*One of Ours* drew the worst she ever got, and even in its case more than half the reviews were positive) was to comfort her publisher for reviews of *Shadows on the Rock*, which with their emphasis on the static, subdued quality of the story, its lack of action, did not seem likely to promote large sales. (In fact, *Shadows* would have enormous sales.) In effect, she was trying to hearten him, as she had earlier tried to hearten herself about *One of Ours*: those earlier reviews were "the worst" and yet, as he knew, Ántonia had enjoyed steady success for well over a decade, so perhaps the same would be true of the new work in which he had invested so much (with a very large first printing). "This time," she continued, "it's only the New York notices that are spiteful," while "papers in the chain of cities across the country" were "all cordial and friendly."[89] That was not entirely true either. Some of the reviewers across the country were quite negative. But perhaps she was letting Fanny Butcher's adulatory review in the *Chicago Daily Tribune* on August 15, which had called *Shadows* "superb" and even better than *Archbishop*,[90] rose color her impression of reviews "across the country."

In referring to New York notices Cather probably had in mind a particular half-dozen: Carl Van Doren's lengthy review in the *New York Herald Tribune Books* (published August 2, 1931), John Chamberlain's in the *New York Times Book Review* (also August 2), Frances Lamont Robbins's in the *Outlook and Independent* of August 5, R. M. Coates's facetiously self-effacing review in the *New Yorker* (August 15), and, most of all, Newton Arvin's in the *New Republic* of August 12 and Granville Hicks's in the *Forum* for September 1931 (which she would presumably have seen by September 2). Of these, only Arvin's and Hicks's could reasonably be called spiteful. Two years later, in an essay called "The Case Against Willa Cather" in the *English Journal*, Hicks would declare that her work exhibited "supine romanticism." Both he and Arvin anticipated that charge in their reviews of *Shadows on the Rock*, accusing her of evading the material realities of her time—essentially, of sentimental escapism. She was deeply offended.

How do the undoubtedly mixed reviews of *Shadows* pertain to Cather's reconstruction of the reviews of *My Ántonia*? Once again, as she did with those earlier reviews, she seems to have so fixated on these negatives that she lost sight of the very positive things that were said even in some of the "New York notices" that she referred to as spiteful. Van Doren, despite pronouncing the new book "dramatically somewhat thin," called it "pictorially rich" and referred to its "excellence," while Chamberlain termed her prose "inordinately beautiful."[91] True, Hicks in particular couched his review as an attack on her career as a whole, making the truly vicious declaration that she was and had always been "a minor artist."[92] Arvin, too, by accusing her of writing "as if mass production and technological unemployment and cyclical depressions and the struggle between the classes did not exist,"[93] implied that her work was irrelevant to the lives of her readers, thereby making a charge that held the potential for undermining her entire literary reputation. Perhaps it was understandable, then, that she returned in distorted memory to the reception of a book whose very structure and theme presented an escape (Jim Burden's) from an unpleasant life to a reassuring past he associates with the generous and life-affirming Ántonia. The objections that reviewers hurled at her in 1931 once again colored her memory of the reviews of that earlier, explicitly "escapist" book, and knowingly or not, she misrepresented them to Alfred Knopf as her "worst" as a mechanism for reassuring herself, as well as him, that this time she would also be vindicated.

Another reason may simply have been the recurrent depression from which she increasingly suffered as advancing age and the deaths of loved ones colored not only her view of the world, but also her memory of her own past. In 1931, when *Shadows on the Rock* was published, Cather was by no means at the end of her career. Major works still lay ahead. But at fifty-eight she was undeniably nearing the end. Beset by the deaths of her father in 1928 and her mother in 1931, she knew she was no longer shielded from the cold blasts of mortality by the presence of the older generation. Just seven years later, on November 6, 1938, she would write to her brother Roscoe explaining that the fundamental wellspring of her art was a deep emotional investment, which she called caring: "I have cared too much, about people and places—cared too hard. It made me, as a writer. But it will break me in the end."[94] Clearly, the caring she referred to extended, as well, to the attacks levied on her by critics in the 1930s. She cared deeply when critics disparaged her work. Her distress over what some, though not all, reviewers said about her novels of 1922 and 1931, *One of Ours* and *Shadows on the Rock*, colored even her memory of the glowing reviews of *My Ántonia*.

NOTES

1. Margaret Anne O'Connor, *Willa Cather: The Contemporary Reviews* (Cambridge: Cambridge University Press, 2001), xi.

2. Ann Moseley, "Historical Essay," in *The Song of the Lark* by Willa Cather, ed. Karl Ronning (Lincoln: University of Nebraska Press, 2012), 589.

3. O'Connor, *Willa Cather*, 37–41.

4. *Alexander's Bridge* was in fact the second novel Cather wrote, though the first to be published. The first was a now-lost manuscript set in Pittsburgh.

5. O'Connor, *Willa Cather*, 45.

6. Ibid., 49.

7. Moseley, "Historical," 589.

8. Ibid., 590.

9. James Woodress, "Historical Essay," in *My Ántonia*, Willa Cather Scholarly Edition, ed. Charles W. Mignon and Kari A. Ronning (Lincoln: University of Nebraska Press, 1994), 392.

10. Andrew Jewell and Janis P. Stout, ed., *The Selected Letters of Willa Cather* (New York: Knopf, 2013), 260.

11. O'Connor, *Willa Cather*, 80. When Cather asked Ferris Greenslet at Houghton Mifflin whether he had seen the review in the *Sun*, which proclaimed, among

other things, that she had "won a complete victory over the reader," and asked for "a little" advertising, he replied, unaccountably, that the Houghton Mifflin publicity department considered it a good review but one lacking in "really quotable nuggets" (Greenslet to Cather, October 22, 1918). In my quotation of this reviewer's statement and at certain other points in this chapter, Ántonia is shown without the accent mark, not by accidental omission but as a reproduction of how the writer has shown it, even if that writer is Cather herself.

12. Jewell and Stout, *Selected Letters*, 260.

13. Ibid., 226.

14. Ibid., 561, 588.

15. Ibid., 261

16. O'Connor, *Willa Cather*, 80–83.

17. Peter Lyon, *Success Story: The Life and Times of S. S. McClure* (New York: Scribner, 1963), xi.

18. Her inaccuracy here is so uncharacteristic that Andrew Jewell, in a private communication dated November 21, 2014, wondered whether there may have been an incidental notice in the *Nation* that has not been identified, in addition to the review reported in the scholarly edition and by O'Connor. I wish to thank Professor Jewell for his reading of an earlier version of this chapter and helpful comments.

19. Jewell and Stout, *Selected Letters*, 265.

20. Ibid.

21. Ibid., 264

22. Ibid. Cather's father's assessment that the frontier-time Nebraska of *My Ántonia* was "exactly the way he remembered it" was echoed, about the same time as Cather's letter to Sergeant, in a letter she received from the superintendent of schools in Saline County, Nebraska, L. J. Bouchal, dated December 2, 1918. Bouchal's impression of the novel, which must have pleased her very much, was that "you have really been able to see things as seen by these people that you write about and feel as they feel" (Love Library, University of Nebraska).

23. O'Connor, *Willa Cather*, 84.

24. Ibid.

25. Ibid., 85.

26. Ibid., 84. Cather also pointed out Bourne's review in the *Dial* in a letter to Ferris Greenslet, written the day after her delightful letter to Roscoe Cather.

27. Jewell and Stout, *Selected Letters*, 272.

28. Ibid., 326. Cather adds in this letter that White's "grapenutsy" manner "really presents his own essentially vulgar personality." Even so, she later developed a real fondness for him and his wife and took pleasure in the way he ribbed her about some of the reviews of *One of Ours*: "When thy Nathan and thy Mencken forsake thee . . ."

29. O'Connor, *Willa Cather*, 88–89.

30. Ibid., 89. In posing this contrast with Dreiser, Mencken referred to Dreiser's title character Jennie Gerhardt (1911). The origins of Cather's title character Lucy Gayheart (1935) have been much discussed. Perhaps Mencken's reference stuck in her mind, even when she was misremembering the tenor of the reviews of Ántonia.

31. Jewell and Stout, *Selected Letters*, 278.

32. O'Connor, *Willa Cather*, 90.

33. Jewell and Stout, *Selected Letters*, 277.

34. L. Brent Bohlke, ed., *Willa Cather in Person: Interviews, Speeches, and Letters* (Lincoln: University of Nebraska Press, 1986), 22, 35, 44.

35. Jewell and Stout, *Selected Letters*, 365, 377.

36. Ibid., 277.

37. Ibid., 362. On October 24, 1924, however, she told a reader who had written to complain about the point of view of *My Ántonia* that she "did not for one minute try to 'talk like a man'" there.

38. Ibid., 278.

39. Ibid., 282.

40. Ibid., 299.

41. Susan J. Rosowski, "Historical Essay," in *A Lost Lady* by Willa Cather (Lincoln: University of Nebraska Press, 1997), 178.

42. Robert A. Thacker, "'As the result of many solicitations': Ferris Greenslet, Houghton Mifflin, and Cather's Career," *Studies in the Novel* 45, no. 3 (Fall 2013): 375.

43. Cather, Unpublished Letters: to R. L. Scaife, October 3, 1918 (Houghton Library, Harvard University).

44. Jewell and Stout, *Selected Letters*, 205.

45. Ibid., 262–63.

46. Ibid., 273.

47. Unpublished letter to Cather, May 3, 1919, Ferris Greenslet, unpublished letters to Willa Cather (Houghton Library, Harvard University).

48. Jewell and Stout, *Selected Letters*, 274.

49. Ibid., 275.

50. Ibid.

51. Ibid., 276.

52. Ibid., 277.

53. Ibid., 279.

54. Ibid., 285–86.

55. Unpublished letters to Scaife (Houghton Library, Harvard University).

56. Jewell and Stout, *Selected Letters*, 289.

57. Ibid., 297.

58. Ibid., 298.

59. James Woodress, *Willa Cather: A Literary Life* (Lincoln: University of Nebraska Press, 1987), 310.

60. Jewell and Stout, *Selected Letters*, 303.

61. Ibid., 324. Cather must have been very pleased, then, to be able to reply to a fan, on November 17, 1922, who had written to express his liking for both Ántonia and *One of Ours*. Ibid., 328.

62. Unpublished letter to Birtwell, Columbia University.

63. O'Connor, *Willa Cather*, 141.

64. Ibid., 124, 125, 127, 128, 138.

65. Jewell and Stout, *Selected Letters*, 335, 339.

66. Ibid., 339.

67. Unpublished letter, October 25, 1923 (Houghton Library, Harvard University).

68. Jewell and Stout, *Selected Letters*, 375.

69. Ibid., 377.

70. Ibid., 538, 539, 557.

71. O'Connor, *Willa Cather*, 95.

72. Jewell and Stout, *Selected Letters*, 404.

73. Ibid., 461.

74. Cather, *My Ántonia: The Scholarly Edition*, 496.

75. Jewell and Stout, *Selected Letters*, 493. Information on translations from Andrew Jewell, ed., "Bibliography of Translations," *The Willa Cather Archive* (Center for Digital Research in the Humanities at the University of Nebraska-Lincoln, 2004–2016), http://cather.unl.edu/translations.bibl.html. Cather may have been slightly off when she wrote her dear friend Carrie Miner Sherwood in 1934 that it had been translated into eight languages.

76. Jewell and Stout, *Selected Letters*, 492.

77. Unpublished letter to Greenslet, October 20, 1930 (Houghton Library, Harvard University).

78. Unpublished letter, Lewis to Cather (New York: J. P. Morgan Library).

79. Jewell and Stout, *Selected Letters*, 506.

80. Ibid., 585.

81. Ibid., 624.

82. Unpublished letter, January 4, 1945 (Chicago: Newberry Library). See also Jewell and Stout, *Selected Letters*, 641–43.

83. O'Connor, *Willa Cather*, 79.

84. Ibid., 89.

85. Ibid., 86.

86. Ibid., 137.

87. Jewell and Stout, *Selected Letters*, 396, 598, 279. She made this same statement, that "from coast to coast there were only two favorable" reviews, "one by Fanny Butcher and one by Grant Overton," in a letter of February 20, 1941, to Viola Roseboro, whom she had known in the old days at *McClure's* (598). If Overton was indeed the author of the unsigned review in the *Sun*, Cather may have been aware of the fact. Or she may have been remembering his praise of her in his book *The Women Who Write Our Novels*, published the same year as Ántonia, which we know she saw (279).

88. Ibid., 454.

89. Ibid., 455.

90. O'Connor, *Willa Cather*, 371, 373.

91. Ibid., 360, 362–63.

92. Ibid., 378–79.

93. Ibid., 370.

94. Jewell and Stout, *Selected Letters*, 561.

Chapter Two

"People in countries who read it in the strangest languages"

The International Reception of My Ántonia

Caterina Bernardini

In her letter dated November 6, 1938, to her brother Roscoe, Willa Cather wrote, "I early learned that if you loved your theme enough you could be as mild as a May morning and still make other people care—people in countries who read it in the strangest languages—Hungarian and Roumanian [*sic*] are the latest. Some day you must come and see my whole bookcase full of translations."[1] As early as 1938, the work of Cather had already been translated, discussed, and celebrated in many countries, and the writer herself had often taken part in decisions involving translations and publications of her books in other languages. In fact, she often voiced concern over the quality of translations and the ability of translators to capture her style.

Of Cather's works, *My Ántonia* was the most frequently published in translation, and it was often the very first novel of the American writer to be translated into a foreign language.[2] And yet the international reception of the book is still quite unexplored. In this chapter, I provide a general overview of the global diffusion of the novel over the past century, and I then discuss some case studies of particular interest, by focusing on translations into—and critical commentaries in—French, Italian, Spanish, and Russian. Although more research into other languages is needed, my study reveals the myriad facts, cultural networks, influencing factors, and participating agents that shape the immensely rich history of *My Ántonia's* cross-cultural reception.

It shouldn't be forgotten that the international reception of Cather's work has not been shaped exclusively by materials in non-English languages. Many international readers and critics, proficient in English, were in fact able to read directly the American editions and reviews or, for example, the inexpensive English-language editions published by the German publishing house Tauchnitz, which Charles Johanningsmeier has recently studied.[3] But as noted by Johanningsmeier, readers of Tauchnitz editions were, in general, "educationally and economically advanced, either cosmopolitan Europeans who had gone to schools where English was taught, or those who could afford to travel either on the Continent or elsewhere in the world." To widen our scope of understanding, then, translations and critical materials in non-English languages must be explored.

While translation choices can effectively render, and sometimes even amplify, the expressive power of a text, they can also, precisely as often feared by Cather, badly alter or completely distort its style and meaning. By closely analyzing key passages that are particularly polysemic, emotionally evocative, and/or challenging, and by taking into account Cather's own comments and decisions about existing or projected translations as they appear in her correspondence with editors and friends, I demonstrate the creative yet vexed role of language in cultural mediation and the complex, dialogic process of interpretation, invention, and revision inherent to translation.

Not only do translations and editions in different languages demand analysis for their peculiarities, but critical articles, introductory notes, and reviews must also be discussed in order to illuminate the reasons why *My Ántonia* was so attractive for non-American readers. I explore the ways the novel interacted with the different local literary and historical-political milieux in which it circulated by examining important acts of mediation by intellectuals and writers like Cesare Pavese (in Italy), Victor Llona (in France), and Vasily S. Yanovsky and Aleksandra K. Savurënok (in Russia), all of whom translated and/or promoted the novel in their countries. Such introductions and critical commentaries in European languages reveal that *My Ántonia* was often presented and marketed as a reflection of American ties to Europe, as well as an innovative literary work, capable of representing an emerging communal, national identity. Cather's depiction of a strong womanhood was also emphasized, together with its optimistic characterization of the immigrant, and of this latter's crucial relationship with a "new" and vast, fascinating land.

"THIS STORY IS NOT FRENCH": CATHER AND VICTOR LLONA

It is perhaps no surprise to hear that *My Ántonia* is the most published novel in Cather's production across the world[4] and that, in many countries, it was the very first novel by the American writer to be published (and, in the case of non-English-speaking countries, to be translated into the local language). This was the case of the Czech Republic (1922), Finland (1934), France (1924),

Germany (1928),[5] Greece (1954), Israel (1948), Iceland (1965), Montenegro (1956), Iran (1956), Kyrgyzstan (2015), Romania (1971), Spain (1955), Thailand (1972), and Pakistan (1990). There are currently (October 2017) forty-nine existing, different translations of the book into thirty-three languages. If we agree with poet Octavio Paz, who argued that "every translation, up to a certain point, is an invention and as such it constitutes a unique text,"[6] we can see Cather's novel as having been uniquely reinvented forty-nine times. And translators of her work often were/are writers themselves.

Cather herself, who had tried to translate from German, French, and Latin in her university years, was well aware of the creative role and mediating responsibility of literary translators. She liked to be informed and to make decisions about new translation projects for her books (including preventing poor translations)[7] and to look at drafts and comment on them. Many of her letters contain her thoughts during this process. Perhaps the most interesting case regarding the translation of *My Ántonia*, one that emphasizes Cather's active involvement in this creative process, is that of Victor Llona and his 1924 translation of the novel into French, which engendered Cather's questions about the translatability of her novel.

Llona was a polyglot writer and translator who had been born in Peru and had moved to France with his family at the age of nine. In Paris, when still very young, he was part of the circle that gravitated around the literary magazine *Nouvelle Revue Française*, which included writers Paul Claudel and André Gide. From 1905 to 1920 he lived (but he also occasionally went back to France) in the United States, both in New York and Chicago. In the United States, he took part in the cultural life of Washington Square and Greenwich Village and met a series of American writers, including Henry James. In 1920 he went back to France, and he started to translate into French the work of some of the American writers he met and/or knew by reputation.[8] As argued by scholar Estuardo Nuñez, Llona was aware of the value and novelty of the work of these writers, and he did not hesitate to start a "gigantic work of translation"[9] once he was back in France.

Cather's trust in Llona was at first high. On December 2, 1920, Cather wrote to editor Ferris Greenslet about Llona, who had proposed his translation into French with the idea of serializing the novel for publication in the *Nouvelle Revue Française*.[10] Cather wrote that she needed to check with some friends in Chicago to understand whether she could rely on Llona, but that his ideas were good. Soon after, she confirmed that all the answers to her inquiries had been reassuring, and she once again praised Llona's ideas: "the man's notes on the first chapter were so good that I would like to have him make the translation. . . . I think he will present the book well. He has worked out some interesting rendering of idiomatic expressions."[11]

But the writer's enthusiasm did not last long. A few months later, in April 1921, Cather wrote to Dorothy Canfield Fisher to ask her opinion about Llona's translation. Cather had reviewed a draft of the first eight chapters,[12] and she felt alarmed: "I am puzzled, because it seems to me about the sort of translation I would make myself with the help of a dictionary—which must mean that it's bad enough! It's too literal, and I fear it's not always grammatical."[13] Cather's judgment of Llona's work with *My Ántonia* would continue to oscillate. In May 1921, she wrote to Laura Hills that she felt it was "done so splendidly."[14] However, in July of the same year, in a letter to Elizabeth Sergeant, she called it "stiffed and flat."[15]

Her dissatisfaction with the translation had at that point become quite high, and she found it overly descriptive and verbose, which conflicted with her style:

> I thought I had written that Damned book once, and was done with it; and now here it is with the same old problems, and in a language I know nothing about. He always uses too many words, and makes the landscape and people too detailed and precise, someway - - - drives in the last carpet tack! When I knock out a dozen words to a page, he says, or writes from Paris, "That's not French!" Well, then this story is not French, and can't be made so; it's absurd to combine a tight precise style with anything so informal and even lax in outline.[16]

This passage is extremely fascinating as it illuminates not only Cather's way of thinking about her novel and style as tight and precise (but not too detailed), but also the fully creative nature of translation as a vexed rewriting process: "here it is with the same old problems." In this same passage, Cather reflects on her own composition struggles and meditates on another crucial issue in translation studies—whether literature can cross lands. "Well, then this story is not French, and can't be made so," she notes. The writer is vehemently reclaiming the original distinction of her work as a novel carved within a precise language and culture. In this sense, then, she also seems to be advocating the cause of a "foreignizing"[17] translation style: Llona should not adapt the language of the novel too much to the French, but should somehow make the original remain present, in its difference, and resonate, in that difference.

In this same line of thought, we need to return to the letter to Dorothy Canfield Fisher I mentioned earlier; in it, Cather expresses her gravest concern with Llona's translation, while, again, making larger statements about both the peculiarities of her style and the nature and purpose of literary translation:

> What is the use of a poor translation for a book where the story is practically zero? There is nothing left!

> What I want to know is; Is there any of the spirit of the book in his translation, or is it such heavy, Chicago French that nothing stands out but clumsy sentences with strangely mixed tenses of the verb?[18]

Cather is here revealing that what most counts in *My Ántonia* is style: the way in which things are articulated—its tone, its spirit. The story per se is minimal, secondary. So her main wonder is whether Llona's translation, for the clumsiness she perceives in it, might be missing the spirit. What is, then, the spirit of *My Ántonia* that Cather wanted translators to catch? What did she want translators to try and recreate in their versions? Likewise, how did she want translators to make clear that "the story is not French" (or Italian, Spanish, Chinese, etc.) and "can't be made so"?

THE PROBLEM OF "COUNTRY":
STYLE AND TRANSLATION

If we take an essential passage from the novel, in which Jim first takes a wagon ride and glimpses the country, we can see how translators into different languages dealt with the problem of "country" as an idea, reflective of Jim's vision and shifting subjectivity. I will transcribe the translations as they are, and I will provide a very literal (to the point of reproducing idiomatic expressions in their naked structure) translation in the endnotes:

> I tried to go to sleep, but the jolting made me bite my tongue, and I soon began to ache all over. When the straw settled down I had a hard bed. Cautiously I slipped from under the buffalo hide, got up on my knees and peered over the side of the wagon. There seemed to be nothing to see; no fences, no creeks or trees, no hills or fields. If there was a road, I could not make it out in the faint starlight. There was nothing but land: not a country at all, but the material out of which countries are made.[19]

I selected this passage because I think it is highly representative of the novel. The language is sharp and concise. Idiomatic expressions are used. The images are limpid, and there are references to objects that are deeply embedded in the geographical and historical context of the novel, such as the buffalo hide and the wagon. The visually poignant scene is paralleled with deep psychological insights. The result is a controlled style that unleashes a powerful lyrical resonance.

Llona's 1924 translation into French demonstrates the difficulty of conveying spirit, style, and the psychological resonance of openness in Jim at this point:

> J'essayai de dormir, mais je me mordais la langue à chaque cahot. D'ailleurs, j'eus bientôt le corps rompu. Quand la paille fut bien tassée, ma couche devint trop dure. Je me glissai avec précaution sous la peau de bison, me dressai sur le genoux et risquai un oeil par-dessus les ridelles. On ne voyat rien: ni haies, ni ruisseaux, ni arbres, pas de collines, pas de champs. S'il y avait une route, je ne

la distinguais point à la mesquine clarté des etoiles. Il n'y avait rien, que de la terre: non pas un pays, mais la matière brute dont les pays sont faits.[20]

Llona's translation is quite well done. It is very literal and mostly straightforward, with the exception of two cases, in which the translator decided to add connotations that were absent from the original. The "faint starlight" becomes for Llona "mesquine clarté des etoiles." While "clarté des etoiles" literally means "clarity of the stars," the adjective "mesquine" indicates something like "petty, mean, ungenerous." And the simple "material" of the last sentence in English becomes "matière brute," literally "raw material." Such interventions are not invasive, and yet they still alter the economy of words of the original passage: "mesquine" adds a negativity that was not present in "faint," and "matière brute" makes the language of Cather's lyrical sentence sound more expected, almost like a set phrase.

The altered economy detracts from Jim's experience. The "wagon" is not directly mentioned in the French passage, while "I had a hard bed" becomes for Llona "my bed became too hard," which, again, is an unnecessary addition. Jim is here entering into a completely new territory. The traveling conditions are hard, he cannot fall asleep, he does not have any real bed at all, and Cather's "I had a hard bed" symbolically renders, in this sense, the feeling of complete estrangement and physical distress that Jim must be feeling. Llona's "my bed," on the contrary, normalizes the image and takes away some of the pathos created by Cather to underline the difficult, unusual, and yet at the same time adventurous experience.

Yet we can see Llona's merit here, in comparison to other translators. He translates "country" as "pays" (which indicates both a national country and a region, a certain space), thus managing to keep the effect of the original. As we will see, many translators of the same passage would not be able to do the same. Let us go back to the entire passage and see how Jole Jannelli Pinna Pintor rendered it into Italian in 1947:

Tentai di dormire ma i sobbalzi mi facevano mordere la lingua, e dopo un pò doloravo in ogni parte; quando poi la paglia fu schiacciata, il mio letto divenne piuttosto duro. Strisciai fuori dalla pelle di bufalo cautamente, m'inginocchiai e m'affacciai sull'orlo del carro. Pareva non vi fosse nulla da vedere: non steccati, non torrenti o alberi, non colline né campi. Se c'era una strada, alla luce tenue delle stelle non era visibile. Null'altro che terra: non la campagna, ma il materiale di cui è fatta la campagna: . . .[21]

Pintor's translation is also literal and it manages well to render the original. But there are some odd choices and imprecisions. At the end of the first sentence of the paragraph, Pintor chose to have a semicolon instead of a full stop, thus uniting two sentences that were separated in the original. She did the same at the end of the paragraph; instead of closing the highly poetic sentence that ends with the words "but the material out of which countries are made" in the original, she used a colon. While it is true that Italian sentences are usually much longer than English ones, this does not seem to justify why Pintor would choose not to retain the brevity of Cather's diction, especially when it is so poetically effective, as in the second case I just mentioned. Pintor also chose to go, as Llona, for "my bed," and even to depersonalize the original "I could not make it out" into a much colder "was not visible." Jim's difficulty, his active, personal, unique attempt—and failure—at seeing the road, so strongly expressed with the use of the phrasal verb "make out," is thus cut from the text. These things, which can at first appear as small and unimportant details, well exemplify how translating choices can have the effect of missing important traits of the tone and, perhaps, spirit of the novel, as Cather would call it.

Finally, Pintor renders "country" and "countries" as "campagna," an Italian term used to refer exclusively to rural areas, something close to "countryside" and not able to carry, as the English "country" does, the multiple semantic connotations of identifiable region, rural land, communal space of belonging and shared identity, and national state. The open-meaning, thought-provoking effect created by Cather's "country" in this sentence is lost. The mythopoetical emphasis on an "America in the making," which is so relevant here and within the entire novel, is lost in translation. Even more problematically, Pintor does not even render the move from the singular to the plural form, which is a crucial feature in the original passage as it amplifies the intense, majestic tone created by the adversative clause. One wonders why Pintor went for "campagna." A limited knowledge of the language seems improbable, given the overall good quality of the translation. Perhaps, then, this could signal some critical shortsightedness, or even a sort of reductive approach. The translator missed Cather's larger point about American communal identity, and anchored the scene to the rural setting of the opening.

Both language and perspective are crucial elements in this scene. Gabriele Baldini, an important Italian scholar of British and American literature, critic, and writer also translated the novel into Italian, just as Pintor, in 1947. But the tone used by Baldini is quite different than Pintor's. While Pintor used ordinary and colloquial words, Baldini used more formal and old-fashioned words like "scotimento" for "jolting," "indolenzito" for "ache," and the quite archaic but visually effective "sdrucciolai" for "slipped from under."[22] Baldini also chose, like Pintor and Llona, to have "my bed" rather than "a hard bed." But he did keep Jim's subjective perspective in rendering "I could not make it out" as "io non sapevo distinguerla" (literally, "I didn't know how to distinguish it"; note the emphasis on Jim's estranged perspective and inability, emphasized by Baldini's choice of using the verb "sapere," "to know"). Baldini also, disappointingly enough, decided to translate "country" and "countries" with "campagna" (rural area). Baldini's and Pintor's 1947 translations remain the only Italian ones available to this day.

For France, the situation is a bit better, with two translations after Llona's: Allan Blaise's[23] in 1967, and Robert Ruard's in 1993. Let us look at how these other two French translators rendered the same passage, investigating different decisions about Jim's subjectivity. Blaise translated "I had a hard bed" as "mon lit devenait tres dur"[24] ("my bed became too hard"), but he kept Jim's subjective perspective. For the word and idea of "country," Blaise chose "paysage" ("landscape, scenery"), which might be the worst possible solution among many he had. Why take away the concrete reference to a country dramatically paired to its raw, primary material, or land, and make it abstract and slightly romantic sounding by turning it into "landscape"? It is unfortunate that Blaise also happened to be the only translator, among the ones I took into consideration, who decided to twist the novel's title into *Mon Amie Ántonia*. The word "amie" in French is the feminine form for "ami," a word that, generally, means "friend" and that can also have a connotation of a loving relationship. Blaise's choice misleads readers and is indicative of a quite reductive and, frankly, problematic overinterpretation that leaves the ambiguity of Jim and Antonia's relationship aside.

Syntactical requirements in other languages also affect style. Ruard, in 1993, went, as the Italians, for "campagne." Interestingly, he chose to separate the phrase that in Cather's text is united by a colon:

> Il n'y avait rien que la terre. Pas la campagne, mais seulement la matière premiere dont la campagne est faite.[25]

Using "pas" ("not") to start a new sentence increases the dramatic and lyrical quality of the sentence. French syntax also comes a little closer than other languages to Cather's use of the affirmative/negative construction. The phrase "there was nothing" is rendered (by Llona, Blaise, and Ruard) with "il n'y avait rien." In other words, in the original and French translations, the negation "nothing" is the direct object rather than the beginning of the sentence (although in the French it does come earlier than the English with the contraction of "ne" in "n'y"). Notice, instead, the Italian "Non c'era altro che" by Baldini and Pintor's "Null'altro che" ("non" is the literal equivalent of "not" and "null'" is the shortened form of "nulla," "nothing"), which set the tone of absence and lack right from the very beginning (while, in the original and in the French versions, readers encounter it only later). Italian language does not offer many options in this sense, as negations have to be structured (with the exception of some dialects and idiolects) with the negative adverb in the first place.[26] "Nothing" cannot be the vision *seen* by Jim, given limits of Italian linguistics.

The same thing is true for Russian translation. Vasily Yanovksy's 1952 translation starts with a beautifully alliterating (double) negation:

Ничего не было, только земля: не страна, а материал из которого страны делаются.[27]

Yanovsky's translation is also interesting as it goes for the word "страна" for "country." "Страна" can be used to indicate a nation, but also a region, a recognizable portion of land with certain natural and geographical charac- teristics, and inhabited by people who share a sense of belonging and a col- lective cultural identity. Therefore "страна" comes closest to Cather's use of "country. " Yanovsky's choice is rooted in a strong critical awareness. In his introduction to the translation, he uses the word "страна" repeatedly when discussing Cather's peculiar sense of the "big land."

But the valid solution of "страна" was not pursued by the duo of transla- tors who next (in 1979) translated the novel into Russian.[28] Irina A. Razu- movskaya and Svetlana P. Samostrelova-Smirnitskaya rendered the passage as follows:

Кру́гом была только земля—не сады, не пашни, а то на чём их создают.[29]

The translators tried to recuperate the affirmative beginning of the original by going for something like "around was only land," but they lost the idea of "nothing but" present in Cather's text. And they did something very strange in the rest of the sentence by having "not gardens, not fields, but what con- stitutes them." The transition from singular to plural is lost, and the word "country" is scattered into two words, two different images. The sharpness of the original passage is significantly decreased by this alteration.

But at least Cather's original sentence was still there. In the first Spanish translation of the book, published in 1955 in Barcelona by Caralt and trans- lated by Julio Fernández-Yañez Gimeno, this sentence is completely gone.[30] Was this the result of a simple inattention or sloppiness? Or was it a deliberate decision of the translator to completely escape the difficulties of this passage? The gap in Gimeno's 1955 text is compensated, if only after a long time, by Gema Moral Bartolomé's rendering, in her 2000 new translation of the novel into Spanish, the polysemity of Cather's use of "country":

No había nada más que tierra: no era un país, sino el material del que están hechos los países.[31]

In Spanish, "país" can mean both a national country and a certain spatial area of land (something like "region"), just as "pays" does in French. This is also true for the Italian "paese," which is even more polysemic than the Spanish and the French. "Paese," in addition to meaning national country and region, can also indicate a small town, not necessarily rural. And yet only Llona, among the French translators, used the term, while both the Italian translators chose "campagna."

While "país," "paese, "pays," and "страна" seem to be ideal renderings of Cather's "country, " the difficulties and alternative solutions found by most translators, perhaps epitomized by the complete erasure of the sentence in Gimeno's version, signal the richness and complexity of the original. This reminds us of how, as Janis Stout eloquently put it, Cather is a "writer of seemingly transparent narratives that turn out to be radically indeterminate."[32] Staying true to the spirit of the novel provokes a variety of interpretations and questions. This sentence also proves pivotal for international critics when they discuss their fascination with Cather's peculiar "sense of the land," as I argue shortly. Analyzing the resonance of "country" across translations concretely demonstrates how the nature of each language and the cultural implications of specific words influence translating decisions and set limitations that can only be partially challenged and overcome. The "untranslatable" is both the curse and the blessing of an activity that remains necessarily faulty, ultimately interpretive, and inherently creative.

BOTH GLOBAL AND PROVINCIAL: MARKETING AND RECEPTION IN EUROPE

While it would be impossible to analyze these single translations in full here, comparisons of this passage reveal that translators of *My Ántonia* were not always able to keep the "tight and precise" style of the original. Italian translations, and often French and Spanish ones too—often because of their linguistic structures—appear to employ longer sentences and more complex syntactic structures. Words that are strictly inherent to the American setting of the original often get translated, instead of being left in the original and accompanied by a footnote, but there are some positive exceptions: Pintor's translation does keep many English words untranslated. The same is true for Llona, as he often left the words intact and added a footnote (I wonder if Cather's direct comments on his draft could have had a crucial impact on this choice).

Connotations of words impact names as well. A funny controversy regards the last name "Shimerda": in Italian, French, and Spanish, the word "merda"/"merde"/"mierda" means "shit," and while most translators decided to go ahead and use the word as it was, a few others decided to change it. Pintor went for "Shimeda," Baldini for "Shiverda," Gimeno for "Shimarde," and Llona did something just incredible: he went for "S . . ." One wonders what a French reader could think this would implicate: that the name was presented as unpronounceable? That it had to be kept secret in the story for some mysterious reason? And what did Cather think about it? Was she aware of it? Llona's translating choice remains puzzling.

In general, translators have been quite successful at transforming and rendering the vivid and lyrical quality of Cather's novel. This could partially be due to the fact that many of these translators were also writers: Llona, Blaise, and Yanovsky, for example, have written novels of their own. This fact is important because these writers were naturally implicated in the networks and milieux in which the reception of *My Ántonia* took shape. Analyzing translators' introductions allows us to explore the ways in which *My Ántonia* has been presented to readers and configured within different literary markets around the world. Many critics saw the novel as an important literary document for the introduction of international readers to the discovery of a part of America and of its history, topics that were unfamiliar to them. This was the point made by Victor Llona in his introduction to his translation, as also discussed by Palleau Papin.[33] But Llona also aimed to underline another trait that would naturally be of great interest for his readers: Cather's ability to describe what he called "the European element" of American history. His introduction situated Cather's work as tied to European influence:

> Miss Cather is perhaps the American writer who loves and best understands the European element to which the United States owe a big portion of their agricultural prosperity, and their major sources of richness. This xenophilia—which is always the sign of a superior intelligence.[34]

The emphasis put by Llona on what he, quite radically, called Cather's "xenophilia," or her attention to the "foreign" element of American history and success, reveals a cutting-edge understanding of the intrinsic cosmopolitanism of Cather's work as well as the marketing of Cather's text to European interests. Another comment by Llona regards the character of Ántonia, "whose bright personality," he writes, "will remain one of the most beautiful creations in literature."[35] This is a common point made by a number of other international critics.

Finally, Llona discusses and praises Cather's writing style by comparing it to that of Russian writer Ivan Turgenev and American poet Walt Whitman. With the Turgenev of *A House of Gentlefolk* and *A Sportsman's Sketches*, Cather "inadvertently"[36] shares "the perfection of colored, but direct and naked style."[37] For the comparison with Whitman, Llona makes reference to Cather's Whitmanian citation in titling *O Pioneers!*, and brings up a comment made by critic Carl Van Doren in an article in *The Nation* in 1921, according to which Cather and Whitman express a similar perception of the spectacle of the world. Whitman was, at that time, in France, one of the few American writers to be quite well known, and Llona's referring to him in an analogy with Cather was perhaps seen as a necessary step. Cather and Whitman, like American literature in general, were appealing to European readers for their focus on "the sanctity and strength of pure beings," "the fundamental beauty of nature and of man," "the simplicity of humble people," and "the modest glory of daily work."[38] But Llona did make sure to underline what he thought was the main differentiating element between Cather and Whitman: as he put it, "a taste for the finest quality, a delicate sense of humor, always retain Cather from being grandiloquent."[39]

Not all critics understood the freshness, innovation, and cosmopolitan character of the novel. The German editors of Tauchnitz, for example, chose *My Ántonia* because they thought that it was an adequate novel to comply with the Nazi's conservative cultural politics, as argued by Johanningsmeier. In Italy, on the other hand, *My Ántonia* was not the first book by Cather to be published, as Italian editors had been privileging, at first, books by the American writer that had some references to the Catholic religion.[40] But Cather's novel was in those same years starting to be appreciated by an Italian critic, writer, and scholar of American literature: Cesare Pavese. Pavese's approach might apparently seem to be close to the idea of the novel as an "anti-avant-garde" work that appealed to the Nazi critics in Germany. He in fact described it (together with other works written by other American writers in those same years) as "provincial." But his view of "provincialism" is far from being a reductive labeling of Cather's work as a piece of "local color." His idiosyncratic use of the word "provincial" was provocative and, actually, positive.

Pavese saw national strength in the novel's penetration of a region. Pavese expressed the desire to write about Cather's novel in a 1931 letter to Arrigo Cajumi.[41] In the letter, Pavese asked Cajumi whether he thought that an article titled "Il villaggio Americano" ("The American village") could be of interest for publication within *La Cultura*.[42] Pavese specifically mentioned the works and writers he would want to concentrate on: *Main Street* by Sinclair Lewis, *Winesburg, Ohio* by Sherwood Anderson, *Spoon River Anthology* by Edgar Lee Masters, *The Grandmothers* by Glenway Scott, and *My Ántonia* by Willa Cather. The article, as described by the Italian writer, would focus on "the literary renaissance that started in 1910 and is still going on, showing how the great discovery of those men was the America of the Midwest, of provinces and of towns."

Pavese felt Italian writers could benefit from the type of national unity emergent from the local. The proposed article was never written, but later that same year Pavese did publish for *La Cultura* an essay[43] that he devoted principally to Edgar Lee Masters, although Lewis, Anderson, and Cather were also mentioned. In it, Pavese described Masters's *Anthology* as the initiator of the realistic description of provincial people with the same renovated energy and an epic, quasi-biblical tone that were also present in the works of Lewis, Anderson, and Cather.[44] In an article about Anderson,[45] Pavese explained what he thought Italian writers had to learn from this "provincial" American literature:

> We might think of the significance, for Italian literature, of the discovery of regions, which went hand in hand with the quest for national unity, a discovery that belongs to the last part of the eighteenth and to the entire nineteenth century. From Alfieri, on down, all the Italian writers try, sometimes and indeed often unconsciously, to achieve a more profound national unity through penetrating always further the character of their own region, thus to achieve the creation of a human awareness and a language rich with all the blood of the province . . . and yet, from Alfieri himself, and then through D'Azeglio, Abba, to Calandra, or even later, we have never had that man and that work in which, in addition to being most dear to us, would truly achieve that universality and originality which would make him comprehensible to all men and not only to his countrymen. This is our still unsatisfied need. Meanwhile, the American novelists of whom I speak have in fact met the corresponding need of their nation and region. We must, therefore, learn from them.

These ideas were put into practice in Pavese's own creative work, which is often set in his native region, Piemonte. The real protagonists of many of his books are the land and its people, the customs and ways of being, all realistically depicted but also filtered through a highly evocative perspective. But the local, in Pavese, is never folkloristic. It is not an arrival, but a departure point, an imaginative core, a mythopoetic microcosm that reflects larger political, social, and existential questions.

From one of Pavese's letters we learn that, as early as 1932—when only a few articles about Cather had come out in Italy, and the only translations available for Italian readers were excerpts from *Death Comes for the Archbishop*—there had been plans for publishing the first Italian translation of *My Ántonia*. As Pavese wrote to Chiuminatto in 1932, a publisher of Turin intended to translate *My Ántonia*.[46] Pavese was referring to the publishing house Frassinelli, with which he had started to collaborate. Even if it is not made explicit in the letter, we can hypothesize that Pavese himself suggested the book to the publisher because he had already read and appreciated it. But

Frassinelli never pursued that project, and *My Ántonia* only appeared in Italian in 1947, when both Longanesi (in Milan) and Einaudi (in Turin) published it, in the translations by—respectively—Gabriele Baldini and Jole Janelli Pinna Pintor. Einaudi was the publishing house for which Pavese had been working since 1934: once again, it seems probable that Pavese actively encouraged, and this time successfully, the publication of Cather's book.

Longanesi also published the book, and in what seems to be a spirit quite close to Pavese's understanding and praising of Cather's work (and of other "provincial" writers) for its renovating, mythopoetic value. An article about the book appeared, in fact, in August 1947 in *Il libraio*, the literary magazine managed by Longanesi and serving as a news bulletin for its publications. In it, critic Giorgio Bubani wrote that Ántonia would soon become a favorite character for Italian readers. These latter would appreciate and admire her for her strong and independent disposition. The traits underlined by Bubani were certainly appealing for the readership of a country that was emerging from wartimes in which women had decisively contributed to economic sustenance and recovery and had just conquered the right to vote (in 1946). And Ántonia had the merit, for Bubani, of embodying and personifying America as well as the Midwest; she suggested a difficult and yet prosperous land, full of optimism. The individual story of Ántonia becomes, according to the Italian critic, the epic depiction of an entire generation of migrants and pioneers. Bubani is particularly struck by the sense of energy and industriousness that dominates the book, praising its intensity:

> All these people launch themselves at work with a sort of fury. It is as if the new land instills in the new people some of its hidden germinating power, of the energies that it contains. The intensity with which people worked for the opening of the Midwest, we believe is quite unprecedented in the history of human life. Perhaps there was never anything like this.[47]

Bubani's emphasis on the land's powerful potential and its impact on people's optimistic minds and industrious lifestyle is quite suggestive, especially when considering, once again, the context in which this review was written: a postwar Italy eager to start a new life.

A similar reading, and a similar fascination with the Midwestern land, seen almost as the real, main protagonist of Cather's novel, came with the introduction to the first translation into Russian, published in 1952 not in the Soviet Union but in New York, by the newly established Chekhov Publishing House for Russian émigré readers.[48] The translation was authored by physician, writer, and Russian émigré (first in Paris and then in New York) Vasily S. Yanovsky. Yanovsky established a parallel between the migrants' experience of *My Ántonia* and that of the Russian émigré community who was the targeted readership of the book. He situated the novel as the industry of a new continent:

> For the Russian reader, presumably, it's going to be very interesting to meet people who are in many respects, as he is: migrants, without the language, without resources, often helpless, but with the ability and savviness of industrious people, craving for a normal, decent life. The mix of languages and customs, hunger, cold, dugouts. . . . It would seem that, alas, this is something rather well known. But at the same time there is also something completely new: not a hostile, brutal nationalism, not masters and slaves, not people of first and second class. But, all around, a frightening, unknown continent, an incomprehensible language, a strange climate. It is hard for the older people. They are sad. Often they don't survive the new conditions, and die. The younger yearningly adapt, work, tirelessly. Look, they built a new house there. . . . Plowed soil here, a new village there. This is how a country grows![49] Like every real artist, Willa Cather unconsciously infects readers with the feeling of a certain strength, an underground spring that stealthily operates in life, with muted strings. Ántonia is equated with the strength that steadily pushes humankind forward, helps to work, to win, to reproduce (and pushes cereals to ripen and seasons to alternate).[50]

Yanovsky also built another connection for his readers. He argued in fact that one could trace, in Cather's writing, something very similar to an important *leitmotif*, in Russian literature, which is the depiction of the endless space of the Russian steppes:

> Willa Cather is enormously endowed with a feeling of landscape. She is moved by a lyrical sense of the big land,[51] of the endless fields of wheat and corn, of the road in the middle of the prairie, the noise of the wheels at night, the starry sky. . . . This is her main connection with Russian writers.[52]

Yanovsky closed his introduction by quoting a passage from the novel that, as he claimed, can be extremely valuable for the Russian reader. The passage he chose describes the Mormon trail and the sunflowers. The Russian translation of the original words "the roads to freedom" is italicized by Yanovsky, and this is particularly striking when thinking that the readership of his translation would mostly be that post–World War II generation of Russian émigrés significantly called "non-returners,"[53] who had flown their motherland (and resisted forced repatriation) in search of political and intellectual freedom.

The hopefulness and vitality emanated by Cather's novel were also emphasized by another Russian critic, scholar Aleksandra K. Savurënok,[54] in her introduction to the 1979 edition (the first one to be published in the USSR).[55] Savurënok's scholarly piece is pretty well documented: the prototype of Annie Pavelka is mentioned, and Cather's style is discussed at length. Savurënok reflected on how the writer is able to build an underground connection of the separate episodes, "not always having a direct link with the destiny of the characters, but essentially important for the full picture," while telling the events "in a way for which the readers feel involved with them," thus achieving "a subjective, lyrical tone."[56] Savurënok concluded, "in this association of an epic amplitude embracing reality and a penetrating lyrism, is contained one of the secrets of the artistic originality of *My Ántonia.*"[57]

The Russian scholar extended her reflections on Cather's writing and explained how the composing principle at the base of *My Ántonia* has much to do with the ideas that Cather would express a few years later in her 1922 aesthetic manifesto, "The Novel Démeublé." Savurënok analyzed Cather's "unfurnished" style[58] and focused on the writer's assertions about the exemplarity of Leo Tolstoy's work in this sense. For Savurënok, Cather's representations of landscape in the novel fully conform to the ideas of "The Novel Démeublé." Landscapes and nature are never, in the novel, simply traditional background elements, but they are "an inseparable part of the emotional world of the characters." As in Tolstoy's novels, they work "as a manifestation of the soul."[59] The narrator does not describe nature, but experiences it.

The vitality, industriousness, and generosity of Ántonia as a character also emerge from her relationship with nature and with the land itself, to which she gives all her interior and physical energy. Ántonia's connection and almost symbiosis with the land derive precisely from her devoted work at it. In this sense, Savurënok discusses the symbolic centrality of the scene of the lone plough in Cather's novel, as contrasted to James Fenimore Cooper's scene of the lonely old hunter in *The Prairie.* If, in Cooper, the hunter tragically epitomizes the human greed that can strip the land of all its natural resources, in Cather the plough stands for the foundational work of the masses of pioneers, domesticating the land. Savurënok closed by reflecting on how many of Cather's works after *My Ántonia* would be characterized by a much more pessimistic view of the world. But the writer's best novels, she concluded, had depicted a world based on the ideal of free work and by hatred for the money-making bourgeoisie,[60] which would be an integral part of American culture, as expressed in the work of those writers who followed her steps: Lewis, Anderson, and Faulkner.

Thus international critics and translators all around the world have interacted with *My Ántonia* and presented it to readers in different languages and in different times. A variety of contexts, approaches, situations, and agendas have shaped these interactions, and critics have often underlined traits that would be of special interest for their specific readership. But it can be safely said that a few patterns emerge from the cases I discuss. First and foremost, even critics who emphasize the European influence in the novel locate the novel's vitality in Cather's depiction of the land and the characters' relationships with it. This particular fascination might derive from a sort of mythical imagination of the Western, endless American space, which commonly inhabits the minds of non-American, and especially European, readers. Second, the appreciation of the communal life described in the novel, with its cosmopolitan nature and with its acute portrayal of social processes of coexistence, makes the novel relevant worldwide. Third, the radiant, independent, modern character of Ántonia epitomizes the novel's vision of strength; her character became an incredible source of inspiration for foreign writers and for actual women in many nations. Finally, Cather's masterful and deeply innovative writing style and use of language proved capable of achieving the most powerful and complex effects with a most sculpted elegance and simplicity: a style that was extremely hard to emulate and often quite hard to translate. Nevertheless, travel across time and national borders *My Ántonia* certainly—and successfully—did.

NOTES

1. Letter from Willa Cather to Roscoe Cather, November 6, 1938, in Willa Cather, *The Selected Letters of Willa Cather*, eds. Andrew Jewell and Janis Stout (New York: Knopf, 2013), 561.

2. See Andrew Jewell, ed., "Bibliography of Translations," in *The Willa Cather Archive* (Center for Digital Research in the Humanities at the University of Nebraska–Lincoln), http://cather.unl.edu/translations.bibl.html.

3. The article, of which Professor Johanninsgmeier kindly sent me a draft, is titled "Willa Cather's Tauchnitz Editions and Their Role in Establishing Her European and Worldwide Reputation, 1926–1947" and is forthcoming in *Resources for American Literary Study*.

4. According to the Worldcat online catalog (http://www.worldcat.org/), and to a series of national library catalogs, the book was published 195 times (including both new editions and reprints) outside the United States. *Death Comes for the Archbishop* and *O Pioneers!* are at the second and third place, having been published 140 and 93 times, respectively. Note that, given the extensive number of languages and countries I am considering and the fact that there could be some gaps and mistakes in the cataloging, the numbers I provide in this chapter should be considered as approximate.

5. The case of Germany is unique as in this same year, 1928, in addition to *My Ántonia*, *A Lost Lady* and *One of Ours* were also published. The Tauchnitz edition of *My Ántonia*, in English, was published in 1935.

6. Paz is quoted in Susan Bassnett, *Translation Studies* (Routledge: London, 1991), 38.

7. See, for example, letter from Willa Cather to Yalthah Menuhin Stix, January 23, 1939, in *The Selected Letters*, 567.

8. In addition to Cather's *My Ántonia* and "Coming, Aphrodite!" Llona translated, among many others, works by Francis Scott Fitzgerald, Edna Ferber, Sherwood Anderson, and Theodore Dreiser.

9. See Estuardo Nuñez, "Semblanza de Victor Llona," *Alpha* 2 (1965): 4. (My translation.)

10. Cather was very flattered by this idea, as she writes to friend Laura Hills in [May 1921]. This letter will be included in *The Complete Letters of Willa Cather*, which will begin publication in 2018 at http://cather.unl.edu.

11. Letter from Willa Cather to Ferris Greenslet, December 14, 1920. This letter will be published in 2018 in *The Willa Cather Archive*.

12. Although she was not fluent, Cather knew French enough to be able to read Llona's translation and to get a sense of the rhythm and tone.

13. Letter from Willa Cather to Dorothy Canfield Fisher, April 10, 1921. This letter will be included in *The Complete Letters of Willa Cather*, which will begin publication in 2018 at http://cather.unl.edu. The letter is also mentioned in Françoise Palleau-Papin's article "Slowly but Surely: Willa Cather's Reception in France," *Studies in the Novel* 45, no. 3 (Fall 2013): 538–58. Papin's article discusses the French reception of Cather and takes into brief consideration the crucial, initiating role of Llona's translation.

14. Letter from Willa Cather to Laura Hills [May 1921]. This letter will be published in 2018 in *The Willa Cather Archive*.

15. Letter from Willa Cather to Elizabeth Shepley Sergeant, July 6, 1921. This letter will be included in *The Complete Letters of Willa Cather*, which will begin publication in 2018 at http://cather.unl.edu.

16. Ibid.

17. By using this term, I am borrowing the concept of foreignization from philosopher Friederich Schleiermacher and from literary scholar and translator Lawrence Venuti, who adopted it as a founding concept for his theories about translation. See, for example, his *The Translator's Invisibility* (New York: Routledge, 1995).

18. This letter will be included in *The Complete Letters of Willa Cather*, which will begin publication in 2018 at http://cather.unl.edu.

19. Willa Cather, *My Ántonia*, Willa Cather Scholarly Edition, eds. Charles W. Mignon and Kari A. Ronning (Lincoln: University of Nebraska Press, 1994), 7.

20. Willa Cather, *Mon Ántonia*, trans. Victor Llona (Paris: Payot, 1924), 17. Back translation: "I tried to sleep, but I bit my tongue at every jolting. By the by, I soon had my body broken. When the hay had been well pressed, my bed became too hard. I slipped with caution under the buffalo skin, I stood on my knees and risked an eye on top of the slatted sides. One could not see anything: not fences, not streams, nor any hills, nor any fields. If there was a road, I could not distinguish it at the mean clarity of the starts. There was nothing, but land: not a country, but the raw material of which the countries are made."

21. Willa Cather, *La mia Ántonia*, trans. Jole Jannelli Pinna Pintor (Torino: Einaudi, 1947), 16. Back translation: "I tried to sleep but the jolting made me bite my tongue, and after a while I was aching in every side; when, then, the hay had become pressed, my bed became quite hard. I slipped out of the skin of the buffalo cautiously, I knelt and peered over the edge of the cart. It seemed that there was nothing to see: not fences, not streams or trees, not hills or fields. If there was a road, at the faint light of the stars, it was not visible. Nothing other than land: not the countryside, but the material out of which the countryside is made."

22. Willa Cather, *La mia Ántonia*, trans. Gabriele Baldini (Milano: Longanesi, 1947), 17. I am not providing a back translation for these terms as they do very literally render the original terms, but it should be noted that they have a connotation of formal and dignified tone that is absent, for example, in Pintor's use of more modern synonyms in her own translation.

23. As noted by March Chénetier in his article "Cather's Reputation in France," in *Willa Cather: Willa Cather: A Writer's Worlds*, eds. John J. Murphy, Françoise Palleau-Papin, and Robert Thacker (Lincoln: University of Nebraska Press, 2010), 28, Blaise was the pseudonym used by Swiss writer Alfred Rosset.

24. Willa Cather, *Mon amie Ántonia*, trans. Blaise Allan (Paris: Vent d'Oeust, 1967), 17.

25. Willa Cather, *Mon Ántonia*, trans. Robert Ruard (Paris: Deuxtemps Tierce, 1993), 15.

26. So an Italian translator who would want to try and render the effect of Cather's original passage would have to distort grammar in a very experimental, foreignizing way.

27. Willa Cather, Моя Антония, trans. Vasily S. Yanovsky (New York: Chekhov Publishing House, 1952), 12. Back translation: "Nothing was there, only land: not a country, but the material out of which countries are made."

28. This edition is interesting also for the presence of original illustrations by E. Kapelyush.

29. Willa Cather, Моя Антония, trans. Irina A. Razumovskaya and Svetlana P. Samostrelova-Smirnitskaya (Leningrad: Chudozhestvennaya Literatura, 1979), 34. Back translation: "Around was only land—not gardens, not fields, but what they are made of."

30. Willa Cather, *Mi Ántonia*, trans. Julio Fernández-Yañez Gimeno (Barcelona: Caralt, 1955), 14. The translation goes directly from "the faint starlight" to "No, there was nothing."

31. Willa Cather, *Mi Ántonia*, trans. Gema Moral Bartolomé (Barcelona: Alba Editorial, 2000), 22–23. Back translation: "There wasn't anything more than land: it wasn't a country, but the material out of which countries are made."

32. See Janis P. Stout, "Seeing and Believing: Willa Cather's Realism," *American Literary Realism* 33, no. 2, Special Issue: Willa Cather (Winter 2001): 168–80.

33. See Palleau-Papin, "Slowly but Surely," 3–4.

34. My translation. See Victor Llona's Introduction, *Mon Ántonia*, viii.

35. My translation. Ibid., xi.

36. Llona seems here to overlook the fact that Cather did know, and admired, Turgenev.

37. My translation. Ibid., ix.

38. My translation. Ibid., xi.

39. My translation. Ibid.

40. For more on this, see my essay, "Religiosa, Provinciale, Modernista: The Early Reception of Willa Cather in Italy," *Willa Cather Newsletter and Review* 59, no. 2 (Fall/Winter 2016): 13–19.

41. See Lawrence Smith, *Cesare Pavese and America: Life, Love, and Literature* (Amherst: University of Massachusetts Press, 2011), 180. Cajumi was one of the major exponents of the literary journal *La Cultura*, with which Pavese had been collaborating since 1930 and for which he published various articles on American literature.

42. Cesare Pavese, *Lettere 1926–1950* (Torino: Einaudi, 1968), 280. My translation.

43. The original article, titled "L'Antologia di Spoon River," was published in *La Cultura* in November 1931.

44. An English translation of this article by Edwin Fussell is printed in Cesare Pavese, *American Literature: Essays and Opinions* (Berkeley: University of California Press, 1970), 43.

45. The original article in Italian, titled "Sherwood Anderson," was published in *La Cultura* in April 1931. The English translation by Edwin Fussell used here is contained in ibid., 31.

46. Pavese, *Lettere*, 326.

47. Giorgio Bubani, "L'Antonia del Nebraska," *Il Libraio*, August 15, 1947: 3. My translation.

48. This publishing house would mostly publish books in Russian, but also a few translations, and *My Ántonia* was among its very first ones. For more on this, see Oleg A. Maslenikov, "Publications of the Chekhov Publishing House, New York," *The American Slavic and East European Review* 13, no. 2 (April 1954): 252–54.

49. My translation. See Yanovsky's Introduction, Моя Антония, viii.

50. My translation.

51. Note that Yanovksy here uses the word "страна," which is the one he chose to translate "country."

52. My translation. Yanovsky's Introduction, Моя Антония, vii.

53. For more on this, see Maslenikov, "Publications," 252.

54. Savurënok was a Faulkner scholar and professor of American literature at the Leningrad State University in the 1970s and 1980s.

55. Willa Cather, *Moia Antonia*, trans. Aleksandra Kirillovna Savurenok (Leningrad: Khydozhestvennaia literatura, 1979).

56. My translation. Savurënok, Introduction, 14.

57. Ibid.

58. She focuses, for example, on the importance, for Cather, of the principle of selecting the right words, quoting the example of the writer's long search for a particular word to describe the color of the corn fields in the fall (which, in the end, she

decided should be "blond"). She also notes how "the first impression in reading the novel is that of an unusual simplicity and rusticity in the style of the storyteller. But this simplicity and rusticity are the product of a painstaking work." See Savurënok, Introduction, 19.

59. Note that Savurënok is quoting here the words of another scholar, but she does not name him/her.

60. Note the radical, communist-sounding terminology, a strong reminder of the political context in which the novel was published.

Chapter Three

Ántonia's Mother Tongue

Reading and Translating (in) My Ántonia

Diane Prenatt

Translation announces itself as a subject in the first pages of *My Ántonia* (1918) with an epigraph from Virgil's *Georgics*: "Optima dies . . . prima fugit." Two-thirds through the novel, Jim Burden translates this sentence as "the best days are the first to flee."[1] In the first edition of the novel, the epigraph appeared on the title page along with the Houghton Mifflin colophon, an image of a classical figure piping on a riverbank and a banner with the French words "Tout bien ou rien" ("[Do] everything well or [do] nothing").[2] The reader who does not read Latin or French might wonder what is lost to him or her. Like readers of *The Waste Land*, who read through, or around, T. S. Eliot's Latin and Greek epigraph and Italian dedication before finding the poem's first line in English, we might wonder whether the novel's meaning is dependent on a text we might not have read. We immediately find ourselves wondering about the issue of translation.

Following the epigraph, *My Ántonia* continues to problematize the communication of meaning when Jim Burden delivers a manuscript to his friend, the unnamed narrator of the "Introduction." The manuscript is his memoir of Ántonia Shimerda, narrated in the first person, which, with the brief "Introduction," constitutes the whole of Cather's novel. Jim's manuscript—like the published novel we hold in our hands as we read—has a material reality that calls attention to itself as a text: Jim carries it in "a bulging legal portfolio."[3] He is unsure about having written it and presents it as something of a work in progress. "'It hasn't any form. It hasn't any title either,'" he comments deprecatingly.[4] He finally writes the title on the portfolio—and then revises it—only when he is about to give it to his friend. "Read it as soon as you can,"[5] he says, but his book ends with a reference to his shared history with Ántonia as "the incommunicable past,"[6] seemingly putting the entire project into question: Can Jim and Ántonia's shared past be translated, after all, to

63

text? Jim's uncertainty about his book, then, suggests a deeper question about the capacity of language to convey and to construct meaning and experience from one person to another, across barriers of language and culture. This question pertains not only to the composition of the manuscript he carries in his portfolio, but also to the story it tells about how Jim and Ántonia assume their respective identities through language and are deeply embedded in languages beyond English.

In *My Ántonia*, reading and translating figure as self-reflexive tropes that illuminate one of the central ideas of the novel: the formation of identity is contingent upon the intersectional axes of ethnicity, nationality, and gender, which are categories of identity constructed through language. Reading and translating function literally and metaphorically to construct Ántonia's personal identity—and Jim's as well—and to transmit ethnic and national culture. As she learns English, the immigrant Ántonia is constructed as a Bohemian-American woman, and specifically a performer of domestic culture as wife and mother. The formation of identity and transmission of culture among European immigrants are recurrent topics for Cather, depicted in such novels as *O Pioneers!* (1913), *Death Comes for the Archbishop* (1927), and *Shadows on the Rock* (1931), and in many short stories (for example, "On the Divide," 1896; "Eric Hermannson's Soul," 1900; "The Bohemian Girl," 1912; etc.). What is striking about *My Ántonia* is the extent to which the novel delineates the act of learning identity and culture through language. Even as the plot traces the growth into adulthood of the main character Ántonia and the narrator Jim, the many references to reading and translating provide markers on the parallel and divergent paths these characters take in the acquisition of identity and culture. Language is as much a barrier as it is a tool for communication. Translation of the mother tongue is both an act of change and appropriation and an unsuccessful quest for communication.

MIXED TEXTS: THE TRANSLATION
PRACTICES OF JIM

Reading is depicted in the very first pages of Jim's story about Ántonia, and the learning of English is presented as a contract between Ántonia and Jim, whose terrain is literacy and who ultimately models translation practices for Ántonia. Recently orphaned and traveling by train from Virginia to his grandparents' home in Nebraska, the ten-year-old becomes absorbed in a *Life of Jesse James*, which, he says, "I remember as one of the most satisfactory books I have ever read."[7] He reads other "texts" as well: he can infer the "different fraternal orders to which [the train conductor] belonged" from all of the "rings and pins and badges" he was wearing. "Even his cuff buttons were engraved with hieroglyphics," Jim notices, "and he was more inscribed than an Egyptian obelisk."[8] The idea of translation, suggested playfully here early in the novel, quickly proves more consequential. The newly immigrated Shimerda family, traveling on the same train, had bought a homestead for "more than it was worth," Jim's grandmother reports later, because the seller, another Bohemian, "was their only interpreter and could tell them anything he chose."[9] The Shimerdas "can't any of them speak any English," the conductor tells Jim, "except [Ántonia], and all she can say is 'We go Black Hawk, Nebraska.'"[10] During their first few weeks in Nebraska, the Shimerdas "could not speak enough English to ask for advice, or even to make their most pressing needs known."[11] It is thus a practical matter that Ántonia is "quick, and very eager" to learn English.[12] Playing with Jim just a few days after they have arrived, she "learned a score of words" when Jim identifies various objects in English ("tree," "sky," "eyes") in response to her repeated question, "What name?"[13] Although Mrs. Shimerda begrudges Ántonia's absence from their hard-pressed household, even she realizes "it was important that one member of the family should learn English," and Ántonia comes "almost every day . . . to have her reading lesson" with Jim.[14]

Ántonia is, in Judith Butler's words, "in linguistic exile,"[15] but Jim confronts language difference as well. His encounters with foreign language are among the earliest childhood experiences he reports. When he hears the Shimerdas being greeted at the Black Hawk train station, he remembers, "it was positively the first time I had ever heard a foreign tongue."[16] In his grandparents' Nebraska, people speak Bohemian, Russian, and German; moreover, the speakers of these different languages can understand one another although he cannot understand them: Mr. Shimerda understands Otto Fuchs's German, and he and Ántonia understand the Russian of Peter and Pavel, who seem to Jim to have come from a place "farther away than China, almost as far as the North Pole."[17] In this first section of *My Ántonia*, "The Shimerdas"—almost half the novel—translation is depicted side by side with the social transplantation of Ántonia's family: "Krajiek was translating for Mr. Shimerda" in conversation with Jim's grandparents;[18] "Ántonia translated" Mr. Shimerda's promise to give Jim his gun someday;[19] Ántonia tells Jim in English the story of the wolves that Pavel had confessed in Russian on his deathbed;[20] Mr. Shimerda explains his family's background to Grandmother Burden "and his daughter translated";[21] "Ántonia undertook to explain" in English her mother's Bohemian directions for cooking the dried mushrooms;[22] after Mrs. Shimerda has prayed in Bohemian at Mr. Shimerda's burial service, she asks Grandfather to pray in English "for the neighbors to understand";[23] Ántonia and Ambrosch argue in Bohemian about the plowing, but Ambrosch switches to English to issue a mild ultimatum to Ántonia in Jim's presence.[24] Otto is "absorbed" in writing a Christmas letter to his mother in Austria: "He spoke and wrote his own language so seldom that it came to him awkwardly."[25] At times, Jim also appears to puzzle over his own language. He has to learn that in Nebraska, one goes "down to the kitchen" as opposed to "out in the kitchen" in Virginia.[26] When his grandfather reads from the Biblical Book of Kings, Jim is "awed by his intonation of the word 'Selah'" although he has "no idea what the word meant."[27] The mix of languages in Nebraska situates Jim as a novice as much as an expert in literate English.

English texts in fact become a lexicon for Jim to interpret his environment. Although not a European immigrant like Ántonia, Jim is understandably disoriented by the death of his parents and his relocation to Nebraska. His reading affirms the landmarks of his known world. The Burdens' scarred and moustached hired man "might have stepped out of the pages of *Jesse James*."[28] In his grandparents' house, Jim reads *The Swiss Family Robinson*, *The Prince of the House of David*, and *Robinson Crusoe*,[29] which illustrate the Anglo-Protestant values that inform his childhood. Similar traditional and popular narratives color Jim's understanding of his childhood experience: the silver and gold prairie cottonwoods look like the trees "in fairy tales";[30] the fall sun lights up the prairie like "the bush that burned with fire and was not consumed" from the book of Exodus;[31] killing the snake in prairie dog town "was a mock-adventure . . . as it probably was for many a dragon-slayer" of chivalric legend;[32] Grandmother thinks Otto reads to Jake "too many of them detective stories";[33] Jim worries that Mr. Shimerda is suffering after death as in the biblical "account of Dives in torment."[34] Grandfather Burden reads the Psalms and "the chapters from Saint Matthew about the birth of Christ," as well as the newspaper.[35] Bodily form even appears to Jim as letters of the alphabet: the snake he killed looks like the letter W; Mr. Shimerda, kneeling before the lighted Christmas tree, forms the letter S.[36] Jim thinks that the faces of his kind, friendly family must have appeared like "open books" to Mr. Shimerda.[37]

A child shaped by middle-class, middle-American literacy, Jim not only makes himself useful by teaching Ántonia to read; he also models the construction of meaning as an act of translation. Under his tutelage, Ántonia's younger sister Yulka, too, "was able to read a little" by Christmas.[38] Jim assembles a book to give her as a Christmas present, with pages made from Grandmother's store of fabric on which he pastes cut-out magazine pictures and "Sunday-School cards and advertising cards I had brought from 'my old country.'"[39] Jim creates an analogy between himself as a transplanted Virginian and Yulka as a Bohemian immigrant: he, too, has a cultural legacy that can be translated into new circumstances. The book he makes for Yulka has a certain resemblance to the bilingual book that Mr. Shimerda has brought from Bohemia—each presents "old country" signifiers translated into a new idiom. In a very concrete way, Jim's Christmas book is a work of artistic appropriation, composed as it is of repurposed materials, and thus it prefigures the book in his legal portfolio, which appropriates Ántonia's life from the country of childhood and translates it into a narrative that gives meaning to his adult world.

Ántonia and Jim's confrontation with the linguistic other is not only an accurate element of what Cather viewed as "the splendid story of the pioneers,"[40] the historical era of European immigration to the plains; it also calls our attention to the constant process of translating and deciphering by which human identity is formed in collaboration with the construction of the world's meaning. *My Ántonia* poses as a memoir written by Jim Burden, and the translation trope complements the generic trajectory of memoir. Jim cannot fully understand the meaning of Ántonia until he is a middle-aged man, his fluency in the world's language indicated by his professional success and marital discontent. The reflective mode of memoir establishes in this novel a pattern whereby Jim reports narrative experience and translates it only later into meaning. The grotesque burial of Mr. Shimerda's body, for example, "cut loose from the pool of blood in which it was frozen"[41] and buried superstitiously under the corner stake of the Shimerda lot, "disturbed and shocked" the community,[42] but years later, the unmowed grave becomes "the spot most dear to" the adult Jim; it takes on meaning as an emblem of "clemency" in the gridded plains.[43] Similarly, as a child, Jim enjoys the playfulness and good cheer of the hired girls in Black Hawk; only later, as a young man, does he understand "clearly, for the first time," "the relation between girls like those and the poetry of Virgil."[44] Jim is "bitterly disappointed" by Ántonia out-of-wedlock pregnancy,[45] but twenty years later, sees her maternity apotheosized as "a rich mine of life."[46] Jim's translation of the events of his childhood narrative into adult meaning echoes the literal translation through which Ántonia and Jim negotiate their personal identities across lines of social, ethnic, and gender difference as well as historical time and personal development.

MOTHER TONGUES:
THE TRANSLATION OF ÁNTONIA

In *My Ántonia*, linguistic difference signals the otherness of additional categories of identity. Ántonia not only learns language at the Burden home; importantly, she begins to acquire the domestic culture that will construct her adult identity. As Ántonia improves her English by reading with Jim, she also learns "about cooking and housekeeping" from Grandmother Burden, "watching her every movement."[47] When the Burden family pays an early visit to the Shimerdas, Mr. Shimerda shows Jim a book "with two alphabets, one English, the other Bohemian," then gives it not to him but to Grandmother Burden, pleading, "Te-e-ach, te-e-ach my Án-tonia!"[48] Grandmother Burden's Anglo-American domestic proficiency becomes the normative standard for the Bohemians' assimilation; the Burdens enact the cultural norm and Grandmother functions as arbiter of the Shimerdas' performance. The Burdens, for example, who enjoy Grandmother's fragrant gingerbread, doughnuts, cakes, pumpkin pies, and currant pudding, are "horrified" by Mrs. Shimerda's "sour, ashy-grey bread."[49] Alarmed that the Shimerdas might be reduced to killing and eating prairie dogs, Grandmother takes them one of her roosters and a sack of potatoes from her garden, bringing Mrs. Shimerda into comportment with her own culinary practice, which included "as much chicken as [the Burdens] could eat and . . . ham or bacon or sausage meat."[50] She is "afraid" of the Shimerdas' dried mushrooms, withered "little brown shavings"[51] that seem to have nothing botanically in common with the "big yellow pumpkins"[52] and juicy watermelons growing in her own garden. Ántonia's explanation of how to cook with the mushrooms as the Bohemians did is lost in translation, and Grandmother throws them away, othering them completely as inedible. Her response to the "stark need"[53] of the Shimerdas' dugout existence imputes domestic incompetence to Mrs. Shimerda: "There's no good reason Mrs. Shimerda couldn't have got hens from her neighbors last fall and had a hen-house going by now," she declares flatly;[54] the Shimerdas' lack of a storage place for vegetables "perplex[es]" her;[55] to Mrs. Shimerda's claims that "all things for eat better in my country," she "dryly" counters, "I can't say but I prefer our bread to yours";[56] and she finally pronounces that the Shimerdas are "wanting in everything, and most of all in horse-sense."[57] Grandmother, with her "polite Virginia way,"[58] her affectionate laughter, and sociable conversation, contrasts with Mrs. Shimerda, who appears furtive and grasping, disgruntled with the limits of the Burdens' charity, angry at the apparent failure of the American dream.

In the Burden home, then, Ántonia is learning to translate in two ways: with Jim, she is translating her native Bohemian language into written and spoken English, and with his grandmother, she is translating Bohemian domestic culture into American. Importantly, with Grandmother, she is translating from an ethnic into a *national* domestic culture. The novel provides no clue to the ethnic origins of the Burdens; they are simply from Virginia, like the Wheelers in Cather's novel *One of Ours* (1922), who are from Maine and Vermont. Grandmother Burden's domesticity is benevolent—Jim "admire[s] the cheerful zest with which [she] went about keeping [her family] warm and comfortable and well-fed"[59]—but she administers her household with "horse-sense"; her practicality and competence are characteristic of the American practice of "home economics" (carried to an oppressive extreme by Enid Royce Wheeler in *One of Ours*). Ántonia is further Americanized in the Harling household, where she continues to develop her proficiency in both language learning and domestic practice. Working as the Harlings' cook and general household help, she "learned English so quickly that by the time school began she could speak as well as any of us."[60] In her essay on Nebraska, appearing in the *Nation* not too long after the publication of *My Ántonia*, Cather would again link linguistic competence and culinary practice:

> Our lawmakers have a rooted conviction that a boy can be a better American if he speaks only one language than if he speaks two. I could name a dozen Bohemian towns in Nebraska where one used to be able to go into a bakery and buy better pastry than is to be had anywhere except in the best pastry shops of Prague or Vienna. The American lard pie never corrupted the Czech.[61]

In this passage decrying the Americanization that displaced so much ethnic culture in Nebraska towns, including the Czech beer gardens and theaters, it is significant that Cather pairs the retention of native language with ethnic food culture: the mother tongue and home cooking.

Fluency therefore becomes a matter of proper homemaking. In the final section of the novel, Ántonia's domestic achievement includes tasks she performed with Mrs. Harling—preserving cherries, tending to the orchard—and she tells Jim, "I'd never have known anything about cooking or housekeeping if I hadn't [worked in town]. I learned nice ways at the Harlings', and I've been able to bring my children up so much better. . . . If it hadn't been for what Mrs. Harling taught me, I expect I'd have brought them up like wild rabbits."[62] But, married to Anton Cuzak, she maintains a Bohemian household. "The American lard pie" was a mainstay of Grandmother Burden's Anglo-American culinary tradition—along with her fried doughnuts, gingerbread, and boiled pudding—and Ántonia pleased the children at the Harling house with American treats like popcorn balls and taffy. But when Jim visits her at the end of the novel, she serves kolaches, the Bohemian pastries, and when she prepares dinner for him, she roasts geese in the Bohemian style; she does not fry or fricassee a chicken as Grandmother Burden or the Widow Steavens would do. She has also reclaimed her mother tongue: "She said they always spoke Bohemian at home. The little ones could not speak English at all—didn't learn it until they went to school,"[63] where they are educated in the national culture. Ántonia is fluent in the American domestic lexicon of Mrs. Burden and Mrs. Harling, but she preserves her first language, literally and figuratively. Like her father's book, her adult life has itself become a kind of bilingual text, expressed materially through her housekeeping.

It is easy to accept at face value Ántonia's praise of Mrs. Harling's motherly model, but the development of her maternal and domestic competence is more complex and contradictory than her claim indicates. Ántonia does not seem able to learn from her own mother, partly because Mrs. Shimerda's personal behavior is so estranging. Mrs. Shimerda is rarely shown acting with kindness or concern toward anyone, and never with any tenderness toward her daughter; we might say Ántonia has been "badly mothered." Mrs. Shimerda's use of language indicates her inability to relate to others. Her tone is accusing,[64] crafty,[65] "envious, complaining";[66] she "shriek[s]," "squeals . . . [and] screams";[67] she "egged [her bickering children] on, chuckling while she gobbled her food";[68] she is a "boastful old thing."[69] The broken English that is often charming when spoken by Ántonia is off-putting when spoken by her mother: "If I got all things like you, I make much better," she brags to Mrs. Burden.[70] She sometimes appears outside the circle of human sociability, almost at the level of her impaired son Marek, whose fingers are webbed like a duck's feet and who barks like a dog and whinnies like a horse. Mrs. Shimerda's most gratifying relationship is with her son Ambrosch, and none of her other children, including Ántonia, receive the attention and approval he does; Ántonia's growth into womanhood is neglected except insofar as it benefits the family economically. The transmission of pragmatic information and skills appropriate to the construction of Ántonia's gender role—what Nancy Chodorow called "the reproduction of mothering"[71]—has been undermined; there is none of the loving instruction in "nice ways" that we see, for example, between Mme Auclair and her daughter Cécile in Cather's later immigrant novel, *Shadows on the Rock* (1931). Ántonia therefore needs such surrogate mothers as Mrs. Burden and Mrs. Harling so that she can be assimilated successfully into American domestic culture. It is not coincidental that Ántonia's fluency in English improves as she cooks and gardens with Mrs. Harling: she cannot learn from her mother how to maintain an American household any more than she can learn from her how to speak English.

On the other hand, *My Ántonia* is not a matrophobic narrative.[72] Rather than fearing that she will become like her mother, Ántonia defends and explains Mrs. Shimerda's unpleasant behavior: "My poor *maminka* . . . is so sad," she tells Mrs. Burden, ascribing her mother's domestic failure to immigrant grief and depression.[73] She draws the Burdens' attention to her parents' "nice bed, with pillows from our own geese in Bohemie,"[74] evidence of competent housekeeping—"nice ways" that belie the crudeness of their current circumstances. Ántonia's compassion reminds us that Mrs. Shimerda is not insulated from an uncongenial environment by the "trifles dear as the heart's blood" that the French colonists of *Shadows on the Rock* brought with them to the new world.[75] Like the Mayflower Pilgrims, the Shimerdas have arrived in an inhospitable land at an unseasonable time, too late to plant a crop or a kitchen garden, too late to build a cabin from the logs "all buried in the snow, along the creek."[76] Ántonia further displaces blame from her mother when she translates Mr. Shimerda's explanation of their situation. In Bohemia,

Mr. Shimerda "made good wages and his family were respected there";[77] the financial cost of immigration was great, and "the snow and the bitter weather had disheartened them all."[78] In a fierce argument with Jim, Ántonia defends her mother's motives in trying to make Ambrosch rich. She takes on her mother's accusatory anger, her blame of the Burdens, in a dispute with Jim and Jake that will estrange the two families for months.

Nevertheless, Mrs. Shimerda's mothering is too harsh to warrant reproduction, as two emblematic scenes in the novel reveal. In the first, Mrs. Shimerda pushes the young Yulka toward her father's coffin, insisting she make the sign of the cross on the dead body. Mrs. Burden interferes, saying she will not allow "that child to be frightened into spasms. . . . Let her alone."[79] In the second, the Widow Steavens has to restrain Mrs. Shimerda from blistering the skin of Ántonia's newborn infant by washing her with "strong yellow soap."[80] In both scenes, which depict very basic mothering, American women intervene to provide a maternal model that replaces Ántonia's experience of her own mother. Remarkably, Ántonia does not reject and repudiate her mother. In fact, without resentment, she reinscribes her mother's narrative with new meaning. It seems true, as the Widow Steavens tells Jim, that Antonia is "a natural-born mother."[81] Like her mother, for example, Ántonia becomes pregnant out of wedlock; instead of enduring a mismatched or coerced marriage, she lives through abandonment by her child's father and goes on to marry happily and have nine more children. Like her mother, she marries a city man and they farm in the country, which "wasn't the kind of life [her husband] had wanted to live,"[82] but unlike Mrs. Shimerda, Ántonia "is got such a warm heart," Anton Cuzak tells Jim. "She always make it as good for me as she could."[83] Ántonia enjoys a thriving partnership of more than twenty years with her husband, unlike Mrs. Shimerda, who was widowed by her husband's suicide and whose real partnership is with her son Ambrosch. Ántonia even names a son "Ambrosch," thereby replacing the image of her cruel and skulking brother with a "very manly" boy "with his pleasant voice and his fine head and eyes."[84] She enjoys a caring and playful relationship with her children, whom she loves and understands as various individuals, unlike her mother who sacrificed attention to her daughters in favor of her oldest son. Ántonia has thus repurposed the materials of her mother's narrative to create a new text suitable to her own life in a new country; she has translated her mother's story.

BEYOND ENGLISH:
MASCULINITY AS TRANSLATION

It is not only the reproduction of mothering that is tied to language use in *My Ántonia*; the novel traces a relationship between reading, translating, and masculine behavioral expectations as well. It is when Jim goes to school in Black Hawk, the space of proper literacy, that he learns how to be a boy: "I could fight, play 'keeps,' tease the little girls, and use forbidden words as well as any boy in my class," he reports.[85] As he matures, his mild antics take on a more sexualized nature as he attends dances and socializes with the hired girls. But he also reads seriously—"Latin that was not in our High-School course"[86]— and delivers a Commencement oration. Language learning is gendered by the social distinctions between country and city life. Ántonia's reading lessons with Jim fall by the wayside as she begins to work in the fields in the spring following her father's death, suggesting that the two activities cannot coexist. When Jim relays his grandmother's suggestion that she begin attending school, Ántonia responds, "I ain't got time to learn. I can work like mans now."[87] In Jim's view, Ántonia has been masculinized by farm work: "her arms and throat were burned as brown as a sailor's";[88] "she ate so noisily now, like a man";[89] "she was too proud of her strength. . . . Ambrosch put upon her some chores a girl ought not to do"[90] and "hired his sister out like a man."[91] Jim sees "less of the Bohemians" once he begins to go to school;[92] in other words, he has less contact with Ántonia the field hand as his own education is formalized. The novel thus poses a binary between domestic work, which is women's work and can accommodate reading lessons, and field work, which is men's work (even when young women do it) and excludes book learning.

Gender and class intersect along the axes of literacy and culture. As an eleven year old, Jim views his relationship with Ántonia as a gendered hierarchy; he resents the "superior tone" Ántonia uses with him because, despite their four-year difference in age, "I was a boy and she was a girl."[93] Ántonia counters with a claim of physical agency that comes with age: "School," she tells Jim, "is all right for little boys," but she has more important work to do; she must put away childish things like reading lessons and help Ambrosch "make this land one good farm."[94] The Shimerdas came to the United States so that Ambrosch could "be rich, with many cattle," and, especially after the death of Mr. Shimerda, they function almost solely on an economic nexus.[95] Ántonia's value resides in her ability to contribute to the family economy by doing strenuous field work, in contrast to the usual gendered division of labor on nineteenth-century American farms enacted, for example, by the Burdens. Grandmother Burden, in fact, worries, "Heavy field work'll spoil that girl. She'll lose all her nice ways and get rough ones."[96] Ántonia herself is aware that she is acquiescing to family expectations based on a false construction of her age; her tears belie the bravado of her claim that she can work "like mans." Crossing the gender boundary in the work world does not liberate her; she is being exploited by Ambrosch, and there is more than a hint of sexual pimping in the statement that he "hired [her] out." Ántonia prefers to do domestic work, and when she is hired by the Harlings, her "nice ways" are restored, along with her English language learning.

Masculinity in a particular class is a matter of discourse. The object of Ántonia's admiration, Frances Harling, has gained access to male discourse by virtue of "her unusual business ability": she "read[s] the markets," and she and Mr. Harling can often be seen "talking about grain-cars and cattle, like two men."[97] Although Ántonia pursues a domestic life with the Harlings that conforms to the normative gender construction of her day, Frances draws her attention as a single woman and her father's business partner. Frances's interest in the local farming community extends to a genuine interest in its people and has developed in her a kind of translating competence: "She was quick at understanding the grandmothers who spoke no English."[98] Frances is a model of the kind of capable businesswoman Lena Lingard and Tiny Soderball will become—women who sidestep the domestic construct embraced by Ántonia, "country girls [who have] come into their own," and become entrepreneurs or the "mistresses" of "rich farms."[99] This development hinges upon the translation between discourses defined by class and gender.

If the country is an environment of mixed languages and untranslatable tongues, Black Hawk embodies education in reading and translation. In Black Hawk, then, both Jim and Ántonia once again take up the work of language learning. Reading and translation receive renewed attention in the last half of the novel through academic exercises, which enlarge the meaning of language learning in the characters' childhoods. For example, as a high school student, Jim observes the social segregation of Black Hawk's "American" and "foreign" inhabitants and predicts the critique of Cather's "Nebraska" essay as he realizes, in frustration, that to the Black Hawk merchant class, "All foreigners were ignorant people who couldn't speak English."[100] He finds this judgment about language competence "very stupid" and characteristic of Black Hawk's "oppressively domestic," "guarded mode of existence [that] was like living under a tyranny,"[101] so inferior to the "awakened and . . . observant" attitudes of young immigrant women like Ántonia who came "at a tender age from an old country to a new."[102] As he continues to study Latin by reading the *Aeneid*—a foundational immigrant narrative—Jim's appreciation for the immigrant culture of his childhood deepens. In the midst of his serious study of Latin at the university in Lincoln (he will later add Greek at Harvard), "the people and places of [his] own infinitesimal past" take up space in his memory.[103] They accrue in importance, he says, "like the image of the plow against the sun" he and the hired girls had seen from the bluff,[104] which he had thought of at the time as "a picture writing on the sun"[105]—a kind of hieroglyph (echoing the train conductor's cuff buttons) that he can now translate from a linguistic vantage point beyond English.

Jim's academic reading and translating prepare him to enter patriarchal discourse as a Harvard-trained lawyer. Reading Virgil and speaking with his tutor about Dante's *Commedia* are educational practices that allow him to assume a position of cultural privilege, an identity in which gender intersects with socioeconomic class.[106] Mr. Shimerda's identity is constructed along similar lines. With his silk cravat and coral stickpin, Mr. Shimerda is refined and urban, a man of some social standing who married the servant he impregnated. He is a violinist and a keeper of folk narratives (for example, the Bohemian story of old Hata and the Russian story of throwing the bride to the wolves). He is, in fact, connected to ancient history through his smile "so full of sadness, of pity for things" (a virtual translation of the "lacrimae rerum" of Aeneas).[107] In the Lacanian sense, Mr. Shimerda is the origin of Ántonia's language learning: when he pleads with Grandmother Burden to use his bilingual book to "'Te-e-ach, te-e-ach my Án-tonia!'" he is advocating the formal learning of language by means of a book. (After Ántonia has abandoned her reading lessons with Jim to "work like mans," one could argue, she shifts to "*écriture* féminine," learning English in a more embodied mode, while doing domestic work for the Harlings.) Ántonia is culturally positioned under Mr. Shimerda's protection, which Mrs. Burden acknowledges when she laments the difference between the rough life Ántonia leads while working for Ambrosch and the life she had led "when she first came to this country . . . and had that genteel old man to watch over her."[108] When her "lovely papa" dies,[109] Ántonia, thrust outside the protection of his gentility, enters a male world not defined by aesthetics and fine feeling but by brutish work, a consequence of the economic bargain struck by Mrs. Shimerda for the success of her eldest child, the cruel Ambrose whose birth occasioned her mismatched marriage.

My Ántonia was published in the last year of the Great War, and the celebration of ethnicity that pervades the novel seems to presage the aftermath of that war, in which the map of Europe was reconfigured to create new nations without respect to the historical ethnic population. The new nation of Czechoslovakia (including the former Bohemia) was one such piece carved out of the defeated Hapsburg Empire. Neither Jim Burden, whose narrative ends in 1916, nor Cather could have known the provisions of the Versailles Treaty, of course, but concern about the effacement of ethnic culture figured in public discourse in the years Cather was writing the novel. Randolph Bourne, who praised *My Ántonia* highly, had called attention to the tension between ethnic and national culture in his 1916 essay "Trans-National America," in which he criticized those who "insist that the alien shall be forcibly assimilated to that Anglo-Saxon tradition which they unquestioningly label 'American,'" while at the same time decrying "the failure of the 'melting-pot.'"[110] The many references in *My Ántonia* to the process of translating from the Bohemians' ethnic language into the national language of their new country call our attention not only to the pragmatic difficulties of assimilation, but also to the difference between ethnic and national identity construction. The focus on food preparation as a site of ethnic culture—the superiority of kolaches to "the American lard pie"—contributes to the sense that ethnic culture is threatened by national culture. Even the Austrian Otto Fuchs's laconic observations about the Bohemians serve to challenge the notion that assimilation to a national culture can efface ethnic identity construction.[111]

It is a little startling to realize that more specific book titles are mentioned in this novel than in *Death Comes for the Archbishop* or *Shadows on the Rock*, both novels about learned, cultivated European men, or in *The Professor's House* (1925), a novel about an American academic. Cather does not focus on the act of translation in the three later novels, although it would have been consistent with their subject matter: the story of a French priest in the American Southwest, interacting with Spanish-speaking Mexicans as well as Native Americans; an American academic, educated in France, who is writing about the Spanish explorers in North America; French colonists in North America. In *My Ántonia*—uniquely in Cather's oeuvre—the acts of reading and translation stand for the construction of personal identity along the intersecting lines of gender, ethnicity, and national affiliation. As much as the novel is about young people growing into adulthood and about immigrants becoming Americans, it is, above all, a novel about the fluency with which the old country of memory is translated into the new country of art.

NOTES

1. Willa Cather, *My Ántonia*, Willa Cather Scholarly Edition, ed. Charles W. Mignon and Kari A. Ronning (Lincoln: University of Nebraska Press, 1994), 256.

2. Jean Schwind, "The Benda Illustrations to *My Ántonia*: Cather's 'Silent' Supplement to Jim Burden's Narrative," *PMLA* 100, no. 1 (1985): 55. Schwind is concerned with the meaning constructed in the novel by the W. T. Benda illustrations and states that "the *pictorial* drama of *My Ántonia* begins on Houghton Mifflin's title page rather than with Benda's first plate" (55; my emphasis).

3. In the revised Introduction of the 1926 edition of the novel, Jim tells his friend that he has worked on the memoir on "long trips across the country . . . in my stateroom" (2), emphasizing its materiality by giving it a history in time and space.

4. Cather, *My Ántonia*, xiii.

5. Ibid.

6. Ibid., 360.

7. Ibid., 4. Jim might be reading Frank Triplett's *The Life, Times, and Treacherous Death of Jesse James* . . . , published in 1882, the year before he travels to Nebraska and the year James died.

8. Cather, *My Ántonia*, 4.

9. Ibid., 19.

10. Ibid., 4.

11. Ibid., 19.

12. Ibid., 26.

13. Ibid., 25–26.

14. Ibid., 29–30.

15. Judith Butler, *Bodies That Matter: On the Discursive Limits of "Sex"* (New York: Routledge, 1993), 149. Butler asserts that when Jim translates for Ántonia, "no name appears to satisfy" (149), but this is inaccurate: the very meaning of this episode is that Ántonia satisfactorily learns English from Jim. She claps her hands "as if . . . amused," for instance, to learn the phrase "blue sky" (*My Ántonia*, 25).

16. Cather, *My Ántonia*, 6.

17. Ibid., 32.

18. Ibid., 40.

19. Ibid., 54.

20. Ibid., 73.

21. Ibid., 75.

22. Ibid., 112.

23. Ibid.

24. Ibid., 120.

25. Ibid., 82.

26. Ibid., 9.

27. Ibid., 13.

28. Ibid., 6.

29. Ibid., 64, 87, 97.

30. Ibid., 21.

31. Ibid., 39.

32. Ibid., 48.

33. Ibid., 94.

34. Ibid., 100.

35. Ibid., 13, 81, 65.

36. Ibid., 44, 84.

37. Ibid., 84.

38. Ibid., 78.

39. Ibid.

40. Willa Cather, "Nebraska: The End of the First Cycle," "These United States," 37, *The Nation*, September 25, 1923, 238.

41. Cather, *My Ántonia*, 110.

42. Ibid., 109.

43. Ibid., 114.

44. Ibid., 262.

45. Ibid., 290.

46. Ibid., 342.

47. Ibid., 30.

48. Ibid., 27.
49. Ibid., 30.
50. Ibid., 64.
51. Ibid., 76–77.
52. Ibid., 16.
53. Ibid., 71.
54. Ibid., 69.
55. Ibid., 72.
56. Ibid., 75.
57. Ibid., 76.
58. Ibid., 71.
59. Ibid., 64.
60. Ibid., 150.
61. Cather, "Nebraska: The End of the First Cycle," "These United States," 37, *The Nation*, September 25, 1923, 237.
62. Cather, *My Ántonia*, 333.
63. Ibid., 324.
64. Ibid., 70.
65. Ibid., 116.
66. Ibid., 58.
67. Ibid., 124.
68. Ibid., 120.
69. Ibid., 86.
70. Ibid.
71. Nancy Chodorow, *The Reproduction of Mothering* (Berkeley: University of California Press, 1978), 34–35, 38, 39.
72. I use the term as Adrienne Rich develops it in *Of Woman Born: Motherhood as Experience and Institution* (London: Virago, 1986). For a nuanced discussion of matrophobia as it intersects with (colonial) ethnicity, see María Dolores Martínez Reventós, "The Obscure Maternal Double: The Mother/Daughter Relationship Represented In and Out of Matrophobia," *Atlantis* 18 (1996): 286–94.
73. Cather, *My Ántonia*, 72.
74. Ibid., 73.
75. Willa Cather, *Shadows on the Rock: The Scholarly Edition*, ed. Frederick M. Link (1931; Lincoln: University of Nebraska Press, 2005), 116.
76. Cather, *My Ántonia*, 74.
77. Ibid., 73.
78. Ibid., 74.
79. Ibid., 112.
80. Ibid., 309.
81. Ibid., 310.
82. Ibid., 355.
83. Ibid., 356.
84. Ibid., 357.
85. Ibid., 141.

    86. Ibid., 220.
    87. Ibid., 80.
    88. Ibid., 117.
    89. Ibid., 120.
    90. Ibid., 121.
    91. Ibid., 143.
    92. Ibid., 122.
    93. Ibid., 41.
    94. Ibid., 118.
    95. Ibid., 86.
    96. Ibid., 121.
    97. Ibid., 145.
    98. Ibid., 146.
    99. Ibid., 195.
    100. Ibid., 194.
    101. Ibid., 252, 212.
    102. Ibid., 192.
    103. Ibid., 254.
    104. Ibid.
    105. Ibid., 237.
    106. Ibid., 254.
    107. Cather, *My Ántonia*, 41. The nonidiomatic wording of the second phrase suggests that it is a deliberate reference to the "lacrimae rerum" Aeneas sheds upon seeing the depiction of the Trojan War on Juno's temple in Carthage (*Aeneid* I. 462). Literally translated "tears of things," the phrase carries a sense of historical nostalgia and regret.
    108. Cather, *My Ántonia*, 149.
    109. Ibid., 110.
    110. Randolph S. Bourne, "Trans-National America," *Atlantic* (July 1916): 86.
    111. "Bohemians has a natural distrust of Austrians . . . it's politics. It would take me a long while to explain" (20); "You can't tell me anything new about a Czech; I'm an Austrian" (126). Judith Butler's statement that Ántonia "belongs to the German-speaking communities derived from a land called 'Bohemia'" (149) appears to be inaccurate.

Part II

TRADITION

Chapter Four

"Live Property"

Cather's 1926 Revisions to the Introduction of My Ántonia and the Specter of Nineteenth-Century Women's Regionalism

Melissa J. Homestead

By 1925, Willa Cather was well settled and content with Alfred A. Knopf, Incorporated, as her publisher. Cather had earlier become dissatisfied with Houghton Mifflin because they were unwilling to pay W. T. Benda for the illustrations she arranged for *My Ántonia*, demanded what she saw as excessive proof correction charges, and failed to market and distribute the novel as aggressively as she thought it deserved. In contrast, her first novel published under the Knopf imprint, *One of Ours* (1922), had been awarded the Pulitzer Prize, and Knopf was aggressively promoting her third, *The Professor's House* (1925), which was selling well. At this crucial juncture and for two reasons, it was in the interest of both Cather and Knopf to have all her novels on the firm's backlist: first, so that the ongoing sale of her novels published in the teens could benefit from Knopf's promotion of her novels of the 1920s, and second, so that funds generated by the ongoing sale of her earlier novels could cross-subsidize Knopf's riskier investment in Cather's newer titles.[1] However, Cather's first four novels, including *My Ántonia*, were still under contract with Houghton Mifflin.

In September 1925, Cather spent three days in Boston on her way to Jaffrey, New Hampshire, and, as she reported to Blanche Knopf, she "had a talk with [Ferris] Greenslet [her editor at Houghton Mifflin] and he said he would seriously consider the question of selling my books to your house and see me later."[2] Blanche Knopf was pleased to hear this. "I hope Greenslet is seriously considering the books," she wrote in reply, "and that we will hear something from him soon. It is certainly something that we want to be working toward now."[3] Greenslet and the Houghton Mifflin firm took their time in responding to Cather's query, which Alfred Knopf repeated in December, asking Greenslet to meet with him face to face the next time he visited New York. Instead, as Greenslet reported to Cather in January 1926, he had writ-

81

ten to Knopf declining to transfer her backlist. After a period of "thinking the matter over [we] were unanimous in feeling very decidedly that we valued the presence of your books on our list very highly, that they were valuable publishing property, and that any price at which we could afford to sell them would be more than he could pay." As a sort of consolation prize, he proposed to Cather a new edition of *My Ántonia* as part of a plan to "increase still further the present sales of your books on our list."

Referring to a conversation they had "several years ago," Greenslet suggested "some change in the introduction and opening machinery" of the novel "with a view to its reissue as a definite new edition." Changes in the text would justify a change in format to a "somewhat larger and more beautiful book" and an increase in price (and, of interest to Cather, a corresponding increase in her royalty per copy sold). He pointed to the novel's "established position as one of the classic American novels" and the "best" of her books as justifying these changes.[4] In a later letter, he explained his objection to the Introduction: he felt that the details of Jim Burden's unhappy life as a middle-aged man in New York City detracted from Jim's first-person account of his Nebraska youth that followed.

Cather indeed made significant changes to the 1926 Introduction of *My Ántonia*. She not only significantly condensed Jim's biography, but also eliminated all references identifying the Introduction's narrator, who ostensibly publishes Jim's manuscript, as either a woman or a professional author. Like Ferris Greenslet, most critics have focused on the Introduction as orienting readers toward Jim's first-person account of Ántonia. In particular, critics have debated whether or not the Introduction ironizes Jim's judgments of her. In contrast, I focus on the Introduction itself as a text that orients readers toward Cather as an author rather than toward Jim's narrative. Looked at this way, Cather's 1926 revisions are an installment in the still-ongoing story of her relationship with Houghton Mifflin. The story of Cather's dissatisfaction with Houghton Mifflin over its handling of *My Ántonia* and her decision to leave the firm for Alfred Knopf, begun tentatively in 1920 with their publication of *Youth and the Bright Medusa* and made decisive a year later when she committed *One of Ours* to Knopf, has long been central to analyses of Cather's career. Robert Thacker has recently complicated this narrative by arguing that Cather maintained a relationship with Greenslet as editor even as she transferred her loyalties to Knopf as publisher.[5] As the case of the revised 1926 *My Ántonia* demonstrates, however, that ongoing relationship remained prickly: even though she undertook the revisions on Greenslet's suggestion and followed some of his suggestions very closely, the revised Introduction nevertheless reflects her ongoing sense of grievance against Houghton Mifflin for what she perceived to be their fundamental misunderstanding of the character and value of her works and, even more fundamentally, of her as an author.

In particular, her letters to Ferris Greenslet and others at Houghton Mifflin reveal her frustration at being classified as a literary regionalist in the manner of nineteenth-century regionalist writers the firm had published, such as Celia Thaxter, Sarah Orne Jewett, and Mary Noailles Murfree, rather than as a serious modern artist moving into the future. Her revisions to the Introduction also, I argue, had a more public function as Cather sought to craft her persona as an author and to stake a place for herself in the 1920s literary scene and in literary history. As I will demonstrate, the 1918 Introduction arguably allied Cather with her female regionalist predecessors on Houghton Mifflin's list, but by cutting herself out of the Introduction, she reoriented herself away from what she framed as a bygone, feminized tradition and staked a place for herself on the modern literary scene of 1926.

UNEASY RELATIONSHIPS: CATHER, REGIONALISM, AND HOUGHTON MIFFLIN

My Ántonia clearly had continuing value for Houghton Mifflin in the 1920s— thus their refusal to sell it to Knopf. In 1925, it was the most profitable of Cather's novels on her backlist with the firm, and as a conservative, old-line firm, Houghton Mifflin relied strongly on its backlist to generate revenue and focused less on promoting and advertising new works (and thus Cather's dissatisfaction with them). As Greenslet noted in 1923 when forwarding her royalty statement, he was "interested to observe the increasing ascendency in sales of MY ANTONIA over all the other books."[6] In that year, *My Ántonia* sold 5,555 copies, more than it had sold in any year since its original publication, while *Alexander's Bridge* sold 131 (a new issue with Cather's new preface had modestly revived sales), *O Pioneers!* 745, and *Song of the Lark* 1,149. In 1924 annual sales of *Ántonia* stood at 4,256, and by the end of 1925, when Greenslet made his proposal for a new edition, sales were 2,882—still considerably higher than her other Houghton Mifflin titles, but a dip that a new edition might remedy.[7]

With full knowledge that *Ántonia* was the most profitable of her books for both her and Houghton Mifflin, Cather agreed to Greenslet's plan. In her letter responding to Greenslet's proposal, however, she both agreed to revise the Introduction and expressed her dissatisfaction with how Houghton Mifflin had been treating her books. She had already heard from Alfred Knopf that Houghton Mifflin refused to transfer her backlist, and she noted tartly, picking up on his language about her book as "valuable property" for the firm, "If the company is not willing to sell the books to [Knopf], then I think it ought to be willing to make some effort to sell them as if they were live property—not merely 'creditable' books on the list, by Charles Egbert Craddock or Celia Thaxter." She also picked up on Greenslet's implicit claim that Cather's body of work in the 1920s showed a decline from the heights she achieved as a Houghton Mifflin author—if Ántonia was her "best" and most popular, then by implication what came later was lesser. She thought it was not "quite fair" that in "pushing" titles published by his firm he should "disparage a book I published last year or the book I will publish next year."[8] Greenslet's description of Ántonia as a "classic" was also a double-edged sword—the word potentially implied that her career as a going concern was over and she and her works were receding into the past.

Cather's reference to Craddock and Thaxter is key to understanding her pique with Houghton Mifflin. Craddock was the pseudonym of Mary Noailles Murfree, who gained fame in the late nineteenth century for her tales about the mountain people of Tennessee, while Celia Thaxter published poetry and sketches set in coastal New England. Both women, like Cather's friend and mentor Sarah Orne Jewett, enjoyed long relationships with the *Atlantic Monthly* and the succession of firms that published the magazine (Ticknor and Fields; Fields, Osgood, and Co.; and Houghton Mifflin). Indeed, Murfree and Thaxter were both friends of Jewett and Jewett's partner in a Boston marriage, Annie Fields, who was also the widow of James T. Fields, partner in Ticknor and Fields.[9] The association of Celia Thaxter, in particular, with the Fields-Jewett ménage would have been fresh for Cather in 1926 because Thaxter featured in *Memories of a Hostess* (1922), a volume of excerpts from Fields's diaries edited by M. A. DeWolfe Howe that Cather reviewed for the *Literary Review* under the title "The House on Charles Street." [10] Thaxter also features prominently in the volume *Letters of Sarah Orne Jewett* (1911), edited by Annie Fields, in which Jewett's letters to Cather appeared. And although Murfree was actually only recently deceased in 1926, the careers of Murfree, Thaxter, and Jewett (who is no less present in Cather's letter for not being named) were largely nineteenth-century phenomena.

Cather chafed at this association with authors whose critical reputations and sales were in decline. The four Thaxter titles still in print from Houghton Mifflin in the 1920s were limping along at a level below viability: *Among the Isle of Shoals* (1874) and *An Island Garden* (1894) were both selling fewer than 100 copies a year, as were volumes of her *Poems* (1896) and *Stories and Poems for Children* (1896) (both in the "Appledore Edition" produced after her death and prefaced by Jewett) and a postmortem *Letters of Celia Thaxter Edited by Her Friends A[nnie] F[ields] and R[ose] L[amb]* (1895), which featured a long biographical portrait of Thaxter by Fields.[11] Murfree's status on Houghton Mifflin's list was also tenuous. By the 1920s, her first collection of stories, *In the Tennessee Mountains* (1884), and her novel *The Prophet of the Great Smoky Mountains* (1885) were still selling in the low hundreds, but most of her other titles had virtually stopped selling or had been allowed to go out of print.[12] Cather's comment about Murfree and Thaxter thus suggests that Houghton Mifflin was treating her like a backward-looking regional writer in the vein of the late nineteenth-century tradition rather than as a serious modern artist whose subject matter happened to be Nebraska and the past.

Literary regionalism did not, of course, disappear entirely with the turn into the twentieth century, and Cather had earlier been equally aggrieved when she felt that Houghton Mifflin had classed her with early twentieth-century regionalists on its list. Indeed, this sense that she was being misclassified as purely a regionalist may have been equally as important in her break from Houghton Mifflin as her quarrel with the firm about the production and marketing of *My Ántonia*. In December 1919, Ferris Greenslet sent her a copy of *The Outbound Road* (1919) by Arnold Mulder. Mulder, a Houghton Mifflin author, wrote regional novels featuring the Dutch Calvinist community in Michigan. "He has a lot to learn," Greenslet conceded, "but I think his feet are in the path of rectitude. I should be interested to know how the book strikes you."[13] Cather did not commit herself to paper, writing back to Greenslet that she would tell him in person what she thought of Mulder when she next saw him. In the same letter withholding her judgment on Mulder, she announced that Knopf would be reissuing *The Troll Garden*.[14] Greenslet, however, was not deterred by either her apparent lack of interest in Mulder or by her announcement about Knopf. He wrote back both pushing Cather toward an understanding about the schedule of Houghton Mifflin's publication of her next new novel, still known as "Claude," and prodding Cather on the Arnold Mulder question. On the latter matter, he wrote, "If you should feel like saying a good word for him sometime in writing we would like to see it and it would help him along."[15] This implies, then, that he was hoping Cather might blurb Mulder.

Around the same time, Roger Scaife, who had handled matters in relation to *Ántonia* in Greenslet's absence, sent her a book by another Houghton Mifflin author of regional fiction, Elsie Singmaster, who published many short stories and novels portraying Pennsylvania Germans, also known as the Pennsylvania Dutch, in the Lehigh Valley region of Southeastern Pennsylvania. "I will read Miss Singmaster's book as soon as I have time," Cather replied wearily:

But I'm not very hopeful. Like everybody who has ever done editorial work on a magazine, I've read scores of her manuscripts. Sometimes they served a useful purpose and we bought them; but there was no more surprise in them than in Kirkman's laundry soap. Even her faults were not interesting. She not only hadn't a voice, she seemingly had no ear; she droned along. However, I'll read her book, since you've been kind enough to send it.[16]

Scaife shifted his ground, sending her Houghton Mifflin's American edition of Irish author Reid Forrest's novel *The Pirates of Spring* instead, suggesting it might "appeal more strongly to your sense of literary values."[17]

Cather clearly wanted Houghton Mifflin to recognize that the artistic value of *My Ántonia* was higher than and distinct from that of regionalist works by Mulder and Singmaster. Shortly after Scaife and Greenslet appealed to her on behalf of these authors, Cather forwarded to Greenslet an excerpt from a letter to Viola Roseboro, Cather's colleague at *McClure's Magazine*, from W. C. Brownell, critic and former editor at rival publishing house Scribner's, about *My Ántonia*. Cather had earlier written about Roseboro's difficulty in securing a copy of the book to give to her friend, so forwarding Brownell's extravagant praise was a kind of rebuke to Houghton Mifflin for what she perceived as an ongoing failure to supply the market properly with copies of her books. Brownell pronounced *My Ántonia* "top shelf," "a truly extraordinary, truly unique, book,—and without any of the ear-marks of conscious 'originality.'" Indeed, Brownell pronounced himself nearly flummoxed by the book's extraordinary quality as it "almost physically floats above the material. . . . I don't mind becoming incoherent, if I convey my notion in the least by my flounderings." He conceded he initially thought the novel "casual and episodical" but came to recognize it as "a picture crowded with real people, made somehow real, given souls." He also praised the modern tenor of Cather's insights, "the tone of literary (and other, for that matter,) breeding, and the sureness of mature sociological philosophy, sound, placid, sweet, forward-looking and 'progressive,' implicit, though nowhere paraded." He thanked Roseboro heartily "for introducing me to one of the undoubtedly most noteworthy and innately distinguished of our authors."[18]

Cather drove home to Greenslet the connection between Brownell's letter and her resistance to being classed with the twentieth-century regionalists on Houghton Mifflin's list. In the same letter in which Cather forwarded Brownell's letter to Greenslet, she queried him, "Do you, yourself, really think I write like Arnold Mulder and Elsie Singmaster?"[19] "No, of course, I don't think you write like Elsie Singmaster, or Arnold Mulder," Greenslet assured her:

That would be a good deal like thinking that [virtuoso violinist Fritz] Kreisler played like an aspiring young amateur. On the other hand, I do think that Kreisler ought to be sympathetic to the aspirations of the amateurs. Mulder is a very

serious hard worker and, personally, I believe that he will some day do work
that will be not inconsiderable. As to Miss Singmaster,—have you read "Basil
Everman"? It is entirely different to my mind and much better than anything
she has ever done before. It contains a real idea, rather intelligently worked out
I think and seems to be pleasing a number of discriminating readers. Of course
she does not belong in the Dostoevsky class, but I do think that she belongs, or
will belong, in the pigeon-hole with your friend, Dorothy Canfield.[20]

Basil Everman (1920), a Civil War novel set on the Gettysburg battlefield,
was something of a departure for Singmaster, but it nevertheless featured
a Pennsylvania German hero. What Cather was registering was that Roger
Scaife and Ferris Greenslet—and thus Houghton Mifflin—saw her as a regionalist, someone whose primary distinction was that she portrayed rural
and small town people and places rather than as a serious modern artist with
an ambitious, "progressive" vision. Although she continued to suggest for
some time that she would allow Houghton Mifflin to publish her next novel,
the idea that Houghton Mifflin classed her with Mulder and Singmaster contributed to her ever-growing dissatisfaction with the firm.

Neither Greenslet nor Cather mentions Jewett in this debate about regionalism and the value of *My Ántonia*. Nevertheless, her editing of Jewett for
Houghton Mifflin shortly before her editing of *My Ántonia* is a key context
for understanding the simmering tensions about Cather's relationship to regionalism in 1926. In 1924, with an eye to the "extension and perpetuation
of Miss Jewett's public" as sales of her works were languishing in the 1920s,
Greenslet persuaded Cather to select and write a preface to Jewett's stories,
a project ultimately resulting in the 1925 publication of the two-volume *Best
Stories of Sarah Orne Jewett*.[21] Cather went into that project with grand plans
to recast Jewett in her own modern image. However, a conflict with Mary
Rice Jewett, the sister and literary executor of the long-dead New England
regionalist, and Theodore Jewett Eastman, Sarah and Mary's nephew, nearly
got Cather fired from the project over dismissive remarks by Cather about
Sarah Jewett reported in the press. Feeling compelled to appease them, she
had made herself over to suit the nineteenth century rather than refashioning
Jewett for the twentieth. In the rousing final paragraph of her preface to the
two volumes that she wrote after she reconciled with Sarah Jewett's heirs, she
classed *Country of the Pointed Firs* (1896) with Nathaniel Hawthorne's *The
Scarlet Letter* (1850) and Mark Twain's *Huckleberry Finn* (1885) as one of
"three American books which have the possibility of a long, long life." In relation to *Firs* in particular, she continues, "I like to think with what pleasure,
with what a sense of rich discovery, the young student of American literature
in far distant years to come will take up this book and say, 'A masterpiece!'"[22]
Through her introduction, then, she had claimed for *Country of the Pointed*

Firs the status of an enduring classic, and Greenslet was now proposing that
she aid Houghton Mifflin in doing the same for her own novel.

THE REVISED INTRODUCTION AND
THE DISAPPEARANCE OF CATHER
AS A REGIONALIST WOMAN WRITER

Even though Cather bristled at being classed with nineteenth-century regionalists, she conceded Greenslet's main point in relation to *My Ántonia*:
that what she called the novel's "preface" was "not very good" because she
"had a kind of complex about it" and revised it repeatedly, making it "la-
borious." She offered to shorten it but defended to Greenslet the necessity
of it on the grounds that the reader needed to "know something about the
unsuccessful personal life of the narrator," Jim Burden, or the body of the
novel would seem "vague."[23] Writing in mid-February, Greenslet, in turn,
defended Houghton Mifflin's intentions: "To sell your books as if they were
'live property' is precisely what we want to do." Cather had asked about timing, and he explained that, given the regular sales of four thousand copies a
year, they had only about two months' worth in stock (that is, six or seven
hundred). Rather than printing more sheets including the Introduction as it
stood, however, he proposed they let the book go out of stock while issuing
an announcement of a new edition to "whet the appetite of the Trade and the
public." He thus proposed that Cather provide a revised Introduction by May
for July publication.[24]

   A comedy of errors briefly ensued. Fanny Butcher, Cather's friend who
was a newspaper book critic and bookstore owner in Chicago, visited Houghton Mifflin's offices after having visited Cather in New York and reported
that Cather was not inclined to revise the Introduction to *Ántonia*. Greenslet
met this exigency by writing Cather a letter that included what he clearly
hoped would be an alluring description of the planned new format for the
novel ("in a slightly larger size, on special quality paper with a tinted top"
with the price raised to $2.50 from $2.00). Citing the "common advantage" of
a higher price, he pleaded for "some change in the Introduction" so that they
could "announc[e] a bona fide new edition" to "greatly increase" at least the
initial sales. In this context of making sure that Cather undertook the work
of revising the Introduction, he gave very detailed instructions about how it
might be carried out:

> I have just been re-reading the book (with very fresh and deep pleasure) and still
> feel that the story would be stronger without any introduction whatever. The at-
> mosphere of the narrator's later life is implicit throughout the last section and is,

I think, more impressive to the reader's imagination that way. The introduction, with its narration of the social activities of Mrs. Burden and its sophisticated background is like a prelude to a symphony that doesn't pre-lude. The reader has to change his base entirely when he starts on the actual story, and doesn't get into the spirit of the thing for a good many pages. Personally, therefore, I should vote for the complete omission of the introduction, and think the classic outline of the story would be clearer and brighter without it. If, however, this seems to you impossible, I wonder whether it wouldn't be feasible to omit all the paragraph that begins on Page x with the world "When Jim" and almost all of the paragraph on the following page which begins "As for Jim." As for the first paragraphs mentioned, I think your own statement "I do not like his wife" sufficiently does for that lady, while Jim's character and temperament—his persistence and romanticism—are sufficiently exhibited in what follows. Three strokes of the blue-pencil, in short, would—at least so it seems to me—do all that is really necessary. Won't you think it over?[25]

Cather opted for scissors over a blue pencil. As Edith Lewis recalled several decades later in a letter to a Patrick Ferry, a book collector, Cather "did what to a book collector would seem a dreadful thing to my first edition of Antonia. She wanted to revise the Introduction, and as she happened to have no copy of her own, she cut out pieces from mine and pasted them together, in order to save the trouble of having them copied!"[26] As Cather wrote Greenslet when she sent him the "revised introduction," "For Heaven's sake don't lose it! I'd never be able to patch it up again." She also asked for a new copy of the novel because she "had to cut into" her only available copy of the book "to make the Introduction."[27]

Cather went far beyond Greenslet's suggestions about cuts, however. He mostly focused on cuts to what amounts to a miniature biography of Jim Burden: the circumstances of his marriage to Genevieve Whitney, his wife's involvement in progressive political and cultural activities (women's suffrage, labor strikes, patronage of young artists), and his support of "young m[e]n with idea[s]" for Western enterprise and development. Cather did (literally) cut this material; however, she also cut what amounted to all sentences suggesting a biographical identification of she herself as the first-person narrator of the Introduction.

Put another way, Greenslet wanted less of Jim Burden's adult life and character in the Introduction, arguing that they did not serve his first-person narrative of his life beginning in childhood. Through the editing of her Introduction, Cather conceded this point. However, she also removed the traces of *her* adult life in the Introduction, the quasi-autobiography of Willa Cather, the Houghton Mifflin author. The first-person narrator of the revised Introduction shares with Jim Burden both a Nebraska childhood and a current status as a New Yorker; however, Cather edited out all references, both in Jim's voice and the narrator's own voice, that identify her as a writer and gender that writer as female. When Jim expresses puzzlement that "you have never written anything about Ántonia," the puzzlement only makes sense if he is following her career as a publishing author who typically takes Nebraska as her subject matter. She responds to his puzzlement by explaining, "I had always felt that other people—he himself, for one, knew her much better than I." She thus proposes a sort of professional-amateur collaboration "to get a picture" of Ántonia in which they would both "set down on paper" their memories of her.[28] Although her claim that she did not know her well is, at first, not explained, in her follow-up encouragement to Jim, a lawyer and business executive, to try his hand at writing, the cause becomes clear: "I told him that how he knew her and felt her was exactly what I most wanted to know about Ántonia. He had opportunities that I, as a little girl who watched her come and go, had not."[29] The 1918 Introduction concludes with the failure of the narrator, a female professional author who spent her childhood in Nebraska but lives in New York, to produce an account of Ántonia. Instead Jim shows up at her New York apartment with a "bulging legal portfolio" and asks "Now what about yours?" She closes, "My own story was never written, but the following narrative is Jim's manuscript, substantially as he brought it to me."[30] Because she has failed, she merely introduces the slightly edited manuscript of her amateur friend.

Few critics have made more than passing mention of the existence of the two versions of the Introduction. Those that do, however, like Sharon O'Brien, focus primarily on how the Introduction orients readers toward the novel and toward Jim as the narrator of the novel proper.[31] In her recent Norton Critical Edition of *My Ántonia*, O'Brien has opted to present the text of the 1918 first edition of the novel but to substitute the 1926 revised Introduction. In her own critical introduction to the novel, O'Brien discusses at length what she sees as the faults of the 1918 Introduction from the perspective of narrative technique. "In the 1918 version," she explains, "the narrator is a woman writer," adding parenthetically, "assumed by most critics to be a version of the author, but I prefer the more abstract concept of 'narrator.'"[32] Drawing on the vocabulary of narratology, O'Brien also makes a judgment based on both aesthetic and thematic grounds in favor of the 1926 Introduction.

Cather's argument with Greenslet about whether he was treating *My Ántonia* like the works of Thaxter or Murfree rather than "live property" suggests that we might productively take a different approach to thinking about point of view in her novel's Introduction. In the context of the tropes, topoi, narrative conventions, and reading practices associated with nineteenth-century regionalism, conflating the frame tale narrator of the 1918 Introduction with Cather herself as author makes sense. In 1926, Cather had very recently been deeply engaged with a text that exemplifies the thematic and formal characteristics of late nineteenth-century regionalism, *The Country of the Pointed Firs*, which constitutes the first volume of *The Best Stories of Sarah Orne Jewett* (1925). Jewett's original readers conflated the first-person narrator of *Firs* with Jewett herself, but this reading convention was not, as O'Brien's remark about the 1918 Introduction to *My Ántonia* might suggest, a mistake. Instead readers deployed interpretive practices that predate the codification of realist aesthetics and the withdrawal of the author as a personal presence in the text. Rather than resisting such a reading, Jewett invited it by making her narrator an author (never identified by name) who resides in Boston and spends the summer in Maine.[33]

Ferris Greenslet implicitly applies this interpretive logic to the Introduction to *My Ántonia* when he writes, "I think your own statement 'I do not like his wife' sufficiently does for that lady, while Jim's character and temperament—his persistence and romanticism—are sufficiently exhibited in what follows." On the one hand, the entire novel is Cather's "own" statement, but Greenslet is making a point about what "Cather"-as-narrator says in the introduction (her "own statement") versus what Jim reveals in *his* first-person narrative that constitutes the body of the novel. Although Greenslet would rather Cather cut the Introduction altogether, his editorial compromise did not involve removing the traces of information that identified Cather-as-narrator, the "you"/I who describes her interaction with Jim Burden on the train and in her New York City apartment—and yet Cather made these cuts as well. Thus on her own initiative she removed all traces of herself as the regional woman writer, disavowing the convention Jewett had used when she created an unnamed female narrator for *Firs* who verbally sketches residents of coastal Maine. If we read the 1918 Introduction as a sort of regionalist sketch that constructs Cather as an author for readers, her decision to cut herself out of the sketch gains specific force: with her scissors and her pen, she simultaneously repositioned herself in literary history and in relation to Houghton Mifflin as the novel's publisher.

As Richard Brodhead influentially observed in *Cultures of Letters: Scenes of Reading and Writing in Nineteenth-Century America* (1993), much late nineteenth-century literary regionalism resonates with the "topoi of vacationing" found in the magazines in which regionalist writing appeared. Magazines such as *The Atlantic* and *Harper's*, which particularly featured regionalist fiction, were full of scenes of genteel tourists and their bags waiting to board the steamships and trains that had made previously inaccessible rural regions open for vacation travel. Brodhead further notes that Jewett in particular "builds her work almost wholly *upon* those topoi."[34] Her first novel, *Deephaven* (1877), featured as its central characters two young women from

Boston vacationing in Maine, and one of them serves as its first-person narrator. In *The Country of the Pointed Firs*, Brodhead argues, the Maine village of Dunnet Landing is "a "place literally of resort for a narrator who comes from afar"—some unspecified urban place, but implicitly Boston—who first encountered it a previous summer on a yachting cruise.[35]

Jewett, Thaxter, and Murfree all used these topoi of vacationing to great effect in their works. In the summer narrated in *Firs*, the narrator approaches Dunnet Landing from the deck of a coastal steamer, plying the waters between Boston and Maine on a regular schedule, rather than on a private sailboat. Thaxter and Murfree's works were similarly deeply embedded in this emerging world of tourism to remote rural regions made newly accessible by expanded interregional transportation networks. Thaxter's father acquired Hog Island, one of the Isles of Shoals off the New Hampshire Coast, rechristened it Appledore, and built a summer resort there. At the suggestion of James and Annie Fields, Thaxter wrote sketches about these beloved islands for publication in the *Atlantic Monthly*, and, as Thaxter's biographer notes, "business at the family hotel increased by leaps and bounds" as a result of the serial appearance of these sketches in 1869 and 1870. When the sketches were collected in 1873 as *Among the Isles of Shoals*, the book appeared both in hardcover and "in a fifty-cent version as a guidebook . . . sold in railroad stations."[36] In the parlor of her cottage adjacent to the hotel, Thaxter ran a notable salon, becoming herself an attraction for visitors who read her book.[37]

As Bill Hardwig argues in *Upon Provincialism* (2013), a study of Southern regional short stories in the context of national magazine culture, "local color fiction of the era closely mirrors travel writing about the South in form, content, and purpose." Further elaborating the importance "that tourist travel writing played . . . specifically in Southern local color writing," he points to "Appalachian regionalist Mary Noailles Murfree [who] gathered much of the material for her writing by traveling to the exclusive mountain resort New Beersheba Springs in the Cumberland Mountains."[38] Contact between resortgoers and the mountain people features in some of Murfree's stories, including her first *Atlantic Monthly* story, "The Dancin' Party at Harrison's Cove" (1878). When Murfree, famous as Charles Egbert Craddock but entirely unknown personally to her publishers, made her first visit to New England in 1884 and befriended Jewett and Fields, she also became a tourist, visiting Thaxter's Isle of Shoals.[39] Brodhead also argues that nineteenth-century regionalism produced rural regions as zones of "inhabitable backwardness" into which the reader could escape from an urban world overrun with non-English-speaking immigrants.[40] Tourism and the construction of the rural were thus intertwined in these texts.

My Ántonia, whether as introduced in 1918 or 1926, does not align pre-cisely with this regionalist mode as theorized by Brodhead: Cather's Ne-braska did not become a tourist destination in the fashion of Maine, and the community represented in the novel features a mix of newly settled English-speaking "Americans" and a polyglot cast of European immigrants who alternate between speaking their own languages to each other and speaking in heavily accented English. Nevertheless, in both versions of the Introduc-tion to *My Ántonia*, the first-person narrator and Jim Burden "happened to be crossing" Iowa by train, and "while the train flashed through never-ending miles of ripe wheat, by country towns and bright-flowered pastures and oak groves wilting in the sun, we sat in the observation car, where the woodwork was hot to the touch and red dust lay deep over everything."[41] Neither ver-sion of the Introduction specifies whether they are traveling east or west, but their conversation about their shared Nebraska childhood implies that each is either traveling toward or has just left that state that both of them associ-ate with the past and childhood. We might thus think of the chance meeting of "Cather" and Jim Burden, particularly in the 1918 version in which the first-person narrator is identifiably an author, as a gentle variation on what Stephanie Palmer identifies as a common motif of nineteenth-century region-alism, the travel accident. "Cather" and Jim, mobile and genteel urbanites, are not stuck in a small town, unexpectedly accommodated by strange local residents, when their train breaks down—that would be the kind of accident that provided the occasion, as Palmer argues, for many works of nineteenth-century local color fiction.[42] Instead a happy accident puts them on the same train traveling across Iowa, giving them an opportunity to reminisce about Ántonia, who may have come from Bohemia as a child but is now immobile and thoroughly localized, as they—the observers—are not.

When Cather eliminated the sketch of the woman writer on the train from the Introduction to *My Ántonia*, the Introduction ceased to resemble a regional sketch. When she shortened the Introduction to her novel of life on the Ne-braska prairies in the late nineteenth century, she removed herself, the adult woman author of the early twentieth century who had spent her childhood in Nebraska. If Houghton Mifflin would not transfer her books to Knopf, then they would not have her surrogate, the regional woman writer, in the Intro-duction to her novel. Arguably, Cather's revisions also shift the novel from a regional to a more modern aesthetic. She had recently published *The Profes-sor's House* (1925), the novel whose form and themes have grounded claims for Cather as a modernist and that inaugurated a shift away from Nebraska and its regional surrogates as the subject matter of her novels (and in 1926, her work on *Death Comes for the Archbishop*, continuing this shift, was well underway). Removing the textual traces of "Cather" in the Introduction to *My Ántonia*, she removed the regionalist woman author.

Of course, as critics have increasingly argued, regionalism was neither exclusively a "woman's tradition," as Josephine Donovan influentially in *New England Local Color Literature: A Women's Tradition* (1983), nor was the *Atlantic Monthly* its only venue.[43] Nevertheless, in her quarrel with Greenslet it is a feminine tradition associated with Houghton Mifflin and the *Atlantic Monthly* that she brings into play and from which she seeks to distance herself. By revising her Introduction, then, she sought to make her novel stand as an autonomous work of art produced by a modern author unconstrained by gender rather than as a regionalist novel contained within a women's literary tradition.

RE-PRESENTING *MY ÁNTONIA* AS A CLASSIC

The new Introduction both did and did not do its office. Houghton Mifflin distinctly shifted its treatment of the new edition even as the firm's marketing focused exclusively on Cather's early career as a Houghton Mifflin author. Greenslet was pleased with the new Introduction, which he saw as an "illustration of the literary maxim, 'The part is greater than the whole.'" Even though Houghton Mifflin had refused to pay Benda for all the illustrations Cather had commissioned in 1918, they now, ironically, of their own accord and without telling Cather in advance had "asked Benda to make a new large oblong drawing for the new edition which we shall use both as an all-over jacket and for end-papers." Greenslet reported Benda "much in the spirit of the occasion" and expected the result to be "very handsome and appropriate."[44] Ironically, Houghton Mifflin also gave the new edition exactly the sort of advertising push Cather thought it deserved in 1928, and particularly advertisements featuring laudatory comments from critics. They featured the novel at the head of an ad "for your summer reading," proclaiming it, "A new and improved edition of the book which Hugh Walpole considers to be 'one of the very finest of all American novels.'"[45] In a similar ad for "new books for Vacation days," they quoted H. L. Mencken's praise, "No romantic novel ever written in America is one-half so beautiful."[46] They also gave it its own ad featuring the W. T. Benda image used on the new dust jacket, describing it as a "new revised edition" and quoting the praise of both Walpole and Mencken; they also reran this ad at the holiday season.[47]

However, the jacket copy for the new edition, which seems to have been devised without Cather's input, highlights the tension between Houghton Mifflin's praise of the novel and their diminishing of Cather's subsequent career as a Knopf author. As was their standard practice, they used the back of the jacket to advertise new novels by authors affiliated with their firm.[48] The copy inside the front and back jacket flaps, however, was devoted entirely to Cather. The front jacket flap copy proclaims, "Ever since the publication of 'My Antonia' in 1918, it has been recognized not only as Miss Cather's greatest book, but as one of the outstanding novels of American literature. It has now been reissued in a striking format with important revisions by Miss Cather and with an illustrated jacket by Benda." The same quotations from Hugh Walpole and H. L. Mencken used in the advertising also appear. Interestingly, in the ads part of H. L. Mencken's praise was omitted without ellipses marking its omission, but the full quotation appears in the jacket copy: "No romantic novel ever written in America, *by man or woman*, is one-half so beautiful" (emphasis added). While Walpole's and Mencken's names carry their own weight, the jacket flap also features an anonymous and more concrete snippet identified as from the *Chicago Daily News*, which frames Cather's novel as distinctly regional: "'My Antonia' is packed with the feel of the country. A scant paragraph sets you out on the plains, and the breath of the wind that billows the long grass never leaves your face." Even as Houghton Mifflin trumpeted the novel's timeless literary value, the specter of regionalism remained.

The praise of critics quoted on the back jacket flap turns to Cather's career beyond *My Ántonia* but encompasses only Houghton Mifflin titles. Indeed, the firm used the same jacket flap copy they used for their 1922 reissue of *Alexander's Bridge*; this reissue appeared in the fall of 1922, at around the same time Knopf published *One of Ours*, but Houghton Mifflin's copy effectively cut Cather's novelistic career off at *My Ántonia*. "Mr. H.W. Boynton," the back flap jacket copy proclaims, "places her 'Song of the Lark' beside 'The Scarlet Letter' and 'The Rise of Silas Lapham." Recurring again to the anonymous reviewer from the *Chicago Daily News*, the jacket flap quotes the critic's praise for Cather's "three novels of the West that stand alone in American literature." Quoting Mencken again, the jacket flap omits only three words that were included in the jacket flap for the reissue of *Alexander's Bridge*: "H. L. Mencken calls *her latest book*, 'My Ántonia,' 'Not only the best novel done by Miss Cather herself, but also one of the best that any American has done.' And he adds, 'There is no other American author of her sex now in view whose future promises so much'" (emphasis added). Mencken notably reversed his judgment when Cather's future appeared in the form of *One of Ours*; and although Houghton Mifflin eliminated his phrase "her latest book," they failed to omit the comma, awkwardly leaving "H. L Mencken calls, *'My Ántonia, '*Not only the best novel . . .'" on the back jacket flap copy of the named novel.

Through this new edition Cather's novel was reborn as a classic, but, ironically, the marketing copy both praises her future as an author and cuts off her career at a moment nearly a decade in the past. The collection of puffs from critics concludes with fulsome praise by two Midwestern newspapers that also place Cather's novel in the regionalist tradition. Reedy's St. Louis *Mirror* proclaims that the novel "does for the prairie country what Bret Harte did for the Far West"—a bit of praise that classes her with a male nineteenth-century regionalist affiliated with Houghton Mifflin and the *Atlantic Monthly*, but whose milieu was the California mining camp—while Detroit *Saturday Night* characterizes "every succeeding novel" by Cather as making it "more and more apparent that her place is in the front rank of American novelists." These quotations from critics are followed by a list of "Books by Miss Cather": *My Ántonia*, *Song of the Lark*, *O Pioneers!*, and *Alexander's Bridge*. Inside the book, facing the title page, all of the titles Knopf issued in the 1920s are appended to this list, but with its marketing face on in producing dust jacket copy, Houghton Mifflin cut Cather short at 1918.

The gambit of the new edition succeeded in market terms: sales of the novel increased. The six months of sales reported in May were in line with previous years at 1,707, but six-month sales in October spiked to 3,745 and stayed high through the next period (3,285 reported in May 1927). When Greenslet sent Cather her copyright statement in October, he called it "goodlooking" and attributed a forthcoming large check to the new edition of *My Ántonia*.[49] Even though Houghton Mifflin had made a modest new investment in the book, they were printing the body of the novel from the original plates (with a few small corrections supplied by Cather), and thus the "escalation clause" in Cather's original contract applied, with royalties being 20 percent rather than the original 10 percent for the first five thousand copies or 15 percent from five to twenty-five thousand copies.[50] Thereafter annual sales dropped back down to under two thousand, but *My Ántonia* remained a steady seller. And while *My Ántonia* remained on their backlist, Cather's authorial surrogate, the regional woman writer in the novel's Introduction, disappeared.

Whether or not we agree with Cather's seeming devaluing and rejection of regionalism is not my point here. Instead I have sought to tease out the logic of Cather's choices as she took advantage of the opportunity Houghton Mifflin presented to her in 1926 to revise the Introduction. Her choices made in this context had lasting effects on how many readers would encounter her novel. The 1926 Introduction was incorporated into yet another artifact of Cather's continuing relationship with Greenslet and Houghton Mifflin, the Autograph Edition of her collected works produced beginning in the 1930s. While the deluxe volumes, each signed by the author, did not sell widely, the Autograph Edition entered the ordinary trade as the Library Edition, filling out many library shelves with a uniform edition of Cather's works. *My Ántonia* remained in copyright until 1993; thus until then only Houghton Mifflin could supply the market with paperback copies suitable for course adoption. The Sentry paperback of *My Ántonia* I acquired in the early 1980s features the revised 1926 edition, with the woman regionalist author of the Introduction removed. Now that the centennial of the novel's original publication is upon us and scholars can quote freely from Cather's letters, we have a new set of texts to interpret and debate as we consider the logic of her revisions in relation to her career in the 1920s and the place of *My Ántonia* in literary history.

NOTES

1. On the economic logic of the backlist, see James L. W. West, III, *American Authors and the Literary Marketplace since 1900* (Philadelphia: University of Pennsylvania Press, 1988), 23, 28.

2. Willa Cather to Blanche Knopf, September 26, 1925, Alfred A. Knopf, Inc., Archives, Box 689, Folder 1, Harry Ransom Center, University of Texas at Austin.

3. Blanche Knopf to Willa Cather, October 5, 1925, in ibid.

4. Ferris Greenslet to Willa Cather, January 6, 1926, Houghton Mifflin Archive, MS Am 1925 (341), Houghton Library, Harvard University, hereinafter WCHM.

5. Robert Thacker, "'As the result of many solicitations': Ferris Greenslet, Houghton Mifflin, and Cather's Career," *Studies in the Novel* 45, no. 3 (Fall 2013): 369–86.

6. Greenslet to Cather, October 25, 1923, WCHM.

7. Sales of Houghton Mifflin titles are documented in their Record of Book Sales, Houghton Mifflin Co. Records, Houghton Library, Harvard University, MS Am 2030 (33). These records end in 1923. In relation to Cather, these figures are corroborated and extended by a document created by Cather and Edith Lewis. Financial Records, James R. and Susan J. Rosowski Cather Collection (MS 228), Box 1, Folder 22, Archives and Special Collections, University of Nebraska–Lincoln Libraries.

8. Willa Cather to Ferris Greenslet, February 15, 1926, in *The Selected Letters of Willa Cather*, ed. Andrew Jewell and Janis Stout (New York: Knopf, 2013), 376. This is the only letter I cite included in this volume.

9. Jewett, Fields, Murfree, and Thaxter all feature in scholarly accounts of the magazine. See Ellery Sedgwick, *The Atlantic Monthly, 1857–1909: Yankee Humanism at High Tide and Ebb* (Amherst: University of Massachusetts Press, 1994), and Susan Goodman, *Republic of Words: The Atlantic Monthly and Its Writers, 1857–1925* (Hanover, NH: University Press of New England, 2011) (Sedgwick gives more space to them than Goodman).

10. With the exception of actresses and Jewett, Howe strongly emphasizes male figures who entered 148 Charles Street before James T. Fields died. Thaxter is thus embedded in a reminiscence of John Greenleaf Whittier. Annie Adams Fields and Mark Antony De Wolfe Howe, *Memories of a Hostess: A Chronicle of Eminent Friendships Drawn Chiefly from the Diaries of Mrs. James T Fields* (Boston: Atlantic

Monthly Press, 1922), 129–31. In her own *Authors and Friends* (Boston: Houghton Mifflin, 1893), Fields gives women equal space, devoting a long chapter to Thaxter.

11. The sketch first appeared in 1894 and was also republished in *Authors and Friends*. Judith A. Roman, *Annie Adams Fields: The Spirit of Charles Street* (Bloomington: Indiana University Press, 1990), 139.

12. Murfree's active career as an author carried on well into the twentieth century. However, her relationship with Houghton Mifflin broke down. They refused both her historical novels, which increasingly occupied her creative energy, and her later Tennessee mountain sketches. These appeared under the imprints of New York and Philadelphia publishers. See Edd Winfield Parks, *Charles Egbert Craddock* (Chapel Hill: University of North Carolina Press, 1941).

13. Greenslet to Cather, December 17, 1919, WCHM.

14. Cather to Greenslet, December 28, 1919, WCHM.

15. Greenslet to Cather, December 30, 1919, WCHM.

16. Cather to Roger L. Scaife, February 21, 1920, WCHM. Scaife's letter transmitting a Singmaster volume to Cather is not extant, so it is not clear what book he sent, although *John Baring*, the other book Singmaster published in 1920, seems likely. On Singmaster, see Susan Colestock Hill, *Heart Language: Elsie Singmaster and Her Pennsylvania German Writings* (University Park: Pennsylvania State University Press, 2009). In particular on her relationship to literary regionalism, see 27–38, and her stories published in *McClure's*, 273–74.

17. Scaife to Cather, February 24, 1920, WCHM.

18. Cather had Brownell's letter retyped, with carbon copies, so she could share it, and it has recently surfaced. "Letter from W. C. Brownell to Miss Roseboro," Charles E. Cather Collection (MS 350), Box 3, Folder 40, Archives and Special Collections, University of Nebraska–Lincoln.

19. Cather to Greenslet, March 24, 1920, WCHM.

20. Greenslet to Cather, March 25, 1920, WCHM. Elsie Singmaster came to Boston in January 1920 to confer about a coordinated promotional campaign for her books in anticipation of the publication of *Basil Everman*, and Greenslet reported to Singmaster that there had been a "pow-wow" with their "selling department" on February 24, 1924. Greenslet to Singmaster, March 25, 1920, Houghton Mifflin Co. Archive, MS Am 1925 (1656). This chronology strongly suggests that Greenslet was pushing Singmaster so hard with Cather because the idea of a blurb from her had come up at this meeting.

21. Greenslet to Cather, February 21, 1924, WCHM. See my "Willa Cather Editing Sarah Orne Jewett," *American Literary Realism* 49, no. 1 (Fall 2016): 63–89, in which I reconstruct a quite different version of this series of events than has previously appeared in scholarship.

22. Willa Cather, "Preface," *The Best Stories of Sarah Orne Jewett* (Boston: Houghton Mifflin, 1925), I: xviii–xix.

23. Cather to Greenslet, February 15, 1926, *Selected Letters*, 377.

24. Greenslet to Cather, February 17, 1926, WCHM. This letter—and some of Greenslet's other letters to Cather about *My Ántonia*—are partially reproduced in *My Ántonia*, ed. Sharon O'Brien (New York: Norton, 2015).

25. Greenslet to Cather, April 9, 1926, WCHM.

26. Edith Lewis to Patrick Ferry, February 3, 1954, Patrick Ferry Willa Cather Collection, Colby College, Waterville, Maine.

27. Cather to Greenslet, [May 1926], WCHM.

28. Willa Cather, *My Ántonia*, Willa Cather Scholarly Edition, ed. Charles W. Mignon and Kari A. Ronning (Lincoln: University of Nebraska Press, 1994), xii. The WCSE uses the 1918 Introduction, and rather than providing the 1926 Introduction as an appendix, its text can only be inferred from the "Rejected Substantives" provided in the textual apparatus (529–31). I thus cite the 1926 Introduction included in the Norton Critical Edition (discussed shortly). Cather, *My Ántonia*, ed. O'Brien.

29. Ibid., xii–xiii.

30. Ibid., xiii.

31. E. K. Brown approves the cuts as making "more profound" Jim's commitment to writing about Ántonia (because not externally motivated). He also characterizes the 1918 Introduction as doing the "book no good" by raising the question of whether it might have been better written by a woman. *Willa Cather: A Critical Biography* (New York: Discus, 1980), 153–54. Jean Schwind, who draws extensively on both sides of the Cather-Greenslet correspondence, analyzes how the Introduction orients readers toward the illustrations as an "editorial" contribution contradicting Jim's romanticism (she finds that the revisions strengthen this effect). See her article, "The Benda Illustrations to *My Ántonia*: Cather's 'Silent' Supplement to Jim Burden's Narrative," *PMLA* 100, no. 1 (1985): 51–67. Richard Harris argues that the revisions to the description of Jim's character reflect Cather's own increasing pessimism; see "Jim Burden, Willa Cather and the Introductions to *My Ántonia*," *Willa Cather Pioneer Memorial Newsletters* 20, no. 3 (Summer 1986): 33–34. Emmy Stark Zitter, who applies autobiographical theory to Cather's use of male first-person narrators across her works, claims the 1926 Introduction makes Jim a stronger target of the woman novelist's irony because she "abandon[ed] the pose of the woman as failed author." See "Making Herself Born: Ghost Writing and Willa Cather's Developing Autobiography," *Biography* 19, no. 3 (Summer 1996): 295. Marilee Lindemann analyzes how women are "figured" in the novel and finds the 1926 version a "sign of Cather's deep skepticism about women's ability to compete in the context to figure themselves in a culturally powerful way"; "'It Ain't My Prairie': Gender, Power, and Narrative in *My Ántonia*," in *New Essays on My Ántonia* (New York: Cambridge University Press, 1999), 119. With a broader frame, taking into account race, region, class, and sexuality, Lindemann makes essentially the same observations in *Willa Cather: Queering America* (New York: Columbia University Press, 1999). O'Brien largely replicates her introduction to the *New Essays* volume in her introduction to the Norton Critical Edition. Focusing on "gender crossing" in the novel, Karen A. Hoffman sees Cather's removal of indications of the narrator's gender as Cather's resisting strict gender dichotomies through the "construction of a figure who eludes gender." "Identity Crossings and the Autobiographical Act in Willa Cather's *My Ántonia*," *Arizona Quarterly* 58, no. 4 (2002): 27. Keith Wilhite seeks to unmoor the novel from its seeming grounding in Nebraska as a place and finds that both versions "merely introduce a sense of uncertainty into the novel" rather than providing a corrective to Jim's narrative as less credible or authentic. "Unsettled

Worlds: Aesthetic Emplacement in Willa Cather's *My Ántonia*," *Studies in the Novel* 42, no. 3 (Fall 2010): 273.

32. Sharon O'Brien, "Introduction," in *My Ántonia*, xv.

33. For the evidence undergirding this assertion, see Melissa Homestead, "'Links of Similitude': The Narrator of *The Country of the Pointed Firs* and Author-Reader Relations at the End of the Nineteenth Century," in *Jewett and Her Contemporaries: Reshaping the Canon*, ed. Karen L. Kilcup and Thomas S. Edwards (Gainesville: University Press of Florida, 1999), 76–98.

34. Richard Brodhead, *Cultures of Letters: Scenes of Reading and Writing in Nineteenth-Century America* (Chicago: University of Chicago Press, 1993), 149 (see also 145). Stephanie Foote also focuses on tourism as constituting late nineteenth-century regionalism generally and *Country of the Pointed Firs* in particular. *Regional Fictions: Culture and Identity in Nineteenth-Century American Literature* (Madison: University of Wisconsin Press, 2001). I do not endorse all aspects of Brodhead's claims about the ideology of regionalism, especially as he applies them to Jewett and to Jewett's influence on Cather. As Tom Lutz argues, readings privileging the tourist-narrator fail to recognize the wider cosmopolitanism produced in a text encompassing both a narrator's perspective and the voices of regional characters. *Cosmopolitan Vistas: American Regionalism and Literary Value* (Ithaca, NY: Cornell University Press, 2004), 30–31, 83–88 (on *Firs*).

35. Brodhead, *Cultures of Letters*, 145.

36. Norma H. Mandel, *Beyond the Garden Gate: The Life of Celia Laighton Thaxter* (Hanover: University Press of New England, 2004), 71.

37. Fields, *Authors and Friends*, 236, 244–46.

38. Bill Hardwig, *Upon Provincialism: Southern Literature and National Periodical Culture, 1870–1900* (Charlottesville: University of Virginia Press, 2013), 3, 11.

39. On Murfree's 1884 visit to Boston, see Parks, *Charles Egbert Craddock*, 123–28. Cather clearly knew "Craddock" was actually a woman. Before Murfree revealed herself in Boston, however, nineteenth-century readers were sure that Craddock was not just a man but a rural mountain man like "his" characters. See Emily Satterwhite, "Reading Craddock, Reading Murfree: Local Color, Authenticity, and Geographies of Reception," *American Literature* 78, no. 1 (2006): 59–88, and Hardwig, *Upon Provincialism*, 45–70. This case speaks to the reading practices associated with regionalism and raises intriguing questions about Cather's thinking about gender and narrative perspective as she revised her Introduction. However, I have been unable to locate any other mentions of Murfree/Craddock by Cather, making the depth of her knowledge of the author and her works purely speculative. Bill Brown also juxtaposes *The Professor's House* with Murfree's *In the "Stranger People's" Country* (1891), a novel about a Native American archaeological site in the Tennessee Mountains, in his discussion of "regional artifacts." *A Sense of Things: The Object Matter of American Literature* (Chicago: University of Chicago Press, 2003), 121,127, 131.

40. Brodhead, *Cultures of Letters*, 133, and see 136–37.

41. Cather, *My Ántonia*, ix; Cather, *My Ántonia*, ed. O'Brien, 7.

42. Stephanie C. Palmer, *Together by Accident: American Local Color Literature and the Middle Class* (Lanham, MD: Lexington, 2009).

43. On regionalism as not exclusively a women's tradition, see Hardwig, *Upon Provincialism*, 12–14. On regionalism beyond *Harper's* and the *Atlantic*, see Nancy Glazener, *Reading for Realism: The History of a U.S. Literary Institution, 1850–1910* (Durham: Duke University Press, 1997), 189–228

44. Greenslet to Cather, May 5, 1926, WCHM.

45. Houghton Mifflin, Advertisement, *New York Times Book Review*, August 8, 1926, 16.

46. Houghton Mifflin, Advertisement, *New York Times Book Review*, August 22, 1926, 16.

47. Houghton Mifflin, Advertisement, *New York Times Book Review*, August 1, 1926, 17; December 5, 1926, 20.

48. Copies of novels with dust jackets intact are notoriously hard to find. On booksellers' websites I have seen images of *My Ántonia* in its new edition but with the back jacket copy listing novels published well after 1926. I am thus not certain which novels Houghton Mifflin featured on the back of the jacket at the moment of issue of the revised edition.

49. Greenlset to Cather, October 23, 1926, WCHM.

50. Agreement between Willa Sibert Cather and Houghton Mifflin Company, January 25, 1918, Houghton Mifflin Company contracts, MS Am 2346 (514), Houghton Library, Harvard University. On the logic of escalation clauses, see West, *American Authors*, 30–31.

Chapter Five

Violence in the Pastoral

Darkness in the Narrative Structure of My Ántonia

Sarah L. Young

The discussion of Willa Cather's modernism has generated interesting and often contradictory perspectives on an author whose work tends to defy categorization. Does she belong to the realist tradition we generally identify with the nineteenth century? Of course she does. Is she also a modernist? Most certainly she is, for reasons developed in arguments by Janis Stout, Richard Millington, Jo Ann Middleton, and many others, who observe that Cather's experiments in form and technique indicate her modernist inclinations. Calling Cather a "transitional" figure is not enough, but it is a useful beginning when observing how her writing develops and why she had such a popular appeal during her lifetime in the earlier portion of the century and continues to attract new circles of readers. When I teach Cather in the company of other "High Modernists," I always get puzzled looks from students who read *My Ántonia* after being introduced to the experimentations of the Imagist poets, T. S. Eliot, F. Scott Fitzgerald, or William Faulkner. They often give sighs of relief as they settle in to *My Ántonia*, feeling like they have found their way back to a "readable" text. As James Woodress suggests, "One of the remarkable aspects of this novel is its appeal to unsophisticated and sophisticated readers alike."[1]

Cather was (and still often is) thought to be a writer extolling the virtues of a vanished past, writing emotional critiques of the vacuity of the modern world, or eulogizing an American Eden. In fact, Cather combines a regionalist sensibility with a romantic tone influenced by her admiration of the pastoral; in novels like *My Ántonia*, which appeals to myriad audiences, she appeared to be writing straightforward prose and readable stories that resonated with a popular audience. In his observations about Cather's readers, Charles Johanningsmeier notes her accessibility:

Indeed, it is evident that Cather's works were popular chiefly because of the intensely emotional, sometimes lachrymose reactions they produced among readers, the type of responses that modernist writers and critics frequently disparaged.[2]

The reaction of today's readers is no different from those of Cather's time, who wrote to her expressing much satisfaction with her works. Whereas high modernists sought to obscure, Cather sought to invite. In *My Ántonia* she rendered an impression of an emotional past that is not completely in line with incidents actually occurring in the novel. Investigation of this gap is the subject of this chapter.

Readers might enjoy her accessibility, but this does not mean she is not experimental in her technique. Johanningsmeier goes on to cite reader Huxton Marly's letter of August 3, 1932, praising "the rugged strength and straightforwardness, the simplicity and utter lack of 'literary' fol-de-rol" in her prose.[3] Her lack of "fol-de-rol" could make it easy to overlook her skill and the complexity of her work because it appears to be so simple. On the other hand, for many readers, *My Ántonia* was neither fish nor fowl:

> The book's radical experiment with narrative form—its limited exposition, episodic structure, interruptions in continuity, shifts in focus, and numerous inset stories—led some critics to wonder whether it should even be called a novel, and if so, whether it belonged to the category of historical fiction, realism, naturalism, or the *Bildungsroman* (novel of growth and development).[4]

As Merrill Maguire Skaggs has pointed out, however, Cather was a constantly evolving writer, one who "always tried a new experiment with every book she wrote."[5] As Skaggs suggests, Cather's new novel *My Ántonia* was a step forward in pioneering the techniques that she would later define in her essays on writing, striving for a kind of simplicity that revealed with suggestion rather than forceful realistic detail. In the relevant and often quoted statements of "On the Art of Fiction," Cather comments on the work and importance of achieving simplicity:

> Art, it seems to me, should simplify. That, indeed, is very nearly the whole of the higher artistic process; finding what conventions of form and what detail one can do without and yet preserve the spirit of the whole.[6]

These statements provide a useful way to think about Cather's works and to consider the progress of her oeuvre over a career that spans several decades and genres. Cather's desire to simplify and to convey a pastoral impression similarly enable us to consider how *My Ántonia*'s realistic details of life on the prairie are subsumed into an impressionist whole, which is quite distinct from the actual details of violence supplied at the margins of the novel.

Cather follows this statement with admiration for the art of Jean-François Millet. Her comments on Millet's "The Sower" indicate both her thoughts about how to write and also another important metaphor for understanding her work:

> Millet had done hundreds of sketches of peasants sowing grain, some of them very complicated and interesting, but when he came to paint the spirit of them all into one picture, "The Sower," the composition is so simple that it seems inevitable. All the discarded sketches that went before made the picture what it finally became and the process was all the time one of simplifying, of sacrificing many conceptions good in themselves for one that was better and more universal.[7]

Cather's inspiration from the visual arts will help us with a useful model for a novel like *My Ántonia*, for in her work is a refinement, a simplicity, and, as she suggests, "the other side of the rug, the pattern that is supposed not to count in a story."[8] So the vision in the novel is occasionally muted, filled with moments of great drama that are touched on and then left behind through the swirling colors and textures of an intriguing pattern. Thus *My Ántonia* is text more like a canvas or a tapestry, pared down into design, and Cather's organizational method affects the tenor of the novel, allowing readers to absorb a variety of emotional responses yet come away from the novel believing that they have experienced the memoir of a bucolic youth. As James Woodress reminds us, the pattern of pastoral is deeply emotional and based on present need rather than past reality:

> The human impulse to remember the past as somehow better than the present, the days of one's youth as happier than the years of adulthood, has a wide appeal. In point of fact, childhood is often unhappy, beset with problems of poverty, broken homes, painful psychological adjustments, but the yearning for the innocence of childhood is undeniably attractive.[9]

A close examination of the text reveals that it is indeed filled with considerable darkness. Why do these moments not overwhelm Jim's memories of Ántonia or of his childhood? Why do they not overwhelm the reader's experience of the novel? How does this novel, with its suicides, violent deaths of various sorts, rape, and adultery—not to mention the pettiness, prejudice, and racism of a small community—manage to evoke nostalgia for an idealized past? Some readers get lost in its lush, vivid prose, losing track of the fact that this Eden on the plains of Nebraska is tinged with great sorrow and crossed by shadows. The effect of this narration lies in the structure and pattern Cather creates to veil but shape these moments of darkness as moments. The novel's construction in intricate patterns allowed Cather to situate rather lurid violence as integrations into scenes of broader scope and contrast. Violence could have overwhelmed the text but it does not; instead the violence—often muted through the voices of several narrators and occurring "off-stage"—defines by contrast the beauty of the novel, highlighting its tone. Cather uses shadows to manage emphasis and create the dimensions of her pastoral canvas.

INSET STORIES: NARRATIVE DESIGN

My Ántonia uses a complex narrative structure to create a novel whose overall effect is often more visual than linear, a series of scenes, written down, as Jim says, without form.[10] The novel always feels visual; it tells its stories through images, vignettes, and tableaus, woven across the tapestry of Jim's memory, exhibiting scenes of symbolic moment even as it chronicles the humble lives of the figures contained in its continuum of fibers. "Seeing" the novel in this way helps to understand the strategically placed inset stories and how they function to color and shape the patterns in Jim's story.

Although it is nominally a first-person narrative, the novel's perspective is often filtered through several narrative voices, holding a magnifying glass to an event here or there, pulling it into the present and then allowing it to fade back into the weaving of the past that comprises Jim's memories. Rather like the plough in one of the novel's most memorable images, the narrative is a series of moments "magnified across the distance" of time, "heroic in size," only to fade back into the memory of the narrative as the plough "[sinks] back to its own littleness somewhere on the prairie."[11] The novel utilizes the tradition of the tableau in many crucial moments: Jim sitting with his "back against a warm yellow pumpkin"; Mr. Shimerda sunk in prayer, "his long body [forming] a letter 'S'";[12] the Lena of Jim's dream "with a curved reaping-hook in her hand . . . flushed like the dawn, with a kind of luminous rosiness all about her";[13] Ántonia standing in her orchard with her hand on the crab tree, a "rich mine of life, like the founders of early races."[14] Such tableaus function as a narrative suspension, concentrating the moment on the image.

Cather's technique is quite clear here, painting the canvas of this novel and creating a dimensional structure one hardly notices but that affects the entire tone of the text. The pastoral and elegiac tone is obvious as it uses memory to examine, interpret, and ultimately mourn the past; however, *My Ántonia* also advances Cather's interest in modernist techniques, especially in her exploration of what she later calls the "novel démeublé" or the "unfurnished novel," wherein the text works by suggestion and imaginative interpretation rather than as a "vivid and brilliant form of journalism."[15] Thus the novel employs a type of literary chiaroscuro, focusing on the "overtone divined by the ear but not heard by it, the verbal mood, the emotional aura of the fact or the thing or the deed."[16] This "aura" is what people find most appealing in *My Ántonia*; they come away imagining they have read a great paean to a romantic or nearly mythological past. The "Optima dies" of Jim's youth dominate particularly the first two books of the novel as he "set[s] the quiet drama going in [his] brain,"[17] celebrating and mourning his lost past. This is a past explicitly offered in preference to his present, with a wife "temperamentally incapable of enthusiasm" who offers no companionship to Jim's "naturally romantic and ardent disposition."[18]

The dominant tone of the novel remains sentimental; it looks beyond rather than ignores the darkness of Jim's actual memories. The violence, darkness, even depravity in this pastoral narrative slinks around corners of neat, clapboard homes; lies in wait under warm summer suns in fecund harvest; strikes with the intensity of a rattlesnake and then fades back into the woven picture of time. Indeed, these shadows are necessary as they intensify the warm, glowing light so often depicted in the visual images associated with this text. As in painting, darkness and shadow define light and focus.

The narrative technique integrates the darkness that edges Jim's memories of his childhood. The effect depends on the contrast of slow, timeless scenes of a child's happy growing up with scenes of occasionally unspeakable violence. The violence must be spoken, however, so Cather uses multiple narrators to introduce this darkness, pulling the stories forward, but keeping both the audience and her narrator, the adult Jim Burden, at a distance from them. That distance begins with Jim's experiences as a child, when he is, for the most part, shielded from direct experience of tragedy. In a sense, the novel is a series of nested narratives, like a shadow box, creating dimension or *trompe l'oeil* in Jim's narrative. The shadows are revealed and then allowed to disappear, lost to the time the novel celebrates.

This complex structure begins with the Introduction, which establishes the initial frame narration by introducing the reader to Jim Burden through the voice of an unnamed "author," who generates the circumstances under which Jim Burden can tell his story. Much has been written about the shifting identity of this unnamed narrator. Clearly an author herself, as Jim asks her why she "had never written anything about Ántonia," this narrative voice dominates the Introduction, offering the reader the chance to see Jim from an outside perspective before we are plunged into his first-person recollection. This narrator offers us considerable detail about Jim, noting his "passion" for the country he travels, working for the railway, his generous mentorship of other young men and their entrepreneurial enterprises, as well as his apparently mismatched marriage to Genevieve Whitney.[19]

As they speak of their mutual childhood friendship with Ántonia, this "author-narrator" and Jim establish her importance in their lives, thinking that perhaps if they both "set down on paper all that [they] remembered of Ántonia," they could "get a picture of her."[20] Jim completes his manuscript, but the unknown author does not; instead she offers his manuscript as "the novel" that we are then to read. Thus the complicated bona fides of the story presented as "My Ántonia" are established.

The odd structure of the Introduction does, in fact, belong to an established literary tradition in examples often much more convoluted than this one. (Consider Emily Brontë's *Wuthering Heights*, for example.) No, the question for Cather readers is essentially, "Why bother?" Why tell the story of Ántonia Shimerda in this way? Given the fact that the unnamed voice of the Introduction disappears and is no longer allowed any commentary on the text, why have her there at all? Jim himself says, "I should have to do it in a direct way, and say a great deal about myself. It's through myself that I knew and felt her, and I've had no practice in any other form of presentation."[21] In fact, his way of presenting Ántonia is rarely "direct" at all; however, establishing his status as an amateur writer, whose work could only be personal, seems important for Cather. In the revised version of the Introduction, she alters his statements: "From time to time I've been writing down what I remember about Ántonia. . . . On my long trips across the country, I amuse myself like that in my stateroom." [22] Even in this revision, Cather wants to suggest amateurism. Obviously, she wants the "manuscript" that follows to be perceived as unartful, unaffected, and without "form." The reality is that the novel is extremely artful and so carefully constructed that it appears simple. This intricate construction suggests Cather's adherence to the tradition of the "realistic" narrative; however, what appears to be realistic or containing an authorial truth value is in fact a conscious manipulation. The "author-narrator" says, "The following narrative is Jim's manuscript, substantially as he brought it to me,"[23] implying that this text is not "written" or "composed" in any conscious way. Of course, the result is a novel that is, in fact, highly "formed" but works hard to appear that it is not.

Cather altered the text of the Introduction in some fairly radical ways for the 1926 publication of the novel. Gone are the details of Jim's marriage, elaborate descriptions of his work and patronage, and even much of the foreshadowing of Jim's later reconciliation with Ántonia. Most particularly missing from this revision are all of the details that might identify his traveling companion, including presumed occupation (writer) and gender (female). There is no pact for dueling manuscripts, only the final product presented apparently unexpectedly to the unnamed person by Jim at a later date. Once again, one might now even more reasonably ask, "Why bother with this introduction at all?" If she was going to revise it to this extent, why not just do away with it?

In a letter to Will Owen Jones in 1919, Cather suggested that the "device" of the introductory chapter is "employed by Russian and French authors, when they wish their narrative to be colored by a certain mood and certain personal feelings throughout."[24] Cather is engaged in what David Shields and Matthew Vollmer call the creation of a "fraudulent artifact." This is a text "purporting to be a particular form of writing . . . which also tells a story, stirs thought and emotion, inspires inquiry, initiates action, and/or calls into question that which is—or has purported to be—real."[25] In this case, *My Ántonia* purports to be Jim's story about Ántonia, and even Cather acknowledged the dangers in such a device: "The method employed in this story is, in itself, dangerous, and usually fakey; but it was the only one to convey the shades of feeling I wished to convey."[26] These "shades of feeling" create the impression of the novel we know, and, as even Jim realizes, this is the Ántonia of his own memories, carefully constructed and moderated.

Then the novel takes on a further complication when Jim allows several other narrators to take over his narrative voice. The narrative continues this process of story-within-story, memory-within-memory, as other narrators to break into "his" story and offer their perspectives—all eventually transmitted through Jim's final narrative:

> The text provides space for a variety of stories as told by multiple speakers: not only about (and by) Ántonia and Jim, but also about (and sometimes by) Jake Marpole and Otto Fuchs, Pavel and Pater, Lena Lingard, Tiny Soderball, grandfather and grandmother Burden [sic], the Shimerdas, the Harlings, Ole Benson and Crazy Mary, Wick Cutter and Mrs Cutter [sic], Gaston Cleric, Mr Cuzak [sic] and the Cuzak offspring, the town, the land, and even specific plants and animals. Cather's novel indicates that such multiple narratives, either they make up a community or simply an individual, are ongoing, are often in conflict, and cannot be resolved into tidy meanings.[27]

Sharistanian goes on to note how these multiple narratives ultimately create a web of ambiguities, but the brilliance of the novel lies in how simply Cather achieves this complexity. Not for *My Ántonia* is there any obvious affectation of "high modern" sensibility even though it is no less a product of skilled artifice. Cather chooses her method to *be* complexity veiled by simplicity, her own response to the "vivid and brilliant . . . journalism" of the realist novel. For her, "the higher processes of art are all processes of simplification," but that simplification is not an invitation to obscurity.[28] In fact, the tapestry of *My Ántonia* seems to us complete, a realistic portrayal of a life, filled in with all the important details of manner, place, and time.

It is not complete, of course. It is a memory—Jim's memory—filled with emotional subjectivism, leaving us to remember that here are only the bits and pieces of his memories: "I didn't arrange or rearrange. I simple wrote down what of herself and myself and other people Ántonia's name recalls to me."[29] And the device of memory allows Cather to paint scenes rather than construct plot outlines. Time becomes flexible, malleable, and subject to the whims of the narrative voice.

The narrative machinations of the Introduction serve to place Ántonia's story one or two more steps beyond the present, beyond the "reality" of the present, generating the melancholic and wistful tone and allowing her to work in a vast anti-temporal memorial past—what Faulkner later described as "not a diminishing road but, instead, a huge meadow which no winter ever quite touches, divided from [us] now by the narrow bottle-neck of the most recent decade of years."[30] Cather embraces a Faulknerian modernist sensibility while comforting the reader with the illusion of a nineteenth-century bildungsroman.

DISTANCING VIOLENCE: NARRATIVE PATTERNS

By 1926, Cather more precisely articulated her modernist philosophy of simplification in "The Novel Démeublé," and looks back to the rather clunky Introduction to *My Ántonia* with an eye toward "emptying the room," as it were. The room, however, is still needed; the stage must be created. She must "leave the scene bare for the play of emotions, great and little,"[31] but the place of action inside the shadow box must remain in order to achieve that *trompe l'oeil* effect and create the necessary distance.

The effect of distance then becomes equally important to the emotional aura of the novel especially as regards the darker elements of the text. The most prominent episodes of violence are reported secondhand, faithfully recounted by the adult Jim Burden as they were relayed to him by others when he was younger: Pavel and Peter's story of the wedding party thrown to the wolves; Mr. Shimerda's suicide; the tramp's death in the threshing machine; Wick Cutter's murder of his wife and his suicide. The story of Ántonia's "shame" is the longest secondhand narrative, told to Jim by the Widow Steavens. In fact, the novel is rife with casual scenes of violence, death, and depravity: Ole Benson's wife Mary chasing Lena with a knife; Wick Cutter's ill use of the hired girls and violent fights with his wife. Even moments of greatest peace and plenty are tinged with danger or death, hiding like the rattlesnakes in Grandmother Burden's garden or in the prairie dog town. All of these scenes are integrated so smoothly into the narrative that the reader hardly notices their effect on the novel. Instead they evoke that "inexplicable presence of the thing not named" that so interested Cather as her writing moved forward.[32]

Cather deftly constructs Jim's memories of his past so that we may see, on this large field of memory, a narrative with depth, color, and accent. The "best days" may be the "first to flee" but these days are not "best" because they are uniformly happy or pleasant; they are highly inflected, deeply colored with overtones of sadness and loss. They are given shadow and intensity by moments of profound fear and scenes of great evil. Jim's narrative need not dwell on the darkness in order for that darkness to be an integral part of his memory, but it needs the darkness, however obliquely presented, in order for us and him to understand his memory.

Jim's recollections even begin with a type of violence, an erasure of identity as he looks up at the night sky from the back of the wagon: "The wagon jolted on, carrying me I knew not whither. . . . If we never arrived anywhere, it did not matter. Between that earth and that sky I felt erased, blotted out."[33] All he has been before is gone, and he is now ready to be born anew into this strange place. It is significant that the adult Jim Burden begins his narrative here because his arrival in Nebraska is the result of tragedy. He comes from the pain of his parents' deaths, and he is entering a strange world completely alone. This is the first moment of his encounter with Ántonia and they are now bound together in this moment of birth and re-creation. They are a juvenile Adam and Eve entering into this fertile and abundant land that offers both the promise of life and the surety of death.

The Edenic nature of Jim's childhood "summer" at his grandparents' farm is evident at every turn in his recollections: the fertile and verdant land is covered with crops, fruit, and plenty, washed in the golden and red tones of the prairie. Prosperity is couched in terms of food: the vast fields of corn and sorghum; Grandmother Burden's gingerbread; her garden full of potatoes and pumpkins; Russian Peter's wheelbarrows of melons; the Burdens' gifts of food to the Shimerdas as they try to hold on through the winter until they can plant and harvest their own food.

Naturally, within this garden of plenty is danger and death, awaiting the ill-equipped or the weak, but Jim encounters these ordeals primarily through other people's experiences and stories, leaving Jim wiser but with less personal trauma. These stories explain to Jim where he is and what to understand. When Jim wakes in his grandparents' home, Grandmother Burden tells him about Otto Fuchs's experience with mountain pneumonia; Otto himself explains how his ear had been frozen off in a Wyoming blizzard. Even as he finds himself absorbed in the "motion" and beauty of the grasses and landscape, Grandmother Burden "call[s] his attention to a stout hickory cane, tipped with copper" on her belt. This is to kill the rattlesnakes that lurk in the garden. "A little girl who lived on the Black Hawk road was bitten on the ankle and had been sick all summer," she tells him. The prairie is not a place for the ill prepared.[34]

This brief allusion sets up the coming "battle" with the great snake that seals Jim's status as hero for Ántonia. The snake that young Jim kills seems to him "like the ancient, eldest Evil,"[35] and though the scene initially presents itself as a moment of great danger, Jim's retelling of the tale from the distance of time softens its significance. The story transforms into a rather comical heroic moment in the life of the boy "dragon-slayer," then the narrator ruefully suggests that the encounter was "fixed" by fate to be less than it appeared. The snake was old and lazy, "had led too easy a life . . . and had forgotten that the world doesn't owe rattlers a living."[36] Jim reduces it, blunting the danger with the adult appraisal that it was not important at all. Thus this event's potential emotional impact on the grandeur of Jim's memory is deemphasized and the reader is offered an amusing tale of a boy's great adventure.

Just as the adult Jim filters his own dramatic snake encounter for his readers, most of the time, other people filter tragedies for Jim Burden as he grows up. They are threads in his story ultimately woven by others that have the effect on the young boy that ghosts stories around a campfire might have. They are close enough and dramatic enough to create a momentary anxiety or fear, but far enough away that a night in his own safe bed will banish those anxieties, leaving them there for his memories to later take up and observe.

The most famous of these inset stories with alternative narrators is the story of Pavel and Peter and the wolves in book I. In fact, Cather does not even allow Jim to understand the story from Pavel's own lips. He speaks in a foreign tongue, pouring out his tale to Mr. Shimerda in a fit of agony, anger, and illness.[37] Jim hears but does not know the story until Ántonia retells it to him in bits and pieces over several days. There is ample evidence that versions of Pavel and Peter's story of the wolves have been a part of Russian folklore for generations, and no doubt Cather probably knew Robert Browning's dramatic poem "Ivan Ivanovich," which offers another version of wolf sacrifice.[38] In addition, much has been made in recent years of the potential inspiration provided by the Paul Powis painting *Sleigh With Trailing Wolves* that hung in the Garber Bank building in Red Cloud at the time of Cather's youth.[39] As Paul Schach points out, the potential "Ur" text, *Les mysteres de la Russie: Tableau politique et moral de l'Empire russe* by Frederic Lacroix, was also rendered in an engraving, depicting the embattled mother about to toss her children to the pursuing wolves.[40] In other words, this is a tale often fashioned in a visual medium and experienced from a distance. Those who experience it firsthand suffer and die, as Pavel does with the burden of it.

The wolves story is also a reminder of the way Cather constructs the novel as a series of tableaus. The Powis painting may well have provided inspiration for the specific story of the wolves, but it may also have suggested the means by which to tell the story of the novel itself. Here again is explicit inspiration from the visual arts, rendered into the novel itself. As Pavel relates his story to Mr. Shimerda, Ántonia and Jim sit spellbound, Ántonia straining to understand Pavel's story, Jim transfixed by the vision of the thrashing man in the bed. The very scene itself is compelling: two children watching by firelight witness the confession of a dying man, a confession made more horrible in its retelling over again by the child Ántonia. Yet the story survives in Jim's memory not as a trauma. He and Ántonia tell the story to one another over and over again, drawing from it a "painful and peculiar pleasure."[41]

Jim's later reaction to Mr. Shimerda's suicide is not quite the same, but this tale also exhibits characteristics blunted by being retold second- and third-hand. Young Jim "listened with all [his] ears" as Otto and Jake recount both what they have seen and what Ambrosch tells them about the suicide and the discovery of the body. The gruesome details are related matter of factly by Otto, and when Jake tries to make a "detective story" out of it, Grandmother and Grandfather Burden shut him down immediately.[42]

Jim repeatedly uses "blunting" techniques to tame violence. When Jim is left alone in the house while the family goes to the Shimerdas', he "felt a considerable extension of power and authority," seeing this as a test of his responsibility. Instead of responding specifically in his own mind to the details of Mr. Shimerda's death, Jim thinks about the stories Ántonia told him of her father's life back in Bohemia. This is a past colored by Ántonia's emotions and transmitted to Jim as a kind of fairyland with music, dancing, and a great forest with a magical white hart belonging to the "nobles." Instead of dwelling on the explicit details of Mr. Shimerda's violent death, Jim imagines Mr. Shimerda's spirit resting in the house before returning to that place he loved where Jim imagines no pain or hunger.[43]

While we might understand a young boy's romanticism, caught up in the strange excitement of the moment, it is interesting that the older Jim Burden also maintains these romantic notions, dwelling into his adulthood on Mr. Shimerda as a sad but inspirational figure. For Jim, Mr. Shimerda's life is redeemed and forgiven by the very land that drove him to his death, "the clemency of the soft earth roads" leaving his grave untouched.[44] The horror of such a death in close proximity to Jim's life is muted and transformed at the time and over the years until it takes on more mythic rather than tragic overtones.

The third horrific tragedy of the early years of the novel is the death of the tramp in the threshing machine, and this event is recounted with what might be called disturbing casualness. Indeed, this story is one of Ántonia's repertoire, told with her "engaging quality" to the young Harling children.[45] Once again, Jim is the recipient of Ántonia's "oddly beautiful tale of the tramp's leap into the threshing machine . . . summing up . . . the nature and possibilities of storytelling in *My Ántonia.*"[46] She entrances her audience with the pace, language, and imagery of the story, but offers only a pragmatic description of how the tramp was "wedged in so tight it was a hard job to get him out, and the machine ain't never worked right since." We might pass over this episode, again influenced by Ántonia's skill as a raconteur and Jim's narrative style, were it not for the reaction of Nina Harling. Nina begins to cry, but Mrs. Harling scolds her for misbehaving: "Stop crying, Nina," she says, "or I'll always send you upstairs when Ántonia tells us about the country." Mrs. Harling is insensible to Nina's response to such a nightmarish story. Ántonia also misinterprets Nina's response: "Don't you cry, Nina. No old tramp won't get you while Tony's here," she says.[47] Not even as he recalls the scene does Jim acknowledge the horror of this story for a child. Mrs. Harling, Ántonia, and Jim, both at the time and as he looks back on it, have clearly absorbed the expectations of an audience for stories: stories are entertainment; they are not personal. They might be instructive, but they do not earn personal emotional capital. They are not about people you know. Even Ántonia, who witnessed the tramp's shocking death, creates a framework for the story that culminates in her reasonable question: "What would anybody want to kill themselves in summer for? In thrashing time, too! It's nice everywhere then."[48] Undoubtedly, she recalls her father's suicide in the dead of winter, making sense of such an event by attributing it to the weather and not to despair or sadness.

The casual way in which this novel in Jim's voice accepts violence and death is reinforced again in the final book "Cuzak's Boys" when Ántonia's son Rudolph tells the final story of Wick Cutter. The scene is reminiscent of the one with Ántonia and the Harling children. Anton Cuzak demurs for a moment, saying, "It's a terrible thing to talk about at supper." But he follows that statement with a cheerful, "Now, all you children be quiet, Rudolph is going to tell about the murder."[49] At this announcement, a cheer goes up among the children. What follows is the macabre but amusing story of Cutter's murder of his wife and then his suicide. As Rudolph explains Cutter's sociopathic but rational solution to his fear that his wife would outlive him and thus have his money, Ántonia just sighs regretfully: "Now would you have thought that man had such a cruel heart? . . . To go and do that poor woman out of any comfort she might have from his money after he was gone!"[50] Once again, we see that these events, blunted by time, distance, and secondhand narration, contain at least a small moral lesson; at most, they are highly entertaining. In the hands of a different author, the lurid details of these deaths would be the focus. However, Cather creates very specialized and controlled scenes for them: a secondhand or thirdhand narrator, sometimes a narrator who is already established as an innocent or as an upstanding character. The audience in all cases includes children, and the actual event is distanced even from its retelling in the novel. Cather makes these editorial choices because Jim

Burden has made them in his recollections of his own life. Jim's narrative itself blunts and distances them.

In fact, the most poignant moment in "Cuzak's Boys" is only casually mentioned in Jim's narration. He does not really seem to understand the moment at all even as he looks back. When he returns to Black Hawk and heads out to see Ántonia, he first meets the boys standing over their dead dog. Jim merely recounts, "This was evidently a sad afternoon for them," and goes on to inquire about how to find the Cuzak home.[51] Why is this scene in the narrative at all? The moment feels excessively raw. But this episode reinforces the unfussy way in which sudden death is accepted by the people in this novel. Later, Ántonia's daughter says in passing to her mother, "[Jan] wants to tell you about the dog, mother. They found it dead." Ántonia pulls the boy to her and allows him to exorcise his pain by telling her the story. Then she "promised him something that made him give her a quick, teary smile."[52] Thus the death of the dog is sandwiched in between dinner, reunions, and reminiscences.

One can justifiably chastise Jim for paying little attention to Jan's pain, focusing only on his own concerns, and perhaps Cather wants to suggest a certain callousness in his attitudes. However, one could also see this as another of the darker threads, the moments in the novel that add dimension and exist as a part but not the whole of Jim's memories.

While there are moments of death or tragedy in the novel, there are even darker threads of murder and depravity. Jim's narrative breaks with his pattern of letting others tell these stories slightly as he recalls in "The Hired Girls" Wick Cutter's attack on him. Cutter's ill use of the hired girls has been vaguely alluded to in Jim's narrative before, but this attack with the clear intention of rape is a moment of terror not muted by a secondhand telling. However, even here, Jim eventually tries to distance himself from the narrative. He is awakened from sleep by Cutter's attack and after struggling in the dark, dives out the window and runs through the street in his nightshirt "just as one sometimes finds one's self behaving in bad dreams."[53] After arriving at the Burdens' house and falling asleep again, he refuses to allow the "story" to be told "abroad" in the town. Then the rest of Cutter's depraved plans are related back to him by others: Grandfather Burden tells the station agent's tale of Cutter's departure; Grandmother Burden and Ántonia tell him about Cutter's mad destruction of Ántonia's bedroom, her clothes and Jim's garments that "had been treated so badly that [he] never saw them again" because Grandmother Burden has thoughtfully burned them. How they were "treated" is unclear and will remain so. Even Mrs. Cutter's tale of Wick Cutter's trick, played on her to get her out of the way, is related to Jim secondhand by Grandmother and Ántonia. The implications of this story are left unsaid. Jim describes how angry he was at Ántonia who "let [him] in for all this digustingness." His concern was not for Ántonia's safety or reputation, but rather for his own, imagining "what the old men down at the drug-store would do with such a theme."[54] In other words, the "story" would be about his embarrassment, not about what could have happened to her. Even the adult Jim's narration concludes not with a discussion of what this attempted rape of Ántonia says about Wick Cutter; instead he completes the description of events by commenting only on Cutter's inefficiency in arranging the attack. This firsthand encounter with depravity and violence unnerves Jim in ways that the stories retold to him never do. In fact, he realizes then the power of the teller of the story to shape the narrative.

Nowhere is the power of the storyteller to reinterpret events more obvious than in the longest inset story of the novel: Widow Steavens's recounting of Ántonia's "shame." In his analysis of the storytelling patterns in the novel, Richard Millington notes how powerfully Book IV, "The Pioneer Woman's Story," recasts Ántonia's abandonment at the hands of Larry Donovan not as a cautionary tale, but as a moment of personal trial, a chance for Ántonia to begin anew:

> The Widow's telling localizes Ántonia's story, cuts it down to size; her rendi-
> tion frees it from its novelistic aura of "tragedy" and its burden of social repre-
> sentativeness, but makes it . . . feel sad in an unusually direct, personal (rather
> than thematic) way. With the assistance of this story, Jim, no longer inclined to
> write Ántonia off, decides to visit her the next day. The title of this section of the
> book, "The Pioneer Woman's Story," emphasizes the counter-novelistic plot;
> the crucial moment in this piece of the narrative is not Ántonia's deflowering
> but the Widow Steavens's storytelling, which saves Jim from his disposition to
> take the novelistic view of Ántonia's life. [55]

The Widow's intervention here is important to the story of Ántonia that Jim is later to write in his own life. Rather than hearing her tale from a less sympathetic voice or as idle town gossip, cheapening her and making Jim feel ashamed for her, he hears her tale simply and directly with the Widow's appropriate but not maudlin sympathy. Misfortune has been recast again as sadness and regret, but not tragedy. The tone here is very reminiscent of the death of Mr. Shimerda from book I when Jim sits quietly feeling the soul of Mr. Shimerda passing through the house, coming at last to a kind of peace. Now, after hearing of Ántonia's heartache, Jim finds himself at the end of the day sleeping in his old room in the farmhouse, "with the summer wind blow-ing in at the windows, bringing the smell of the ripe fields" coming home to his childhood, resolving its pattern as the windmill does, "making its old dark shadow against the blue sky."[56] Once again, Cather mutes the heartbreak of

Antonia's circumstances by pulling us out of the particular and individual tragedy and back to the larger tapestry of the novel. The windmill recalls the plow of the earlier chapter: a clear shape in shadow that eventually diminishes against the larger background.

For many readers, *My Ántonia* is the best of Cather's works, and it is easy to see why when we peel back the novel's technique, seeing the novel as a compromise of realist technique modified by Cather's growing modernist thoughts about the possibilities of narrative structure. As Wallace Stevens said about Willa Cather, "you may think that she is more or less formless. Nevertheless, we have nothing better than she is. She takes so much pain to conceal her sophistication that it is easy to miss her quality."[57] Cather was clearly writing with a sophisticated form in mind for *My Ántonia*, and what she produces is something that requires us to look at the text with an eye attuned to the visual. Cather pulls us into the world of Jim's memory as it spreads itself out on the page. Even while Jim colors his experiences in the misty reds and golds of a Nebraska pastoral, we see cruelty, death, sadness, and pain pulsing through the text. The book is "ruthless, poetical, tremendously alive," said Latrobe Carroll in 1921, and we are relentlessly drawn into the picture it creates.[58] Cather is given considerable latitude as a result of her choices in structure here; the world she creates is the world of Jim's memories, the world of Faulkner's meadow, filled with brilliant, sensual details, brought into stark relief by the shadows passing over them. As Jim recalls and reinterprets his own youth, he has already returned to Black Hawk and reunited with Ántonia. His memories of their past together are influenced by having "come home to [himself]," reconciling himself with all of what Ántonia means to him and to his past.[59] The days of his youth are thus washed with the glow of reunion, allowing him to integrate the story of his connections with Ántonia firmly into his own life, confirming the nostalgic vision of his youth.

NOTES

1. James Woodress, *Willa Cather: A Literary Life* (Lincoln: University of Nebraska Press, 1987), 294.

2. Charles Johanningsmeier, "Cather's Readers, Traditionalism, and Modern America," *Cather Studies* 10, no. 48 (January 2015): 48.

3. Ibid., 38.

4. Janet Sharistanian, Introduction to *My Ántonia* by Willa Cather (Oxford: Oxford University Press, 2006), vii.

5. Merrill Maguire Skaggs, *After the World Broke in Two: The Later Novels of Willa Cather* (Charlottesville: University Press of Virginia, 1990), 2.

6. Willa Cather, "On the Art of Fiction," in *On Writing: Critical Studies on Writing as an Art* (New York: Knopf, 1949), 102.

7. Ibid., 102–3.

8. Willa Cather, *Willa Cather in Person: Interviews, Speeches, and Letters*, ed. L. Brent Bohlke (Lincoln: University of Nebraska Press, 1986), 77.

9. Woodress, *Willa Cather*, 298.

10. Willa Cather, *My Ántonia*, Willa Cather Scholarly Edition, ed. Charles W. Mignon and Kari A. Ronning (Lincoln: University of Nebraska Press, 1994), xiii.

11. Ibid., 238.

12. Ibid., 83–84.

13. Ibid., 218.

14. Ibid., 342.

15. Willa Cather, "The Novel Démeublé," in *Not Under Forty* (1922; Lincoln: University of Nebraska Press, 1988), 40.

16. Ibid., 41–42.

17. Cather, *My Ántonia*, xii.

18. Ibid., xi.

19. Ibid., x–xi.

20. Ibid., xii.

21. Ibid., xii.

22. Willa Cather, *My Ántonia*, ed. Janet Sharistanian (Oxford: Oxford University Press, 2006), 198.

23. Cather, *My Ántonia*, xiii.

24. Willa Cather, Andrew Jewell, and Janis P. Stout, eds., *The Selected Letters of Willa Cather* (New York: Knopf, 2014), 277.

25. David Shields and Matthew Vollmer, *Fakes: An Anthology of Pseudo-Interviews, Faux-Lectures, Quasi-Letters, "Found" Texts, and Other Fraudulent Artifacts* (New York: W. W. Norton, 2012), 13.

26. Cather, Jewell, and Stout, eds., *The Selected Letters of Willa Cather*, 277–78.

27. Sharistanian, Introduction, in *My Ántonia*, xxiii.

28. Cather, "The Novel Démeublé," 48–49.

29. Cather, *My Ántonia*, xiii.

30. William Faulkner, "A Rose for Emily," in *Collected Stories of William Faulkner* (New York: Vintage International, 1995), 129.

31. Cather, "The Novel Démeublé," 49.

32. Ibid., 50.

33. Cather, *My Ántonia*, 8.

34. Ibid., 15.

35. Ibid., 46.

36. Ibid., 47–48.

37. Ibid., 51–54.

38. Paul Schach, "Russian Wolves in Folktales and Literature of the Plains: A Question of Origins," *Great Plains Quarterly*, January 4, 1983, 71.

39. Cather, *My Ántonia*, 410–11.

40. Schach, "Russian Wolves in Folktales," 76.

41. Ibid., 59.

42. Ibid., 93–94.

43. Ibid., 96–98.

44. Ibid., 114.

45. Ibid., 173.

46. Richard H. Millington, "Willa Cather and 'The Storyteller': Hostility to the Novel in *My Ántonia*," *American Literature* 66, no. 4 (1994): 695.

47. Cather, *My Ántonia*, 173.

48. Ibid., 174.

49. Ibid., 349.

50. Ibid., 352.

51. Ibid., 319.

52. Ibid., 326.

53. Ibid., 241.

54. Ibid., 242.

55. Millington, "Willa Cather and 'The Storyteller,'" 707.

56. Cather, *My Ántonia*, 310.

57. Wallace Stevens and Holly Stevens, *Letters of Wallace Stevens* (New York: Knopf, 1966), 381.

58. Cather, *Willa Cather in Person*, 22.

59. Ibid., 360.

Part III

TRANSGENDER

Chapter Six

Boyhood and the Frontier

Nostalgia and Play in My Ántonia

Martin Woodside

The role of Jim Burden in Willa Cather's *My Ántonia* remains one of the novel's most complex and intriguing features. Jim's move west to Nebraska as a child mirrors Cather's own, and much of his early experience in the novel seems crafted from Cather's memories. Critics have long focused on Jim Burden's importance to the text, speculating about how his presence complicates Cather's representation of perspective and consciousness, its construction of gender and sexuality, and its framing of memory and nostalgia.[1] Jim has been read as a Virgil figure, an unreliable narrator, deluded by repressed sexual desires, and an intermediary, negotiating the tensions of Cather's frontier and his own longing for primitive connection. However, *My Ántonia*'s evocation of the nineteenth-century Boy Book remains a logical but unexplored lens on the novel's genre and style. In particular, the novel shares much with Hamlin Garland's novel *Boy Life on the Prairie* (1899), and comparing these texts reveals vivid interactions between ideas of childhood, child development, and American pastoral mythology in the early decades of the twentieth century, when psychological explanations of boyhood and masculinity received urgent attention, obtaining the status of a national imperative.

It should be noted that any influence Garland's fiction had on Cather was likely indirect. While Cather's Pioneer Trilogy remains some of her most popular work, her earliest fiction approached Western themes warily. What's more, while she did admire iconic Western writers, such as Frank Norris and Mark Twain, the young Cather had nothing but disdain for Garland's work.[2] Nonetheless, *My Ántonia*'s most direct literary antecedent may well be *Boy Life on the Prairie*. Both *Boy Life* and *My Ántonia* were drawn from the childhood experiences of the authors, and, as Neil Gustafson points out, in migrating from East to West, "both [authors as] children did have a similar experience—at the same age," shared experiences that left a clear mark on their work.[3] The frame of Cather's novel folds in a reminiscence that closely mirrors Garland's, situating the frontier as a dynamic space of and for boyhood. Much like Lincoln Stewart, Cather's Jim Burden is uprooted and sent west as a child. Also like Lincoln, Jim is initially alienated by his new surroundings before forging deep connections with the land. Like Garland, and in fact much more so, Cather's novel is also about the power of memory to collect, sustain, preserve—and even create—the past.

Garland's novel filters boyhood nostalgia through the lens of the frontier, presenting the untamed West as both a literal and metaphorical space of boyhood. In doing so, he creates the prototype for a different type of Boy Book, one that defines boyhood and the frontier through and against each other, providing a model Willa Cather later revisited—and revised—for her own meditation on boyhood and nostalgia in *My Ántonia*. While clearly influenced by Cather's own childhood, *My Ántonia* makes no claim to autobiography, and, if anything, this brief frame emphasizes Jim Burden's position in relation to the text, which becomes less a memory of childhood and more an artifact of his desire to explain and recall it.

Ultimately, memory and nostalgia drive both novels as they attempt to reconcile the timeless space of boyhood with the inevitable growth of actual boys into men, a process paralleled by the vanishing space of the prairie as settlers proliferate and civilization booms. This confrontation between the civilized pioneer and untrammeled nature has dominated American frontier mythos, from Frederick Jackson Turner's "The Significance of the Frontier in American History" to R.W. B Lewis's archetype of the American Adam.[4] And this idea of the West as a collision of the savage and civilized, a sort of incubator, where the distinct American character is forged by the interaction between the settler and the savage, while dangerously facile, has wielded significant rhetorical power in American culture and is a major theme in both of these novels. Jim may well serve as Cather's artistic proxy in *My Ántonia*, but he's also very much a participant in the racist ideology of boyhood development that permeated American culture in the early modern period. Through Jim, Cather's interactions with—and reconfigurations of—the Boy Book become visible in comparison with *Boy Life on the Prairie*.

BOY BOOKS AND THE FRONTIER

The figure of the bad boy dominated the American Boy Book during the second half of the nineteenth century. Anne Scott MacLeod describes Mark Twain's *Tom Sawyer* and Thomas Bailey Aldrich's autobiography as prototypical Boy Book novels, in which "Aldrich and Twain consciously repudiated the moralism that dominated children's literature before the Civil War."[5] Thumbing their noses at more didactic fiction for boys, Boy Book authors celebrated the essential goodness of their young heroes, a goodness made possible by their mischievous boyhood antics. These novels offered an adult recollection of childhood "badness" celebrated rather than regretted. For authors of these books, and presumably their adult readers as well, boyish misdeeds paved the way to successful American manhood. If fictionalized bad boys seemed to promote reckless, even immoral, behavior, that behavior ultimately served to reinforce the essential moral purity of their protagonists. As David Macleod puts it, the boys imagined in these novels "had a crude sense of honor, lied only when absolutely necessary, and always respected women."[6]

In a broader sense, the American Boy Book served as a bulwark against the feminine and the domestic, a form of resistance to the notion that boys needed close supervision and moral guidance. Kenneth Kidd describes these novels as "defined against advice writing and domestic fiction."[7] The novels are liberated from "all things feminine," telling the story of the author's own evolution from "gentle boy-savagery into both manhood and literary vocation."[8] The construction of boys as "gentle savages" is a lynchpin of the Boy Book and foundation piece for emerging nineteenth-century ideologies of boyhood development. Psychologist and leading voice of the American Child Study Movement G. Stanley Hall played a prominent role in shaping those ideologies into his theory of racial recapitulation, a key tenet of Hall's influential model of education.[9]

Hall's doctrine of racial recapitulation framed boyhood as a crucial site for revitalizing white middle-class manhood in the final decades of the nineteenth century. Reacting to antimodernist fears—often projected against the swelling populations of American cities and their increasingly nonwhite populations—Hall developed a model for preserving white power by developing Anglo-Saxon boys into ideal American men. Boys, Hall suggested, had unique access to the primitive, and he argued for allowing them to fully indulge savage whims. Hall's theory created a racial hierarchy. As David Macleod asserts, for educators like Hall, "preadolescent boyhood seemed the ideal time to build masculinity," allowing the boy to increase his potential to develop into an ideal specimen of manhood.[10] That specimen was, of course, white, as the inherently racist dimensions of Hall's recapitulation theory dictated he must be. As savages, all boys may have been equal. As potential men, each boy could only develop to the limits imposed by their species.

Much like Hall's work, Boy Books offer a (pseudo) scientific study of the American boy. Frank Norris, writing at the turn of the century, describes these books as targeting "the average American businessman" by appealing to his "early phases of primitive growth." In dredging up those long lost days,

Norris goes on, the Boy Book provides a value that is "vaguely scientific," offering "the study of an extinct species."[11] The boy's value, then, comes from his ability to facilitate the development of the adult man and, ultimately, he's celebrated not for his presence (as a boy) in the everyday world but for the presence of his memory, his status as an "extinct species" in the excavation of adult reminiscence. Looking back, Boy Book authors imagined the prospect of a brighter future. As Maria Jacobsen describes it, the genre "was steeped in nostalgia, it idealized the past," and, at the same time, "it also presented a view of boyhood that could be used for the present."[12] Drawing on idyllic recreations of their own remembered youth, Boy Book authors provided a useful tool for adult pedagogues and caretakers eager to mold the next generation of American boys into the right kind of men.

In refining this model, Boy Book fiction narrowed its range considerably by geography and, correspondingly, by race and class. Like Aldrich, many prominent Boy Book authors—including Charles Dudley Warner, William Dean Howells, and even Mark Twain—lived in and/or wrote of the rural small town, and the genre promoted, as Kidd puts it, "a language of delinquency that separated middle-class white kids from the criminal classes."[13] For white middle-class boys in the idealized small town, acts of mischief fit the script of "savage play" advocated by Hall and other character builders. For immigrant boys in the crowded inner city, acting "bad" connoted juvenile delinquency and served as a threatening harbinger of future criminal behavior. In balancing these visions of proper and improper boyhood, Boy Book fiction also drew heavily on pastoral nostalgia. These books pined for the vanishing farming communities of the Northeast, as G. Stanley Hall does in his own 1890 memoir of boyhood. Looking back to his own golden past in Ashfield, Massachusetts, Hall claims to "know nothing more sad in our American life than the decay of these townlets."[14] As Kidd points out, Hall's memoir participates in a larger late nineteenth-century narrative closing of the frontier farm, a closing punctuated by Turner's 1893 frontier thesis.[15]

Turner's frontier functions as a place where the pioneer confronted the savage—referring both to the landscape itself and those who occupied it, suggesting that, through this confrontation, the European becomes American. Driven by new—and still unrefined—theories of evolution and the flawed science of Lamarckian genetics, child study pedagogues like Hall pushed a model of child development that drew on the same ideological ballast. Looking back to the heroic soldiers of the American Revolution, Hall argues, "such a people cannot be conquered for war and blockade would only drive them back to more primitive conditions."[16] Turner also lauded the primitive strengths the American pioneer, a distinctive product of the collision between savage and civilized. As he writes, the "American development has exhibited not merely advance along a single line but a return to primitive conditions on a continually advancing frontier line, and a new development for that area."[17]

Much like Hall's theory of racial recapitulation, Turner's thesis attempts to reconcile the story of America's past with a vision of the nation's future. For each of these models, the past served as a critical tool for shaping that future. As Mary Lawlor notes, Turner's theory offers a model of "evolutionary determinism" that sustained "a rich nostalgia for what was left behind in the sweep of history."[18] The American Boy Book also mines nostalgia, using the myth of the pastoral to turn the vanishing family farm into a powerful vehicle for American futurity. In moving the Boy Book to the frontier, Hamlin Garland attempts to sustain this narrative, marking both the frontier and boyhood alike as timeless spaces, perpetual resources to fuel the narrative of white American progress. The distinct similarities to *My Ántonia* identify a broad developmental ideology hidden behind the story of Ántonia, an ideology to which Cather's novel clearly responds.

TIMELESS BOYHOOD SPACE ON THE PRAIRIE

In *Boy Life on the Prairie*, Hamlin Garland offers a distinctive wrinkle on the Boy Book formula. At first glance, the novel reads like a standard exercise in nineteenth-century boyhood reminiscence, not unlike the novels of Aldrich, Warner, and Twain. "In his home in the city," Garland rhapsodizes toward the book's conclusion, "the middle-aged man of country birth hears the wind blowing through the branches of a sparse elm and instantly is transformed to the prairies of Iowa, to the harvest field of twenty years ago."[19] All told, Garland utilizes many Boy Book conventions in *Boy Life on the Prairie*—its semi-autobiographical story, its celebration of unfettered (middle-class) boys at play, and, most importantly, its privileging of boyhood, as Jacobson describes it, as a "condition of being that is truly vanished forever."[20]

For all of that, Garland's novel—which is not strict autobiography; the author produced a separate book, *Son of the Middle Border*, for that purpose—stands apart through its use of the frontier to focus and articulate notions of idealized and developing boyhoods. While Twain's work in *Adventures of Huckleberry Finn* and its aborted sequel, *Tom and Huck Among the Indians*, gestures to similar themes, *Boy Life on the Prairie* is the rare Boy Book projecting American boyhood through the space of the frontier. Deemphasizing bad boy fiction's rhetoric of mischief, *Boy Life on the Prairie* defines boyhood through the balance of work and play. Ultimately, the novel betrays, as Macleod puts it, "not merely a sentimental longing for the past but a strongly felt discontinuity between past and present, a sharp sense of the

contrast between the beauty of the rural past and the bleakness of industrialized contemporary life."[21] Bleakness and drudgery are frequently associated
with Garland's portrayal of rural life, and it's unsurprising that those themes
appear in *Boy Life on the Prairie*. More surprising is how subdued they are,
how lightly Garland treads in respect to the bulk of his frontier fiction, and
how freely *Boy Life on the Prairie* indulges in wistful nostalgia.

The novel's nostalgia exists in tension with its presentation of the hard
labor of the protagonist's childhood. In the novel, twelve-year-old Lincoln
Stewart moves west to Sun Prairie, Iowa, and a childhood defined by punish-
ing work and hardscrabble living. Despite these conditions, Garland romanti-
cizes life on the prairie as a space of natural boyhood. In doing so, he stresses
Lincoln's deep and abiding connection to the land, with the child's development from boy to man closely paralleling the land's development from wild
prairie to domesticated farm. That Lincoln eventually outgrows this space of
boyhood and returns east is inevitable; he is no longer a boy, and the open
land is no longer open. The loss of boyhood is, in fact, synonymous with the
loss of the "open" frontier, and it works for Garland as a powerful engine of
memory, a space enshrined in nostalgia and always just out of reach.

Garland writes in the third person in *Boy Life on the Prairie*, interspers-
ing his prose sketches with poetry. A number of these sketches were first
published in *American* magazine in 1887 and then enhanced and augmented
when *Boy Life on the Prairie* was published as a novel in 1899. Garland's
introduction to that edition is cagey about whether or not the book should be
read as autobiography, but the characters here are given fictional names and
the stories, whether drawn from real-life experience or not, are clearly fictionalized. In his 1929 introduction to the book, Garland encourages the reader to
view these characters as analogues for himself and his childhood friends, but
he also retains the veil of fiction—for instance, the main character remains
Lincoln Stewart not Hamlin Garland.

First published in 1918, with illustrations by W. T. Benda, Cather's *My
Ántonia* is narrated in the first person by Jim Burden, looking back at his
own childhood in and around the fictional town of Black Hawk, Nebraska. In
the book's Introduction, a second narrator—who may or may not be Cather
herself—encounters Jim Burden on a westbound train. Both Burden and the
narrator grew up in Black Hawk, and they reminisce about their time there,
particularly about Ántonia, a Bohemian whom they both strongly associate
with prairie childhood. Both the narrator and Jim promise to write up their
recollections of Ántonia and compare notes. The narrator confesses that her
own story "was never written," but offers the novel that follows as "Jim's
manuscript, substantially as he brought it to me."[22] While clearly influenced

by Cather's own childhood, *My Ántonia* makes no direct claim to autobiography, and, if anything, this brief frame emphasizes Jim Burden's position to the text, which becomes less about his childhood and more about his desire to recall, explain, and possess it.

Unsurprisingly, Garland's novel follows the Boy Book script much more closely than Cather's, immersing the reader thoroughly in Lincoln's point of view. Lincoln himself is deeply involved in the homosocial world of boy's play, and the absence of any significant characters beyond his boyhood circle of friends is startling. Mothers, sisters, and girls from town garner occasional reference. Native Americans are evoked but never present. Likewise, the migration flows that sustained prairie life are completely absent. In short, *Boy Life on the Prairie* is a story about white middle-class boyhood. In this way, Garland's novel explains how the land gives shape to a distinctive vision of American boyhood and how that vision becomes a tool for fixing the landscape as a symbol of American progress and ideal manhood, erasing other genders and races.

Cather's novel does no such thing. It serves as a recollection of childhood and a meditation on westward expansion, but it directly addresses the blending of communities and addresses class, race, gender, migration, and immigration. It takes as its subject how the developing civilization of the prairie brings disparate powerful forces into unpredictable collision. As Jan Goggans argues, *My Ántonia* explores the interaction between the "landscape and the migrant and immigrant farmers who attempted to transform their crops." In this way, she continues, the novel "tells the story of how Americans received the tide of immigrants that characterized the late nineteenth and early twentieth century in this country," and how those groups negotiated their relationship to each other, and to the Western landscape.[23] Rather than celebrating the solitary figure of the pioneer as symbol of white American manhood, Cather's novel interrogates that figure through the recognition of the prairie as a diverse, dynamic community.

Despite this key distinction, Cather's novel, filtered through Jim, largely remains a novel that advances an ideology of white boyhood. Early in the Introduction, Cather's narrator describes how Jim—though his adult life has been to some degree a disappointment—retains a boyish passion, one that remains rooted to the land, both the idea and the fact of it. What's more, as Cather's narrator quickly points out, he serves as a kind of guiding spirit for this passion in others: "If a young man with an idea can once get Jim Burden's attention, can manage to accompany him when he goes off into the wilds hunting for lost parks or exploring new canyons, then the money which means action is usually forthcoming. Jim is still able to lose himself in those big Western dreams."[24] Ultimately, both *My Ántonia* and *Boyhood and the Prairie* revolve around those "big Western dreams." Memory and nostalgia drive both novels as they attempt to reconcile the timeless space of boyhood with the inevitable growth of actual boys into men, a process paralleled by the vanishing space of the prairie, including its racial elements, as civilization spreads.

Garland's novel privileges boyhood as a sacred space and positions the rural farm as an ideal place for a boy to grow into the right kind of man. Lincoln moves exclusively in the world of boys and men, so that his days and nights cohere closely to the vision of late nineteenth-century boyhood culture E. Anthony Rotundo describes, wherein boys immersed themselves in "backyards, streets, parks, playgrounds, and vacant lots," free spaces where boys largely governed their own play.[25] Of course, Lincoln plays in fields and rivers rather than streets and vacant lots. Moreover, unlike the boys Rotundo describes, or the roguish heroes of Aldrich and Twain, Lincoln has little time for character-building pranks, spending most of his time working on the farm. In fact, his growth in the book closely parallels the growth of the farm, pegged to the seasons of planting and harvesting the family's corn crop. The emphasis on harrowing work separates Lincoln's boyhood from Boy Book fiction and, notably, from *My Ántonia*. Still, while these daily labors prove long, demanding, and even painful, they also promise great reward, as Garland describes in his account of seeding time:

> Day by day, the boys walked their monotonous rounds upon the ever-mellowing soil. They saw the geese pass on to the north, and the green grass come into the sunny slopes. They answered the splendid challenge of the solitary crane, and watched the ground sparrow build her lowly nest. Their muscles grew firm and their toil tired them less.[26]

As the boys cultivate the land, the land cultivates them. However, as Lincoln grows up, he becomes increasingly tired of the monotonous toil of farming. He cannot wait to leave and eventually goes east for schooling. As with Jim, this is a sure sign he is losing his connection to the land—to the space of boyhood itself. As Lincoln notes earlier, "All the boys he knew—all the young men talked of 'the west,' never of the east; always of the plains and the mountains and cattle-raising and mining and Indians."[27] Yet at sixteen, Lincoln notes that the "lonely toil of the farm made each year more irksome," while he and his friend Rance "planned ways of escape." Escape pulls Lincoln east, where his primitive strength can be refined in a more civilized environment. Nevertheless, the process ensures a nostalgic return—both literally and figuratively in Lincoln's case—to the West, a space where memory simultaneously creates and erases.

MEMORY AND PLAY: CATHER'S REVISION

Notably, both Lincoln Stewart and Jim Burden first experience the prairie through a sense of timelessness and erasure. In both cases, the boys arrive at night. Lincoln feels "as though he had suddenly been transported into another world, a world where time did not exist; where snow never fell, and the grass waved forever under a cloudless sky. Awe filled his soul as he looked, and he could not utter a word."[28] Jim Burden remembers "nothing but land—slightly undulating," recalling "the feeling that the world was left behind, that we had got over the edge of it, and were outside man's jurisdiction. . . . Between the earth and that sky I felt erased, blotted out."[29] This sensation of nothingness comprises a central theme in *My Ántonia*, serving as an extended meditation on the powers of memory.

Much has been written about the importance of memory in Cather's work, and to *My Ántonia* in particular. Sheryl Meyering describes "the power of memory" as "Cather's central focus," noting that in *My Ántonia* "the reader experiences not so much a succession of events as a succession of memories."[30] This effect creates a strange distancing, as the reader, like Jim Burden himself, struggles to piece together a series of feelings and images to structure the memory of Jim's lost childhood. Jim's boyhood, much like Lincoln's, remains out of reach—symbolized by the vanishing prairie itself, so that, as it does for Lincoln, Jim's memorializing of the vanishing prairie creates a space for boyhood to thrive in the imagination. Jim's inability to control his memories symbolizes his inability to control the past and, of course, Ántonia herself. This lack of control represents a key feature in the novel, one that reveals Jim's personal struggles, while also speaking to, as Lisa Marie Lucenti puts it, the communal aspects of memory and "collective attempts to silence and subdue the ghosts of a communal past."[31]

The workings of memory are more transparent in *Boy Life on the Prairie*. Lincoln returns to Sun Prairie for the first time as an adult and finds, like Jim, the absence of past landmarks:

> A changed world in 1884, a land of lanes and fields and groves of trees. . . .
> No prairie sod could be found. Every quarter-section, every acre was ploughed.
> The wild flowers were gone. . . . The very air seemed tamed and set to work
> at windmills whose towers rose high above every barn, like great sunflowers.[32]

As Garland describes it in his introduction, he is writing of "a vanished world—that of the prairie—much more deeply buried than my words at the ending of this book would indicate."[33] As an "historian of homely Middle Border family life," Garland can preserve that absent world, enmeshed as it is with the timeless space of boyhood.[34]

The distinctive workings of memory point to different tensions at work in each of these novels. In *Boy Life on the Prairie*, Garland struggles to reconcile the frontier landscape as a space of work, one that punishes the body and suppresses the sprit, and an idealized space of play, one that nourishes the imagination and cultivates the spirit. Lincoln struggles to balance the effects of work and play, and ultimately can do so in the past tense only through the act of nostalgia; he has to leave the prairie in order to preserve it. In this way, the novel conforms to the broad conventions of the Boy Book, while participating fully in Hall's project of using the space of the West to develop Anglo-Saxon boys into robust American men.

A different tension plays out in Cather's novel, though she too requires distance from her frontier childhood in order to process it. In Cather's case, that distance represents an attempt to maintain authorial objectivity. Thinking back on her young immigrant playmates, the inspiration for many of the characters populating Cather's fictional prairie landscapes, Cather expressed concerns about her ability to represent them accurately. "I was not at all sure, however, that my feeling about the Western country and my Scandinavian friends was the truth," she told *The Philadelphia Record* in 1913; "I thought perhaps that going among them so young I had a romantic personal feeling about them."[35] Struggling to suppress romantic sensibilities—and to avoid being criticized as a romantic writer—Cather struggles against nostalgia in order to offer a realistic portrayal of her formative years on the prairie and the playmates that made such a deep impression upon her.

Of course, these comments come five years prior to the publication of *My Ántonia*, a novel that is far less direct in its representation of prairie life than *O Pioneers!* and Cather's early short fiction. In *My Ántonia* the tension between romance and realism remains, but the process of memory is further complicated by Jim Burden's own fraught relationship to ideal boyhood. If Lincoln Stewart fits squarely in the Boy Book mold, Jim Burden is much harder to pin down. He comes to the plains as an orphan. His grandparents do not require him to work, and Jim's main childhood playmate is Ántonia. Even she drifts apart to begin working in the fields, leaving Jim increasingly isolated. In the second part of the novel, "The Hired Girls," Jim's grandparents move to town, but he remains aloof from his peers. In fact he has little use for the kind of play Lincoln revels in and spends most of his time with Ántonia and her peers, the hired girls from which this section takes its name. He pointedly decries the town's smug attitude toward these girls, who were "considered a menace to the social order," calling it "stupid" and claiming, "I knew where the real women were, though I was only a boy; and I would not be afraid of them, either!"[36]

These real women dominate Jim's consciousness and Cather's novel, and in this way Cather radically reworks the Boy Book model. In Jim's memories, the prairie is dominated by young immigrant girls like Ántonia, who, he describes, had been "early awakened and made observant by coming at an early age from an old country to a new."[37] It is not Jim but these hearty girls who transform the land and, in turn, are transformed by it. Tweaking Hall's rhetoric of the savage and civilized, Jim describes the hired girls as "almost a race apart" and the "refined" town girls in Black Hawk as dull and formless. "When one danced with them, their bodies never moved inside their clothes," Jim complains; "their muscles seemed to ask but one thing—not to be disturbed."[38] Living in Black Hawk, Jim quickly comes to disdain the "refined" residents who turn their nose up at these girls. For Jim, the hired girls are stronger and heartier; their only problem came in the way their "beauty shone out too boldly against a conventional background."[39]

In fact, the girls serve as the chief mechanism for Jim's efforts at calibrating his memory and holding on to the distant sensations of the childhood he's left behind. After he leaves town to go to school in Lincoln, Nebraska, Jim continues to revere these immigrant girls. Lena Lingard in particular becomes a potent signifier for Jim's vanishing boyhood. After leaving Black Hawk initially, Jim turns away from Ántonia, attempting to turn away from prairie life itself, and takes Lena on as a lover; she had long been an object of desire for Jim. After seeing her in Black Hawk, dressed up in the fashion of a town girl, Jim recalls her as a child herding cattle on the range. Back then, Jim notes, he always "thought of her as something wild, that always lived on the prairie."[40] The whiteness of her skin makes such an impression upon Jim that she seemed to him "more undressed than other girls who went scantily clad."[41] While the herding life makes other girls "rough and mannish," Jim is struck by Lena's softness, "the unusual color of her eyes—a shade of deep violet—and their soft, confiding expression."[42] Lena stands at the threshold of an idealized boyhood and manhood, a wildness romanticized and domesticated, a love object not quite attained. Poignantly, Lena's articulation of her past is more akin to Lincoln's hard labor narrative, and she betrays little nostalgia for it.

Lena signifies the pull of the past for Jim, which is distinctly romanticized by Jim and Jim alone. Two years into his studies in Lincoln, Lena surprises him with a visit. She is living in Lincoln now, making a living as a dressmaker, and Jim invites her in. As they talk, his mind drifts to the past, remembering the wild Lena and "how she used to run barefoot over the prairie until the snow began to fly."[43] After Lena leaves, Jim notes, "the room seemed much pleasanter than before. Lena had left something warm and friendly in the lamplight." In her laugh, he can "hear them all laughing—the Danish laundry girls and the three Bohemian Marys. Lena had brought them back to me."[44] Lena, like the narrator of the Introduction, provides a path back to Jim's imagined boyhood, and in that moment he decides "if there were no girls like them in the world, there would be no poetry. I understood that clearly, for the first time. This revelation seemed to be inestimably precious. I clung to it as if it might suddenly vanish."[45] In part, the precarious nature of this poetic past results from the fact that it does not exist for Lena at all.

Jim's relationship with these girls—easily the most powerful figures in the novel— remains a subject of great debate among Cather scholars, just as the emphatic "My" in the title remains a bone of contention. Terence Martin situates Lena and Ántonia through their significance to Jim and his efforts to resolve what Martin calls the "drama of memory." He describes Jim's relationship with Lena as "an unproductive nostalgia, an indulgence in Romantic melancholy."[46] For Burden, Martin argues, "the reality of memory" is achieved through Ántonia, who ultimately serves "as a basis for happiness." Martin's analysis is compelling. At the same time, Jim's ultimate rejection of Lena as a muse holds significant ramifications for the novel's construction and projection of ideal boyhood. After all, Lena provides a powerful connection between Jim and his earliest recollections of boyhood, recalling the simplest sensations of boy life on the prairie—joys taken not in active play, but rather in the sensation of nothingness. These feelings of nothingness recall Jim's desire to be erased or blotted out. These feelings are in fact echoed by a recurring dream Jim later has about Lena, in which the girl "came across the stubble barefoot, in a short skirt with a curved reaping-hook in her hand, and she was flushed like the dawn, with a kind of luminous rosiness all about her. She sat down beside me, turned to me with a soft sigh and said, 'Now they are all gone, and I can kiss you as much as I like.'"[47] In some sense, this kissing represents Jim's longing for the rural dream that exists in his imagination.

Blanche Gelfant offers one of the earliest and most influential assessments of Lena's relationship with Jim, arguing that this relationship points to Jim's stunted growth. "When he finds love," Gelfant claims, "it seems to him the safest kind—the narcissistic love of the man for himself as a boy." Gelfant describes this as a kind of regression in Jim, one common in Cather's fiction, wherein "the self defies change and establishes its immutability."[48] Jim's dream is central to Gelfant's analysis, which demonstrates how "desire and fear clearly contend with one another."[49] Jim imagines the Western landscape as both seductive and terrifying, the terror stemming from Jim's aversion to accept the natural "cycle of growth, maturation, and death."[50] Gelfant is right to note Jim's fear and aversion, but it is the landscape itself that terrifies him, not just the erotic charge he gets from Lena. In other words, it is not the cycle of life that terrifies him but the loss of the imagined landscape, that vital resource for cultivating frontier boyhood into fully realized manhood.

Annette Kolodny famously describes the frontier as a flexible symbol for a wide range of patriarchal rhetoric. The frontier, she argues, is "America's oldest and most cherished fantasy: a daily reality of the harmony between man and nature based on the experience of the land as essentially feminine—that is, not simply the land as mother, but the land as woman, the total female principle of gratification."[51] As mother, as lover, and in various other guises, the frontier has proven a durable vehicle for several forms of male fantasy, offering male thinkers and writers "the repeated invitation to experience pastoral realities."[52] Jim's efforts to remember his frontier boyhood and provide a narrative frame for his relationship with the hired girls map neatly onto Kolodny's argument. In showing his struggles, his failure to control his relationships with either Lena or Ántonia, Cather shows Jim's inability to harness the space of the prairie as a vehicle for male fantasy.

Jim's posture between Ántonia and Lena therefore reveals tension within him as he grows, attempting to situate himself in relation to his prairie boyhood. Jim confesses that he wished he could dream about Ántonia as he does about Lena but admits he never does. Gelfant suggest this failure demonstrates the different role these women play for Jim: "Lena, the archetypal Woman, beckons him to full sexuality. Ántonia, the eternal Mother lures him back through her children, Cuzak's boys, to perennial childhood."[53] Oddly, Gelfant sets "woman" and "mother" in opposition to one another. Ultimately Jim turns to Ántonia because Lena offers no connection to the land, first leaving Black Hawk and then Nebraska altogether to live as an independent woman. For Jim, Lena remains a symbol of vanishing boyhood. Ántonia, on the other hand, provides a source of perpetual renewal. This process is actually set in motion as soon as the Burden family moves to town. Jim starts to dismiss the notion of boyhood as timeless; in fact, he takes the adults around him to task for their failure to understand as much: "When boys and girls are growing up, life can't stand still, not even in the quietest of country towns; and they have to grow up, whether they will or no. That is what their elders are always forgetting."[54] This realization presents Jim, however, with a dire need to grasp an eroding connection.

If the dream of erasure (sexual or otherwise) proves illusory, the figure of Ántonia offers a durable link to the land and a more effective vehicle for sustaining it as a regenerative space. For Jim, *My Ántonia* is an exercise in memory, and as Lucenti points out, "Jim's memory work is the attempt to provide Ántonia with a home so that she can then house him."[55] When Jim first returns home, he finds Ántonia living back on her family farm, having been abandoned with her infant child by the railroad man Larry Donovan. Jim confesses to Ántonia, "I think of you more often than anyone else in this part of the world. I'd have liked to have you for a sweetheart, or a wife, or

my mother or my sister—anything that a woman can be to a man."[56] Walking
in the twilight with Ántonia, Jim "felt the old pull of the earth, the solemn
magic that comes out of those fields at nightfall. I wished I could be a little
boy again, and that my way could end there."[57] But Jim knows he cannot be
a little boy again, and, despite the novel's frequent evocations of death, he
wants to live.

Ultimately, Ántonia's most important role is that of creator, of mother; the
title of the book's final section declares as much: "Cuzak's Boys." Returning to his hometown twenty years later, Burden is overjoyed to find Ántonia
having settled down, taken a husband, Cuzak, and given birth to a large brood
of healthy children. There are girls as well as boys, of course, but these matter little to Jim. It is through Ántonia's boys that he ultimately satisfies the
demands of memory. Here on the Cuzak farm, Ántonia has achieved a sort
of domestic Eden, most clearly typified by the family's "fruit cave," an oft-
cited metaphor for Ántonia's earthbound nature and potent fertility. In *Boy
Life on the Prairie*, Lincoln transformed the land, while the land became a
tool for mediating the self. In *My Ántonia*, Jim does not work the land, and
he needs Ántonia, a nonwhite other, to negotiate his identity and evolution
from primitive to civilized.

Certainly, this final section of *My Ántonia* serves as a rebuke to the Boy
Book formula reproduced in *Boy Life on the Prairie*. Cather's novel rejects
outright the model of the Western as male fantasy, as Susan Rosowski forcefully argues. Cather, she claims, "sent Adam packing and claimed paradise
for women, restoring them to psychosexual identification with nature and
appropriating for them the promise of nature's wildness."[58] Ántonia, Rosowski argues, stands out as the prime example of this trend in Cather's work.
Indeed, Ántonia cuts a powerful figure, and, as Rosowski claims, a more
complex rendering of the "earth mother" archetype than that for which she is
often given credit. Still, her main function in the novel is as a conduit between
Jim and the vanished landscape, an imagined world nourished by Jim's boyhood memories, but, more importantly, sustained by the new generation of
Cuzak's boys. In the novel's final pages, Jim returns to Black Hawk and finds
the town depressing. He quickly shakes this feeling, noting "my mind was
full of pleasant trips I meant to take with the Cuzak boys, in the Bad Lands,
and up to the Stinking Water. There were enough Cuzaks to play with for
a long while yet."[59] The land becomes a space of boyhood play once again.

Ultimately it is through these boys that the frontier is preserved as a space
of boyhood, even as the literal space of Jim's boyhood vanishes beneath his
feet. The fact that they are Bohemian boys preserves Jim's boyhood in the
tradition of Hall's recapitulation thesis, even as it destabilizes and moves forward a potential future of white American masculinity. As the novel ends, the

connection between boyhood and the Western landscape is stronger than ever. Jim retraces the old road that first brought him to the prairie—now grown over from disuse: "I had the sense of coming home to myself," Jim writes, "and of finding out what a little circle man's experience is." [60] Speaking of Ántonia, he continues, "Whatever we had missed, we possessed together the precious, the incommunicable past." For Jim, Ántonia has become more than a wife, a sweetheart, or a mother, helping to construct his identity through the imagined frontier. In this way, *My Ántonia* radically alters the structure of Boy Book, while preserving the frontier as a vital space of developing boyhood.

NOTES

1. On Cather and memory, see Lisa Marie Lucenti, "Willa Cather's *My Ántonia*: Haunting the Houses of Memory," *Twentieth Century Literature* 46, no. 2 (Summer 2000): 193–213. For Jim, memory, and mediation, see Catherine D. Holmes, "Jim Burden's Lost Worlds: Exile in *My Ántonia*," *Twentieth Century Literature* 45, no. 3 (Autumn 1999): 336–46. For more on Jim as mediator, see Joy Cooney, "A Mediating Presence in Cather's *My Ántonia*," *The Explicator* 69, no. 3 (2011): 142–45. For Jim's repressed sexuality and its impact on his role as narrator, see Blanche H. Gelfant, "The Forgotten Reaping-Hook: Sex in *My Ántonia*," *American Literature* 43, no. 1 (March 1971): 64.

2. Sue Thomas, *Willa Cather* (Savage, MD: Barnes and Noble Books, 1990), 57–59.

3. Neil Gustafson, "Willa Cather and Hamlin Garland: Parallel Early Lives," *Willa Cather Newsletter and Review* 49, no. 1 (2005): 9.

4. Frederick Jackson Turner, "The Significance of the Frontier in American History, *American Studies at The University of Virginia*, 2014, http://xroads.virginia.edu/~hyper/turner/chapter1.html. R. W. Lewis Adams, *The American Adam: Innocence, Tragedy, and Tradition in the Nineteenth Century* (Chicago: University of Chicago Press, 1955). For more on the savage and civilized in frontier mythos, see Henry Nash Smith, *Virgin Land* (New York: Vintage Books, 1957).

5. Anne Scott MacLeod, *American Childhood: Essays on Children's Literature of the Nineteenth and Twentieth Centuries* (Athens: University of Georgia Press, 1994), 72.

6. David I. Macleod, *Building Character in the American Boy: The Boy Scouts, YMCA, and Their Forerunners, 1870–1920* (Madison: University of Wisconsin Press, 1983), 53.

7. Kenneth Kidd, *Making American Boys: Boyology and the Feral Tale* (Minneapolis: University of Minnesota Press, 2004), 52.

8. Ibid., 62.

9. Macleod, *Building Character*. For a thorough analysis of Hall's recapitulation theory through the lens of race, boyhood, and masculinity, see chapter 3 in Gail Bederman, *Manliness & Civilization: A Cultural History of Gender and Race in the United States: 1880–1917* (Chicago: University of Chicago Press, 1995).

10. Macleod, *Building Character*, 55.

11. Quoted in Marcia Jacobson, *Being a Boy Again: Autobiography and the American Boy Book* (Tuscaloosa: University of Alabama Press, 1994), 2.

12. Ibid., 11.

13. Kidd, *Making American Boys*, 79.

14. G. Stanley Hall, "Boy Life in a Massachusetts Town Thirty Years Ago," in *Proceedings of the American Antiquarian Society*, 1890, 127, http://www.american-antiquarian.org/proceedings/44769428.pdf.

15. Kidd, *Making American Boys*, 36.

16. Hall, "Boy Life," 127.

17. Turner, "The Significance of the Frontier."

18. Mary Lawlor, *Recalling the Wild: Naturalism and the Closing of the American West* (New Brunswick, NJ: Rutgers University Press, 2000), 43.

19. Hamlin Garland, *Boy Life on the Prairie* (New York: Frederick Ungar Publishing, 1959), 166.

20. Jacobson, *Being a Boy Again*, 3.

21. Macleod, *Building Character*, 102.

22. Willa Cather, *My Ántonia*, Willa Cather Scholarly Edition, ed. Charles W. Mignon and Kari A. Ronning (Lincoln: University of Nebraska Press, 1994), xiii.

23. Jan Goggans, "Social (Re)Visioning in the Fields of *My Ántonia*," *Cather Studies* 5 (2003): 153.

24. Cather, *My Ántonia*, xi.

25. E. Anthony Rotundo, *American Manhood: Transformations in Masculinity from the Revolution of the Modern Era* (New York: Basic Books, 1993), 35.

26. Garland, *Boy Life on the Prairie*, 67.

27. Ibid., 90.

28. Ibid., 2–3.

29. Cather, *My Ántonia*, 7–8.

30. Sheryl Meyering, "Fleeting Moments of Beauty: A Literary Analysis of *O Pioneers!* and *My Ántonia*," in *Understanding* O Pioneers! *and My Ántonia*, ed. Sheryl L. Meyering (Westport, CT: Greenwood Press, 2002), 13.

31. Lucenti, "Willa Cather's *My Ántonia*," 194.

32. Garland, *Boy Life on the Prairie*, 311.

33. Ibid., vii–ix.

34. Ibid., vi.

35. "Special Correspondence," with P. A. Kinsley, *Philadelphia Record*, August 10, 1913, accessed September 18, 2016, http://cather.unl.edu/bohlke.i.05.html.

36. Cather, *My Ántonia*, 218.

37. Ibid., 192.

38. Ibid., 192–93.

39. Ibid., 195.

40. Ibid., 160.

41. Ibid.

42. Ibid.

43. Ibid., 259.

44. Ibid., 262.

45. Ibid.

46. Terence Martin, "The Drama of Memory in *My Ántonia*," *PMLA* 84, no. 2 (March 1969): 304–11; Cather, *My Ántonia*, 218.

47. Cather, *My Ántonia*, 218.

48. Gelfant, "The Forgotten Reaping-Hook," 64.

49. Ibid., 65.

50. Ibid., 66.

51. Annette Kolodny, *The Lay of the Land: Metaphor as Experience and History in American Life and Letters* (Chapel Hill: University of North Carolina Press, 1975), 4.

52. Ibid., 136.

53. Gelfant, "The Forgotten Reaping-Hook," 68.

54. Cather, *My Ántonia*, 187.

55. Lucenti, "Willa Cather's *My Ántonia*," 195.

56. Cather, *My Ántonia*, 312.

57. Ibid., 313.

58. Susan J. Rosowski, *Birthing a Nation: Gender, Creativity, and the West in American Literature* (Lincoln: University of Nebraska Press, 1999), 79.

59. Cather, *My Ántonia*, 358.

60. Ibid., 360.

Chapter Seven

The Nebraskan Neverland

The Archeology of Children's Fantasy Fiction in My Ántonia

Holly Blackford

In her chapter "Traces of J. M. Barrie's Peter Pan in Willa Cather's *The Professor's House*," Rosanna Walker analyzes the intertextuality of *Peter and Wendy* in Cather's 1925 novel.[1] The youth Tom Outland appears in the Professor's life suddenly, lacking a precise birthday and given an approximate age—like Peter Pan—by how many teeth he had when he was adopted. The Blue Mesa that Tom discovers and defines as a space of purity is a Neverland space, which becomes a symbol for the Professor's lost original youth as he looks back on his life and feels that his "unmodified" boyhood has nothing to do with the events and demands of manhood. Godfrey St. Peter's study in his old house, which he refuses to leave, has a window looking onto Lake Michigan, which likewise signals his escape from the confines of his demanding, female-governed family. The infusion of the eternal boy Tom Outland into the Professor's story communicates desire for authenticity, given a fallen, materialist, modern America. Cather's appreciation of Barrie and Barrie's inspiration from the American frontier embody a dexterous transatlantic mobility, which we can also use to illuminate the complexities of male psychology, national history, and desire for myth making in Cather's earlier *My Ántonia*.

Jim Burden's reflections on nineteenth-century settlement of the Plains draw upon the vexed relationship of Peter and Wendy in Barrie's 1911 novel.[2] Cast as a perennial boy who "never seems to me to grow older" by the narrator of the Introduction,[3] Jim stands for continual motion and flight embodied by trains. Jim is always traveling and fueling Western dreams of other men. Indeed, in the vivid landscape sections of the opening portions of the manuscript he writes, he is identified with the flight of an owl who leaves a shadow in his wake. Jim's memory of childhood in Nebraska contains images of grasslands as neverending spaces yet edges off which he might float, suggesting a Neverland space. The opening Introduction situates Jim's posture on the train in the observation car looking out on a landscape that evokes sensory memories of being "buried" and "stifled" in wheat and corn.[4] The rhythm of flight and return to a Nebraskan Neverland situates Jim as the boy who circumvented a linear developmental pathway by the structure of flight and return as his life principle.

Just as the Professor in Cather's *Professor's House* feels his feet firmly on the ground again when he encounters his seamstress Augusta, a Wendy figure who represents the reality of earth for Professor St. Peter, Jim circles around Ántonia and Mrs. Harling in the same way that Peter circles around Wendy and Mrs. Darling to work through paradoxical feelings toward origins, mothers, and maternal landscapes. Creating a Nebraska Neverland that mythologizes childhood and a pioneer past in an unmapped landscape, a cultural geography theorized as child psychology in Barrie's Neverland, Jim reworks Peter's vexed feelings about flight and return, desire for and fear of enclosed spaces and dominating women. Peter wants to hold onto Wendy but fears and resents commitment to women, just as Jim holds onto "his" Ántonia but flees and neglects to return to her for twenty years. He fears the shock of seeing her grown up.

Jim's reinvention of Ántonia as a mythic mother of the prairie, "a rich mine of life, like the founders of early races,"[5] his closing of Mrs. Harling's gate and embrace of exile; these Peter Pan moments symbolize his enterprise of creating frontier mythology from selective fragments of memory. The Neverland, as Barrie presented it in *Peter and Wendy*, is a space of floating, swirling fragments of personal and cultural history, what Fredric Jameson names "the political unconscious."[6] Just as Peter has rare instances of "painful" dreams that "had to do, I think, with the riddle of his existence,"[7] Jim pushes terrifying dreams and realities of murder, suicide, abuse, and the like to the margins of his consciousness, as analyzed by Sarah L. Young in this volume. Just as Barrie's swirling Neverland becomes organized into the imperialist adventure story of piracy and its defeat by loyal subjects to the Crown, Jim's consciousness eventually organizes into "the pioneer woman's story" and "Cuzak's boys," the final books of the novel. Jim's one dream of Lena, which is a transitional device between childhood and myth, centers on *a hook*. The reaping hook she carries in his dreams renders sexuality and the career woman as the looming ending to Neverland mythology. On the last night of his childhood in the country with Ántonia, Jim and Ántonia witness a summer storm and they observe "one black cloud, no bigger than a little boat . . . kept moving westward" amid lightning flashes that "looked like deep blue water."[8] Images of shadows, islands, hooks, and mother longing signal Cather's subtle engagement with Barrie's children's fantasy of British imperialist history and her application of Barrie's project to American mythography.

In her letters, several of which name Barrie and his voiced admiration of her works, Cather names J. M. Barrie as a hero of her early youth,[9] praising in particular his *Sentimental Tommy*[10] and his late play "The Boy David" for "how wonderfully Barrie does the future man in the boy."[11] In this, Cather and Barrie overlap. Peter Pan is an extensive study of male identity choices and the cost of those choices—the tragic consequences of exile from one's original meaning and context. Peter Pan is intimately associated with death, and Jim Burden voices death drives in his radical embrace of eradication and continual identification with Mr. Shimerda, whose suicide Jim views as a "return" to Mr. Shimerda's longed-for home in the past. Both Mr. Shimerda's grave and Ántonia's Bohemian community of children become Neverland islands around which Jim continues to circle after his other anchors have disappeared. This was not the first time Cather evoked children's fantasy literature in her novels; at the end of this chapter I will compare her use of *The Wizard of Oz* in *O Pioneers!* to her use of *Peter and Wendy* in *My Ántonia* to distill the point that the very concept of the Neverland, Peter Pan's world, led her to innovative thinking about the lost world of childhood and the landscape of national history. Ultimately Peter Pan offered Cather an opportunity to show how the artist could use childhood and selective memory to shape a nation's need for mythic origins in Neverland.

NEVERLAND AND "THE WHOLE ADVENTURE OF OUR CHILDHOOD"

In *Peter and Wendy*, the Neverland is introduced as a geography of the child mind, a geographical mapping of child psychology remapped in *My Ántonia*. The Neverland resides inside the child and it is unmappable because it refuses to stay still:

> Catch [doctors] trying to draw a map of a child's mind, which is not only confused, but keeps going round all the time. There are zigzag lines on it . . . and these are probably roads in the island; for the Neverland is always more or less an island, with astonishing splashes of colour here and there.[12]

As a child first acquainting himself with the Plains, Jim Burden detects motion in the landscape, and he celebrates the lack of roads and fences, which allows him free range with Ántonia. The land with "no fences," through which he can "drift along," indeed has splashes of color, the "damp spots" found at the edges of the "pale-yellow cornfields," the "rich copper colour" of the smartweed, and "the narrow brown leaves . . . curled like cocoons about the swollen joints of the stem."[13] The land is essentially pregnant, and like a fetus

Jim can hear the corn growing in the night. Like Carl in *O Pioneers!*, also an artist figure, Jim prefers the wild nature of the landscape to the cultivated farms and paved roads of the postsettlement period.

Jim continually emphasizes the feeling of endlessness in the land when a child; this endless feeling gives him the illusion that he could float off in space, die, and return to nothingness, a death drive anchoring *Peter and Wendy* as well. Mrs. Darling remembers Peter Pan as an escort to dead children so they are not frightened, and Peter Pan collects children who fall out of their prams, ruling an underworld and doing "some things" to children so they continue to fit in the underground tree.[14] As Jim enters the new land without landmarks and trees, he feels "erased, blotted out," yet "so much motion" in the grass that "the whole country seemed, somehow, to be running."[15] Actual buffalo have moved on because of settlement, but he detects the archeological trace, registering "motion in the landscape; in the fresh, easy-blowing morning wind, and in the earth itself, as if the shaggy grass were a sort of loose hide, and underneath it herds of wild buffalo were galloping, galloping."[16] This archeological sense that national history resides in the empty grasses and child mind is also true of the Neverland, where fragments of British history, folklore, and banal elements of child life mix democratically.

Barrie pioneered this rudimentary idea of the historical and personal unconscious in the child's Neverland. The Neverland contains everything from gnomes "who are mostly tailors" to "first day at school, religion, fathers, the round pond, needlework, murders, hanging, verbs that take the dative, chocolate-pudding day, getting into braces, say ninety-nine, threepence for pulling out your tooth yourself, and so on; and either these are part of the island or they are another map showing through, and it is all rather confusing, especially as nothing will stand still."[17] Of course, there are also Indians and pirates with historical fame in Neverland, whose descriptions allude to various trade routes, public schools, and even Charles II. These along with "one very small lady with a hooked nose"[18] nonsensically stream in child consciousness. If Jim finds out "what a little circle man's experience is," this circle is coordinated with "a great circle where Indians used to ride," "faintly marked in the grass."[19] If Jim in dreams can take on histories like that of Peter and Pavel and combine their Russian landscape with Virginia, it is given precedent by the swirling mix of personal and cultural histories of the Neverland, which is located in the child mind and cannot be precisely mapped. Its openness means it is a reservoir of everything underneath and in the historical past of the mainland.

The curious mix of Jim's embeddedness in landscape and disappearance through flotation and flight also derives from the impossible Neverland space (you cannot *land* in it). Jim feels he can walk "through the red grass and over the edge of the world,"[20] an edge mirrored by the location of his first exchange with Ántonia at the edge of Squaw Creek, "the ground itself stopped—fell away before us so abruptly that the next step would have been out on the treetops."[21] Cather was interested in unexpected canyons, cliffs, crevices, and edges in the Southwestern landscape, where, significantly, traces of ancient civilizations and their ritualistic lives could be found in such edges and crevices. Thea in *The Song of the Lark* goes to Panther Canyon, based on Walnut Canyon where Cather went in 1912, and finds "one of those abrupt fissures with which the earth in the Southwest is riddled; so abrupt that you might walk over the edge of any one of them on a dark night and never know what had happened to you."[22] In this spot, Thea loses and finds herself, her sense of the sacred, and her understanding of what real art can be. Feeling that the grasses of Nebraska are the edge of the world, Jim thinks, "The light air about me told me that the world ended here; only the ground and sun and sky, and one would float off into them, like the tawny hawk which sailed over our heads making slow shadows on the grass."[23] When one flies one leaves a shadow, much as Peter loses his shadow in the Darling nursery and Tom Outland in *The Professor's House* leaves a blanket, described as his skin, which still smells of his Southwestern adventures. The issue of shadows embedded in the landscape recurs throughout *My Ántonia*, evoking the introduction of Peter into the Darling household in pursuit of his shadow, which Wendy reattaches for him. The entire novel of *My Ántonia* could be defined as Jim's efforts to reattach his shadow with memories of Ántonia. He cannot do it alone.

If the hawk in flight makes a "slow shadow" on the land, embedded much as Jim burrows in nooks and crannies throughout the first book, Jim "raced [his] shadow home"[24] after he encounters Mr. Shimerda looking at him "as if [he] were down at the bottom of a well"[25]—as if Jim were not quite real and the soon-to-die man knows this. Jim feels that his shadow, in concert with Ántonia's, forever resides in the landscape of their childhoods: "How many an afternoon Ántonia and I have trailed along the prairie under that magnificence! And always two long black shadows flitted before us or followed after, dark spots on the ruddy grass."[26] The ambiguity about whether the shadows come before or follow the two children is symbolic of the status of child memory in the novel; is it an acute, raw perceptual device, registering something authentic, or is it a shadow of an "incommunicable past"[27] at once healing to reconstruct and registering a hopeless fantasy of escape from the discontents of modern civilization? When Jim leaves Ántonia at the end of "The Pioneer Woman's Story," he "could almost believe that a boy and girl ran along beside me, as our shadows used to do, laughing and whispering in the grass."[28] Jim at the end, feeling "like a boy in [Ántonia's sons] company," finds his shadow walking singly and peacefully beside him "over the close-cropped grass,"[29] but the meaning of this singular shadow is unclear. It is one shadow, not two, which could mean he locates his wholeness in the discovery of Leo, a new Peter Pan figure, who is covered in light fur, goatlike ("like a little ram"[30]), mischievous, and his mother's favorite.

The Introduction in which the narrator and Jim collaboratively construct a narrative of childhood in the Plains is reminiscent of the fact that the name "Peter" first arises in the children's minds when Mrs. Darling sorts their mental contents at night. Similarly, the name "Ántonia" arises in the co-reminiscence of the narrator and Jim in the Introduction. Somehow Ántonia is supposed to capture "the whole adventure of our childhood,"[31] a curious ascription of the adventure genre because *My Ántonia* is hardly an adventure novel. Mrs. Darling finds that Wendy's mind "began to be scrawled over with" the name Peter Pan,[32] and the name Ántonia anchors Jim's reminiscence, over which he scrawls "My Ántonia." It would be tempting to view Ántonia as the Pan figure, especially because she "presides" at the heart of this Nebraskan Neverland and is decontextualized from her culture of origin. But it is Jim, not Ántonia, whom the narrator of the Introduction identifies as the boy who never seems to get any older, which is highly reminiscent of the first words of Barrie's novel, "All children, except one, grow up." Ántonia also observes at the end of the novel to Jim, "You've kept so young, yourself. But it's easier for a man," as if men are exempt from the rules of nature.[33]

Barrie's identification of the Neverland as child psychology, remembered longingly and in traces by adults, is instructive because the Neverland is a matter of personal and cultural perception. If you line up the individual Neverlands, they would have a sort of "family resemblance,"[34] much as figures in the Nebraskan landscape have a family resemblance for Jim. Although Ántonia, Tiny, and Lena have individuality for Jim, they are lumped into "the hired girls," and the Danish girls of the laundry as well as the three Bohemian Marys begin to slide together in Neverland fashion. The way in which memories blend and swirl into patterns, while particular figures emerge and recede, suggests Barrie's Neverland; after delineating how John's Neverland differs from Michael's and Wendy's, Barrie's narrator explains that the word Peter is in all of them, but in Wendy's he emerges more fully and takes on "an oddly cocky appearance."[35] The Neverland is therefore a topographical embodiment of how the child mind and memory operate.

Cather deploys a similar theory of topographical memory. Distinct occurrences in Jim's life, such as the story of Peter and Pavel escaping the wolves, merge into patterns and images that blend with other fragments in life, much as certain elements of Ántonia are individual and certain things blend in Jim's mind with patterns. This happens when Jim sees Lena through a Virgilian lens; when he dreams of Peter and Pavel's sled sailing through a landscape "something like Nebraska and something like Virginia";[36] when he imagines Mrs. Shimerda's mushrooms "had been gathered, probably, in some deep Bohemian forest";[37] when he intuits Ántonia's vibrant personality through her battered appearance and remembers "the pictures" she calls up in him; and when he imagines the deceased Mr. Shimerda stopping in his grandmother's kitchen before heading home to Europe. All these mental blends speak to the Neverland as governing principle: personal and cultural pasts, some re-counted in stories, blend in the consciousness of childhood. Childhood, as Barrie constructed it, is essentially an extinct geographical site ripe for arche-ological excavation and recontextualization. This is likely why Jim sees not only a cloud like a boat on his last night in the country with Ántonia, but also images of "some splendid seacoast city, doomed to destruction."[38] Only in the child mind can Pompeii and pudding day coexist with the same equivalence.

Taking place at "clay cliffs" and an "edge" at Squaw Creek, the initial exchange between Ántonia and Jim mirrors the first interchange between Peter and Wendy, signifying a romance that is not quite romantic. Wendy asks for a kiss and Peter, not knowing what a kiss is, holds out his hand, so she gives him a thimble. In return, he gives her his "kiss"—an acorn button. The exchange is a request for commitment from Wendy, but Peter has no idea what she seeks. He is both developmentally behind Wendy and less worldly. This is carried through to the end; even after their return Wendy asks Peter whether he would like to speak to her parents about a sweet subject, and he says no.[39] Jim's meeting of Ántonia establishes similar issues. She seeks the word for his eyes and the sky—the word *blue*—and he "had no idea what she wanted" until after several tries.[40] He does not seem developmentally ready for physical attraction. For her, he embodies the sky; and for him, she embod-ies earth and nesting throughout the text, equated with warm earthy colors and later myths of earth mothering. Ántonia's father commands Jim to teach Ántonia English, but the exchange culminates in her attempt to give him a ring and his horror at this. As a reverse suitor relationship mirroring Wendy throwing her sexuality at Peter and Peter's oblivion and resistance to it, Jim's stance mirrors his nonsexual stance throughout the novel. While it is clear that Jim is four years younger than Ántonia, it is not clear whether Peter is younger than Wendy; in the novel, their size is the same. However, it is clear that Peter chooses boyhood as a protection from female sexuality, which is thrown at him by multiple figures (Tiger Lily, Tink, Wendy).

This early exchange between Jim and Ántonia is also reminiscent of Peter and Wendy's "exchange" because in it Peter is both shamed and proud of his freedom from cultural markers. Wendy has multiple names, siblings, family, and context, whereas Peter has only the "shortish" name Peter, no address, and pure freedom. The scene in which Jim meets Ántonia emphasizes *her* familial context; she has multiple siblings, the chatter of language surrounding her, and a context that Jim cannot possibly understand—a past. In contrast, Jim is an orphan in a fairly silent new family, with the freedom of a horse to rove at will but with no words about his own past with his parents. The acceptance of sexuality from Ántonia (the ring) would give him context, something resisted throughout the novel. Even when Ántonia, Tiny, and Lena try to predict Jim's vocation, he resists commitment. When Jim returns to Ántonia after college, he lists the various contexts he could have taken up with her: "I'd have liked to have you for a sweetheart, or a wife, or my mother or my sister—anything that a woman can be to a man."[41] These incompatible and hardly past-tense possibilities circulate, but they are never real, and the early exchange and suggestion that Ántonia is developmentally ahead, more sexual, and more worldly as well as context-based define Jim's hesitation at commitment in the terms of Peter Pan's.

As much as Barrie's text resists precise ties to women that would define male roles, it is packed with longings for mothers and women. The paradox of rejecting and longing for women and mother is one of the deepest ties between the two novels. As Penelope Schott Starkey writes of *Peter and Wendy*, the escape fantasy embodied by Peter's flight, the moment he hears his mother contemplating how he will grow to manhood, is contradicted by the novel's foregrounding of mothering—the maternal Wendy who cares for the lost boys the moment she arrives by setting up housekeeping and routines for them, giving them medicine and mending their clothes; the pirates who feel the game is up because the boys have a mother; the worship of Mrs. Darling as an ideal mother leaving the window open for her children's return; and Peter's transport of Wendy to Neverland to give the lost boys a mother.[42] Jim's construction of Ántonia as an earth mother becomes overt by the end, and she participates in it as well, saying, "Jim, I loved you children almost as much as I love my own," grouping Jim with the Harling children.[43] Her governance of a land of "Cuzak's boys" makes sense in the context of Wendy, Queen of the Lost Boys' world. The idea that Ántonia's household is mostly boys could be a matter of Jim's perception; the section is titled "Cuzak's Boys," but it is clear there are many girls there and they are a major support system for Ántonia and a big part of the fun in the house. Yet Jim does not see them as comprising the mythic title of his manuscript.

Throughout the text, the motherless Jim confronts rhythms of mourning and longing for the company of strong women—Ántonia, his grandmother, the Harlings, and even Lena. They dominate his imagination, and he enjoys being dominated. As Ann Fisher-Wirth argues about his relationship to landscape, Jim alternates between burrowing in womblike spaces and facing the terror of absorption in open spaces, much as a child interacts with the body of the mother.[44] Jim's circulation around the lively, playful, artistic household of the Harlings is particularly reminiscent of Peter Pan's hovering around the window of the Darlings, and Mr. Harling is ostracized much as Mr. Darling. Jim will not come near if Mr. Harling is home and he is jealous of the attention Mrs. Harling must give her husband if he is there, as if he is a child of hers as well: "On winter nights, the lights in the Harlings' windows drew me like the painted glass. . . . Of course, if Mr. Harling was at home, if his shadow stood out on the blind . . . I did not go in."[45] The root of Jim's circulation, as for Peter, is the family and storytelling that occurs there; stories of "adventure" can be found there. For example, Ántonia tells the story of the tramp there. The idea that Jim circles around the Harlings can be seen in that chapter, which begins by praising Ántonia's housekeeping and ends with observations of her husky voice and similarity to her earthy mistress: "There was a basic harmony between Ántonia and [Mrs. Harling]. . . . They loved children and animals and music, and rough play and digging in the earth."[46] The chapter is an example of the way the novel operates in circles that contain horrors in idyllic frames, much as the many horrors at the margins of Jim's consciousness are contained by his cycles of flight and return to an idyllic countryside. Neverland works the same way; it is remembered as an ideal place of play: "We too have been there; we can still hear the sound of the surf, though we shall land no more."[47] But it is a place of murder and mayhem.

Part of this longing for mothers is also resentment, which also periodically surfaces in Jim as he resents Ántonia being a dominant figure as well as an excellent storyteller, much as we find a rival storytelling and artistic struggle between Peter and Wendy. In the chapter in which Wendy tells her story of the Darling children, Peter plays his pipes and interrupts her story to explain "the truth" about mothers—how they shut windows and move on. The power struggle over storytelling is also apparent in the narrator, who draws attention to his role in shaping the stories told; he tells the reader there are many adventures he could select, spending a long paragraph debating which adventure to tell and finally flipping a coin.[48] He is competing with Mrs. Darling and Wendy, who tell stories like Cinderella and attract Peter. The unique narrator of *Peter and Wendy* also vacillates in his relationship to the characters; sometimes he aligns with adults and those who "shall land no more" in Neverland, but sometimes he aligns with children: "Off we skip like the most heartless things in the world."[49] Often he is a trickster author: "One thing I should like to do immensely, is to tell [Mrs. Darling], in the way authors have, that the children are coming back. . . . This would spoil so completely the surprise. . . . How delicious to spoil it all."[50] He concludes that both reader and narrator are not wanted: "Nobody really wants us. So let us watch and say jaggy things, in the hope that some of them will hurt."[51] In fact, he fluctuates in attitude toward Mrs. Darling from "I despise her"[52] for her patient vigil to declaring he likes her best of all.

This odd fluctuation similarly characterizes Jim's fluctuations between praising Ántonia's vitality and judging her coarse manners. In one moment he is revolted by her shoveling her food, in another he is upset she has to work and put away childish things, and in the next breath images of her "vibrant personality" come through. The upshot, as with Jim in relation to Ántonia, is that we never know quite what to make of the Neverland, which is because we do not know how to come to terms with shifting, unmappable landscapes; in Neverland, childhood amorality, savagery, and hedonism lurk alongside fond memories of innocence, asexuality, and playfulness. Peter Pan tells Hook "I'm youth, I'm joy"[53] as if he is not the same rascal who laughs when the Darling children fall asleep and plummet, who blows out the stars, who messes with Neverbird nests, who expects obedience in his games and tires of them quickly, who insists to Wendy they are just playing mother and father, who impersonates and takes the place of Hook on the Jolly Roger, who steals the Darling children for a long period of time, and who tries to prevent their return. Cather seems to have understood and seen the potential of a trickster narrator who embodies Neverland's zigzag.

The great "romance" between Wendy and Peter, which never culminates, also defines the romance between Jim and Ántonia, which flirts with but never reaches sexual maturity. This is not so much childhood asexuality, as we would expect Cather to like, but the prolonging of the realm of play, which has both hostile and appreciative elements and remains open to fluctuation. Peter Pan's role is to keep Wendy guessing about his adventures and feelings toward her:

> [Peter] often went out alone, and when he came back you were never absolutely certain whether he had had an adventure or not. He might have forgotten it so completely that he said nothing about it; and then when you went out you found the body; and, on the other hand, he might say a great deal about it, and yet you could not find the body. Sometimes he came home with his head bandaged, and then Wendy cooed over him and bathed it in lukewarm water, while he told a dazzling tale. But she was never quite sure, you know.[54]

Peter embodies the unmappable Neverland space of which you can never be certain; he embodies "the whole adventure of childhood," but this adventure cannot be precisely named. Similarly, one is never sure whether Jim has "mock adventure[s]"[55] such as the snake, or what exactly is his relationship to the "peculiar pleasure"[56] of hearing stories of hardship and death on the prairie. The destructive sadomasochism of enjoying such "adventures" is simultaneous with the constructive nature of storytelling; it is this theory of art, the child mind, play, and hedonism that Peter Pan embodies with his lack of memory, his perpetual and extreme creativity, and his reflection of the Neverland (a communal construct) itself.

Jim is a figure of displacement from the beginning of the novel, identifying with displaced immigrants, which are cultures in ruins, and particularly the homeless, past-longing Mr. Shimerda. But his own situation is unclear: is it sympathetic or voyeuristic? Is he out for compassion or sport? The narrator of the Introduction explains that Jim has a particular sympathy toward women, and Peter Pan has a special courtesy toward women. Jim's meditations on his past before feeling "blotted out" by the Plains and domination by Ántonia are as "impossible" as Peter's dreams because they are as absent. We know nothing about his past except that the "window" is shut. Yet both youths suggest originary traumas of separation from mothers, both the place and person of the mother, which gives them a free-floating existence that cannot be pinned down. In other words, the "boys" are also fractured, which gives them insight into cultural traditions undergoing destruction and rebirth into something new.

Because the normative pathway to sexual maturity is not reached and even defined, Peter Pan has often been queered in critical reception histories and plays, where women play the trousers role. This queering of arrested development is also an issue for Cather's Jim because of questions about Cather's sexuality[57] and readings of the way Jim shies away from sexuality.[58] Indeed, the one area in which Jim and Peter Pan actually differ is masculinity; Jim's time with boys is not represented—though he claims he does roam and fish with boys—and he maintains a housewifely eye, judging manners, ashy bread, and Ántonia's systematic housekeeping at the end. Indeed, if Wendy's decision to return to her parents is engendered by Peter's refusal to be the partner she wishes, Jim's leave-taking of Ántonia is much more violent in its rupture; the sexual assault by Wick Cutter, when Jim is taking the place of Ántonia, initiates the far safer distance Jim can have with a Virgilian lens. In fact, the one time Jim dashes out the window, Peter Pan's threshold, is in this scene as he escapes the grotesque feminized sexuality he feels has been cast upon him. Directly, he is in college perched at a window, which he likes to keep open, much as the Professor in *The Professor's House*. This is a safe distance from Neverland and it is precisely when Jim takes up his Virgilian stance on "country girls." The point is that Neverland is safest when one cannot actually go there—when one is no longer a child and therefore no longer vulnerable to (reaping) hooks and pirates in the form of grotesque cutters.

This is rather why Barrie's Peter Pan has been discussed as "the impossibility of children's literature" because children do not exist except as defined and used by adults for their own purposes,[59] a definition encompassing

Cather's extremely self-conscious project of Jim's memory and child reminiscence. Ántonia and Nebraska only acquire meaning from the observation
car in Jim's mobile view. Just as Ántonia captures "the whole adventure of
our childhood,"[60] impossibly because *her* story is different and she is often—
like Wendy—cooking and cleaning for "the children" who are remembering
her on the train, Wendy is the anchor around which the Peter Pan mythology,
as constructed mythology, revolves. Ántonia, even at twenty-four, is "ever
so much more than twenty," Jim's age when he encounters her with her first
child. Like Wendy, Ántonia offers her children and Jim seizes upon them as
ways to reimagine his boyhood and relationship with Ántonia. If a British tale
of romance with the pretense of adventure defines the pioneer myth Cather
authored, it is partly because Barrie uniquely combined *two* origin myths in
his novel, in which he focused on Wendy as the protagonist more so than in
his 1904 play. Wendy is involved in a distinct tale of female sexual development, negotiating breaking away from her mother by taking on the myth
of Persephone, reaching out for an underworld figure and negotiating her
partial return.[61] Similarly, as Evelyn Helmick has explained, the Persephone-
Demeter myth structures Ántonia's story.[62] To this I would add that there is
a strong embedded tale of Ántonia rejecting her own mother Mrs. Shimerda
and reaching out for a different world, but facing the inescapable pattern of
her mother's life and negotiating its transformation. The story of Persephone
concerns the female desire for continuity yet change, rather than radical fractures, departures, and displacements.

As in *Peter and Wendy*, the male developmental story is placed alongside
the female one. John, Michael, Peter Pan, and Hook operate in a different
bildungsroman involving not so much sexuality as capitalism, fair treatment,
"good form," piracy, and loyalty. Jim's tale of education, leave-taking, and
modernity is set against a female origin tale of Peresphone sexuality and
Demetrian motherhood. Jim is given the adventures of Jesse James on the
train and the "brother" figures he encounters, Otto and Frank, temper later
models of the New England intellectual Gaston Cleric and the different male
pathway he is set to follow. On a final picnic with "the hired girls," whom Jim
begins to objectify, he is asked to discuss Coronado's search for gold and he
explains the discovery of two Spanish artifacts in Nebraska, a metal stirrup
and sword with a Spanish inscription. Although muted, fragments of masculine traditions reside in the landscape next to "timeless"[63] female concerns
with negotiating sexuality, womanhood, and motherhood. Cather, following
Barrie's lead, gives them equal due and demonstrates their coexistence and
irreconcilability in terms of narrative arc.

This model, set by Barrie, uniquely combined Wendy's romance plot and
development with adventure motifs, and neither is given precedence over

the other. Jacqueline Rose argues about *Peter Pan* that part of its impossibility is how "children's fiction has never completely severed its links with a philosophy which sets up the child as a pure point of origin in relation to language, sexuality and the state."[64] The unique combination of gendered origin myths, the sexual and the capitalist, makes Cather's *My Ántonia* and *Peter and Wendy* dialogically classic, for unlike in *The Professor's House* the female origin myth is given its due. The male perception of the country as a virgin, maternal landscape is set alongside "the pioneer woman's story" of negotiating sexuality, relationships, social perceptions, and mother-daughter dynamics at the center of self. Like Wendy, who is a strong character in her own right and who expresses her desires without shame, Ántonia has her own sense of herself and it often conflicts with Jim's vision of her. This is because Ántonia operates rather like the Spanish artifact; she is a fragment in Jim's geographical unconscious that he is excavating and recontextualizing according to the narrative he wishes to tell. She is always incomplete in his representation.

NATIONAL HISTORY IN CHILDREN'S FANTASY: FROM OZ IN *O PIONEERS!* TO NEVERLAND IN *ÁNTONIA*

Cather's concern with civilizations in fragments and ruins is apparent throughout her fiction, and understanding this explains why the Neverland as a concept held appeal for her. As a geography of the mind, Neverland presents child consciousness as a swirling mix of chocolate pudding and hangings, which for Jim is likewise a curious mix of murders, suicides, sexual assaults, and celebration of country landscape and fond memories of Christmas. Neverland is also a reflection on a history of imperialism and colonialism, present in fragments that wash up on the shores of meaning. Border zones between cultures embody the destructive and constructive impulses immortalized in Neverland as the meeting of island and empire, and also the meeting of child and the past. The Bohemian mushrooms and Mr. Shimerda's gun, Otto's Austrian Christmas figures and unexplained sentiments about Bohemians, the story of Russian Peter and Pavel, the Indian circle of which no one knows the real meaning, the Spanish stirrup and sword, the racist perceptions of Blind D'Arnault, who, like Mr. Shimerda, is a fragment of Jim's Southern past: these are all presented as decontextualized fragments mixed in the Nebraskan Neverland, which are recontextualized into something new and uncertain. The concept of immigration allowed Cather to reconceptualize one of her favorite themes—the extinct culture that leaves behind a relic, whose lack of context is precisely its archeological value and possibility.

Cather often used the motif of the Southwestern cliff-dwellers to define the way in which civilized cultures face extinction and leave behind de-contextualized fragments, which are inspiring in their very ambiguity. Her description of her trip to Blue Mesa was published in 1916, and in it she voiced admiration for the way the dwellings work in concert with the natural landscape and represent the dignity of a people with a sense of design.[65] At the same time she preferred her own stories of them and saw them, like others did in her time, as ways to rival European history. In *The Song of the Lark*, she demonstrated the effect that seeing Southwestern ruins had on her when Thea finds Indian women's pottery and celebrates them as capturing life in a vessel—as art itself. Ántonia's first residence on "clay cliffs" at the edge of Squaw Creek, where trees are golden like a fairy tale, resembles Cather's imagination of Blue Mesa, which in *The Professor's House* becomes an ideal Neverland space Tom wishes to map and catalogue but also protect and keep pure from mercenary interests. Cliff-dwellers, in Cather's lifetime, were also used to consider extinction of the most settled Indian tribes and panic about immigration,[66] but Cather tended to view the rise and fall of civilizations as the natural order of things.[67]

As early as 1909 Cather used the idea of the inaccessible mesa where the cliff-dwellers perished to define boyhood dreams and ideals, again likely inspired by Barrie's work. In "The Enchanted Bluff," she presents the Mesa as a Neverland space that cannot be reached and mapped but remains a space of fantasy for youth. Cather's partner Edith Lewis comments on how the Mesa mythology functioned for children growing up in the West: "'children knew about them before they were conscious of knowing about them.'"[68] But the combination of children's fantasy as historical geography suggests Cather's active engagement with the way in which children's fantasy writers were constructing idealized spaces to register children's interactions with national history. If the imprint of Peter Pan can be felt in both *My Ántonia* and *The Professor's House*, the imprint of another children's fantasy text, L. Frank Baum's *Oz* books, can be felt in *O Pioneers!* The difference between Cather's use of Baum's specifically American progressive utopia and Barrie's regressive Neverland in the British seas is instructive for thinking through not only how Cather understood childhood and national mythology, but also why *My Ántonia* should utilize Barrie's model rather than Baum's as a way to situate Jim's relationship to "the pioneer woman's story."

O Pioneers!, the novel in which Cather found her voice and natural subject, is a forward-moving account of transformation in the Plains, which is apparent when her use of Baum's Oz is considered. The transformation in land between parts I and II of *O Pioneers!* is highly reminiscent of Dorothy's sudden cyclone transport between gray Kansas and the colorful farms of Oz in Baum's *The Wonderful Wizard of Oz. O Pioneers!* begins with images of a fairly hostile landscape resistant to human habitation. The land is the "great fact," but human efforts on it are like "feeble scratches on stone left by prehistoric races."[69] This is similar to the beginning of *The Wizard of Oz* in which the landscape is completely gray and unmarked, the grass and even house "as dull and gray as everything else," even Aunt Em: "The sun and wind had changed her, too. They had taken the sparkle from her eyes and left them a sober gray; they had taken the red from her cheeks and lips, and they were gray also."[70] Between parts I and II of *O Pioneers!*, however, the land transforms quite suddenly for the reader into "a vast checkerboard, marked off in squares of wheat and corn; light and dark, dark and light . . . one can count a dozen gaily painted farmhouses; the gilded weather-vanes on the big red barns wink at each other across the green and brown and yellow fields."[71] The sudden splash of color, the neat checkerboard farms, and the winking weathervanes mirror the sudden transport of Dorothy into Munchkinland, a land of neat farms, perfect fences, and bright color. It is an idealized vision of agrarian settlement and progress. For Cather, this transformation signals both progress and regret; characters like Carl miss the wild landscape, whereas the visionary intuitive Alexandra is a successful businesswoman whose connection to the land has produced a feudal kingdom. It is highly reminiscent of Dorothy's walk through the successful farms, when all Munchkins emerge from their houses to bow to her because she is responsible for killing the witch that kept them in bondage. Her farmhouse has transformed a kingdom.

In *O Pioneers!*, the main point of alluding to Oz is to use Baum's text as a precedent for exploring a social utopia in which there is shared governance between male and female rulers, especially Princess Ozma, Glinda, and Dorothy herself, who shares many characteristics with Alexandra and who is similarly surrounded by incomplete men. With Dorothy Alexandra shares the calm level-headedness of the planner; the Oz narrator often remarks of Dorothy how surprising it is that things do not phase her, and she is never as scared as you might predict a girl of ten would be. Both Dorothy and Alexandra are machinelike and placid in their command of situations. Just as Alexandra's reveries quickly shift to practical farm plans, while Scarecrow and Tin Man in front of Dorothy debate which is happiness, brains or heart, "What worried [Dorothy] most was that the bread was nearly gone, and another meal for herself and Toto would empty the basket . . . she was not made of tin or straw, and could not live unless she was fed."[72] Although a little uncanny for a ten-year-old orphan, this placid and practical nature works well with a forty-year-old Swedish woman who is never so much in repose as when she is thinking about farm plans, such as where to build her pig corral. The very embodiment of the pioneer with machinelike placidity and an odd combination of conservatism and outspokenness, a real head for business and slow innovation on the resistant land, Alexandra is highly reminiscent of the persistent, practical Dorothy who demands accounts when people like the Wizard fail to deliver on promises.

The men around Alexandra also share kinship with the men surrounding Dorothy's journey; the inflexible Oscar resembles Scarecrow, the shady Lou resembles the Wizard, Emil resembles the Tin Man, the great lover who slices off his parts with his own axe because a witch has enchanted it, and Carl firmly resembles the Lion. Lion believes he lacks courage, and he has an intimate link with Dorothy (both are "meat" and share the same needs), as Carl does with Alexandra. In fact, Dorothy secretly feeds the Lion when they are captives of the Wicked Witch. One line of the Lion's directly mirrors Carl's. Lion says after living in Emerald City, "City life does not agree with me at all. . . . I have lost much flesh since I lived there, and now I am anxious to show the other beasts how courageous I have grown."[73] Carl, too, in the context of explaining to Alexandra that city life is unsatisfying and transient, admits he liked the country better when it "was a wild old beast."[74] Lion is the King of Beasts but he needs Dorothy to learn that about himself. The men and the land need Alexandra as much as she needs them, and the role of Oz in imagining an American utopia lurks behind Cather's social progressiveness in *O Pioneers!*

It is likewise important that Cather found inspiration in an American children's source that sought to shift dependence from European to American landscape. As Cather would have read in Baum's preface, Baum's expressed intent in creating a fairytale for American children was to depart from Europe and create tales for modern children:

> A series of newer "wonder tales" in which the stereotyped genie, dwarf and fairy are eliminated, together with all the horrible and blood-curdling incidents devised by their authors to point a fearsome moral to each tale. Modern education includes morality; therefore the modern child seeks only entertainment in its wonder tales and gladly dispenses with all disagreeable incident.[75]

This was a rather new view of American children's fantasy as possibility rather than an impoverished lack of historical and cultural material. Bemoaned by Nathaniel Hawthorne and other American writers, the youth of the country was seen as sterile and uninspiring rather than "a rich mine of life, like the founders of early races." American writers in Cather's time were self-consciously reaching inward for organic material. Van Wyck Brooks in his 1908 *The Wine of the Puritans* theorized that America lacked cultural traditions because Puritans separated from their authentic childhood in the Middle

Ages by leaving their adult nation. As Susan Hegemen analyzes, intellectual thinkers in the early twentieth century theorized in this fashion:

> With the separation from Europe, America had been disastrously severed in some deeply emotional way from its roots. To lose contact with its proper "childhood" in the European Middle Ages is for America to have lost something like its race memory of traditional lore, superstition, and irrational custom—the things that Brooks saw as conducive to the creation of rich, authentic cultural traditions.[76]

Material for children is typically culled from this folklore, as Barrie's work on boyhood would demonstrate and Baum sought to alter.

By 1917 the Pueblo Indians were understood to possess a uniquely "American" cultural and artistic tradition by which to be inspired and from which to borrow. Eastern Pueblo Indians of the Rio Grande basin became accessible to tourists and held dances and festivals; they were understood to be historically related to the Anasazi, ruins of intense archaeological and aesthetic interest to Cather and others:

> Indeed, as Benedict suggested in the Zuñi chapter of *Patterns of Culture*, the Anasazi ruins hinted at a romantic history, and in their grand antiquity, even offered a plausible historical substitute for Europe's Middle Ages, that moment of cultural "childhood" which, Brooks had argued, America otherwise lacked.[77]

Cather's recurrent interest in the Anasazi ruins as a geography that could fuel an American Neverland vision in "The Enchanted Bluff" and *The Professor's House* suggests her continuing efforts to determine what national history could comprise a young landscape. Her theory in *My Ántonia* is that the Plains could showcase a small, select exhibit of ruins and artifacts, which could take on rich meaning in the eye of the artist. Whereas Barrie's Neverland is "crammed" with material in a "compact" fashion,[78] in *My Ántonia* highly select artifacts of other cultures, times, and traditions are as sparse as trees on the landscape, details that, Jim says, make them "so precious."[79] Cather liked the "uncluttered" nature of the mesa, as articulated in her "Mesa Verde" essay, and this was a quality she sought in her writing. As Jim explains, "It must have been the scarcity of detail in that tawny landscape that made detail so precious."[80]

Depicting Ántonia's family as cliff-dwellers whose location resembles the Blue Mesa that Cather idealized and that her later Peter Pan figure (Tom Outland) discovers, *Ántonia* suggests that Cather thought deeply about childhood encounters with cultural traditions as they swirl and combine in personal reminiscence. While *My Ántonia* seems to allude to Oz's yellow-brick road at least once, in the Sunflowers that pave the road West and make it look like a ribbon of gold, the fact that she shifted from Oz to Barrie's Neverland in thinking about the Plains suggests deepening interest in psychology as an excavation of archeological traces and the importance of this vision to national myth. Even without a "cramped" common Neverland of shared history, Jim encounters traces to sort and incorporate into myths of the past. While the Oz series moves forward and "upward" to introduce more wondrous creatures and communities that approximate an increasingly multicultural community, Barrie's *Peter and Wendy* moves distinctly backward and regressively underground into realms of death and the past, to create a vision of stopping time. The rich stock of a Neverland as an expression of British history and folklore for children, "cramped" and ripe for excavation, became in *My Ántonia* a sorting and sifting of the past until one woman alone could encapsulate "the whole adventure of our childhood."

Significantly, *My Ántonia* features Barrie's mythology to define Jim's efforts to construct a meaningful Neverland from the interaction of immigrant cultures on the Plains, of which he is appreciative but outside it, like Peter "looking through the window at the one joy from which he must be forever barred."[81] Peter expresses traumatic separation from life sources and origins, as do most of the characters in Cather's fiction. The reflection of history and mix of cultures in Jim's community can be defined as swirling mixes and fragments in orientation to which he shifts as he prepares to fly to Black Hawk, to Lincoln, to New York, to perpetual train life, much as the tawny hawk leaves and imprints a shadow even in his flight. *Peter and Wendy* allowed Cather to situate the Plains as a register of cultural fragments that in Jim's imagination are sorted into an unreal landscape that is best before it could be mapped but that could, in the model of Barrie's construction of British mythology, be distilled into arresting images of settlement: the plough in the setting sun, the earth and sky meeting and leave-taking, the two origins of gendered consciousness Jim and Ántonia, whose imprecise relationship mirrors and somehow sustains the childhood fantasy of the unmarked frontier and a nation's need for origin myths. As Tony Watkins explains in his account of children's literature, national ideology is reflected in the landscape of children's fantasy. Cather's active engagement with children's fantasy writers Baum and Barrie signal her project of thinking about the stories that become national treasures; they begin in the consciousness of children and in *My Ántonia* linger in an expressly American archeology of the Neverland.

NOTES

1. Rosanna Walker, "Traces of J. M. Barrie's *Peter Pan* in Willa Cather's *The Professor's House*," in *J. M. Barrie's Peter Pan In and Out of Time*, ed. Donna R. White and C. Anita Tarr (Metuchen, NJ: Scarecrow Press, 2006), 127–55.

2. J. M. Barrie, *Peter Pan* (*Peter and Wendy*) (New York: Puffin, 1911).

3. Willa Cather, *My Ántonia*, Willa Cather Scholarly Edition, ed. Charles W. Mignon and Kari A. Ronning (Lincoln: University of Nebraska Press, 1994), xi.

4. Ibid., ix.

5. Ibid., 342.

6. Fredric Jameson, *The Political Unconscious: Narrative as a Socially Symbolic Act* (Ithaca, NY: Cornell University Press, 1982).

7. Barrie, *Peter Pan*, 174.

8. Cather, *My Ántonia*, 134.

9. Unpublished letter from Cather to Viola Roseboro, April 11, 1941, University of Virginia.

10. Ibid.

11. Letter from Cather to Mrs. William Stix, January 23, 1939, in *The Selected Letters of Willa Cather*, ed. Andrew Jewell and Janis P. Stout (New York: Knopf, 2013), 567.

12. Barrie, *Peter Pan*, 13.

13. Cather, *My Ántonia*, 27, 28.

14. Barrie, *Peter Pan*, 102.

15. Cather, *My Ántonia*, 8, 15.

16. Ibid., 15.

17. Barrie, *Peter Pan*, 13–14.

18. Ibid., 13.

19. Cather, *My Ántonia*, 360, 60.

20. Ibid., 16.

21. Ibid., 24.

22. Willa Cather, *The Song of the Lark*, *Project Gutenberg*, produced by Judith Boss, Marvin Peterson, and David Widger, accessed March 11, 2015, not paginated.

23. Cather, *My Ántonia*, 16.

24. Ibid., 41.

25. Ibid., 40.

26. Ibid., 39.

27. Ibid., 360.

28. Ibid., 314.

29. Ibid., 334.

30. Ibid., 323.

31. Ibid., xii.

32. Barrie, *Peter Pan*, 15.

33. Cather, *My Ántonia*, 325.

34. Barrie, *Peter Pan*, 14.

35. Ibid., 15.

36. Cather, *My Ántonia*, 59.

37. Ibid., 77.

38. Ibid., 134.

39. Barrie, *Peter Pan*, 229.

40. Cather, *My Ántonia*, 25.

41. Ibid., 312.

42. Penelope Schott Starkey, "The Many Mothers of *Peter Pan*: An Explanation and Lamentation," *Research Studies* 42 (1974): 1–10.

43. Cather, *My Ántonia*, 324.

44. Ann Fisher-Wirth, "Out of the Mother: Loss in *My Ántonia*," *Cather Studies* 2 (1993): 41–71

45. Cather, *My Ántonia*, 169.

46. Ibid., 174.

47. Barrie, *Peter*, 14.

48. Ibid., 113.

49. Ibid., 152.

50. Ibid., 215.

51. Ibid., 216.

52. Ibid.

53. Ibid., 206.

54. Ibid., 110–11.

55. Cather, *My Ántonia*, 48.

56. Ibid., 59.

57. Judith Fetterley, "*My Ántonia*, Jim Burden, and the Dilemma of the Lesbian Writer," in *Lesbian Texts and Contexts: Radical Revisions*, ed. Karla Jay, Joanne Glasgow, and Catharine R. Stimpson (New York: New York University Press, 1990), 145–63.

58. Blanche Gelfant, "The Forgotten Reaping-Hook: Sex in *My Ántonia*," *American Literature* 43, no. 1 (March 1971): 60–82.

59. Jacqueline Rose, *The Case of Peter Pan: The Impossibility of Children's Fiction* (Philadelphia: University of Pennsylvania Press, 1984).

60. Cather, *My Ántonia*, xii.

61. Holly Blackford, *The Myth of Persephone in Girls' Fantasy Literature* (New York: Routledge, 2011).

62. Evelyn Helmick, "The Mysteries of Ántonia," *Midwest Quarterly* 17 (1976): 173–85.

63. Julia Kristeva, "Women's Time," in *Feminisms: An Anthology of Literary Theory and Criticism*, second edition, ed. Robyn Warhol-Down and Diane Price Herndl (New Brunswick, NJ: Rutgers University Press, 1997), 860–79.

64. Rose, *The Case of Peter Pan*, 8.

65. Willa Cather, "Mesa Verde Wonderland Is Easy to Reach," *The Denver Times*, January 31, 1916, 7, reproduced in *The Willa Cather Archive*, ed. Andrew Jewell (Center for Digital Research in the Humanities: University of Nebraska–Lincoln, 2004–2013), 14, accessed March 7, 2014.

66. Michael Tavel Clarke, "Lessons from the Past: The Cliff Dwellers and New Historicism," *Western American Literature* 42, no. 4 (Winter 2008): 395–425.

67. See my chapter on Cather's *My Ántonia* in my forthcoming book, *Alice to Algernon: The Evolution of Child Consciousness in the Novel* (Knoxville: University of Tennessee Press, 2018).

68. Quoted in Sharon O'Brien, *Willa Cather: The Emerging Voice* (New York: Oxford University Press, 1987), 405.

69. Willa Cather, *O Pioneers!* (New York: Bantam, 1989), 13.

70. L. Frank Baum, *The Wonderful Wizard of Oz*, ed. Jack Zipes (New York: Penguin, 1998), 7.

71. Cather, *O Pioneers!*, 49.

72. Baum, *Wonderful Wizard*, 28.

73. Ibid., 91.

74. Cather, *O Pioneers!*, 75.

75. Baum, *Wonderful Wizard*, 3.

76. Susan Hegemen, *Patterns for America: Modernism and the Concept of Culture* (Princeton, NJ: Princeton University Press, 1999), 73.

77. Ibid., 108.

78. Barrie, *Peter Pan*, 14.

79. Cather, *My Ántonia*, 52.

80. Ibid.

81. Barrie, *Peter Pan*, 225.

Chapter Eight

"Obliterating Strangeness"

Willa Cather, Truman Capote, and the Influence of My Ántonia

Thomas Fahy

When the Capote family moved from a Connecticut suburb to Park Avenue in 1942, Truman had only one goal in mind—to become a great American writer like Willa Cather. He didn't seem troubled by the Japanese attack on Pearl Harbor six months earlier or by the fact that he needed to retake his senior year of high school. He was single minded about writing, and after landing a part-time job as a copyboy at *The New Yorker*, his dream of getting published seemed within reach. The magazine, however, only hired Capote— along with a variety of sketchy assistants—as an act of desperation. Most of the staff had left because of the war, and *The New Yorker* needed the help. At any other time, someone with Capote's flamboyance, childlike appearance, high-pitched voice, and writerly aspirations would never have been considered. Not only did his demeanor run counter to the typical copyboy, who was expected to remain invisible and silent, but his submissions to the fiction department also irritated editors, who did not view employees as potential writers. Not surprisingly, they rejected all of Capote's work.

The eighteen-year-old Capote did not become discouraged, however. He continued to dedicate himself to his craft, spending as much time as possible reading and writing. It was during one of these afternoons that Capote had a strange encounter. A winter storm was pummeling the city with "fist-sized" snowballs, so he decided to ensconce himself in the warm stillness of the New York Society Library. When he finally left the building, he noticed a woman desperately trying to hail a cab. He had seen her at the library on several occasions and offered to help. "Her eyes were the pale blue of a prairie dawn on a clear day," he remembered, and a turquoise necklace adorned her neck.[1] She wore a beautiful sable coat over a tweed suit, and her bobbed black-and-white hair struck him as mannish. After finding a cab proved hopeless,

Capote offered to walk the stranger home. They soon stopped at a restaurant on Madison Avenue for a hot cup of tea—well, Cather drank tea; Capote ordered a double martini—and they began talking about literature. The woman inquired about his favorite American authors. "I love Willa Cather," he replied. "*My Ántonia* and *Death Comes for the Archbishop*. Have you read her two marvelous novellas—*A Lost Lady* and *My Mortal Enemy?*"[2] Cather nodded and sheepishly admitted that she wrote those books. A flabbergasted Capote swallowed his martini in one gulp: "How could I have been so stupid? I had a photograph of her in my bedroom. Of course she was Willa Cather!"[3] Cather subsequently invited Capote to dinner at her Park Avenue apartment. In his essay "Remembering Willa Cather," he describes the elegant apartment and her partner, Edith Lewis. The pair looked "so alike one could be certain they had decorated the apartment together. There were flowers everywhere— masses of winter lilac, peonies, and lavender-colored roses. Beautifully bound books lined all the walls of the living room."[4] Sadly, Capote never finished this recollection, and these were the last words he ever wrote. He died the following day, one month before his sixtieth birthday.

It seems fitting that Capote would begin and end his literary career talking to and writing about Willa Cather. Not only was she one of the few writers whom he praised openly throughout his life, but *My Ántonia* also provided the literary model that would shape much of his fiction. As an aspiring writer, reading Cather must have felt like a homecoming for Capote. Cather, in addition to being a Southerner, offered a kind of literary permission for the type of spaces, characters, and ideas that fascinated him. In a sense, she obliterated the strangeness of his upbringing. Cather infused Midwestern life with a lyricism that gave Capote the tools to transform his small-town world—with its broken marriages, absent parents, bizarre spinster caretakers, a cantankerous African American housekeeper without teeth, a tomboyish companion who defended him from bullies, and an aunt whose only connection with the outside world came from her annual ritual of making Christmas fruitcakes and medicine—into something of lasting beauty.

Capote's debt to Cather has been given little critical attention, but upon closer examination, one can see the profound imaginative, structural, and thematic impact of *My Ántonia* on *Other Voices, Other Rooms* (1948), a coming of age story about a teenager who learns to accept his homosexuality. Since his mother's death, Joel Harrison Knox has been staying with his aunt, but he decides to leave after receiving an unexpected invitation to live with his estranged father, stepmother, and effeminate older cousin, Randolph. From the outset, Joel worries that his father, Ed Sansom, will reject him for not being "taller and stronger and handsomer and smarter-looking," but his fantasies about finding a masculine role model are shattered soon after he arrives.[5] Sansom, the former manager of a prizefighter, became paralyzed after

Randolph accidentally shot him. Grief and guilt have consumed Randolph ever since. When Joel tries to leave town after going to the circus, he catches pneumonia, and Randolph nurses him back to health. Joel's delirious state enables him to recognize his burgeoning affection for Randolph. In the closing moments of the novel, Joel sees Randolph dressed as a lady and goes to him. This decision, however, seems to necessitate Joel's isolation from others. His friendship with Idabel Thompkins, a tomboy who has recently discovered her own homosexuality, ends when her family sends her away to live with other relatives. Likewise, his deep affection for Missouri ("Zoo") Fever, a young African American woman who works for Amy and Randolph, does not last either. Her experiences with spousal abuse and rape position her too solidly in the real world for Joel. He wants to be protected from the social realities of racial and sexual violence, not exposed to them, so he chooses to live with Randolph instead.

In this debut novel, Capote reworks several critical moments of *My Ántonia* to craft Joel Knox as a queered Jim Burden. Specifically, Capote uses the encounter with the snake, the pseudo-rape of the protagonist, and the sexual exploitation of a "hired girl" to condemn the persecution of sexual and racial otherness. As with much of Cather's work, Capote's fiction views rigid, social definitions of gender as harmful. They promote barriers between men and women. They fracture relationships. They induce self-hatred. And in the context of a heteronormative society, they fuel intolerance for any expression of sexual identity that deviates from the norm. Jim Burden and Joel Knox have been taught the same message about masculinity: to be a man is to be heterosexual. These characters, however, struggle profoundly with these assumptions and, as a result, experience varying degrees of repression. Lastly, these authors link the intersection between gender and sexuality with a racist ideology that exploits nonwhite women in America. For Cather and Capote, homophobia exists alongside racial intolerance. The hired girls (whether young immigrants in Nebraska or African Americans in the South) are sexualized and exploited in large part because of their marginalized status. The violence (potential and literal) experienced by them exposes the ruthless hierarchies that punish sexual and racial otherness, and it illustrates a failure at the heart of an American project that proclaims democracy and possibility, tolerance and inclusiveness.

"YOU IS JUST LIKE BIG MANS": SNAKES, SEXUALITY, AND MANHOOD

Jim Burden's battle with a sixty-six-inch rattlesnake has become one of the most discussed scenes in *My Ántonia*, suggesting its importance for understanding the narrator's complex—and conflicted—relationship with gender and sexuality.[6] While David Porter's biography *On the Divide: The Many Lives of Willa Cather* views this moment in terms of Judeo-Christian mythology, Susan J. Rosowski situates Cather in the tradition of literary romanticism and reads Jim as a failed Saint George figure.[7] For Rosowski, Jim's heroism is undercut by the old, lazy snake and the actual risk facing Ántonia during the encounter. Blanche H. Gelfant finds a similar failure on Jim's part but attributes it to his sexual fears of women: "[Jim's] recapitulation of the past seems to me a final surrender to sexual fears. He was afraid of growing up, afraid of women, afraid of the nexus of love and death. He could only love that which time had made safe and irrefragable—his memories."[8] Jim's framing of this moment, however, suggests that safety can also be found in reestablishing conventional gender roles. As Lisa Marie Lucenti has argued, Jim's adventure with the snake attempts to return Ántonia "to her proper place as a girl. Her pride at being able to work in the field was, for Jim, a threatening elision of gender difference, and the snake episode works to subdue that pride."[9] These efforts fail, however, and Ántonia, who works, eats, and runs like a man, continues to reject traditional gender roles. Jim's ongoing anxiety about these gender transgressions makes him a rather ambiguous figure throughout the story, neither male nor female. He becomes, according to Hermione Lee, "an androgynous narrator who mediates between male and female world."[10] Such ambiguity also raises questions about his sexuality. Jim himself acknowledges such a possibility: "People said there must be something queer about a boy who showed no interest in girls of his own age, but who could be lively enough when he was with Tony and Lena or the three Marys."[11] Queer theorists such as Marilee Lindemann, inspired by Sharon O'Brien's groundbreaking psychobiography *Willa Cather: The Emerging Voice*, have examined the lesbian subtext of masculine desire in Cather's texts.[12] However, critic John P. Anders, drawing on the work of Judith Butler and Eve Sedgwick as well as the field of masculinity studies, interprets such moments as evidence of the way male "homosexuality can be felt throughout Cather's fiction, whether as a dimension of friendship, delineated within a single character, or implicit in the narrative voice."[13] More specifically, he sees "Jim's passivity, his detached admiration of the hired girls, his 'queer' adolescent habits, his lack of interest in marrying Ántonia, and his seemingly loveless New York marriage" as evidence of his "homosexual temperament."[14]

As this brief overview suggests, the critical readings of the snake scene focus almost exclusively on Jim, but because Ántonia initiates the journey to prairie dog town, it is also worth examining its importance for her character and Cather's message about the immigrant experience in America. Ántonia wants to explore the subterranean world of dogs to discover "whether [the holes] ran straight down, or were horizontal, like mole-holes; whether they had underground connections; whether the owls had nests down there, lined with feathers. We might get some puppies, or owl eggs, or snakeskins."[15] In many respects, Ántonia is a subterranean dweller as well. The Shimerda home has been dug out of a hillside, and this dark, smoke-filled "hole" has more in common with the living quarters of dog town than Black Hawk. Ántonia and her sister, Yulka, even sleep in a burrowed space within the home: "In the rear wall was another little cave; a round hole, not much bigger than an oil barrel, scooped out in the black earth. When I . . . peered into it, I saw some quilts and a pile of straw."[16] Ántonia's curiosity about prairie dog town therefore reveals her interest in the rich complexities, beauty (feathered nests and puppies), and possibilities (owl's eggs) that exist beneath the surface. Just as Mr. Shimerda "wanted [Jim's family] to know that they were not beggars in the old country; he made good wages, and his family were respected there,"[17] Ántonia communicates a similar message to Jim here. There is more to her and her family than their hovel and her shaky command of English suggest. Cather makes this connection between Ántonia's family and the prairie dogs explicit when Jim describes Krajiek's snake-like exploitation of them: "They kept him in their hole and fed him for the same reason that the prairie dogs and brown owls housed the rattlesnakes—because they did not know how to get rid of him."[18] On one level, the snake imagery captures one danger of immigrant life—exploitation by other immigrants. On another level, the rattlesnake in dog town represents the dangers of the land itself. For those who are unprepared for the challenges of farming, the land can be ruthless and deadly. Not long after the snake adventure, for example, winter comes, and Cather offers two contrasting views of the heavy snowfall. For Jim and his family, a blizzard can provide the opportunity for a "country Christmas" with cozy fires, hearty meals, and a freshly cut Christmas tree. While Jim makes Ántonia and Yulka a picture book with "scenes from a circus," the wintry conditions function like the rattlesnake, a devouring "circus monstrosity" for the Shimerdas.[19] Their winter is devastating—characterized by hunger, deprivation, and despair—and it culminates in Mr. Shimerda's suicide.

Cather also presents this subterranean dog world as a metaphor for Jim's anxieties about masculinity and his suppressed sexuality. He begins the scene by expressing his frustration over the gender roles that Ántonia seems hellbent on violating: "Much as I liked Ántonia, I hated a superior tone she sometimes took with me . . . but I was a boy and she was a girl, and I resented her protecting manner."[20] Throughout her life in Nebraska, Ántonia rejects the kind of socially prescribed femininity that comforts Jim ("Oh, better I like to work out of doors than in a house! . . . I not care that your grandmother say it makes me like a man. I like to be like a man.").[21] The problem for Jim is that her masculine performance is arguably better than his. He spends most of his time at home (particularly in the kitchen), while Ántonia works tirelessly in the fields. Certainly her efforts make a more meaningful contribution to the community. She cultivates the land to produce something of value, whereas Jim takes on the role of a consumer, passively benefiting from the labor of others, as Daniel Worden argues:

> *O Pioneers!* and *My Antonia* depict Nebraska as a space where female masculinity prospers. In this frontier territory, the novels make a case for female masculinity as an authentic subject position. . . . This dislocation of masculinity from the male body disrupts patriarchal entitlements, while at the same time reworking marriage and family relations.[22]

I would add that this interior landscape also contains the potential to disrupt patriarchal norms. As Jim examines one of the dog's holes with two entrances, he notices "where the two corridors united, and the floor was dusty from use, like a little highway over which much travel went."[23] The image of intermingling paths contrasts his adherence to rigid categories, and it offers the metaphoric possibility of viewing gender and sexuality differently—of accepting female masculinity and masculine femininity, of placing heterosexuality and homosexuality on a continuum of sexual identity. Jim's rigidity, however, prevents him from seeing or accepting these possibilities.

His visceral disgust with the snake also functions as a tool for Cather to critique the heterosexist expectations surrounding masculinity. When he first encounters the gigantic rattlesnake, its size, writhing motion, and "abominable muscularity" nauseate him.[24] Jim's thin, boyish body stands in stark contrast to the snake's muscular strength, and his emotional response to killing it ("I struck now from hate")[25] can be understood as an expression of resentment. He struggles with the social pressures to perform a certain type of masculinity, and this moment of having to "prove it" makes him ill: "I suppose I looked as sick as I felt." Not surprisingly, he swats away Ántonia's handkerchief as she tries to wipe the sweat (and fear) from his face. In truth, Jim simply cannot escape the constant reminders of his own physical inadequacies. No one at his grandparents' farm, for instance, includes Jim in outdoor labor—neither as an opportunity to teach him about farming nor to encourage him to earn his keep. Many of his behaviors are interpreted by the town as "queer" and atypical for a boy/man. His awkward kiss with Ántonia ends in rejection and infantilization ("'And you'll always treat me like a kid, I suppose.' . . . 'I expect I will'").[26] And late in life, his emotionally and physically distant marriage ("she lives her own life")[27] leaves him traveling around the country with young men eager to speculate and exploit the landscape in "mines and timber and oil."[28] Jim may not be able to perform a masculinity defined by physical strength and callous sexual conquest (as Larry Donovan demonstrates with Ántonia), but he can have an unsatisfying marriage. These masculine expectations, in other words, have forced him to reject the possibility of homoerotic desire or of pursing a less conventional lifestyle that could make him happy in the present. Instead he can only find happiness in nostalgia. In the context of *My Ántonia*, nostalgia reveals Jim's need to return to a time before the complexities of sexuality, or as Judith Fetterley explains, "Reunited at last to Ántonia, he is also reunited with a past before the domination of sexual definition where one might be tomboy and love one's Ántonia to one's heart's content."[29] Even in the closing moments of the snake adventure, Jim undercuts his victory as a "big mans" by admitting that the snake was old and lazy: "So in reality it was a mock adventure; the game was fixed for me by chance, as it probably was for many a dragon-slayer."[30] Jim's hopes to achieve the kind of manhood that the farmhands (Otto and Jake), the Russians (Pavel and Peter), and Ántonia possess is shattered. It is a merely another moment of fantasy and myth.

Capote recognized the importance of this scene as well—so much so that it inspired him to refashion it in *Other Voices, Other Rooms*; read alongside *My Ántonia*, Capote's version, in which Joel Knox encounters a gigantic viper, teases out the queer implications of Cather's text and reinforces its challenge to gender and sexual norms. Both scenes begin with narrators seeking to reaffirm gender categories that have come into question because of a tomboyish girl. The subsequent encounter with a monstrous snake provides the perfect opportunity to perform a feat of masculine strength and, in the minds of the young boys, to reestablish conventional—and reassuring—gender identities. The narrators amplify the significance of the moment by casting it in terms of fantasy (specifically dragon slaying). However, both scenes end in disappointment, and in the context of Capote's narrative, Joel's failed masculine performance reveals the novel's powerful critique of the ways these norms generate self-repression and self-loathing on the part of gay Americans.

Much like the subterranean networks of dog town in *My Ántonia*, Capote depicts a landscape with obscure spaces and shadowy interiors as a metaphor for the challenges facing homosexuals at the time. When Idabel tries to convince Joel to run away with her and to join the circus, they huddle in the "shade of the house where tulip stalks leaned around, and elephant leaves, streaked with silver snail tracks, hung above their heads like parasols."[31] Although the tomboyish Idabel is much closer to embracing her homosexuality, Joel still hopes to achieve some version of heterosexual masculinity. This description of the foliage reflects his ongoing attempts to hide his homosexuality from himself and others. When Joel's stepmother calls out from the upstairs window to chastise him for leaving his invalid father, "she could not see them, though, for the elephant leaves were a camouflage."[32] Joel has, in fact, been camouflaging himself both as heterosexual and as the masculine boy he thinks his father wants him to be. At the same time, Capote suggests that homosexuality was an identity most felt the need to camouflage in 1940s America. Idabel, for instance, believes she must run away with the circus and identify as a "freak" for being a lesbian; Randolph feels the need to cross-dress and sequester himself in a decaying house to live as a gay man, and ultimately Joel chooses Randolph's insulated world as a pathway for embracing his sexuality. For Capote, these limited and problematic choices serve to indict a heterosexist society that leaves gays with few opportunities—if any—for living openly.

The landscape also foreshadows the futility of the protagonist's efforts to perform a successful version of heterosexual masculinity. Before going to the traveling show with Idabel, Joel insists on a detour to the Cloud Hotel in the hopes of getting a magic potion to protect them from harm. The potion and mysterious hotel, which has been abandoned for years, reflect his ongoing desire to escape concerns about his sexuality and to embrace a comforting fantasy world. The name of the hotel itself "evoked a kind of mist-white palace floating foglike through the woods,"[33] and this description captures Joel's discomfort with being grounded in the real world and with being seen clearly by others. He prefers the freedom of foglike obscurity because difference—physical (for example, his thin, unmuscular body that reminds Idabel of a "plucked chicken")[34] and sexual—terrifies him. Even the idea of a hotel, with rooms designed only for temporary occupation, appeals to Joel's desire to resist the permanency of labels and definitions—particularly heterosexual/homosexual and masculine/feminine. On the way to Cloud Hotel, Joel and Idabel come across a "forsaken mill" on stilts above the river "with a strange unfinished look, as though its builder had been frightened and fled his job midway."[35] In the context of a bildungsroman, this unfinished structure operates as a clear metaphor for Joel's journey into maturity, and the builder's fear suggests that the finished product might not be what he intended or desired. Joel certainly worries about his own outcome, yet he presses forward with his quest for heterosexual and masculine norms. The first obstacle on the journey is crossing the river over a rotted beam. The dark, "bottomless olive" water beneath him is discomforting. Unlike Jim Burden, who glimpses into the underground world of the prairie dog tunnels, Joel averts his eyes: "[He], stepping gingerly, using his sword to balance, made his eyes avoid the dizzy deep creek moving so closely below, kept them, instead, aimed on the opposite bank where, in sunshine, laden gourdvine burst from red clay green and promising."[36] Instead of looking into the muddy, dizzying waters of his own sexuality, Joel yearns for the sunny, "promising" bank of green vines grow-ing out of red clay. The clay, which is acidic and deficient in nutrients, can still produce something beautiful, and Joel hopes that his own deficiencies can be transformed as well, that he can burst forth from his troubled, lonely upbringing. Because Joel still clings to heterosexual masculinity as the only positive alternative for himself, however, Capote depicts this moment as one of paralysis, not possibility. Joel immediately fears that "always he would be balanced here suspended between land, and in the dark, and alone."[37] He re-mains suspended between what he knows about himself (his homosexuality) and his desire for heterosexual norms. As Capote suggests, this suspension represents the internalization of heteronormative prejudices that are damag-ing and isolating for gay Americans.

In this psychological state of suspended animation, Joel's body also be-comes paralyzed with fear at the sight of the snake, and this scene, which occurs near the end of *Other Voices, Other Rooms* (as opposed to Cather's early placement), signals the protagonist's last-ditch effort to perform het-erosexual masculinity before accepting the more freeing impulses of his own bodily desires. Unlike Jim and his spade, Joel literally carries a sword that his caretaker, Zoo Fever, gave him as a gift. Strapped to his waist, he imagines himself as a brave, chivalrous knight: "Then, facing a fence of brambles, he unsheathed his sword and cut an opening. 'After you, my dear Idabel,' he said, bowing low."[38] As with the dynamic between Jim Burden and Ántonia, Joel's investment in fantasy stems, in part, from his frustration with Idabel's refusal to see herself as a girl. She takes Ántonia-like pride in embracing mas-culine characteristics, and this blurring of male and female raises unsettling questions for Joel about himself. As Idabel explains, "I never think like I'm a girl. . . . I want so much to be a boy: I would be a sailor."[39] She even chal-lenges gendered language: "'Florabel. That damned bastard.' 'A girl can't be a bastard,' he said. 'Oh, she's a bastard all right.'"[40] She recognizes words and their socially prescribed meanings as inadequate for her unconventional experiences and desires. Joel tries to negate her manipulation of language and goes as far as to interpret her invitation to run away in terms of marriage ("Out West you don't have to be but twelve years old to get married.").[41] Idabel vehemently rejects such a possibility and does so by first challenging gendered language: "Who the hell said I wanted to get married? Now you listen, boy: you behave decent, you behave like we're brothers or you don't behave at all."[42] She redefines their boy-girl relationship as fraternal, and her use of the word "boy" is belittling and emasculating in this context. Joel responds by viewing their adventure as an opportunity to reaffirm a clear gender division between them, and he does so with rhetoric strikingly similar to Jim's: "After all, no matter what Idabel said, he was a boy and she was a girl and he was damned if she was going to get the upper hand again."[43] Joel's attitude about gender makes him insist on taking the lead when crossing the rotted beam, and he hopes to perform his masculinity in a more convincing manner than Idabel. Upon seeing the cottonmouth snake as "thick as his leg, long as a whip,"[44] Joel cannot move. His paralysis is part fear, part recognition. The snake "sees" Joel, and its eyes recall his father's perception of him as an inadequate son. The snake's eyes, in other words, signal a recognition of his failed masculinity. Idabel repeatedly urges Joel to strike the snake with his sword, but she must use the weapon herself to kill it: "'Bastard,' she hollered, closing her eyes, swinging the blade like a sickle, and the cottonmouth, slapped into the air, turned, plunged, flattened on the water: belly up, white and twisted."[45] This too has been a mock adventure (to borrow Jim's phrase). Earlier in the narrative, the reader learns that Idabel has done battle with snakes: "The time that snake bit me, I lived a week in a terrible place where everything was crawling, the floors and walls, everything. Now all that was plain foolishness."[46] Idabel is the battle-hardened warrior here, not Joel, and her past experiences have grounded her in the real world, recognizing the venom-induced visions as "plain foolishness."

In the aftermath of the snake encounter, the adventurers attend the circus where Idabel falls in love with a dwarf named Miss Wisteria, and this expression of same-sex desire further draws out the implications of the snake sequence. She successfully slays the dragon/snake because she has accepted her sexuality and defined femininity in her own terms. Just as Jim mocks his heroism, Joel is horrified by his failure, yelling "no" as Idabel kills the snake. She is true to herself, and in the fictional world of Capote's novel, this achievement of identity is heroic. Yet Capote does not freeze Joel in this moment forever. Unlike Jim, whose nostalgic vision of the past suggests a return to the time before the complexities of sexuality, Joel uses his encounter with the snake to move closer to accepting his repressed sexuality.

"TRULY, I WAS A BATTERED OBJECT": RAPE, HIRED GIRLS, AND BOYS IN BED

Sexual assault plays an important role in both *My Ántonia* and *Other Voices, Other Rooms*. Each protagonist experiences a figurative rape, and these moments establish an important link between the condemnation of sexual violence against nonwhite women and the persecution of homosexuals. In *My Ántonia* Jim does not waste any opportunity portraying Wick Cutter as quite possibly the worst human being in Nebraska. Every passing reference reinforces his characterization as brutal, dishonest, lecherous, and petty.

Many farmers need to be rescued from the "clutches of Wick Cutter," "the merciless Black Hawk money-lender."[47] He is a "rascal," "an inveterate gambler," and "a poor loser."[48] He even chooses to kill his wife and himself to prevent her family from inheriting his money. In addition to all of these charming qualities, Cutter is also a rapist, and his assault on Jim has typically been read in these terms. As Judith Fetterley argues, "Surely Jim has literally taken Ántonia's place and experienced the rape intended for her. The physical repulsion, awareness of sexual vulnerability, sense of shame so profound as to demand total isolation—all are intelligible in the responses of a woman to an attempted rape."[49] By making Jim a surrogate victim for Ántonia, Cather offers a glimpse into the depths of exploitation facing immigrant women and the culture of silence surrounding it, but the homoerotic overtones of the scene have broader implications as well.

Prior to the rape, Cather has already revealed the social forces that limit these young women and make them vulnerable to sexual abuse. The "hired girls" become domestic servants because no other work is available to them in Black Hawk. They can't be schoolteachers, Jim explains, because of their ethnicity (they're "almost a race apart") and poor command of English, which is the most commonly expressed bias against them: "all foreigners were ignorant people who couldn't speak English."[50] This preoccupation with language, however, acts mostly as legerdemain; it deflects attention away from a much more profound concern—the threat the girls pose to class hierarchies:[51] "The country girls were considered a menace to the social order. Their beauty shone out too boldly against a conventional background."[52] Jim goes on to explain that the local men lacked the courage to break with social convention and marry these girls. Social respectability and deeply engrained hierarchies hold too powerful a sway over them. Yet this dynamic reveals something far more troubling. Because these women are not marriage material, the men *want* them to remain "hired girls" (a term that equates them with prostitutes) in order to continue seeing them as exploitable, sexual objects. In fact, the men of Black Hawk routinely have sexual liaisons with the girls. Two of the "three Marys," for instance, work for bachelors and get pregnant, a condition that forces them to leave town temporarily. Sylvester Lovett, who falls madly in love with Lena Lingard, chooses to marry a "widow six years older than himself" to escape the "predicament" (that is, social stigma) of marrying a hired girl.[53] And Ántonia herself gets duped and impregnated by a man who abandons her. Jim's failure to acknowledge this layer of exploitation reveals his need to objectify them as well. He may identify with their outsider status, but objectifying them gives him a way to feel like an insider—at least for a while. After his friendship with Lena, he offers merely a demeaning interpretation of her picture at the end of the novel: "Yes, it was exactly like Lena,

I told her; a comely woman, a trifle too plump, in a hat a trifle too large, but with the old lazy eyes, and the old dimpled ingenuousness still lurking in the corners of her mouth."[54] This photograph provides Jim with another opportunity to prove to himself that she does not fit in—as her too plump body and oversized hat suggest.[55] She is nothing more than a body to interpret and to demean as a way to deflect attention away from his own shortcomings.

In addition to Cutter's vile, lecherous nature and the social context limiting the hired girls, Jim's physical description of Cutter provides critical insight into the assault as well. Certainly, the feminization of Cutter raises questions about his sexuality: "I detested his pink, bald head, and his yellow whiskers, always soft and glistening. It was said he brushed them every night, as a woman does her hair. His white teeth looked factory-made. His skin was red and rough, as if from perpetual sunburn; he often went away to hot springs to take mud baths."[56] The passive voice here ("It was said") implies that the town views Cutter as an androgynous figure—both a brutish exploiter of hired girls and womanish. As Jim explains, "he was so fastidious and prim about his place. . . . It was a peculiar combination of old-maidishness and licentiousness that made Cutter seem so despicable."[57] It makes sense that Jim would continue to use passive voice. He doesn't want to take ownership of these interpretations because the town views him in similar terms, as not quite male or female. Jim may not have a reputation for being licentious, but at some level he recognizes that people could also view his "queer" behavior with distaste. The shared gender ambiguity between these men helps explain Jim's disgust over Cutter's combination of fastidious, old-maidishness, and licentiousness. Cutter blurs the line between masculine and feminine, heterosexual and homosexual. He defies the very categories that Jim has used to suppress his own sexual desires and to limit his happiness.

Without recognizing Cutter's gendered and sexual ambiguity, a number of details about the assault on Jim simply don't add up, and these elements suggest Cather's intention for the reader to view this scene as more than a foiled attempt to rape Ántonia. First, Jim's decision to sleep in Ántonia's bed at the Cutter house—as opposed to a couch or lounge chair downstairs—makes little sense; given Cutter's characterization in the novel, it is implausible that Jim would not recognize the sexual subtext and potential risk facing Ántonia. Jim's grandmother, for instance, has warned her about the risks of working for Cutter: "You know what that man is. It will be the ruin of you."[58] His sexual affairs with and possible assaults of two Swedish girls are notorious, and both incidents leave the girls "worse for the experience."[59] He even continues to torment one of them by visiting her in Omaha whenever he desires. So why does Jim sleep in that bed when the Cutters leave town? His choice seems to function as a passive, tentative attempt to experience some type of intimate or sexual encounter with another man. Despite the risk of substituting himself for Ántonia, Jim has no other outlet for same-sex desire in Black Hawk. Second, Cather makes it clear that both men recognize the homoerotic subtext of the moment. Cutter's rage can be understood as a response both to being duped and to the way this substitution (a young boy for a young girl) implicates Cutter's own ambiguous sexuality: "The man became insane; he stood over me, choking me with one fist and beating me in the face with the other, hissing and chuckling and letting out a flood of abuse."[60] His laughter here could signal some recognition of irony; in another context and with another set of expectations, Cutter might possibly have been fine with finding a boy in bed. (This might also explain why Jim's description of Cutter—with his bald, pink head and soft, glistening whiskers—is evocative of a penis.) Nevertheless, according to Jim, Cutter's abusive remarks are not addressed to him but instead focus on Ántonia's presumed promiscuity and his assumption that Jim is her lover. Jim, however, has been trying to pull off the same ruse for the entire book. He wants the reader to see him as Ántonia's would-be lover, as a missed opportunity, but the performance breaks down in this scene. Jim cannot interpret this act of substitution as a chivalric gesture to protect his beloved's virtue. Instead he hates Ántonia for "all of this disgustingness": "I lay with my disfigured face to the wall and felt no particular gratitude [for taking Ántonia's place]."[61] Jim sees himself as victim because Cutter's beating serves as an aggressive rejection of his homosexuality. He has left Jim "a battered object,"[62] and his damaged body—with a nose like a "blue plum" and his swollen, "hideously discolored" eye—visibly marks him as different. It signals his deviance from the norm and demands a public explanation that Jim wants to avoid for fear of gossip: "If the story once got abroad, I would never hear the last of it. I could well imagine what the old men down at the drug-store would do with such a theme."[63] This "theme" is clearly homosexuality ("there must be something queer about a boy who showed no interest in girls of his own age"),[64] and he learns from this encounter the importance of suppressing and silencing same-sex desire.

Finally, the scene concludes with one more strange deflection; it refocuses the reader's attention on Wick Cutter's marriage and lets him off the hook to some extent for his sexual exploits. Jim attributes Cutter's actions to a perverse investment in tormenting his wife: "Perhaps he got the feeling of being a rake more from his wife's rage and amazement than from any experiences of his own."[65] After establishing Cutter as "notoriously dissolute with women,"[66] these concluding remarks are quite surprising. Jim is suggesting that Cutter values the perception of rakishness more than the acts themselves. The feeling of impropriety trumps truth for Cutter. This claim also implies that Cutter's notorious reputation has been exaggerated. His lascivious behavior could change, and his sexual proclivities (whether acted on or not) could diminish: "His zest in debauchery might wane, but never Mrs. Cutter's belief in it."[67] How do we explain this shift of focus and softening toward Cutter? Once again, Jim's characterization reveals more about himself than Cutter. Bringing the enraged Mrs. Cutter into the narrative at this point reaffirms Cutter's heterosexuality and arguably Jim's when it is most in doubt (that is, while Jim assumes the role of a sexual assault victim). Cutter's marriage keeps the focus on the heterosexual implications of the assault, not the fact that this incident is partially a story about a boy in bed with a man. By casting doubt on the public perception of Cutter, Jim tries to undercut any possible gossip about himself and his own sexuality. He wants his version of events on record. He wants to remind the reader that rumor is not truth and that the impulses driving human nature can be mysterious to others as well as to the self. As such, we should not judge Cutter's secret desires—or Jim's—too harshly. Despite this misdirection, we cannot forget the source of his battered body. Cutter's rage was partially fueled by homophobia, and Cather uses this moment to connect the mistreatment of homosexuals with the exploitation of nonwhite or immigrant women.

Capote also presents Joel as a rape victim of sorts in order to condemn heterosexist norms. While skinny dipping with Joel, Idabel starts telling bawdy jokes that neither of them fully understand. Idabel's performance, however, rings false ("Idabel's jokes were even for her none too clear; the manner in which she told them was not altogether her own"),[68] and she admits to learning them from another boy: "He's awful tough, Billy Bob is. I remember back in fourth grade we had that mean Miss Aikens, and she used to beat Billy Bob's hands raw with a ruler, and he never cried once."[69] Capote uses this borrowed, obscure piece of humor to highlight the way young people inherit problematic ideas about gender and sexuality. Such jokes are a means for passing along attitudes about sex. The kids' failure to recognize this crass humor reflects the lack of understanding they have about their own sexuality. Discovering the truth about oneself is particularly difficult in a heteronormative environment, as Idabel's explanation for the jokes illustrates. She attributes them to Billy Bob and his manliness, and one message emerges: real men tell lewd jokes. More seriously, Idabel's definition of masculinity involves toughness and emotional control, which pressures Joel to put on a performance of his own. He denies ever crying and then kisses her. For Joel, the gesture serves as an attempt to play out a heterosexual romantic fantasy with her (a role he thinks he needs to perform for his father and society) and to communicate feelings that he knows men shouldn't express verbally: "And he wanted to touch her, to put his arms around her, for this seemed suddenly the only means of expressing all he felt."[70] When Idabel subsequently wrestles him to the ground, a shard from her sunglasses cuts his buttock during the assault (as if he were losing his virginity): "'Please stop, I'm bleeding.' Idabel was astride him, and her strong hands locked his wrists to the ground. She brought her red, angry face close to his: 'Give up?'"[71] Joel experiences a figurative loss here. His determination to find social acceptance through heterosexuality is shattered once again. He is beginning to learn that he must craft an understanding of masculinity that makes room for sensitivity, emotional expression and, ultimately for Joel, homosexuality.

Although Joel is not substituting for an actual sexual assault here, Capote does include the rape of a hired girl to link the persecution of homosexuality with the objectification and mistreatment of African American women. In the South at the time, "hired girls" are African American women, and the sexual assault on Joel's caretaker, Zoo Fever, is one of the most violent and disturbing moments in the text. Zoo's violent rape on her trip to Washington, DC, which Capote based on an actual incident in Alabama in 1944,[72] serves as a reminder of the ways race and sexuality intersect to oppress black women. Exhausted from carrying a quilt filled with her belongings and walking for an entire day, Zoo decides to rest by the roadside. She is gazing at the stars overhead and nursing her blistered feet when several men in a red truck stop. The driver, an older man with a cigar, then pushes her into a ditch, tears open her dress, and invites the three boys with him to rape her. Meanwhile, an African American man, "who rode in back squatting on top of a mountain of watermelons,"[73] stands guard with a rifle to prevent her from screaming and trying to escape. When the white boys finish, they ask the driver to take a turn, but he refuses, claiming that he doesn't like to be watched. His refusal causes the others to laugh. In response he "[squats] impotent at her side like a bereaved lover . . . and '[pushes] that cigar in [her] belly.'"[74] Zoo notes the sailor's uniform on one of the boys as well, and this detail—like her choice to go to Washington, DC—underscores the hypocrisy of American democracy at the time, which presented itself as a model for those struggling against oppression around the globe. Instead of protecting her, this sailor participates in her assault, suggesting that the government (as represented by this man) tacitly endorses racial and sexual abuses. Zoo has been used as a tool for white labor, a sexual object, and now an outlet for white rage when the impotent driver figuratively rapes her with his cigar. Burning her flesh brands her the victim of male power. For Capote, hierarchies that privilege whiteness, men, and heterosexuality perpetuate a system of abuse. Randolph, for instance, accepts the physical abuse of Pepe, the man he still loves, even as he turns his aggression toward Amy, slapping and threatening her. Amy, in turn, verbally abuses Zoo. Throughout *Other Voices, Other Rooms*, this cycle of violence reflects hierarchies that have disproportionately harmed African Americans and homosexuals.

CONCLUSION: THE BURDEN OF *MY ÁNTONIA*

In addition to the powerful impact of *My Ántonia* on *Other Voices, Other Rooms*, Cather's remarkable novel inspired aspects of the other two novels Capote completed in his lifetime—*The Grass Harp* (1951) and *Breakfast at Tiffany's* (1958). In these subsequent works, however, Capote retreats from an explicit treatment of homosexuality into a Jim Burden nostalgia, which makes his sociopolitical critiques much more subtle. Capote seems most comfortable with narrators that position themselves as outsiders with insider access—watching but not participating in romantic entanglements that are the focal point of their obsession. For instance, *The Grass Harp* functions to some extent as a nostalgic meditation on self-discovery and love. Its narrator, a lonely lawyer figure much like Jim, recalls a childhood friendship with Riley Henderson and a small group of mavericks who retreat to a tree house to escape the oppressiveness of town. Collin Fenwick cannot find a way to express his sexual desires for Riley, which leaves him to wallow in nostalgia and to idealize a time before adulthood, before sexual maturation.

Both Collin and Joel Knox are also similar to the nameless narrator of *Breakfast at Tiffany's*, who retrospectively tells the story of a captivating, enigmatic, and morally problematic figure named Holly Golightly. By reminiscing about the 1940s, the narrator distances himself from the sexual politics of the late 1950s, and though he allows Holly to give voice to daring attitudes about sexuality (acknowledging her own attraction to women and endorsing gay marriage), he keeps himself at a safe distance from such risky sentiments. Certainly, one of Capote's messages in all three books is that love should not be defined by social convention. Just as Jim tells Antonia ("I'd have liked to have you for a sweetheart, or a wife, or my mother or my sister—anything that a woman can be to a man"),[75] all of Capote's main characters yearn to define love as a powerful connection between two people that transcends conventional thinking and social prejudices about sexuality. Each novel has an Ántonia figure at its center, and as with *My Ántonia*, Capote's books raise troubling questions about the construction of masculinity and femininity in relation to sexuality and the prejudices that instill fear and self-hatred in those who fall outside of heteronormative standards and white power hierarchies. Yet the insistence of these narrators on looking back—on situating stories in the past—keeps them from acting with a greater degree of social and political engagement. (For Joel, he is not looking back per se, but his persistent dreamlike fusion of childhood fantasy with reality distances him from the world outside his imagination.) The politics of these books stem from measured thoughtfulness and retrospection, not public protests and sit-ins. Certainly, Cather and Capote challenge ethnic and sexual biases in America and, as such, call for change. But by relying on narrators that fail to heed such a call, these authors don't insist on immediate action from their readers. They demand awareness, but this is only the first step toward social change. In this way, one could argue that the narrative approach of Jim Burden proved to be both liberating and limiting for Capote. It celebrates lyrical beauty and social consciousness without providing a pathway for achieving change—change that Capote, through his celebrity and flamboyant sexuality, may have been able to do much to facilitate.

NOTES

1. Truman Capote, *Portraits and Observations: The Essays of Truman Capote* (New York: Random House, 2007), 506.

2. Ibid., 506.

3. Ibid., 507.

4. Truman Capote, "Remembering Willa Cather," *Vanity Fair*, November 16, 2006, http://www.vanityfair.com/news/2006/11/capote-200611.

5. Truman Capote, *Other Voices, Other Rooms* (1948; New York: Vintage International, 1994), 51–52.

6. Although my focus here is on gender and sexuality, a number of other critical approaches have provided dynamic ways of reading this moment as well. For instance, Carol Steinhagen and Steven Trout have recently offered ecocritical readings of the snake scene, arguing that "Jim's display of aggression against a hated 'pest' conveys the ecological impact of that culture as its members speedily transformed the Great Plains from a wilderness of tall grass and prairie-dog towns to the patchwork of enclosed, mechanically-harvested fields that we see today." See Carol Steinhagen, "Dangerous Crossings: Historical Dimensions of Landscape in Willa Cather's *My Ántonia, The Professor's House,* and *Death Comes for the Archbishop,*" *Interdisciplinary Studies in Literature and Environment* 6, no. 2 (Summer 1999): 63–82; Steven Trout, "Seeing the Rattlesnake in Willa Cather's *My Ántonia,*" *Interdisciplinary Studies in Literature and Environment* 12, no. 1 (Winter 2005): 109. Additionally, postcolonial critics have situated *My Ántonia* in contemporary concerns about American empire. Guy Reynolds's *Willa Cather in Context: Progress, Race, Empire* (New York: St. Martin's Press, 1996) situates Cather's work in the debates surrounding immigration and assimilation at the time, and more recently, Michael Gorman uses the snake scene to critique Jim's erasure of American colonial history and its impact on Native Americans: "Jim's slaughter of the rattlesnake resembles the dirty political reality in which his future employer, the railroad, was complicit. In other words, Jim's vicious beating and near beheading of the aged sidewinder corresponds to the manner in which the U.S. military and railway industry colluded to eliminate Native American claims to territory in the Central Great Plains." See Gorman, "Jim Burden and the White Man's Burden: *My Ántonia* and Empire," *Cather Studies* 6 (2006): 38.

7. See David Porter, *On the Divide: The Many Lives of Willa Cather* (Lincoln: University of Nebraska Press, 2010); Susan J. Rosowski, *The Voyage Perilous: Willa Cather's Romanticism* (Lincoln: University of Nebraska Press, 1986).

8. Blanche H. Gelfant, "The Forgotten Reaping-Hook: Sex in *My Ántonia*," *American Literature* 43, no. 1 (March 1971): 64.

9. Lisa Marie Lucenti, "Willa Cather's *My Ántonia*: Haunting the House of Memory," *Twentieth Century Literature* 46, no. 2 (2000): 198.

10. Hermione Lee, *Willa Cather: Double Lives* (New York: Pantheon, 1990), 153.

11. Cather, *My Ántonia*, 209.

12. Marilee Lindemann, *Willa Cather: Queering America* (New York: Columbia University Press, 1999); Sharon O'Brien, *Willa Cather: The Emerging Voice* (Cambridge, MA: Harvard University Press, 1997).

13. John P. Anders, *Willa Cather's Sexual Aesthetics and the Male Homosexual Literary Tradition* (Lincoln: University of Nebraska Press, 1999), 3.

14. Ibid., 67.

15. Cather, *My Ántonia*, 42.

16. Ibid., 72.

17. Ibid., 73.

18. Ibid., 31.

19. Ibid., 78, 44.

20. Ibid., 41.

21. Ibid., 133.

22. David Worden, "'I Like to Be Like a Man': Female Masculinity in Willa Cather's *O Pioneers!* and *My Antonia*," in *Violence, the Arts, and Willa Cather*, ed. Joseph R. Urgo and Merrill Maguire Skaggs (Madison, NJ: Fairleigh Dickinson University Press, 2007), 273.

23. Cather, *My Ántonia*, 43.

24. Ibid., 44.

25. Ibid.

26. Ibid., 217.

27. Ibid., xi.

28. Ibid.

29. Judith Fetterley, "*My Ántonia*, Jim Burden, and the Dilemma of the Lesbian Writer," in *Gender Studies: New Directions in Feminist Criticism*, ed. Judith Spector (Bowling Green, OH: Bowling Green State University, Popular Press, 1986), 55.

30. Cather, *My Ántonia*, 48.

31. Capote, *Other Voices, Other Rooms*, 172.

32. Ibid., 175.

33. Ibid., 177.

34. Ibid., 132.

35. Ibid., 178.

36. Ibid., 179.

37. Ibid.

38. Ibid., 177–78.

39. Ibid., 132.

40. Ibid., 172.

41. Ibid., 174.

42. Ibid.

43. Ibid., 179.

44. Ibid.

45. Ibid., 181.

46. Ibid., 130.

47. Cather, *My Ántonia*, 146, 49.

48. Ibid., 207, 203.

49. Fetterley, *My Ántonia*, 143.

50. Cather, *My Ántonia,* 192, 194.

51. It is not my intention to suggest that foreign language does not play an important role in the novel. I am simply arguing that the bias against non-native speakers masks other fears as well. For an insightful interpretation of foreign language in *My Ántonia*, see Guy Reynolds's discussion of Cather's celebration of bilingual communities in *Willa Cather in Context*, 81–83.

52. Cather, *My Ántonia*, 195.

53. Ibid., 197.

54. Ibid., 339.

55. Cather also uses Lena's career as a dressmaker to comment on the objectification of these women as well. As Lindemann has argued, "the seductive, violet-eyed Lena Lingard earns her living as a dressmaker, catering to the tendency in consumer culture to view women's bodies as objects of display and exchange" (*Willa Cather*, 68).

56. Cather, *My Ántonia*, 203.

57. Ibid., 204.

58. Ibid., 201.

59. Ibid., 203.

60. Ibid., 188.

61. Ibid., 189.

62. Ibid.

63. Ibid., 189–90.

64. Ibid., 166.

65. Ibid., 191.

66. Ibid., 162.

67. Ibid., 191.

68. Capote, *Other Voices, Other Rooms*, 133.

69. Ibid., 134.

70. Ibid.

71. Ibid., 135.

72. Capote based Zoo Fever's experiences on the gang rape of a young sharecropper named Recy Taylor. For more on this incident, its role in the early Civil Rights Movement, and its function in Capote's novel, see my chapter on *Other Voices, Other Rooms* in *Understanding Truman Capote* (Columbia: University of South Carolina Press, 2014).

73. Capote, *Other Voices, Other Rooms*, 215.

74. Ibid., 216.

75. Cather, *My Ántonia*, 312.

Part IV

TRANSHUMAN

Chapter Nine

Hysterical Resistance

Desire and Narrative in My Ántonia

Monroe Street

At the end of *My Ántonia*'s 1918 Introduction, Jim Burden rather cautiously delivers a manuscript to the New York apartment of a longtime friend. Although we never learn who exactly this friend is, we do know—as does Jim—that he or she is an established writer, and it is perhaps this knowledge that accounts for Burden's self-consciousness as he presents his work: "Here is the thing about Ántonia," he notes with an air of uncertainty. "Do you still want to read it? I finished it last night. I didn't take time to arrange it; I simply wrote down pretty much all that her name recalls to me. I suppose it hasn't any form. It hasn't any title, either."[1] In light of the fact that Jim's formless "thing" serves as the primary narrative content of the novel Cather thought of as her finest, his remarks here seem almost conspicuously self-deprecating. Bracing his friend for what he fears may be a disappointing read, Jim presents *My Ántonia* as a hurried and unrevised compilation of associations, a mere assemblage of "all that [Ántonia's] name recalls." How, then, to make sense of this unflattering review of the novel—furnished by its own figurative "author," no less—in light of Cather's own insistence until the end of her career that "The best thing I've done is *My Ántonia*"?[2]

Or perhaps the question worth asking is whether there may in fact be something quite compelling about the apparent "formlessness" of Jim's narrative—and Cather's favorite novel. A brief consideration of the sexual politics of traditional narrative suggests precisely this. As Judith Roof has argued, many of our most seemingly "well-told" stories support a narrative logic that implicitly suppresses queer and deviant forms of sexuality. In *Come As You Are: Sexuality and Narrative*, Roof exposes the formal similarities of stories as seemingly opposed as Freud's chronicle of normative sexual development and lesbian tales of "coming out."[3] In both of these cases, we are given a narrative that Roof designates as "heteroideological"—that is, one whose ending

185

suppresses the deviant desires encountered mid-plot.[4] In Freud, the queerness of children—or "infantile perversion"—is transformed perhaps just a bit too tidily into adult heterosexual object-choice. Meanwhile, the lesbian "coming out" story works toward the opposite—but no less reductively resolved—pole of the sexual binary: the queer subject's realization of her decidedly homosexual identity. Roof then traces the form of such overly well-told stories of sexual development to the form of the marriage plot. While not predicated on literal matrimony, the function of the "heteroideological" ending is nonetheless to bring together and stabilize the polymorphous, heterogenous dimensions of sexuality under the aegis of a coherent social structure: the heterosexual couple in the case of Freud; the unambiguously homosexual individual in the case of the "coming out" tale.

In light of Roof's work, the apparent "formlessness" of *My Ántonia* can be thought of as one way in which Cather's novel refuses to comply with the heteroideological terms of the marriage plot—and, generally speaking, conventional narrative form. Indeed, in Jim's episodic chronicling of his relations with Ántonia, there is a sustained ambivalence that characterizes the relationship, an ongoing tension between attraction and renunciation that is never fully resolved. Although Jim and Ántonia end up marrying, their respective marriages are characterized by indifference, stemming more from circumstance than romance. Meanwhile, as is made evident in the Introduction, Jim's writing of his narrative—in other words, the novel itself—is premised on Burden's ongoing interest in Ántonia, one that persists in spite of the matrimonial commitments each has made.[5]

Of course, a brief look around the Cather library reveals *My Ántonia* to be but one among many of her novels that could be said to resist the terms of "heteroideological" narrative. As Christopher Nealon observes,

> It cannot be said that Cather wrote dramatic fiction, if by that term we mean novels organized around a marriage plot. When characters marry in her novels, the marriage is never the consummation of narrative drives; indeed, characters more often start out married and conveniently suffer separation.[6]

Leafing through Cather's oeuvre, one is hard pressed to find a heterosexual romance that isn't either ambivalent, tormented, or tepid. From the unsentimental Thea and Fred of *The Song of the Lark*[7] to the hardened distance of Sapphira and Henry in her final novel,[8] Cather wrote ceaselessly of lukewarm couples.

One prominent consequence of Cather's apparent predilection for such dispassionate displays of heterosexuality has been an ongoing critical interest in mining her novels for the signs of latent homoeroticism—and *My Ántonia* is no exception in this regard. Yet if Cather leaves us hard-pressed to find an unambiguously satisfied heterosexual couple in her work, her rendering of same-sex friendships[9] is often ambiguous to the point that we question whether such bonds are to be taken as homosocial or homoerotic. Unlike the "heteroideological" work of which Roof is so critical, one routinely comes away from Cather's text with no clear sense that either heterosexuality or homosexuality is an object of particular interest.[10] Although Cather's texts have inspired countless gay and queer readings, critics such as Joan Acocella have pointed out that this hermeneutic fervor may have less to do with Cather's nuanced portrayals of sexuality and more to do with the politics of the feminist canon.[11] For Judith Butler as well, Cather's ambiguous figuration of the erotic presents a fundamental challenge to those looking to align her with the legacy of lesbian fiction: "It is not easy to know how to read gender or sexuality in Willa Cather's fiction. Cather has appeared not to place herself in a legible relation to women or to lesbianism."[12]

Thus, lack of "form" for which Jim criticizes his narrative in the early pages of *My Ántonia* might then be thought of as one particular way in which the novel contributes to a body of work that consistently refuses to depict sexual romance as abiding by the conventions of either heterosexuality or homosexuality. Haphazard as Jim may allege it to be, his text nonetheless advances a narrative project in line with the one Susan Rosowski describes in "Willa Cather's Subverted Endings" as a "search for alternatives to the End, particularly as mandated by socially imposed gender conventions."[13] The subversions of such conventions are numerous in *My Ántonia*'s ending. Although Ántonia does indeed marry a man (Anton Cuzak) and can also be seen more figuratively as "wed" to the Nebraska land she's made a life of tilling, neither of these outcomes amount to the consummation of her and Jim's relationship for which conventional romance enthusiasts may have hoped. What's more, it is not at all clear that there remains much in the way of requited passion (if there ever was any) in Ántonia's marriage to Cuzak. Indeed, Cuzak's passions are decidedly elsewhere—and rather queer at that: his late nights on the town and extended reveries on the virtues of opera lend him more the air of a Wildean urbanite than a Nebraskan fruit farmer.[14]

Further unsettling what scraps of a marriage plot there are in *My Ántonia* is Jim's own ambiguously homoerotic involvement with Ántonia's family in the closing chapters of his narrative. Although Jim finds Ántonia compelling enough to write a book in her honor, his romantic interest wanes by the novel's final episode, in which he reserves much of his attention and affection for her husband and boys. Indeed, Jim shows an almost brazen fondness for Cuzak and his male children: not only does Burden title Book V "Cuzak's Boys," within this episode he also promises to return the following summer for the express purpose of treating said "boys" to an outing in the mountains.[15] As Jim's narrative ends, it is thus by no means clear whether he is still drawn to Ántonia or whether his once romantic feelings for her have moved on in the direction of the male characters with whom she cohabitates.

What further sense are we to make, then, of *My Ántonia*'s refusal of a conventional marriage plot—that is, the novel's resistance to rendering sexuality in unambiguously homo- or hetero-terms? Or, shifting the emphasis somewhat, how does the narrative form of *My Ántonia* encourage us to understand the way that Jim's sexuality works, given that his desire doesn't appear to be clearly gay or straight? Past commentators on sexuality in the novel have tended to approach such questions by way of what we know about Cather's *own* desire from her biography—notably her relationships with Louise Pound, Isabelle McLung, and Edith Lewis. Cather's assumed homosexuality thus informs classic gay readings of the novel such as those by Timothy Dow Adams[16] and Judith Fetterley.[17] For Fetterley in particular, an understanding of Cather as first and foremost a "lesbian writer" factors in centrally to her analysis of the novel's failed marriage plot. Cather's presumed lesbianism thus works in tandem with the absence of matrimony between Ántonia and Jim to produce a reading of this manifestly heterosexual relation as a homosexual affair in disguise. The real reason our protagonists can't marry? Jim is but a poorly masked Willa Cather, and the setting is the late nineteenth century; the prospect of a union between Willa and Ántonia is literally inconceivable.

One of the wagers of the present chapter is that a Lacanian psychoanalytic approach might open up another way of understanding the relationally ambiguous and unresolved aspects of Jim's narrative, such as its foiled marriage plot. While Fetterley aptly characterizes the tumultuous story of Jim and Ántonia's relationship as a "drama of renunciation,"[18] my primary proposal here is that we read this "renunciatory" passion not as the sign of Jim's lesbianism but as aligning with a psychoanalytic understanding of hysterical desire. In addition, I suggest that Freud and Lacan's formulations of hysteria allow us to account more closely for the ways in which the novel actively resists interpretations like Fetterley's—that is, those that reduce Jim and his desire to gendered categories of analysis. In this regard, my reading falls in step with the view Sharon O'Brien evolves in one of her more recent studies of Cather's work. When reading Cather, we ought "not assume that male characters are simply 'masks' for a lesbian consciousness. . . . Nor should we assume that the overt heterosexual story is the fake 'cover' story, the hidden lesbian story the 'real' one."[19] O'Brien's remark alludes to the ways in which an interpretive preoccupation with gender—and particularly cross-gendered identification[20]—can lead to reductive decodings of Cather's subtle depictions of sexuality.

Knowing—or thinking we know—all too well of Cather's own love for women, we fall prey to a kind of hermeneutic mode of reading in which all moments of ambiguity seem to point in one direction: that of lesbianism and, more broadly, homoeroticism. While psychoanalytic interpretation is often criticized on similar grounds—that is, for all too masterfully reducing a text's complicated social dynamics to, say, Freud's model of Oedipal desire or phallic symbolism—Lacan's work both challenges and provides ways around hermeneutic analysis of this sort.[21] My use of analytic theory here will thus be in the service of describing how desire in *My Ántonia* resists being decoded in terms of gender. Instead I propose that we make sense of Jim's sexuality as modeled on one of Lacan's formulations of hysterical desire—as a desire for an unsatisfied desire.[22] In the pages ahead, I develop the implications of this deceptively simple-seeming formula and place it in conversation with both the content of Jim's tale—notably, his indeterminate relations with Ántonia and Lena—as well as *My Ántonia*'s narrative form.

FRUSTRATING DESIRE: HYSTERIA AS A RELATIONAL STRUCTURE

Hysteria's long conceptual lineage, dating as it does at least as far back as Hippocrates, is beyond the scope of this chapter. However, in the interest of clarifying my usage of the term, I wish to explain several of the most important ways in which a psychoanalytic approach to hysteria departs from popular and medical conceptions of the condition.[23] Put briefly, such conceptions typically understand hysteria to be a pathological illness and also one that is decidedly linked to the biology of the female body—two postulates that Freud's work resists.

It is perhaps the unfortunate consequence of a widely publicized and well-justified critique of Freud's oft-misogynistic writing that the socially progressive inflection of his work on hysteria has been obscured. Elided thereby is Freud's reconceptualization of hysteria, which he took to be neither a medical disorder in the biological sense nor a condition specific to women. Indeed, as early as 1886, Freud was an outspoken proponent of French psychiatrist Jean-Martin Charcot's theories regarding *male* hysteria, even going so far as to deliver a lecture on the topic to the Vienna Society of Physicians.[24] Failing to gain much interest among his medical colleagues, yet determined to demonstrate how hysterical symptoms could be analyzed in both men and women, Freud subsequently withdrew into private practice, where he began an analysis of *his own* self-described hysteria. Throughout his epistolary correspondence with physician Wilhelm Fliess in the late 1890s, Freud can be seen analyzing a number of his own psychosomatic (or "conversion") symptoms: nasal infections, migraines, and episodes of melancholia that had emerged in connection with the death of his father in 1896.[25] As Mark Micale suggests, Freud continued to cogitate on Charcot's ideas regarding male hysteria during this period, and it was likely such rumination that inspired his subsequent conception of "universal bisexuality" among humans—the nonessentialist notion that as infants we identify with adult caretakers of both genders and thus emerge into the social world as, originally, bi-gendered subjects.[26]

In addition to offering a less sexist way of understanding hysteria than biological and medical conceptions that had linked it to the female body, psychoanalysis can also be seen as working to depathologize hysterical suffering. Rather than treating conversion symptoms as stemming exclusively from a diseased body in need of fixing, Freud elected to approach them as forms of symbolic expression. As psychoanalyst Patricia Gherovici asserts, "the clinical revolution introduced by Freud began by restoring subjectivity to the hysteric"[27] through its refusal of a medical model—that is, by refusing to understand the patient as reducible to "a set of organs, symptoms, and clearly ascertainable complaints."[28] Instead Freud invented free association as a technique for allowing the hysteric's complaints to speak and be heard.

Listening closely, Freud also soon noticed that embedded in the structure of the hysterical complaint was a message addressed to the medical establishment itself. By presenting the physician with a confusing and mutable array of somatic symptoms that were baffling to extant medical wisdom, the hysteric could effectively lead the doctor to the limits of his or her medical knowledge. Hard pressed to cure psychosomatic ailments by way of objectivist science, the medical physician would then be revealed by the hysteric as at least partly impotent, his or her curative knowledge lacking.

By way of psychoanalysis, hysteria thus becomes conceivable as neither a gendered condition nor a medical pathology but instead as an inventive practice of social and epistemological protest against the knowingness of doctors. Yet such protest extends toward not only the *medical* physician but also the psychoanalyst. Consider, for instance, one of the most widely known and frequently reinterpreted "works" of hysteria: the dream of the butcher's wife, which Freud recounts in *The Interpretation of Dreams*. Here Freud's primary reason for presenting the dream is its alleged resistance to his theory that all dreams represent the fulfillment of wishes. The dream itself—in which the butcheress tries *but fails* to procure salmon for a dinner party she is to host—appears to stand as a direct affront to Freud's thesis: where in it, the butcheress wonders, are we to identify anything resembling a fulfilled wish?[29]

Ever attached to his theory, Freud counters the butcheress' challenge with an explication of the desire latent in her dream. His patient, Freud claims, has identified herself in the dream with a friend in whom her husband has recently taken interest, and who is one of the invited guests to the aforementioned soirée. The "I" of the dream thus represents not the dreamer herself but a rival for her husband's affection. It is this rival—known by the butcheress to adore smoked salmon in real life—who is depicted in the dream as desiring and failing to obtain this delicacy. For Freud, the dream represents and fulfills the butcheress' latent wish to frustrate the desire of her friend and rival.

In demonstrating how the butcheress' dream in fact supports rather than challenges his wish fulfillment theory, Freud might appear to have fended off his hysterical patient's resistance to it. But as Lacan points out, in responding as he does to the butcheress Freud overlooks how the dream could be "motivated by no other desire than to provide Freud, who has explained to [the patient] his theory that dreams are desires, with proof that they are nothing of the kind."[30] Such a wish, Lacan suggests, is hardly an extraordinary one among hysterical patients and in fact serves as an integral diagnostic marker for distinguishing hysteria from other psychic structures. Rather than following Freud and others in understanding the hallmark of hysteria to be the mysterious somatic ailments that routinely accompany it, Lacan instead insists that the condition be understood structurally, as a particular manner in which certain subjects relate to their own desire and that of the Other.[31] Accordingly, one of the most well-known ways in which Lacan formulates the condition is by way of the hysterical patient's paradoxical desire "to posit . . . desire in relation to [the analyst] as an unsatisfied desire."[32] In addition to avoiding the psychiatric pitfalls of diagnosing a condition like hysteria in terms of poorly defined clusters of symptoms, Lacan's structural definition also eradicates any traces of biological essentialism lingering in Freud. Insofar as hysteria is understood as a way in which the subject relates to desire and the Other, the anatomy of the body is of no consequence in establishing a diagnosis—and thus neither is the subject's gender.

Following Lacan, we can see how nonessential the butcheress' identification as a woman has to do with the way in which her dream baffles Freud's interpretive capacities. Rather than her *gender*, it is the *form and function* of her wish—to articulate unsatisfied desire—that presents Freud with difficulties. Such a wish not only complicates Freud's theory of dreams, but also exposes the limitations of Freud's own "desire to recognize the dream's desire."[33] Indeed, Lacan's hysteric might always manage to frustrate Freud's wish to have his interpretation honored by the patient as the correct one. For in attempting to have the butcheress "recognize" her desire as satisfied by her dream, Freud deprives her of her wish to be unsatisfied. Freud's interpretive intervention is thus in some sense self-defeating: it *produces* dissatisfaction where it had intended to quell it. Such is the logic undergirding what Diana Fuss calls hysteria's "powerful resistance to interpretive mastery": driven by a desire for an unsatisfied desire, the hysteric remains capable of dissolving any interpretation that would satisfy his or her wish by naming it as such.[34]

Within Lacan's thinking on hysteria, it is thus possible to unpack at least three distinct forms that hysterical desire might assume. In the case of the butcheress' dream, for instance, there emerges a wish to present *her own desire* as unsatisfied. But this aim also coincides with a second wish (the one Freud identifies): to *dissatisfy the Other*—or, rather, to reveal the Other as lacking and therefore desiring. For the butcheress the Other is both her salmon-loving friend as well as Freud himself, whose own desire to "recognize desire" she works to frustrate. From there emerges a third distinct wish: *to preserve desire as a subjective inclination that resists being recognized, known, or named.* Returning to *My Ántonia*, we can discern how the groundwork above allows Jim to be understood as a hysterical subject in relation to both the women remembered in the novel as well as the desire which circulates between himself and them. The first two of these three hysterical projects emerge repeatedly in Jim's relations with Ántonia and Lena, while the third—a resistance to the interpretation of desire—is made manifest at the level of the novel's framed narrative form, by way of which Jim ironically satisfies the unnamed narrator of the Introduction by presenting his frustrated desire in manuscript form.

NARRATIVE HYSTERIA: THE NAMELESS WRITER

Beginning with *My Ántonia*'s Introduction, we might admit that Jim's relation to the narrator hardly seems imbued with any of the hysterical forms of antipathy just described. Sitting in the observation car of a train barreling across Iowa, Jim and his childhood friend are downright amicable as they watch red dust fly by and fall into a collective reverie of the "Bohemian girl whom we had known long ago and whom both of us admired."[35] Of course, the narrator makes no secret of disliking Jim's wife Genevieve Whitney, described as a "restless, headstrong girl . . . who liked to astonish her friends"—indeed, one who finds her husband's "quiet tastes" irritating.[36] But these comments are confined to the narrator's private thoughts rather than spoken outwardly to Jim, and the narrator's distaste with Whitney would hardly seem a hysterical complaint designed to antagonize. Indeed, it would seem to be by way of encouragement rather than hysterical games that Jim's friend inspires him to write the account of Ántonia we will read in Books I through V: "I told him how he knew her and felt her was exactly what I most wanted to know."[37] Meanwhile Jim, although initially tentative to write—"I've had no practice," he claims—hardly seems hysterical himself. Obediently seeking to satisfy the narrator's request, he delivers the manuscript to the narrator's apartment soon after they return to New York.

But while in the Introduction there is little indication of hysteria in the *spoken* relation between Jim and the narrator, a closer look at the latter's possible motivations for taking interest in Jim's narrative—even before it is written—complicates this picture. Consider how, far from thrilled about Jim's marriage to Whitney, the narrator incites him to write of his feelings for another woman—Ántonia—instead. An innocent request? Hardly. Recall that after presenting the unflattering portrait of Whitney, the narrator expresses candid in-credulity at the fact that she "wishes to remain Mrs. James Burden" and thus, by extension, that Jim remains married to her.[38] Then, in the paragraph that follows immediately thereafter, Jim is portrayed as more than a bit of a flirt: "he meets new people with . . . impulsiveness" and "his . . . solicitous interest in women is as youthful as it is Western." Given the rather demure, socially aloof persona Jim subsequently adopts in his manuscript, these comments seem as much a product of the narrator's wishful thinking as they are of a piece with Jim's own self-presentation. In other words, the narrator's description of Jim reflects the narrator's desire to view Jim as an "impulsive" and "solicitous" man of the West, indifferent to his wife and prone to straying. Might we not then wonder whether the narrator's wish for Jim to write about Ántonia represents a hysteri-cal effort to incite a bit of trouble in Burden's otherwise placid marriage?

Further evidencing the narrator's desire to meddle with matrimony is the unsettled outcome of Jim's romance with Ántonia that his narrative chroni-cles. In my preliminary discussion of the novel's narrative form, I noted the way in which Ántonia's tepid marriage to Cuzak serves as a primary vehicle through which Cather resists what Roof has called "heteroideological" end-ings. Such resistance is also reflected within the novel through the writer of the Introduction, who desires to read Jim's text in spite of knowing full well at the outset that he will not marry Ántonia. In other words, the text the name-less writer wishes to read is one of love that will go unrequited rather than be resolved. The Introduction's narrator thus is not quite the "ideal reader of [Jim's] future text" that Judith Butler suggests him or her to be.[39] Indeed, the logic of the nameless writer's textual desire runs rather far afield from the narrative wisdom espoused by more canonically minded narrative theorists like Peter Brooks. While for Brooks's conventional reader, the "desire of the text (the desire of reading) is . . . desire for [knowledge of] the end," the nameless narrator of *My Ántonia* seems indifferent to the satisfaction of knowing how a story will pan out.[40] The story the narrator requests is not only one in which the desire of the Other (Jim) will go unsatisfied, but also one whose narrative conclusion he or she already more or less knows in advance. In other words, the narrator desires a text in which his or her would-be "desire for the end" has already been frustratingly fulfilled at the outset. And yet, this foreknowledge that Jim's manuscript will conclude unsatisfyingly for both its writer and reader appears to support, rather than dissolve, the text's desirability for the nameless narrator. Far from an "ideal," the writer of *My Ántonia*'s Introduction delights in a kind of narrative hysteric more easily seduced by a story that frustrates than one that satisfies.

If so far I have been alluding to the ways in which the nameless writer's desire for Jim's text might be understood as hysterical, it's also worth situating this claim in the context of the narrator's complicated gender identity. Indeed, Cather's investment in decoupling desire from gender can be seen in the revisions she made to the character of the nameless narrator between 1918 and 1926. In the 1918 edition of *My Ántonia*, the first-person narrator is explicitly feminine, but by the text's 1926 publishing Cather has removed any and all references to this nameless character's gender.[41] Many critics—Butler among them—have understood the genderless 1926 narrator as first and foremost a device whereby Cather has attempted to camouflage her own autobiographical presence in the novel.[42] But I propose that Cather's changes to the Introduction be seen as an argument against the importance of the reader's knowledge of this character's gender. Indeed, from the perspective of narrative function, it isn't the nameless writer's *gender*, but his or her *wish* for Jim to write that assumes primary importance in the Introduction. It is the narrator's desire for Jim's narrative that gets the novel rolling, and the narrative consequence of this desire—Jim's writing of the text—is obviously just as evident in 1926, when the narrator has no apparent gender, as it is in 1918, when she is feminine. In other words, both avatars of the narrator effectively seduce Jim into authoring the work that will serve as the main text of Cather's novel. Cather's revisions might thus be read as suggesting not so much an indifference to gender as the possibility of an engendered mode of desiring. And if the narrator's desire for Jim's text is in certain respects hysterical, this certainly has little to do with whether he or she is a man or a woman—for in fact, at least in 1926, he or she is neither.

While Cather's revised presentation of the Introduction's narrator decouples hysterical desire from this character's status as a man, woman, or neither, a similar attenuation of hysteria's traditional gendering can be seen within Jim's narrative—particularly in his relations with Ántonia and Lena Lingard. In turning now to the main narrative of *My Ántonia*, I am interested in the way Jim's text presents hysterical desire as discernible not only in the text's two main feminine characters, but also, perhaps more fundamentally, in Jim himself. Indeed, it is by way of Jim's pursuit of dissatisfaction with Ántonia and Lena that the novel resists reducing hysterical passion to the feminine, suggesting the apparently hysterical women represented in Jim's narration to be a function of his own desire. Whereas *My Ántonia*'s Introduction subtly keys in on the narrator's hysterical desire to upset the matrimonial satisfactions of the *Other* (e.g., Jim and his wife Genevieve), the main text of the novel reveals Jim's hysteria as a commitment to frustrating *his own desire* for Ántonia and Lena.

THE HYSTERICAL MANUSCRIPT:
JIM'S RENUNCIATORY DRAMA

Throughout much of his manuscript, Jim constructs a narrative in which it appears to be manifestly *feminine* desire—that of Ántonia and Lena Lingard rather than his own—that operates hysterically. In other words, Jim presents Ántonia and Lena as actively working to frustrate the Other's (in many cases, his own) desire. This characterization begins to surface almost immediately in Jim's text. For instance, here's how Jim describes the first extended interaction he has with young Ántonia, during which she probes him for the English names of objects within view:

> Ántonia pointed up to the sky and questioned me with her glance. I gave her the word, but she was not satisfied and pointed to my eyes. I told her and she repeated the word, making it sound like "ice." She pointed up to the sky, then to my eyes, then back to the sky, with movements so quick and impulsive that she distracted me, and I had no idea what she wanted.[43]

Our first real impression of Ántonia is thus of a demanding young "Bohemian," one who is not easily "satisfied" and whose bodily "movements" are "quick" and "impulsive," effectively thwarting Jim's wish to please her. A hysteric in the making, Ántonia kindles in Jim a frustrated wish to help her by expressing her own enigmatic dissatisfaction. Eager to ascertain the object of Ántonia's verbal desire, Jim is left guessing, having "no idea" what it might be.

Of course, we subsequently learn how Jim learns to satisfy, more or less, Ántonia's epistemic wish to learn English by way of the "reading lessons" alluded to throughout Book I. When the relationship turns romantic, however, Ántonia's elusive desire once more proves challenging. This registers most potently during the scene near the end of Book II in which Ántonia staves Jim off following a dance at Fireman's Hall. After consenting to a goodbye kiss, Ántonia pulls away in disgust, Jim having apparently approached the embrace a bit overzealously.[44] Granted, Ántonia's reticence here may well be motivated as much by a commitment to her new gentleman caller Larry Donovan as by a wish simply to frustrate Jim's desire. But oddly enough, Ántonia makes no mention of Donovan to Jim. Instead she simply berates him, not only for his uncouth advance toward *her*, but also for the "nonsense" he's been up to with Lena Lingard. It would thus appear that, were Ántonia to have things her way, Jim would have no access to physical affection whatsoever. Advocating that Jim go "away to school and make something of [himself]," Ántonia insists that he remain an almost exclusively intellectual figure in her life—an ambiguously platonic friend rather than one whose romantic yearnings she is willing to entertain.[45] If in this scene Ántonia at first evinces an ambivalent romantic interest in Jim—she invites his embrace and then rebuffs it—she ultimately emerges as a superegoic figure of sorts, advocating against Jim's seeking physical affection of any kind. Once more, Jim's text seems to encourage a reading of Ántonia as hysterically working to frustrate his desire.

In Jim's portrayal of Lena Lingard—his other main love interest—the hysterical caricaturing of a feminine character is perhaps even more pronounced. Indeed, in Jim's earliest descriptions of Lena, we are encouraged to think of her as something of a tease. Not only does the "miraculous whiteness" of Lena's legs and arms lead her to "seem more undressed than other girls who went scantily clad," but she also regularly welcomes Jim and other men into her company while working the fields in this alluring state.[46] Indeed, it is by such means that she attracts the attention of Ole Benson, one of her "fat and lazy"—and, we might add, *married*—neighbors on the Norwegian encampment.[47] In light of Jim's unflattering description of Benson, we are given to wonder how Lingard could possibly be attracted to him; nonetheless, she routinely allows him to spend afternoons with her tending the fields. Yet, Lena's kindling of an affair with Benson leads nowhere, and their fling ends with his being driven "out of his head, until he had no more sense than his crazy wife [Mary]." All told, we learn from this episode of Lena's ability and willingness to engage and frustrate not only Ole's desire, but also that of his spouse. Indeed, deprived of her husband's wandering affections, Mary eventually comes after Lingard in a fit of jealous rage, armed with an ominously suggestive corn knife, no less.[48]

Given her apparent penchant for stirring up unsatisfied desire in the Other, it should perhaps come as no surprise when Lena later admits of her interest in "wild" men rather than the married ones. "Men," she tells Jim, "are alright for friends, but as soon as you marry them they turn into cranky old fathers, even the wild ones. They begin to tell you what's sensible and what's foolish, and want you to stick at home all the time. I prefer to be foolish when I feel like it, and be accountable to nobody."[49] Here Lena alludes to one of the most significant relational aims of hysterical structure: frustrating desire in the Other so as to ensure its ongoing presence. In this passage, marriage is conceived as a social structure whereby desire might become all too easily satisfied and thus stultified. According to Lena, matrimony not only immobilizes women, who as wives are expected to *"stick* at home," but it also stands to nullify the capacity of "men" to pine after their spouses. As wives women become dangerously "accountable" to their husbands—that is, all too available—and their spouses consequently become "cranky" and controlling toward women rather than able to be excited by them. Lena thus rather brilliantly implies how, too secure in their wives' capacity to satisfy their wishes, married men *themselves* become hysterical characters. In behaving poorly, Lena's hypothetical husbands render themselves unappealing to their hypothetical spouses, frustrating the desire of all involved. Nothing is more unsatisfying, Lena suggests, than the illusory satisfaction conferred by marriage.

Indeed, throughout her relationship with Jim in Book III, Lena can be seen actively fending off the stifling of desire induced by matrimony and other more "accountable" forms of intimacy. Evidence of this can be discerned in Lena's quite visibly independent lifestyle: she owns a thriving business, entertains Jim and other guests in her own private residence, and makes few demands for Jim's company.[50] Of course, it would be more than myopic to reduce Lena's well-earned independence to a hysterical project of kindling frustrated desire in the Other. But within the context of Jim's narrative, Lena's vehement self-reliance and relative unavailability—represents a key dimension of her character that allows Jim to sustain his desire for her.

Indeed, the odd way in which Jim represents the ending of their affair reveals his attachment to imagining Lena as noncommittal—that is, as the one who withholds and renounces desire in their relationship. Although it is clearly Jim who initiates the breakup, having decided to uproot from Nebraska to attend Harvard, he nonetheless works to portray Lena as the one in charge: "At last she sent me away with her soft, slow, renunciatory kiss. . . . She always kissed one as if she were sadly and wisely sending one away forever."[51] Note how Lena is positioned here as the active, "renouncing" subject while Jim appears passive: it is he who is "sent . . . away" by her, rather than the other way around. As with Ántonia, with Lena too: an embrace that proves more "renunciatory" than satisfying; a feminine Other refusing Jim's embrace.

Already I have been hinting at the role Jim plays as narrator in constructing Ántonia and Lena as the agents of what Fetterley calls *My Ántonia*'s "renunciatory drama." Rather than take Jim's account of his feminine love interests as self-transparent, we might do well to read his account not only for what it tells us about Ántonia and Lena, but first and foremost for what it reveals

about Jim. That Jim so blatantly exaggerates Lena's responsibility for the dissolution of their relationship alerts us to the possibility of reinterpreting the
hysteria he imputes both to her and Ántonia as a function of his own narrative
imagination and his own desire. By extension, if we recall Lacan's suggestion
that the hysteric often wants nothing more than "to posit . . . desire . . . as an
unsatisfied desire," we might then take Jim's manuscript as a hysterical form
of writing, one through which he elaborates his desire as repeatedly let down
by the women in his life. While hysteria in *My Ántonia* can be imputed to
the diegetic actions of Lena and Ántonia, it is perhaps most fundamentally a
function of Jim's narration.

Evidence of Jim's hysterical investment in rendering his own desire unsatisfied appears at several telling moments in his narrative. A backward glance
at the scene in Book II mentioned earlier, for instance, reveals how Jim in
fact plays an active role in producing his own rejection. For starters, when he
leans in to kiss Ántonia he already knows full well that she is involved with
Larry Donovan and is thus predisposed to resist his physical advances. It is
also he who prompts Ántonia to lash out against his involvement with Lena.
When Ántonia refuses to continue making out with him, Jim immediately
insists that "Lena Lingard lets me kiss her," which effectively provokes Ántonia to proscribe such pleasures.[52] Note, however, that Jim's remark serves
as more than just an invitation for Ántonia's prohibitory response; it is also
in itself a hysterical complaint. In evoking Lena as he does here, Jim not only
makes his own dissatisfaction clear, but also positions Ántonia as lacking by
way of the comparison—a move by which he attempts to engage her envy
and desire for the "nonsense" he pursues with another woman.

Further evidence of the hysteria Jim brings to his relationship with Ántonia
emerges in Book IV, when he returns to Black Hawk for the summer after
finishing at Harvard. Over the course of Jim's visit, we witness the extent of
the effort he is willing to exert so as to guarantee that his love for Ántonia will
remain unconsummated. While at the end of this episode Jim affirms having
wanted "to have Ántonia for a sweetheart, or a wife," his earlier behavior on
betrays his anxiety at the prospect of realizing this wish.[53] Indeed, Jim's response to the news of Ántonia's failed relationship with Larry Donovan—and
by extension her renewed availability for marriage—is rather odd. Instead
of expressing anger with Donovan for having left Ántonia single, pregnant,
and destitute in Denver, Jim instead reports having felt "disappointed" with
Ántonia, callously noting how he is unable to "forgive her for becoming an
object of pity."[54] How to make sense of this sudden coldness on Jim's part,
this obstinate refusal to sympathize with Ántonia's plight? While it is far
from clear that Ántonia is in fact the "object of pity" Jim makes her out to be,
it is evident at this moment that she is once again *single* and thus available

for him to pursue should he so please. Signaling Jim's nervousness at this prospect is the way he uses the language of forgiveness in this passage. It is as though he feels Ántonia, having betrayed his trust that she would forever remain unavailable to him, now owes him an apology. Indeed, Ántonia's newfound spinsterhood might be the very reason Jim avoids her for the first half of his summer in Black Hawk, attempting "to shut [her] out of [his] mind." In fact, it isn't until he learns of how preoccupied Ántonia is with her newborn baby,[55] a child she "loves as dearly *as if she'd had a ring on her finger*,"[56] that Jim deigns to meet her face to face. In other words, it is only upon conceiving of Ántonia as once again unavailable—her love having been invested elsewhere, in her child—that Jim allows himself to see her.

If Jim's hysterical desire subtly subtends his interactions with Ántonia and his discursive characterization of Lena, it is perhaps most powerfully on view in his account of the dreams he describes at the end of Book II, just after Ántonia turns away from his embrace. Given the evocative effects produced by Jim's sequential narration of these two dreams, I quote from this passage at length:

> Toward morning I used to have pleasant dreams: sometimes Tony and I were out in the country, sliding down straw-stacks as we used to do; climbing up the yellow mountains over and over, and slipping down the smooth sides into soft piles of chaff.
>
> One dream I dreamed a great many times, and it was always the same. I was in a harvest-field full of shocks, and I was lying against one of them. Lena Lingard came across the stubble barefoot, in a short skirt, with a curved reaping-hook in her hand, and she was flushed like the dawn, with a kind of luminous rosiness all about her. She sat down beside me, turned to me with a soft sigh and said, "Now they are all gone, and I can kiss you as much as I like."
>
> I used to wish I could have this flattering dream about Ántonia, but I never did.[57]

At first glance, these two dreams might hardly seem hysterical, each depicting at least one rather clearly fulfilled wish. Noting that the dreams appear in Jim's narrative in such close proximity to his unsuccessful attempt to embrace Ántonia, we might take the first as responding to this event with a nostalgic wish to return to an earlier moment in his childhood friendship with Ántonia—that is, a moment in which the question of physical intimacy had yet to become problematic.[58] Or, approaching the first dream's manifest "text" as punning on the act of "rolling in the hay," we might even take it as the camouflaged expression of a much more sexually forward wish on Jim's part. Meanwhile, the wish fulfilled by Jim's second dream is all but self-evident, given the dream's overtly sexualized mise-en-scène: the erect corn "shocks," Lena's "short skirt" and "luminous rosiness," not to mention the seductive words she offers Jim. Desiring to be sexually "flattered" by Lena, Jim imagines a landscape in which no one else is around to proscribe such "nonsense" (as Ántonia has just done in the preceding scene).

But although Jim introduces these dreams as "pleasant," the single line of reflection he offers after summarizing them makes clear the hysterical dissatisfaction they induce when considered in sequence. Taken together rather than in isolation, the two dreams serve as the basis for a wish that neither of them satisfy: Jim's desire to have the second, more "flattering" dream be "about Ántonia" instead of Lena. By narrating the dreams in direct sequence, Jim facilitates their comparison—one that illuminates the dissatisfying elements of each. By contrast to the seductive scene taking place in the second dream, Jim's oneiric romp in the "straw-stacks" with Ántonia appears platonic, infantile, unexciting. At the same time, the allure of the second dream is significantly reduced by its narrative proximity to the first: that is, it features Lena rather than the more desirable Ántonia.[59] We might also note that the second dream—seductive as its content may seem—never fully realizes Jim's wish to kiss his lover. Instead, substituting in the dream for the physical act of kissing is the verbal description of it provided by Lena's speech. What's more, even this speech is itself equivocal with regard to Lena's *desire* to kiss Jim: in saying she "*can* kiss [him]," Lena doesn't actually say that she *wants* to do so. Jim's desire thus emerges from not only the first, but also the second of his two dreams as, to a considerable degree, unfulfilled. The wish enabled by this narrative sequence is perhaps none other than Jim's hysterical longing to engineer scenarios in which his desire will be frustrated.

HYSTERICAL FORM: THE UNKNOWABLE ORIGINS OF DESIRE IN *MY ÁNTONIA*

My suggestion so far has been that hysteria in the main text of *My Ántonia*—while it may appear to manifest first and foremost in the characters of Ántonia and Lena—is to be understood as a function of Jim's own narration and the structure of his desire that subtends it. Such is one of the significant ways in which *My Ántonia* could be said to resist conventional notions of hysteria as a feminine pathology: although hysterical, the novel's primary narrator is, after all, not a woman. And yet by embedding Jim's hysterical narrative within the frame of the Introduction, Cather takes this resistance to the gendering of hysteria—and, more broadly speaking, the gendering of desire—one step further. By presenting Jim's text as a work he creates at the urging of the Introduction's nameless narrator, Cather sets up the possibility that Jim's hysterical narration stems as much from the influence of his audience as himself. Earlier on, I argued it to be the narrator's narrative hysteria—

his or her desire for Jim's manuscript—that leads Jim to compose it. With this in mind, we cannot overlook how Jim may well have written relational malaise into his text for the purpose of paradoxically satisfying his reader's interest in reading an account of frustrated romance. To whom, then—Jim or the nameless narrator—can we attribute the wish for dissatisfied desire that consumes so many of the relationships depicted in the novel?

Insofar as it leads readers to such a question—which we may well be unable to answer definitively—the framed structure of *My Ántonia* might in itself be thought of as a form of hysterical resistance to masterful interpretations of desire in the novel. In other words, the framing of Jim's text by the novel's Introduction frustrates our interpretive wish to be certain about the nature of Jim's desire by preventing us from extricating that desire from the influence of the nameless narrator. Such a move has a considerable impact on our own interpretive desire as readers. As Lacan indicates, an interpretive or epistemic impulse of this kind is actually at the heart of desire itself: "desire becomes bound up at that junction with the Other's desire" where "*the desire to know* lies in this loop."[60] Lacan's comment allows us to understand the narrative frame of *My Ántonia* as more than just an intellectual exercise in that as it serves to performatively provoke our interpretive passion. Insofar as it prevents us from disentangling Jim's narration and the hysteria subtending it from that of the nameless narrator, Cather's narrative frame interminably frustrates our "desire to know" the structure of either character's desire on an individual basis.

My Ántonia's narrative frame might thus be thought of as one of the primary formal strategies whereby the novel resists interpretations seeking to understand Jim's desire by reference to categories of sexual orientation. By preventing us from knowing Jim's desire as his own, the novel's structure works against our interpreting and "orienting" desire in terms of categories—that is, "straight," "gay," and even "trans"—which assume an individual, gendered subject in whom desire originates. As daring as queer readings such as Fetterley's may have once seemed, the suggestion that Jim's desire be read as lesbian still assumes—in a way that may be unwarranted, given the formal structure of the novel—that his sexuality can be grounded in terms of his own individual identity. Implicit in the conceptual logic of lesbianism is an individual subject (and an object) to whom a gender can be ascribed. *My Ántonia* calls to question whether the desire that attends Jim's narrative can be known in such individualized and gendered terms by presenting both Jim's narrative and the desire subtending it as having been created under the influence of two authors—one identifiably male, the other not. As Butler notes, the collaborative authorship that emerges between Jim and the nameless narrator at the beginning of *My Ántonia* is one of the novel's innovations over which interpretation stumbles. In the reader's progression from the Introduction onto "Jim's" text, "it is unclear whether Jim has taken the place of [the nameless] narrator or whether the narrator now more fully possesses him."[61] It is perhaps by leading us to such interpretive impasses that *My Ántonia*'s formal hysteria most productively prompts us to revise how we conceive sexuality. As the collaboration of two or more authors, desire in *My Ántonia* might ultimately be thought of as an intersubjective enigma, belonging wholly to no one.

NOTES

1. Willa Cather, *My Ántonia*, ed. Doris Grumbach (1918; Boston: Houghton Mifflin, 1988), 2.

2. Mildred R. Bennett, *The World of Willa Cather* (Lincoln: University of Nebraska Press, 1961), 203.

3. Judith Roof, *Come As You Are: Sexuality and Narrative* (New York: Columbia University Press, 1996).

4. Note here that Roof's use of the term "heteroideological" can be understood as referring not only to the implicit heterosexism of the narratives she designates as such, but also their resolving of sexual "otherness" (or "hetero"-ness) into normative forms of sexual identity and relational structure.

5. Willa Cather, *My Ántonia*, Willa Cather Scholarly Edition, ed. Charles W. Mignon and Kari A. Ronning (Lincoln: University of Nebraska Press, 1994), xii.

6. Christopher Nealon, "Affect Genealogy: Feeling and Affiliation in Willa Cather," *American Literature* 69, no. 1 (1997): 6.

7. Willa Cather, *The Song of the Lark* (1915; New York: Dover, 2004). In *Willa Cather and the Politics of Criticism* (Lincoln: University of Nebraska Press, 2000), Joan Acocella observes just how incidental to the plot of *The Song of the Lark* this marriage is—incidental to the point of the reader's easily missing the fact that Thea and Fred do in fact become wed to each other.

8. Willa Cather, *Sapphira and the Slave Girl* (1940; New York: Vintage, 2010).

9. In *My Ántonia*, one thinks of not only Pavel and Peter, but also the more fleeting references to Mr. Shimerda's "love" for his musician friends in the "old country." See Cather, *My Ántonia*, 86.

10. See Acocella, *Willa Cather and the Politics of Criticism*.

11. One of Acocella's major claims is that queer and lesbian readings of Cather reflect an attempt to reclaim her work as central to the feminist canon—in spite of the challenging, sometimes misogynist views of women that Cather expressed. Ibid., 43–49.

12. Judith Butler, "'Dangerous Crossings': Willa Cather's Masculine Names," in *Bodies that Matter: On the Discursive Limits of "Sex"* (New York: Routledge, 1993), 143.

13. Susan J. Rosowski, "Willa Cather's Subverted Endings and Gendered Time," in *Cather Studies 5: Willa Cather's Ecological Imagination*, ed. Susan J. Rosowski (Lincoln: University of Nebraska Press, 2003), 76–77.

14. Cather, *My Ántonia*, 348.

15. Ibid., 357.

16. Timothy D. Adams, "My Gay Ántonia: The Politics of Willa Cather's Lesbianism," *Journal of Homosexuality* 12, no. 3–4 (1986): 89–98.

17. Judith Fetterley, "*My Ántonia*, Jim Burden, and the Dilemma of the Lesbian Writer," in *Lesbian Texts and Contexts: Radical Revisions*, ed. Karla Jay, Joanne Glasgow, and Catharine R. Stimpson (New York: New York University Press, 1990), 145–62.

18. Ibid., 153.

19. Sharon O'Brien, "Introduction," in *New Essays on My Ántonia*, ed. Sharon O'Brien (New York: Cambridge University Press, 1999), 21.

20. I would be remiss to describe this method of interpreting sexuality by way of cross-gendered identifications between characters without mentioning the work of Eve Sedgwick. In her influential book *Between Men: English Literature and Male Homosocial Desire* (New York: Columbia University Press, 1985), Sedgwick famously uses this method to analyze homoeroticism: desire is understood as intersubjective and displaceable, hence the possibility of understanding the heterosexual love two men feel for a woman as a displacement of a homoerotic attachment to each other. Such displacements abound in Sedgwick's reading of *The Professor's House* (1925) wherein we are encouraged to see Cather's lesbianism as having undergone two coded transformations in the making of her text—one across the axis of gender and another across the axis of object-choice. The result? A patently homoerotic relation between not two women, but two men: Professor Godfrey St. Peter and pupil Tom Outland. See Sedgwick, "Across Gender, Across Sexuality: Willa Cather and Others," *South Atlantic Quarterly* 88, no. 1 (1989): 53–72.

21. Jacques Lacan, *The Seminar of Jacques Lacan, Book XI: The Four Fundamental Concepts of Psychoanalysis, 1964–1965*, trans. Alan Sheridan (New York: Norton, 1981), 11.

22. Ibid.

23. At the beginning of *Seminar XI*, Lacan is unusually clear in opposing psychoanalysis to hermeneutics. For one of the most rigorous genealogies of hysteria published in recent years, see Patricia Gherovici, *Please Select Your Gender: From the Invention of Hysteria to the Democratizing of Transgenderism* (New York: Routledge, 2010), 41–65.

24. Ibid., 65.

25. Diana Fuss, *Identification Papers* (New York: Routledge, 1995), 23.

26. Mark Micale, *Approaching Hysteria: Disease and Its Interpretations* (Princeton, NJ: Princeton University Press, 1995), 166.

27. Gherovici, *Please Select Your Gender*, 57.

28. Ibid., 56.

29. Sigmund Freud, *The Standard Edition of the Complete Psychological Works of Sigmund Freud*, Vol. 4, Pt. 1: *The Interpretation of Dreams*, trans. James Strachey (1900; London: Hogarth Press, 1956), 147.

30. Jacques Lacan, *Écrits: The First Complete Edition in English*, trans. Bruce Fink (New York: Norton, 2006), 518.

31. In Lacanian theory, one way of understanding the concept of the "Other" (with a capital "O") is as the set of assumptions and expectations that an individual subject projects onto those "little others" (other people) with whom he or she interacts. In the clinic, it is often the analyst who embodies the Other for the patient insofar as the latter will transfer onto the relatively neutral figure of the analyst particular thoughts and feelings he or she has developed with regard to significant figures in his or her life, quoted as parents, lovers, and so on.

32. Lacan, *Seminar XI*, 12.

33. Lacan, *Écrits*, 518.

34. Fuss, *Identification Papers*, 31.

35. Cather, *My Ántonia*, xi.

36. Ibid., x.

37. Ibid., xii.

38. Ibid., xi.

39. Butler, *Bodies that Matter*, 147.

40. Peter Brooks, *Reading for the Plot: Design and Intention in Narrative* (Cambridge, MA: Harvard University Press, 1992), 104.

41. Toward the end of the 1918 Introduction, the narrator enigmatically notes that Jim "had had opportunities [with Ántonia] that I, *as a little girl* who watched her come and go, had not" (Cather, *My Ántonia*, ed. Grumbach, xii–xiii; italics mine). The ambiguity of the passage leaves us uncertain as to whether it is the narrator's age, her gender, or some combination of the two that limits her "opportunities" with Ántonia. Similarly, the precise nature of these "opportunities"—are they chances at romance? friendship?—is never specified.

42. Butler, *Bodies that Matter*, 148–49.

43. Cather, *My Ántonia*, 25.

44. Ibid., 216–17.

45. Ibid., 217.

46. Ibid., 160.

47. Ibid., 161.

48. Ibid., 162–63.

49. Ibid., 282.

50. Ibid., 258–61.

51. Ibid., 284–85.

52. Ibid., 217.

53. Indeed, Jim's awkward use of the past perfect to phrase this wish—to have had Ántonia as a "sweetheart"—can be seen as reflecting a hysterical wish. That is, Jim constructs the possibility of his romancing Ántonia as a chance long gone in spite of the fact that at this moment in his narrative the opportunity is still open. Ibid., 312.

54. Ibid., 290.

55. Ibid., 295–96.

56. Ibid., 309–10; my italics.

57. Ibid., 218.

58. Indeed, connections might be drawn between material in Jim's dream—notably, the "yellow mountains" with their steep, "smooth sides"—and Jim's very first

excursion on the prairie with Ántonia, in which they come to the edge of a "steep drawside" and look out at the "gold tree tops" below. Ibid., 24.

59. Lena's desirability in the dream is further complicated by the "reaping hook" she carries. It is by way of this attribute that Jim's unconscious links her to Crazy Mary, the unsavory wife of Ole Benson who attacks Lena with the same weapon (a "corn knife") earlier in the book. Ibid., 161.

60. Lacan, *Écrits*, 679; my italics.

61. Butler, *Bodies that Matter*, 147–48.

Chapter Ten

The Image of Nature in the Past in *My Ántonia*

Fangyuan Xi

Cather is known for her famous Nebraska novels, as well as her descriptions and representations of the American West. Most of Cather's novels are based on her childhood memories of Willow Shade, the Nebraska prairie, and Red Cloud. When writing novels, she felt the power of uprooted memories in her mind. However, she also drew upon her perceptions of Native American culture to define her views of nature and the idea that nature evokes the past as well as an interactive principle between humans and nature. While most of her readers have focused on the content of her memories,[1] the devices by which Cather uses nature to connect past, present, and future have not been interpreted sufficiently. Specifically, Cather uses the train journey and a process of losing the self in nature to develop her biotic theory of human connection to nature and the historical past. Above all, the way Cather depicts nature *as* the past, without giving any impression of abruptness and contradiction, is crucial because it leads us to understand the effect of her skillful renditions of individual growth through nature.

Some writers prefer to use phantasmagorical images to reflect the psychological world of the character or to present the past memory and the past story, while others use the dramatic monologue to display characters' feelings and to describe what happened in the past. Cather, however, does not adopt these styles. Instead of using dreams or dramatic monologue, she employs two intricate and delicate media to connect the present world with the past: the train, as connective journey, and human immersion in land as a process of loss and reconstruction. These media recur throughout Cather's works, and comparing how they function allows us to analyze an ecocritical sensibility rooted in both industrial and primitive symbolism.

This chapter investigates how the image of nature in the past is represented in Cather's *My Ántonia* and her other works. The first part of this chapter aims to interpret how the image of the train acts as a direct means to connect the past and the present, or bring the protagonist back to the past, while the second part will discuss the way Cather employs a remarkable method to represent the relationship between the character and the surrounding landscape. As a whole, this chapter explicates and interprets Cather's intention to situate nature in the past and by doing so reject the detachment from nature that both the train and the outside observer of the traveler might at first suggest.

THE IMAGE OF THE TRAIN

In this section, the various functions of the image of the train in Cather's novels and stories will be discussed. The image of the train represents on the one hand social change during nineteenth-century America, and, on the other hand, a new relationship to landscape and nature. Moreover, I investigate the narrative effect of the train and the way in which the image of the train reinforces the connection to the past.

Trains played an important role in Cather's life. As Mark Facknitz observes, Cather's seventy-four years align precisely with the golden age for the development of the railroad: "Cather was born four years after the completion of the Transcontinental Railroad, and by the time she died the railroads were already beginning to wane, giving way to highways."[2] In Cather's early short stories, the train, as one of the most important methods of transportation, frequently appears. For instance, at the beginning of "The Bohemian Girl,"[3] "The trans-continental express swung along the windings of the Sand River Valley,"[4] and in "The Sculpture's Funeral,"[5] "The night express shot, red as a rocket, out of the eastward marsh lands, and wound along the river shore under the long lines of shivering poplars that sentineled the meadows, the escaping steam hanging in gray masses against the pale sky and blotting out the Milky Way."[6] Cather observes the social changes that the railroad brought, but rather than resist modern industrial civilization, she subtly and unobtrusively integrates the image of the train into the text.

The railroad, as a product of modern civilization, exerted a significant influence on American society during the nineteenth century. It reduced the distances between different places. Bringing the industrial civilization to the traditional primitive villages and transporting labor forces to cities, it demonstrates human yearning for a prosperous and wealthy civilized city.

In *The Machine in the Garden*, Leo Marx points out that the development of the machine is a symbolic instrument of power, and the train is the embodiment of human triumph over nature:

In the 1830's the locomotive, an iron horse or fire-Titan, is becoming a kind of national obsession. It is the embodiment of the age, an instrument of power, speed, noise, fire, iron, smoke—at once a testament to the will of man rising over natural obstacles, and, yet, confined by its iron rails to a pre-determined path, it suggests a new sort of fate.[7]

Referring to the historical context of the time, "with the trains Cather implies a network of journeys and transferences."[8] As the important transportation in the Midwest, the trains bring the migrants to settle in the prairie and develop the West.

The train not only changed people's way of life and people's perception of space, but also shaped the surrounding landscape. William Cronon argues that during the second half of the nineteenth century, the American landscape was transformed in many respects. According to him, the rise of the railroad, especially the completion of the Transcontinental Railroad, exerted a great influence on every aspect of society and even on the landscape of America at that time. Viewing the railroad as a combination of first nature (original prehuman nature) and second nature (artificial nature), he argues that "[humans] assimilated the railroad to the doctrine of natural advantages, merging first and second nature so that the two became almost indistinguishable,"[9] and that "wherever the rails went, they brought sudden sweeping change to the landscapes and communities through which they passed."[10]

Marx remarks that the description of the train crossing the wilderness or the machine appearing suddenly in the forest is a symbolic metaphor in the landscape for the intrusion of civilization into the primitive natural world. It also constructs a contrast between the urban and the pastoral: "it is a variation upon the contrast between two worlds, one identified with rural peace and simplicity, the other with urban power and sophistication, which has been used by writers working in the pastoral mode since the time of Virgil."[11] The train is the quintessential machine in the garden. Marx observes that this symbolic landscape appears frequently in nineteenth-century American literary works: "The ominous sounds of machines . . . reverberate endlessly in our literature,"[12] which attracts many writers: "indeed it is difficult to think of a major American writer upon whom the image of the machine's sudden appearance in the landscape has not exercised its fascination."[13]

By dwelling on train imagery, Cather integrates the rural landscape and the industrialized one in her novels. She does not resist modern urban culture when depicting landscapes. In Cather's novels, the country and urban spaces are connected as well as the landscapes of civilization and wilderness. The train is the metaphor for the connection or merge of these two aspects and even pushes forward the plot development and narrative effect. Take "Paul's Case"[14] as an example. Paul takes a train to New York, the big city that he is always longing to visit, and commits suicide by jumping off the train. Or in *O Pioneers!*,[15] Carl Linstrum takes the train back from the East to the Midwest Nebraska prairie with the purpose of marrying Alexandra at the end of the novel. As is seen in these scenes, by means of the train, the different places and landscapes, or the wilderness and the civilization, the country and the city are connected and juxtaposed in one story. The train, by changing people's way of life and humans' perception of space, symbolizes the infusion of industrial civilization into the primitive natural wilderness. In addition to this function of the metaphor, the image of the train embodies the image of nature in the past by connecting past and present in the journey to establish and strengthen the pastoral and nostalgic atmosphere in the novels.

My Ántonia is generally considered one of Cather's most successful novels about the frontier and has established her fame in American literature. In the beginning of the novel, Jim Burden, a middle-aged legal counsel for Western railways in New York, travels back to a Nebraska town where he had spent his childhood with Ántonia. Jim Burden and the narrator "I" are sitting in the train, and the landscape outside the train reminds them of their childhood experience:

> While the train flashed through never-ending miles of ripe wheat, by country towns and bright-flowered pastures and oak groves wilting in the sun, we sat in the observation car, where the woodwork was hot to touch and red dust lay deep over everything. The dust and heat, the burning wind, reminded us of many things.[16]

It is the train that combines the original nature with the artificial nature, namely the landscape outside the observation car with the hot woodwork covered with red dust inside. In this scene, the train, a symbol of the intrusion of modern industrial civilization into the wilderness and the natural world, embodies human triumph over nature. Facknitz thinks the train leads the narrative into two directions: first, it delivers Jim to escape to the nostalgia-infused West and "Ántonia's garden"; second, the train "moves east and penetrates through the geographical, social, and class distances that separated Burden from Ántonia."[17] In addition to this metaphor and narrative effect, the image of the train connects the present with the past. If life is like a long journey, recollection is almost similar to taking a train into the past with the previous landscape reviving once again. In this sense, the train can transport people not only in space, but also in time. Like a time machine, it takes the characters back into the past or forward into the future in Cather's novels. At the beginning of the story, the orphan child Jim travels to the Nebraska prairie for the first time to meet his grandparents. The train acts as an agency, a medium that brings Jim from the present into the past, from the East to the West, from his middle age to his childhood.

The same occurrence can be seen in another short story, "The Treasure of Far Island,"[18] in which the train serves as an important agency connecting the present to the past. The story begins with the famous young playwright Douglass Burnham taking the train back to his old Nebraska home, recalling his childhood memories and friendships:

> As the train rumbled over a trestle built above a hollow grown up with sunflowers and ironweed, he sniffed with delight the rank odor, familiar to the prairie bred man, that is exhaled by such places as evening approaches. . . . I'm getting home sure enough. And heavens! there's the island, Far Island, the Ultima Thule; and the arched tree, and Spy Glass Hill, and the Silvery Beaches; my heart's going like a boy's.[19]

The train from the East, swinging into the valley, is akin to the train in *My Ántonia*, moving from civilization into the country filled with childhood memories. Like Jim, Douglass is taking the train from the East back to his hometown in Empire City, Nebraska, where he had spent his innocent childhood days twelve years ago. The train acts as the agency and a tool for the protagonist to revisit his childhood. He delights in watching the shining curves of the river and is excited when sniffing the familiar odor of the prairie. His childhood experience is to be revived, and time is to flow backward in this episode.

The short story clarifies the meaning of the train as a journey backward in personal time. The familiar names of place bring forth nostalgic yearning in his mind. At the end of the story, we realize that the whole plot was constructed by the protagonist's recollection of his childhood experience and friendship. The next day after his arrival, Douglass goes to a party with the locals and meets his old childhood friend Margie, when their childhood memories are revived. Douglass and Margie talk and recall the good old days, until Douglass asks Margie if they can go back to Far Island where they used to play as children together. They venture out and dig up the treasures that they had buried there in their childhood. They are satisfied with the fantastic experience they used to have on the island, and Douglass feels that it is so real that he seems to go back to his childhood again: "He felt as a boy might feel who had lost all his favorite marbles and his best pea shooter and the dog that slept with him, and had found them all again. He tried to follow, step by step, the wonderful friendship of his childhood."[20]

Similar to *My Ántonia*, throughout the whole story the train works as an agency that brings the protagonist back to his childhood, where he can recapitulate and rejoice the nostalgic places and the good old days all over again. In a word, by using the image of the train, Cather directly connects the country and the city, and the present and the past together. Published in 1918 and looking back at the late nineteenth century, Cather's faith in connective devices proliferates. The journey backward in time and space to an open prairie in fact rearranges the relationship between human and nature, overcoming the detachment that occurs in a postindustrial context.

As Facknitz points out, it is the train, the device of much importance, that connects the different places, fulfilling the urge of migration,[21] which Urgo claims to be "the keystone of American existence."[22] The train as a metaphor directly or indirectly influences Cather's writing. Based on her own experience, she introduces the railroad, the transportation system of the time, into the landscape to enlarge the space and the mobility of the novel. It is the "trains not wagons [that] bring Cather's migrants westward to the prairie; eastward, trains take them to education, careers, money, war, and European culture."[23] With the help of the train, the space is enlarged and becomes mobile rather than static in the novel.

Although Cather emphasizes mobility and migration to the new place, she does not advocate abandoning the past. Urgo believes that Cather's emphasis on transit or migration hinges on the idea of forgetting the past: "her emphasis on transit—including the great fact of migration—reinforces the idea that the past must often be forgotten if one is to succeed in transferring self and value to a new environment."[24] It's true that Cather migrated from Nebraska to Pittsburg then to New York; however, she frequently returned to Nebraska or the American Southwest to search for the past. She was concerned more with connection to the past, as she argues in "Escapism": "fired with some more vital feeling than contempt, you will see how automatically the old and false makes itself air before the new and true."[25] For Cather, the connection to the past that is built by the train is more vital than separation.

THE CHARACTER AND THE LANDSCAPE

When we come to a prairie, we feel a sense of freedom. When we live in the city, we are aware of the noise. Similar to nonhuman animals, humans have a sense of space, and in the context of this spatial awareness, humans comprehend the world rationally. Cather used her fiction to revisit many places in her life; a sensitive writer who captures the sentiment exquisitely, she observes, smells, and feels places. In *My Ántonia*, the train brings Jim back to Ántonia and to the prairie, and then the train "delivers the body to a still center, a place at which he conceives of the utter absence of being, as if the train could still bring one to a threshold of wilderness."[26] Jim's experience in the prairie intersects with another related topic—how Cather theorizes the relationship between the character and the landscape.

Travel between locations seems to have fueled Cather's abilities to consider connective devices. Martha Robertson compares Cather to a famous American painter Georgia O'Keeffe and mentions that "*Death Comes for the Archbishop* (1927) was Cather's last novel set in the American Southwest, whereas O'Keeffe continued to live and work in New Mexico until her death in 1986."[27] Although Cather visited the Nebraska prairie and the American Southwest many times, indulged in the primitive beauty of the wilderness, and invested strong emotion in the landscape, she did not choose to spend the rest of her life in Nebraska or in the Southwest and, unlike O'Keeffe, returned to New York City. For Cather, Nebraska is her hometown, where she grew up in her childhood; meanwhile, Nebraska is also the destination for her traveling, where she as an adult stayed for only short-term visits. It is these two different identities and perspectives in these places that help Cather experience the delicate difference between inside and outside the place, which situates her interest in the interrelationship between humans and the landscape: "from the outside you look upon a place as a traveller might look upon a town from a distance; from the inside you experience a place, are surrounded by it, and part of it."[28]

Cather does not only describe the landscape, but also depicts the emotional relationship between the landscape and humans. When writing these novels, she pays much attention to the way characters in the novels perceive the landscape, nature, and surrounding spaces. Their perceptions frequently have a symbolic meaning in her novels. This section will discuss the way Cather represents the past and nature by portraying the natural landscape and by describing the relationship between the character and the landscape.

The emergence and the development of the term "landscape" are inextricably associated with the development of the human's inner self. The term "landscape," according to the *Oxford English Dictionary*, was first used in 1603, signifying the scenery in a painting: "A picture representing natural inland scenery." From 1725, "landscape" began to signify the land or natural scenery perceived through an individual's viewpoint: "A view or prospect of natural inland scenery, such as can be taken in at a glance from one point of view." Considering the historical background at that time, such as the development of modern science, the Reformation, and the industrialization and the commercialization of society, it is not surprising to see the evolution and development of the word "landscape." From that time on, humans began to realize their own points of view, created and modified by their own inner selves, and began to be segregated and separated from nature. According to J. H. Van den Berg, the Dutch psychiatrist, the birth of nature is inseparably associated with human consciousness of inner self. He takes Da Vinci's world famous painting *Mona Lisa* as an example. He believes that *Mona Lisa* and Luther's manuscript embody the same spiritual expressions. Mona Lisa's smile, in his view, is a sign of the abundant inner world and the secret, hidden inner self. Furthermore, he points out that the landscape in this painting has extraordinary significance, which symbolizes human's estrangement from nature:

> At the same time she [Mona Lisa] is the first (it is unavoidable) who was estranged from the landscape. The landscape behind her is justly famous; it is the first landscape painted as a landscape, just because it was a landscape. A pure landscape, not just a backdrop for human actions: nature, nature as the middle ages did not know it, an exterior nature closed within itself and self-sufficient, an exterior from which the human element has, in principle, been removed entirely.[29]

"Landscape," as natural scenery from the human viewpoint, separates the human from nature and destroys the original bond between human and nature. In the introduction of *Landscape and Memory*, Simon Schama voices a similar assertion: "For although we are accustomed to separate nature and human perception into two realms, they are, in fact, indivisible."[30] Leslie Marmon Silko also maintains that the term "landscape" is actually misleading: "So long as the human consciousness remains within the hills, canyons, cliffs, and the plants, clouds, and sky, the term landscape, as it has entered the English language, is misleading."[31] Silko believes that the relationship between humans and their surroundings is not correctly described by a portion of territory, for when humans stand on a mountain peak or a high mesa edge, they already become a part of the surroundings. So the term "landscape" is misleading because it is based on dualism of the subject and the object, or the viewer and the view, as well as on homocentrism of the dominant human and the subordinate surroundings: "This assumes the viewer is somehow outside or separate from the territory he or she surveys. Viewers are as much a part of the landscape as the boulders they stand on. There is no high mesa edge or mountain peak where one can stand and not immediately be part of all that surrounds."[32]

In Cather's novels, humans' separation from and integration with the surrounding landscape are of great significance, which deserves discussion and analysis. Cather occasionally allows the characters to merge into the landscape as a part of it, while sometimes keeping them out of and detached from the landscape as a viewer or an outsider. She displays these two distinct depictions delicately and exquisitely. When the character is merged into the landscape, gradually losing his or her selfhood, he or she sometimes comes up with half collective memories of the historical landscape—the landscape that tells about what happened there in the past. This sympathy between the character and the surrounding landscape in the past forms one of Cather's important ways of representing the past and nature in her novels.

In "Dangerous Crossings: Historical Dimensions of Landscape in Willa Cather's *My Ántonia, The Professor's House,* and *Death Comes for the Archibishop*," Carol Steinhagen classifies the dangerous crossings that appear frequently in Cather's three representative novels: "movement from one geographical region to another, movement from one isolating shelter like attic rooms into society, movement from conception to art, and movement from life to death."[33] What she regards as the most dangerous crossing is the one that leads man into the realm of all-ness. This is dangerous because it diminishes the self in modern society, separating it from the historical background that allows it to experience the collective memory. In a sense, the dissolution of the ego or consciousness means the death of the individual and the inner self:

> To truly cross into the realm of all-ness is dangerous because it separates the individual from those literary and historical forces that have given her a sense of selfhood and allowed her to participate in the collective memory that has created a shared sense of landscape. It is, as Cather recognized, a kind of self-destruction.[34]

The self-destruction here means the loss of the inner self, the vanishing of the subjective ego. When a human being keeps selfhood awake, he or she is finally estranged from the landscape. When one completely merges into the landscape, one's inner self is lost and unable to feel anything around it, and one can achieve a sense of oneness with nature, gain sympathy with the landscape, and experience a land and participate in the collective memories engraved in the landscape. Steinhagen's term of the "dangerous crossings" is a thought-provoking perspective that raises ideas about the relationship between human and the landscape in Cather's novels. There are many other such dangerous crossings in her works than what Steinhagen deals with in her article. In *My Ántonia*, there are some other episodes that also represent the way a character participates in the collective memory and the historical landscape. For example, Jim's experience in the garden and Jim's illusion of the motion in the red grass demonstrate not only Jim's journey to a personal past, but also to a historical past. Furthermore, whereas Steinhagen discusses Jim's dangerous crossings in the novel, his separation from the landscape is ignored. In fact, however, Jim's first visit to the Nebraska prairie is actually a typical example of his separation from the landscape as an observer.

JIM BURDEN'S EXPERIENCE IN *MY ÁNTONIA*

My Ántonia begins with the story of Jim Burden, a ten-year-old orphan who moves from Virginia to the West to live with his grandparents in Black Hawk,

Nebraska. As a boy who lived in pastoral Virginia for ten years, Jim has only a limited experience in the world, and the wilderness and emptiness of the Nebraska landscape overwhelm him the moment he arrives in the Nebraska prairie at night. Jim's first impression of the prairie is detached:

> There seemed to be nothing to see; no fences, no creeks or trees, no hills or fields. If there was a road, I could not make it out in the faint starlight. There was nothing but land: not a country at all, but the material out of which countries are made.[35]

Jim's first impression of Nebraska is described when he "peered over the side of the wagon."[36] Obviously, the episode is narrated from the viewpoint of Jim as a traveler or an outside observer because Jim looks on the place from a distance. He feels literally separated from the landscape, not yet experiencing the place from inside. He claims that the Nebraska prairie as a natural scenery or an alienated object is something he has never seen before. He realizes that the scenery here is very different from the pastoral scenery in Virginia; there is no fence, no creek, and no mountain or trees here. The empty and primitive prairie changes his inherent and familiar aesthetics of the landscape. Jim's encounter with the wilderness and the primitiveness of the prairie symbolizes humans' yearning to return to the early primitive stage where human beings and nature are still together, which is derived from Cather's own experience.

Although Cather was not an orphan like Jim, her visit to the Nebraska prairie and Jim's obviously overlap. She herself had an impression that is very similar to his: "The land was open range and there was almost no fencing. As we drove further and further out into the country, I felt a good deal as if we had come to the end of everything—it was a kind of erasure of personality."[37] Young Cather was apparently overwhelmed by the primitive landscape of the prairie because it was so vast that she felt her own self shrink into nothingness. In other words, she felt as if she reached the boundary between human and nature, and her consciousness of her inner self disappeared.

Jim deeply feels the mysterious power of the prairie as he stays there, just like Cather did: "I had the feeling that the world was left behind, that we had got over the edge of it, and were outside man's jurisdiction."[38] Jim regards this place as being beyond human control, and he further describes this feeling: "Between that earth and that sky I felt erased, blotted out."[39] Steinhagen asserts that the word "erased" is symbolic and meaningful because it "suggests not just a dangerous but a fatal crossing into a world without landscape."[40] Jim's inner self is so overwhelmed by the vast and immense wilderness of the prairie that it is on the verge of being extinguished.

Jim's mind continues to be profoundly impressed by the Nebraska prairie as the plot develops, but in it he detects motion akin to the railroad journey, which reconstructs the contours of the land as well as the self. He begins to explore his new surroundings to find a larger cornfield and a sorghum patch. Walking westward, he finds out that as far as his eyes can reach there is nothing but rough shaggy red grass as tall as he is. Standing among the tall red grass, he has other impressions of the prairie as follows:

> As I looked about me I felt that the grass was the country, as the water is the sea. The red of the grass made all the great prairie the color of wine-stains, or of certain seaweeds when they are first washed up. And there was so much motion in it; the whole country seemed, somehow, to be running.[41]

> I can remember exactly how the country looked to me as I walked beside my grandmother along the faint wagon-tracks on that early September morning. Perhaps the glide of long railway travel was still with me, for more than anything else I felt motion in the landscape, in the fresh, easy-blowing morning wind, and in the earth itself, as if the shaggy grass were a sort of loose hide, and underneath it herds of wild buffalo were galloping, galloping.[42]

The motion in the landscape becomes a critical metaphor in the novel. It is not realistic for a ten-year-old boy to have this shrewd intuition or deep insight about the land. The description of the grassland cited here seems to be more of the voice of the author herself than Jim's. Cather first visited the Nebraska prairie in 1883 at the age of nine. Almost thirty years later, before she gave up her work in *McClure's* to concentrate on writing, she made a trip to the Southwest again in 1912. The journey to the West made Cather recollect her childhood memories, to which she began to be devoted. Presumably she attained a new realization of a series of events in American history, including the different social changes that happened in her lifetime, and the influence of the Westward Movement, which she employed as the background of the plots in her novels. After she came back to New York, she composed a series of prairie novels, including the most influential *O Pioneers!* and *My Ántonia*.

The land where Jim Burden stands does not actually quake but he intuits that it once did. What makes the description remarkable is that a historical connotation is hidden in the landscape: the motion in the landscape is in fact an implication of the Westward Movement. The story of *My Ántonia* is based on young Cather's memory of the Nebraska prairie in 1883. When Cather first visited there, the herds of wild buffalo could not be seen anymore. But around ten years before, there were plenty of them as well as other wildlife running freely on the land, making the land seem to shake. What Jim is hearing and feeling is a situation that existed ten years before in the Nebraska prairie. Since then, the Westward Movement had made the place the frontier between the wilderness and the civilization. The motion in the landscape is the product of Jim's imagination, which demonstrates the process of conquering the wildness in American history.

As he is standing among the red grasses and indulging himself in the amazing landscape, Jim attains this historical connotation through his integration into the landscape and the diminishment of his consciousness. The paragraph between these two quotations fully explains what happens in his mind: "I had almost forgotten that I had a grandmother, when she came out, her sunbonnet on her head, a grain-sack in her hand, and asked me if I did not want to go to the garden with her to dig potatoes for dinner."[43] Jim admits that he had nearly forgotten the fact that he was with his grandmother there. This shows that he is so much enchanted by the landscape that he becomes unconscious and forgets things around him. As the scene when Jim arrives at the Nebraska prairie and observes the surrounding landscape as a viewer, this episode also suggests that his consciousness of an inner self starts to disappear and begins to be merged with the historic landscape as a part of it.

On some occasions, Jim loses his self to be a part of the landscape, while on others he is aware of the surrounding environment as an observer. Cather applies this ambiguity to represent an intricate relationship, which might be called the corresponding sympathy or the imaginary empathy, between humans and the landscape. This sympathy is transient, yet it provides Jim with the past story of the landscape to show the reader through his imagination the scenery of the Nebraska prairie of the past when the buffalos were still galloping there.

What Jim has imaginatively seen in the red grass leads him into the depth of the wilderness. He believes that if he goes further through the red grass, he would reach the end of the world where only the sun and the sky would exist and he would fly like a tawny hawk. Jim indulges himself in his imaginary perception of the red grass and becomes so sympathetically united with the prairie that he becomes unaware of almost everything until his grandmother suggests to him to go to her garden. He goes there a quarter mile away from the house and tells his grandmother that he would like to stay up there for a while. He feels content that he will be left alone in the garden so that he can enjoy the new feeling of lightness. He sits down and leans his back against a warm yellow pumpkin in the middle of the garden, dissolving into the landscape and the surrounding natural scenery again:

> All about me giant grasshoppers, twice as big as any I had ever seen, were do-
> ing acrobatic feats among the dried vines. The gophers scurried up and down
> the ploughed ground. There in the sheltered draw-bottom the wind did not blow
> very hard, but I could hear it singing its humming tune up on the level, and I
> could see the tall grasses wave. The earth was warm under me, and warm as I

crumbled it through my fingers. Queer little red bugs came out and moved in slow squadrons around me. Their backs were polished vermilion, with black spots. I kept as still as I could. Nothing happened. I did not expect anything to happen. I was something that lay under the sun and felt it, like the pumpkins, and I did not want to be anything more. I was entirely happy. Perhaps we feel like that when we die and become a part of something entire, whether it is sun and air, or goodness and knowledge. At any rate, that is happiness; to be dissolved into something complete and great. When it comes to one, it comes as naturally as sleep.[44]

Compared to the scene of the waving red grass, Jim's perception of nature in his grandmother's garden is more comprehensive and profound. According to Steinhagen, this situation provides Jim with an opportunity to cross into some new imaginative viewpoint: "At this primitive stage in his own life history Jim Burden is open to the opportunity for a 'natural' cessation of consciousness, an effortless crossing into the realm of all-ness that he experiences in his grandmother's garden."[45] By crossing into there, Jim merges into the surroundings and gains more profound realization of the history of the landscape. While his experience in the red grass relates to the vast prairie only in a historical sense, his experience in the garden recapitulates the evolution of organisms. He sees the insects, grasses, vines, feels the earth, hears the wind. He is completely absorbed into the natural landscape and realizes the whole ecosystem is interdependently and organically operated with human beings included.

Humans have always considered themselves the rational creatures. With the rapid development of industrialization and urbanization, the rational human beings insist that they are superior to other creatures because they have knowledge and reason and begin to conquer, transform, and sometimes exploit nature. The organically equal and profoundly varied natural world was replaced by the binary opposition of human and nature. However, when Jim considers himself to be only "something that lay under the sun and felt it, like the pumpkins," his inner self shrinks considerably and is freed from reason and knowledge. He gradually dissolves into the organic natural world to perceive and realize that he is at the mercy of the system of the whole ecological world as much as the animals, plants, and other organisms. According to Aldo Leopold, human beings only serve as one part of the biological chain. He argues "the community concept" and "the land ethic" as follows:

Man is, in fact, only a member of a biotic team is shown by an ecological interpretation of history. Many historical events, hitherto explained solely in terms of human enterprise, were actually biotic interactions between people and land. The characteristics of the land determined the facts quite as potently as the characteristics of the men who lived on it.[46]

Through Jim's epiphany in the garden, Cather recovers and restores the essential, biotic relationship between human and nature. The world that Jim perceives and experiences in the garden is the one where humans are restored to nature, the one that presumably existed and was sustained before the emergence of human knowledge and art. Along with Jim's other perception of the landscape in the novel, these two episodes in the initial part illustrate Cather's remarkably deliberate way of restoring the relationship between the character and the landscape.

NATURE IN THE PAST

Through the protagonist's encounter and sympathy with the landscape, Cather represents nature in her novels with its own old story that has been forgotten to be recollected by humans. Cather's location of nature in the past provides the reader with an occasion to experience retrospectively the relationship between human and nature in ancient times and introspect the one in modern times. For this theme Cather drew inspiration from her interpretation of Native American culture as well as her own memories of open space.

As Holly Blackford discusses in the introduction, Cather, like her contemporaries, interpreted Native American culture archeologically as an authentic past culture more holistically biotic in its interactions with nature and landscape. In part I of *The Song of the Lark*,[47] Ray's comments on the modern people's misconception of the Native American are telling of Cather's own views. Living for a long time in Mexico and knowing much about the people, he approves of their natural way of living and believes that modern people misjudge them. He sniffs at the remarks in the geography book that the Native Americans mastered the art of forging metals and cut houses out of rock by using metals. He believes that civilization, in the real sense, began with metals: "I guess civilization proper began when men mastered metals."[48] Since humans mastered the art of forging metals, they have always been determined to control and alter nature, whereas, in his view, Native Americans never attempted to learn that art. Ray's statement, so to speak, is of satire or irony, which on the one hand foreshadows Thea's experience in Panther Canyon, and on the other arouses a reflection on the human-nature relationship ranging from ancient to modern times, sentiments tied to early twentieth-century interpretations of Native American culture and ruins in the Southwest.

Contemporary Native American writer Leslie Marmon Silko follows and promotes a similar line of thought, locating a more significant relationship with nature in less modernized cultures. She compares the Pueblo people with technologically advanced cultures in terms of how they view and treat nature.

Her thoughts help us interpret the reason why Cather frequently equates biotic theories of human-land interaction with the Pueblo people. According to Silko, the term "landscape" misleads us with respect to human-nature relationships. Silko discusses the ancient Pueblo's imagination and their modest attitudes to nature, which reminds us of another way of man's living in the past:

> Standing deep within the natural world, the ancient Pueblo understood the thing as it was—the squash blossom, grasshopper, or rabbit itself could never be created by the human hand. Ancient Pueblos took the modest view that the thing itself (the landscape) could not be improved upon. The ancients did not presume to tamper with what had already been created. Thus realism, as we now recognize it in painting and sculpture, did not catch the imaginations of Pueblo people until recently.[49]

Silko supposes that, although modern cultures partially appreciate the art of the ancient Pueblo people through their apparently simple and ingenuous painting or sculpture, they still do not understand fully the natural imagination. Traditional Pueblo perspectives evince a distinct way of viewing and treating nature, which is profoundly different from the way of technologically advanced societies. Respecting and esteeming nature with a humble and modest attitude, traditional Pueblo individuals recognize a natural law rather than seek to conquer, change, improve, and disturb nature.

Silko's remarks remind us of Cather's view, expressed in *Death Comes for the Archbishop*, of how Native American and European settlers treat nature differently:[50]

> Father Latour judged that, just as it was the white man's way to assert himself in any landscape, to change it, make it over a little (at least to leave some mark or memorial of his sojourn), it was the Indian's way to pass through a country without disturbing anything; to pass and leave no trace, like fish through the water, or birds through the air.[51]

> It was the Indian manner to vanish into the landscape, not to stand out against it. The Hopi villages that were set upon rock mesas were made to look like the rock on which they sat, were imperceptible at a distance.[52]

Cather equates "the Indian's way" and "the Indian manner" with valuing embeddedness in land more than domination. The Native American and the European approach create completely different ways of treating nature. The former consider themselves a part of nature and try to discern and obey its law, conforming to the surroundings of the natural environment. On the other hand, the settlers change the natural law and have nature work for and serve human beings. In Cather's view, the European tendency to dominate rather than interact with nature is a human-centered, damaged worldview and an anthropocentric way of thinking. Just as, Steedman articulates, the inner self became important in the early twentieth-century theory of human subjectivity,[53] modern psychology separated the human self from nature, viewing and evaluating nature as an object apart from individuals. Cather traces this to history, arguing that the art of forging metals and the development of industrial civilization largely increased humans' desire to conquer and improve nature in order to make it serve human need. Cather's intention of making comments on the contrast between the Native American and the modern people is to lead us to reflect on modern people's attitudes to and treatment of nature as well as the discrepancy between human and nature.

In a word, what Cather emphasizes more is the nature of the past and the connection between ancient and modern times, which also explains why Cather used the train as the time machine device to enhance this connection. In "Mesa Verde Wonderland Is Easy to Reach," Cather shows her belief that the train takes people to the places that were previously difficult to reach, bringing the great convenience and enjoyment of modern times: "The journey to the Mesa Verde, which was a hard one in Nordenskjöld's time, is now a very easy one, and the railways runs within thirty miles of the Mesa."[54] The Mesa Verde is not "an inconveniently situated museum," and it tells us the "story of an early race, of the social and religious life of a people indigenous to the soil."[55] With the help of the railways, the modernized transportation device, the remote Mesa Verde is no longer inconvenient; meanwhile, during the journey, the natural scenery brings aesthetic enjoyment to people and the historical landscape brings them back to ancient times. For Cather, this historical enjoyment and connection are vital and significant, raising people's consciousness of the completely different mode of life between ancient Pueblo and modern Americans. The Mesa people were "absolutely unenterprising in the modern American sense";[56] however, their personal attitude toward and interpretation of nature demand the deepest reflection and consideration.

NOTES

1. Latrobe Carroll did an interview with Cather after the publication of *My Ántonia*, and during this interview Cather talked about the vast influence of her childhood memory to her writings: "the memory that goes with the vocation. When I sit down to write, turns of phrase I've forgotten for years come back like white ink before fire." See Latrobe Carroll, "Willa Sibert Cather," *The Bookman* 53 (May 1921): 212–16.

2. Mark A. R. Facknitz, "Changing Trains: Metaphors of Transfer in Willa Cather," in *Cather Studies* 9: *Willa Cather and Modern Cultures*, ed. Melissa J. Homestead and Guy Reynolds (Lincoln: University of Nebraska Press, 2011), 71.

3. "The Bohemian Girl" (1912), in *Willa Cather's Collected Short Fiction 1892–1912*, ed. Mildred R. Bennett (Lincoln: University of Nebraska Press, 1965), 3–42.

4. Ibid., 3.

5. "The Sculpture's Funeral" (1905), in *Willa Cather's Collected Short Fiction 1892–1912*, 173–86.

6. Ibid., 173.

7. Leo Marx, *The Machine in the Garden: Technology and the Pastoral Ideal in America* (New York: Oxford University Press, 1964), 191.

8. Ibid.

9. William Cronon, *Nature's Metropolis: Chicago and the Great West* (New York: W. W. Norton, 1991), 72.

10. Ibid.

11. Marx, *The Machine in the Garden*, 19.

12. Ibid., 15–16.

13. Ibid., 16. Willa Cather is listed as an example.

14. "Paul's Case" (1905), in *Cather: Stories, Poems, & Other Writings*, ed. Sharon O'Brien (New York: Library of America, 1992), 468–88.

15. Willa Cather, *O Pioneers!* (1913) (Lincoln: University of Nebraska Press, 1992).

16. Willa Cather, *My Ántonia*, Willa Cather Scholarly Edition, ed. Charles W. Mignon and Kari A. Ronning (Lincoln: University of Nebraska Press, 1994), ix.

17. Facknitz, "Changing Trains," 77.

18. "The Treasure of Far Island" (1902), in *Willa Cather's Collected Short Fiction 1892–1912*, 265–82.

19. Ibid., 265–66.

20. Ibid.

21. Facknitz, "Changing Trains," 70.

22. Joseph R. Urgo, *Willa Cather and the Myth of American Migration* (Urbana: University of Illinois Press, 1995), 39.

23. Ibid., 71.

24. Urgo, *Willa Cather and the Myth of American Migration*, 39.

25. "Escapism," in *Willa Cather on Writing* (Lincoln: University of Nebraska Press), 26.

26. Facknitz, "Changing Trains," 70.

27. Martha Robertson, "Messages from the Far-Away: Willa Cather's and Georgia O' Keeffe's Visionary Landscape of the American Southwest," *Language and Culture: Bulletin Institute for Language Education* (2007): 79–98.

28. Edward C. Relph, *Place and Placelessness* (London: Pion Limited, 1976), 49.

29. Van den J. H. Berg, *The Changing Nature of Man: Introduction to a Historical Psychology* (New York: W. W. Norton, 1983), 231.

30. Simon Schama, *Landscape and Memory* (New York: Vintage Books 1996).

31. Leslie Marmon Silko, "Landscape, History, and the Pueblo Imagination," *Antaeus* 57 (Autumn 1986): 882–94.

32. Ibid., 884–85.

33. Carol Steinhagen, "Dangerous Crossings: Historical Dimensions of Landscape in Willa Cather's *My Ántonia, The Professor's House, and Death Comes for the Archbishop*," *Interdisciplinary Studies in Literature and Environment* 6, no. 2 (Summer 1999): 63.

34. Ibid., 66.

35. Cather, *My Ántonia*, ix.

36. Ibid.

37. James Woodress, *Willa Cather: Her Life and Art* (Lincoln: University of Nebraska Press, 1975), 31.

38. Cather, *My Ántonia*, 7.

39. Ibid., 8.

40. Steinhagen, "Dangerous Crossings," 66.

41. Cather, *My Ántonia*, 14–15.

42. Ibid., 15.

43. Ibid.

44. Ibid., 17–18.

45. Steinhagen, "Dangerous Crossings," 66.

46. Aldo Leopold, *A Sand County Almanac, and Sketches Here and There* (New York: Oxford University Press 1987), 205.

47. Willa Cather, *The Song of the Lark* (1915), in *Early Novels and Stories*, 291–706.

48. Ibid., 397.

49. Silko, "Landscape," 885.

50. Willa Cather, *Death Comes for the Archbishop* (1927), *Later Novels*, ed. Sharon O'Brien (New York: Library of America 1992), 273–460.

51. Ibid., 419.

52. Ibid.

53. Carolyn Steedman, *Strange Dislocations: Childhood and the Idea of Human Interiority 1780–1930* (Cambridge, MA: Harvard University Press, 1995).

54. Willa Cather, "Mesa Verde Wonderland Is Easy to Reach," *The Denver Times*, January 31, 1916, 7, archived at *The Willa Cather Archive*, ed. Andrew Jewell (Center for Digital Research in the Humanities: University of Nebraska–Lincoln, 2004–2013), 1–4, accessed July 10, 2016, http://cather.unl.edu/nf056.html.

55. Ibid.

56. Ibid.

Chapter Eleven

My Ántonia

Keatsian Negative Capability and the Dissolution of Boundaries

Jim Cody

John Keats's theory of negative capability provides a useful way to analyze Cather's technique of seeing nature from an experiential perspective. In a letter to his brothers on December 21, 1817, Keats articulated his definition of negative capability: "At once it struck me, what quality went to form a Man of Achievement, especially in literature, and which Shakespeare possessed so enormously—I mean Negative Capability, that is when man is capable of being in uncertainties. Mysteries, doubts, without any irritable reaching after fact and reason."[1] This definition has been understood as a poet's extreme empathy with his or her subject. In *My Ántonia*, there are two subjects: nature and Ántonia, to whom Jim Burden attempts to apply the negative capability he displays in his connection to the natural world. However, whereas representations of nature establish the novel's credibility and negative capability, the subject of Ántonia increasingly frustrates Jim and threatens to evoke his present, broken life. Jim struggles to keep the narrative about Ántonia and increasingly deploys less credible, romanticized language about her, indicating that the real project of the novel is to recapture the essence of his connection to nature. The application of this need to Ántonia is an increasing failure.

Cather enjoyed Keats's poetry. As James Woodress writes, "she delighted in the poems of Campbell, Moore, Longfellow, Keats, Arnold, Poe, and Byron that she found in the family bookcase."[2] While visiting Mrs. Fields, widow of the publisher in Boston who lived on Charles Street, Cather got to see a lock of Keats's hair that was given to Mrs. Fields from Joseph Severn, a close friend who stayed with Keats in Italy in his last days.[3] Cather even adorned her 5 Bank Street apartment with a bust of Keats inherited from Mrs. Fields. More specifically, Woodress names "The Eve of St. Agnes" as "one of Cather's favorites"[4] and "Endymion" as a work that "fed her creative imagination throughout her life."[5] This poem about a youth's ardent-hearted searching for the moon goddess clearly mattered to Cather, who continually referenced the moon in life-changing moments of her characters, such as Thea Kronberg, Captain Forrester, and Carl and Alexandra in the last scene of *O Pioneers!*, evidence of an "Endymion" influence on her writing.

Perhaps confidence in her own negative capability encouraged her to take on the ghost writing task of McClure's autobiography in 1913. Hermione Lee says that Cather herself wrote in a letter, "Ghosting McClure's autobiography trained her to appropriate the colours of a man's voice and personality" and "was the inspiration for Jim's narration in *My Ántonia*." Lee cites the claim as made both "revealingly and disingenuously." That such a claim could do both is reflective of how the concept of negative capability may have shape shifted into Cather, resulting in what Lee refers to as "her deep and lifelong obsession with doubling." Lee defines doubling as "the split self, symbolically projected."[6] And if, as Keats says, "a Poet is the most unpoetical of anything in existence, because he has no identity, . . . continually filling some other body" by virtue of imagination, a "split" is certainly needed to convey a subject's essence. Lee theorizes that the split belongs "to a powerful tradition in American writing," and she goes on to reference writers like Hawthorne whose "guilty Reverend Dimmesdale [nurses] a hidden scarlet letter" and Henry James's "failed hero Roderick Hudson, caught between art and love."[7]

Jim Burden is a case study in the multiplicity of dimensions brought on by a broken life. The complexity of his yearnings reflects a range of conflict within, so large that it can only be released into the vastness of open spaces. In *My Ántonia*, Jim Burden is akin to the swallow in Cather's poem "The Old Cliff Dweller," released of his burdens when given opportunities to "[fly] from wall to wall all the days of summer / Over the old trails [he] knew when he was young."[8] Cather uses the natural environment in *My Ántonia* to illustrate the enormity of her narrator's broken life, which the shift to Ántonia cannot heal.

NATURE AND ÁNTONIA IN TENSION

The Introduction to *My Ántonia* focuses on the fact that *My Ántonia* is Jim's memory, and Cather believed that first-person novels best conveyed feeling rather than action.[9] Memory creates a kind of fragmentation of the self. We are not fully alive in the present when immersed in memories. And as Lisa Marie Lucenti notes, when memories are used to represent another, as Jim Burden uses them in his depiction of Ántonia, they "are essentially and frighteningly out of [our] control."[10] Lucenti refers to them as "invasive memories," which have in their capacity what Lucenti sees in Cather's treatment of memory, "always disfigured and disfiguring—a relentless prying at the sutures of cosmetic design."[11] For Jim Burden, this is the case, but his longing for the past is in his control, at least initially.

Less under control is the life he lives in the present. The friend (perhaps Cather herself) on the train discusses his "frigid, unhappy marriage."[12] His wife "has her own fortune and lives her own life."[13] He also works as a railroad attorney in New York City, "a practitioner of the law that helps the railroads develop—that is to say annihilate the open prairies," but travels often, away from his office.[14] He tells that narrator that he has been writing about Ántonia for quite some time, intimating that the past was becoming for him "better than the present, the days of [his] youth . . . happier than the years of [his] adulthood."[15] He tells her, "From time to time I've been writing down what I remember about Ántonia. On my long trips across the country, I amuse myself like that, in my stateroom."[16] Burden is ready for a departure from his present, a need to arrive at a place where the past could become a reality again, which he believes lies in Ántonia.

The vehicle he attempts to use to get back to childhood is Ántonia. As William Barillas states, "the central theme of *My Antonia* is the nostalgic (and tragically futile) desire to recapture the innocence of childhood when material and social success has not fulfilled spiritual and emotional needs."[17] For both of them, the Cather character on the train and Burden, Ántonia "seemed to mean . . . the country, the conditions, the whole adventure of [their] childhood." It is Burden who lets the narrator "see her again, feel her presence, reviv[ing] all [her] old affection for her."[18] Burden has come to a point in his life when he sets up the binary opposition of a "fixed unchanging idyll" against his "real world," "subject to time and decay."[19] His memories of Ántonia become a pastoral in which he not only restores Ántonia, but also revives the landscape of his childhood so he can blend back into it before the disappointment of his adult life diminishes him.

Much of what Cather has characters experience makes them seek sanctuary from their present lives. Guilt (Frank Shabata), regret (Harry Gordon), grief (Godfrey St. Peter), abandonment (Marian Forrester, Claude Wheeler), loss of all kinds (Lucy Gayheart, Alexandra Bergson, Myra Henshawe), and threat (Nancy Till) send her characters floating back to a past where life seemed better or more fulfilling. And when the worst believed to happen actually happens, crawling from the wreckage necessitates the preservation of what one thinks was the happiest times in one's life. For Jim Burden, as John J. Murphy explains, memories of Ántonia become a "memoir of a middle-aged lawyer whose failed marriage leaves him unloved and alone and whose childhood in Nebraska at the end of the pioneer period becomes in retrospect the happiest time of his life, the period of potential and expectancy before the disappointment of adulthood."[20] When the Cather surrogate meets Jim on the train, their conversation, dominated by memories of Ántonia, nurtures Jim's nascent rejection of his present life. The train, as Fangyuan Xi argues in the previous chapter, becomes a womb for Jim to seek the self he has lost, the self central to making him feel whole again.

Jim breaks the stranglehold of binary opposition between two selves by creating a third self, one that seeks an answer to Claude Wheeler's question about death, "Was there no way out of this world besides this?"[21] He leaves his present self by attempting to create a pastoral memoir of *his* Antonia in which his own "real self" can be reclaimed and restored.

This is not without danger. Lee identifies two kinds of pastorals, both with potentially harmful grappling hooks that reduce meaning into binaries that should not be trusted. She defines the "soft pastoral" as "a romance, a dream of celebration, carnival, song, and love: guiltless, prelapsarian gratification, innocent hedonism, to which tender feelings of nostalgia are attached." Yet it "has the death's head within it."[22] So while fecundity, restoration of community, and life-giving forces abound in the soft pastoral, it contains an elegiac presence. One may conjure so many pleasing images of Cather's prairieland in *My Ántonia* well after reading it, but what never really goes away either are the suicide of Mr. Shimerda, Pavel and Peter's tale of "[feeding] the bride to the wolves,"[23] or Mr. Cutter's murder of his wife. The "death's head" pervades the narrative body of Jim's Ántonia.

Cather also composed *My Ántonia* out of material that fits the hard pastoral. Lee describes the "hard pastoral" as "a realist narrative of labour and endurance." It is contained within a golden age, "recalled as an idyllic, vanished period of harmony between man and nature."[24] Though nature and humankind are severed, the value and rewards of hard work and the dignity it provides are evident. Ántonia's pride in her strength,[25] the determination to "wander for miles along the edge of the cornfields for ground-cherries,"[26] the "dried mushrooms . . . gathered, probably in some deep Bohemian forest,"[27] and becoming "a rich mine of life, like the founders of early races"[28] are the rewards of toil in *My Ántonia*.

The "something complete and great" into which Jim desires to dissolve in the context of his memoir of Ántonia is the natural environment. However, the natural environment is most effectively recreated when Ántonia is not present. Jim's negative capability, in retrieving that part of his past that was the prairieland with such exactness, is his resounding achievement as a narrator. By fulfilling his wish to be part of something "complete and great," he succeeds in recreating the world in which Ántonia lived. In that landscape, we can place our own version of Ántonia. The exactness of Jim's description of the natural environment brings us as close to her as anyone can get via someone's memory. The invitation Jim Burden gives us to revisit this landscape every time we read *My Ántonia* helps make it the "continuously changing work" that Susan Rosowski calls it.[29]

Jim Burden has the same gift that Lee observes in Cather: she "translates her landscapes, and the figures in them, into landscapes of the mind."[30] But through Jim's negative capability (which is really Cather's, of course), the opposition caused by his raging unconscious and conscious narrative battle subsides when he renders the natural environment surrounding and encompassing Ántonia with details that evoke life. When he is properly distanced from Ántonia in his memories and immerses himself in the natural environment of his past, the narrative is at its closest in recreating Ántonia. Rosowski sees Jim's narrative tied to "a successful balancing of the world of ideas and the world of experience through imaginative fusion."[31] For the purposes of my claims here, I translate Rosowski's "world of ideas" into Jim's unconscious world and her "world of experience" into Jim's conscious efforts to undermine the validity of his unconscious. To use Rosowski's third term, "imaginative fusion," I see the unconscious and conscious paradoxically working at odds to defuse binaries in Jim's narrative, but fusing them imaginatively allows him penetration into the natural environment, which renders his past with accuracy. Part of that past allows glimpses of an objective view of Ántonia.

In two of her earlier novels, *O Pioneers!* and *The Song of the Lark*, Cather shows her narrative ability to blend characters into the natural environment to reveal their predicament, situation, or essence. When characters in these novels are subsumed into the landscape, their individual contribution to their space in that landscape emerges. Often what characters think or feel when they are forced or choose "to be dissolved into something complete and great" says something significant about who they are and how they distinguish themselves from others. Early on in *O Pioneers!*, when Alexandra and Emil return to their Nebraskan prairie from town with Carl's assistance, "the little town behind them had vanished as if it had never been, had fallen behind the swell of the prairie, and the stern frozen country received them into its bosom."[32] At that moment, we learn something about Emil. Cather initiates his character development by having him share his feelings about being received into the prairie's bosom. Cather writes about Emil, "It was from facing this vast hardness that the boy's mouth had become so bitter; because he felt that men were too weak to make any mark here, that the land wanted to be let alone, to preserve its own fierce strength, its peculiar, savage kind of beauty, its uninterrupted mournfulness."[33] In this moment of dissolution, Cather invites us into who Emil is and who he will become. He will never feel comfortable working the land. He will be disassociated from it, resisting all efforts to tame it, to make it habitable and arable. Emil, engulfed by the landscape, projects the part of his self resistant to the natural environment, which will act as a compass for his actions, decisions, and behavior through-out the rest of the novel.

A similar self-immersion into the natural world happens to Thea Kronberg early on in *The Song of the Lark*. However, this one comes "from within, not from without."[34] Cather sometimes lets the interior world of a character spread itself onto the landscape to merge the self into the space of the natural environment. In this instance, Thea's feelings project themselves onto the landscape "as if her heart were spreading all over the desert."[35] This sensa-tion comes at the end of chapter 13 of the "Friends of Childhood" section, when she is only fifteen years old and before she experiences the death of Ray Kennedy and her voyage to Chicago, where she will establish her identity as a world-class opera singer. These feelings are the result of Dr. Archie sharing his view on life that human beings really "only have about twenty able, wak-ing years."[36] Her deep conversation with Dr. Archie triggers in Thea a convic-tion that she has just entered an adult world that she has never experienced before, and she leaves his office "happy, flattered, and stimulated."[37] The joy she feels within permeates (shall I say like music can?) into everything she sees, both natural and built places: "white, moonlit streets," "stars and the bluish night," "quiet houses," "familiar trees," "people in those little houses," and even to "the unknown world beyond Denver."[38] And this drives her to a kind of doubling—an "either/or" splitting in two, being torn "between the desire to go away forever and the desire to stay forever."[39]

She is young though and these adult feelings and thoughts are new to her. She is drawn to a simplistic binary opposition, but Cather allows her readers to see how her "heart spreading all over the desert" is much deeper, much more conducive to determining a part of her that later on in the novel she asserts she will never let go: "As long as she lived that ecstasy was going to be hers. She would live for it, time after time, height after height." And she would protect it from anyone "bent upon taking [it] away from her."[40] This "it" is mysterious, a thing not stated, there only to be felt at this point in the novel perhaps, but it is established the night her heart encompasses the landscape of that desert. Though it is contained later when she goes home to her room and "lay[s] on the floor in the moonlight, pulsing with ardor and anticipation," her heart's conveyance onto the landscape produces in her the understanding of "the thing that Old Dumas meant . . . that to make a drama he needed but one passion and four walls."[41] This passion would never leave her and she would give it artistic expression and outlet for the rest of life. The "it" found is later determined to be her "wholeness and inner well-being," which in Cather no one should ever lose.[42] A sense of completeness defines what she yearns for, what her soul cries out for, and what makes her feel like she belongs in this world.

Similar dissolutions happen to Jim Burden, but his blending into the landscape is complicated by his narrative effort to recreate truths about Ántonia, ones that elude him when she is too close for the comfort of his narrative goals to objectify her. The truth revealed about Jim when Jim uses his negative capability to capture the landscape is his sincere effort to be a reliable narrator. When his negative capability filters into recreating the natural environment, like Cather succeeds in doing for Emil and Thea, something about Ántonia's self is revealed. When he aims directly at her, he misses the mark; the projection of his self into her life disrupts opportunities to narrate her life objectively. Cather defined imagination as a combination: "Imagination is a response to what is going on—a sensitiveness to which outside things appeal. It is a composition of sympathy and observation."[43] Jim's recapturing of the Nebraskan landscape shows his "appeal" for "outside things." His sensitivity toward the natural environment that surrounds Ántonia reveals, as Cather also says, "the quality writers must have."[44] His sympathy toward it combines with his skill of observation to create art. Ann Fisher-Wirth writes, "Jim's vocation is art. He exists only as the (fictive) creator of this highly artful novel."[45] That said, when Jim's "sympathies" for Ántonia dominate his narrative, Goggans is correct in saying that it is "such a huge mistake for readers to see Ántonia only as Jim does."[46] I contend, however, that it is a mistake for readers not to see the natural environment as Jim does. To do so opposes Jim's skill as an artist, a fact Fisher-Wirth defends, and undercuts what Cather wants us to witness in Jim's narrative ability to use his imagination to dislodge the emotions he has for Ántonia, to recreate her objectively.

Throughout the novel, Cather helps us witness the struggle Jim undergoes alternating between narrating Ántonia and *My Ántonia*. Prior to any description of her, except when he first sees her, "a girl holding oilcloth bundles," Jim includes, in his first description of the natural world around his new home, a strong sense of movement: "As I looked about me I felt that the grass was the country, as the water is the sea. The red of the grass made all the great prairie the color of wine-stains, or of certain seaweeds when they are first washed up. And there was so much motion in it; the whole country, seemed, somehow, to be running."[47] This is a description of the landscape that evokes life. Land is depicted as water, undulating, ebbing, flowing; the color of wine connotes life, fertility; and "running," a gerund, captures motion and stillness, an evocation of being fully alive but frozen as the lovers forever about to kiss and the "melodist, unwearied, / For ever piping songs for ever new" in Keats's "Ode to a Grecian Urn."

Images of Ántonia evoke motion and stillness as well, but they are seen through the prism of Jim's sentiments toward her. Perhaps reflective of a more directly Catherian narration, the descriptions of landscape sustain a memorable intensity throughout the novel. Murphy sees a distinction between what is Cather and what is Jim in how she is able to "distinguish her vision from the character Jim when his becomes colored by feelings she might not share."[48] Murphy sees a separation between different kinds of narration despite Burden's first-person point of view. Jim's moments of objectivity, mainly in his descriptions of the natural environment, also reveal evidence of how aware he is of his flawed narration elsewhere. But as Goggans asserts, "our understanding of Jim Burden's limitations is the only way to fully appreciate the complexity of *My Antonia*."[49] What is particularly complex, in addition to what Goggans purports to be "a time marked by shifting social boundaries and new means of constructing identity,"[50] is Jim's psychological struggle to recreate Ántonia to suture his fractured life. The intensity of the natural environment descriptions helps his credibility as a narrator. The sentimentalized, romantic, luminous, and emotive descriptions when Ántonia is present (or getting near) reflect Jim's wish to restore his own life by putting himself back in hers.

A closer look at the colored world of Jim's narration when it includes Ántonia is needed. Jim captures the movement of the landscape as a "loose hide" of buffalo "galloping, galloping,"[51] which leads to the end of that chapter with the penultimate gravestone passage about dissolving "into something complete and great."[52] I contend that Jim has practiced such dissolving with the negative capability he shows in capturing the natural environment's motion with such precise image-making metaphors. In the following chapter, which includes Jim's meeting Ántonia, the description of nature is altered; it loses the feeling of objectivity as a result of Jim's anticipation of Ántonia. As she gets closer to being part of the narrative, the cottonwoods' "yellow leaves and shining white bark made them look like the gold and silver trees in fairy tales."[53] This enhanced description of the cottonwood trees is an instance when Murphy sees Jim use "details in the landscape [that] are surrealistically singled out."[54] Jim's earlier efforts to render the landscape's motion with exactness contrast sharply with this surreal picture—as from a fairy tale rather than Nebraska.

Jim's first description of Ántonia is equally as fanciful. He immediately sets her off, like the cottonwoods, by her accented name, "An-tonia," and she is "prettier" than her sister. Her eyes "were big and warm and full of light, like the sun shining on brown pools in the wood. Her skin was brown, too, and in her cheeks she has a glow of rich, dark colour. Her brown hair was curly and wild- looking."[55] It is as if he cannot describe her without assimilating her into the natural world's description. Jim displays a negative capability earlier when describing the movement of the landscape, but here nature is used to glorify Ántonia, to associate her with the light and wildness of nature. And then the first activity they do together is run: "In a moment we were running up the steep drawside together, Yulka trotting after us."[56] The motion of the landscape he described with such precision before dovetails into his first direct encounter with Ántonia, making both him and Ántonia "surrealistically singled out" as extensions of nature. They continue to run "toward Squaw Creek" until there is no ground left, where they stand "panting on the edge of the ravine, looking down at the trees and bushes that grew below." The wind is strong there, and Antonia's eyes are "fairly blazing with things she could not say."[57] The panting, the strength of the wind, and her blazing, incommunicable eyes come across as heightened details. She and Yulka learn Jim's name, and Antonia offers him a ring, which Jim finds "reckless and extravagant," words perhaps that describe Jim's own narration here and elsewhere when he tries to recreate memories of scenes with Ántonia in them.

Rarely is Ántonia absent until book III, "Lena Lengard." Within Ántonia's vortex, Jim seems incapable of describing the natural environment with the negative capability his imagination summoned before she appears. By the end of book I, vivid details illuminate Ántonia's body instead of nature. In the ending garden scene, Ántonia throws off the sunbonnet forced upon her by her grandmother, letting her hair fly in the breeze. Jim even remembers "beads of perspiration [that] used to gather on her upper lip like a moustache."[58] He also recounts how "she would toss her head and ask [him] to feel the muscles swell in her brown arm."[59] Her proximity in Jim's memory seems almost too much for him. The last image of Ántonia in book I is of her putting "her arms under her head and lay[ing] back, looking up at the sky."[60] Jim has narrated her with a sensuality that enlivens, breathing life and a life force onto the page, which underscores her appeal and attraction. Having returned to her in this way through his memory and the vehicle of narration and knowing full well he can never again be a part of her life or that she can never be a part of his, he must detach, recoil. He must channel his narrative energies into a place where he still can be part of something "complete and great." That place is the natural environment, but it will take him until book III to disengage himself from the memories of Ántonia that are just too painful to continue peeling off the layers. Book III is Jim's deliberate effort to frustrate a narration that otherwise would have the impact of turning his pastoral about Ántonia into an elegy of his own life.

FAILURE

When Jim invites the natural environment to press upon his memories of Ántonia is when he is most able to negate himself and allow the narrative to be Ántonia's. Conversely, the moments when he has himself stand out, making Ántonia the backdrop to her own memoir, when he takes her "place," so to speak, is when he verges on returning to his present self where he also fights to assert his identity. As Rosowski notes, in the scene at the end of "The Pioneer Woman's Story," when Jim informs Ántonia of his plans to leave for New York to study law, "there is strikingly little of Ántonia in this meeting."[61] When Jim has Ántonia fade from the narrative, he disrupts it from luring him into something "complete and great." When he diminishes in the presence of Ántonia, when "there is strikingly little of" him, the natural environment becomes an all-encompassing presence in the narrative.

However, the restoration of Ántonia is marked with failure. He had the opportunity to be in her life, to be a vital part of her life, but he missed it. Maybe that's why, when Ántonia is "strikingly not there" at the end of "The Pioneer Woman's Story," Jim admits wanting to have had her "for a sweetheart, or a wife, or [his] mother or [his] sister."[62] He cannot have her back again, even if he still feels that she really is a part of him. But what if he has to in order to survive? What if the life he chose is so fractured, so unfulfilling that intolerable grief would consume him? What if his life cannot be sustained without the part of him that he feels is her? In Cather's work, the pursuit seems to matter more than the results, especially when that pursuit involves "fashion[ing] an existence that would free the expressive self."[63] Cather gives Burden the gift of that pursuit. As Vivian Gornick observes, "in the pursuit of the deepest self there is salvation, and in the absence of that pursuit there is a kind of death-in-life."[64] In Jim's pursuit, what he finds is not Ántonia and not a way to put his life back in hers. Instead he finds within his narrative imagination a negative capability, present mainly when he describes the natural environment, preserving his native Nebraskan landscape in the process. When Jim unburdens himself of reviving Ántonia and from reinventing himself to be such a part of her life, he demonstrates an ability to be negatively capable enough to "become a part of something entire."[65] That is when he becomes part of a grand mosaic that is the natural world—that is, when he approaches making the pastoral more than a vehicle for living in the past. Cather uses Jim Burden's need to put his life back together to help "pastoral values endure in the new materialistic age."[66]

Jim tries to let Ántonia become what Rosowski calls "a vital source of meaning." His defeated self as a railroad attorney in a loveless marriage supports Rosowski's view that "the male myths of adventure have led to pointless wondering and lonely exile."[67] But he cannot write about her in any negatively capable ways because she is such a part of him, or at least a part of his past and memory that cannot be objectified. Jan Goggans observes the strain Jim undergoes "to make Ántonia fit into the story."[68] Only when he writes about the landscape can he really capture Ántonia's "vital source." She embodies the landscape; she "has always been at home with herself and her place."[69] Goggans asserts that Ántonia "does the best 'job' of establishing herself at a place and beginning to construct identity in relation to that place."[70] When he keeps her there, in "place," belonging to the environment around her, he captures her essence and works toward reclaiming his own, especially the part of him that is her.

A microcosm of Jim's struggle while narrating Ántonia life as he remembers her occurs months later, after their train ride together, when Jim shows up at the Cather character's doorstep with "the thing about Ántonia" in hand. He makes the claim, "I suppose it hasn't any form," affirming an artlessness to the memoir's shape, brought on, he asserts, by "simply [writing] down what of herself and myself and other people Ántonia's name recalls to me."[71] What a name recalls certainly is iffy business. But he labels it "Ántonia" while sitting at his friend's desk in the next room, and then adds the word "My," which, the narrator says, "seemed to satisfy him." That Jim wrote "Ántonia" first matters. It signifies that he viewed it initially, even for a few seconds, as an objective rendering of her life. But it is not and cannot be even close to that if Jim is the storyteller. The possessive "My" changes the point of view and his own perspective on what the text is. This text is not wholly Ántonia, not an impartial attempt to capture her as a source of meaning. It's colored, tainted, and distorted, a life imbued by Jim's subjectivity. But the "My" comes second, an afterthought, a correction maybe. Either way, I think Cather suggests a writing process at work here. The narrative will ebb and flow with objectivity and subjectivity. It will reflect a conscious effort to capture her and maybe a sub- and/or unconsciousness at play that coats it with Jim's desperate desire to possess her, to maintain the satisfaction of "making it '*My Ántonia*.'"

Jim's struggle to keep "the thing about Ántonia" actually about Ántonia is seen when he asserts his identity in places better reserved for Ántonia in a memoir about her. The story of the snake, for instance, really becomes Jim's story. Interpretations of it include the scene displaying his removal of the snake from Eden or his own wish to rid his narrative of sexual desires.[72] Either way, saving her from the snake positions him in the foreground of the story with Ántonia in the background. Jim becomes the plough "left standing in the sun," with Ántonia as the sun, and Jim, "heroic in size," "a picture writing" on the narrative that is Ántonia's.[73]

But like the plough before the setting sun, Jim's snake story is "forgotten"; Jim has it sink "back into its own littleness" calling it a "mock adventure" and attributing his slaying of the snake to its being "old and lazy."[74] Jim undercuts his own version of the story's worth in Ántonia's narrative. He makes a conscious effort to shed the narrative of epic features, yet it's as if he cannot help his unconscious longing to will an invented identity of his own into Ántonia's life. He goes as far as to say that it was "fixed for me by chance," mocking how "many a dragon-slayer" whose glorified reputations equally were inflated by the benefits of a stacked deck.[75] He dims his own patriarchy in this instance specifically and patriarchy in general by the end of "The Shimerdas" chapter. By doing so, he vaults his own credibility as Ántonia's storyteller.

The end result of the snake story for Jim is that Ántonia "liked [him] better from that time on and she never took a supercilious air with [him] again."[76] I think the same could be said for anyone reading *My Ántonia*, including the author from the train journey Introduction. In other words, Jim's authenticity as a narrator is achieved by evidence of his conscious efforts to self-correct his memory's interpretation of events. Jim's burden ultimately is that he cannot be relied upon to tell Ántonia's story, but he acknowledges that when he changes the title in front of the Introduction's narrator. His narrative is as smelly and oozing as the poison coming from the crushed head of the snake, especially when he recounts scenes involving him and Ántonia. He cannot detach himself from his strong feelings for her, which is most noticeable when his memories bring him back to scenes of close proximity to her. William J. Stuckey feels that Jim's problem is he cannot get Ántonia into romantic focus until he is far enough away to keep from seeing the things that make her unromantic."[77] I disagree. His memories with her are too painful. The nearness of her in his mind through memory conjures up lost opportunities, suffering from unrequited love and what could have been, too intolerable for him to face especially in light of his present crisis. He retreats into the past to be with her, to recreate her, and to idolize her. What makes him reliable though as her memoirist is his own awareness of this authorial flaw.

Book III is Jim's attempt to counter the "invasive memories" keeping him from the narrative task of writing a "thing" that can at first earn the title Ántonia. In a sense, too, it is Jim's return to "straining to make Ántonia fit into the story."[78] In "The Hired Girls," straining is replaced by an ease or complacency of narration. Introduced "to the world of ideas" by Gaston Cleric when he experiences what he calls a "mental awakening," Jim returns to a narration that evokes Ántonia.[79] Detached from the encroaching closeness of Ántonia's presence in his memory, he remembers places and spaces with vividness. He can describe his workspace with "a commodious green-topped table placed directly in front of the west window which looked out over the prairie." Jim recalls, "In the corner at my right were all my books, in shelves I had made and painted myself. On the blank wall at my left the dark, old-fashioned wall-paper was covered by a large map of ancient Rome. . . . Over the bookcase hung a photograph of the Tragic Theater at Pompeii."[80] Jim is able to conjure up color, position, perspective, and arrangement. His powers as an artist ("Jim's vocation is art"[81]) seem rejuvenated. He vivifies a story Cleric shares with him about a "solitary day [Cleric] spent among the sea temples at Paestum: the birds flying low over the flowering marsh grasses, the changing lights on the silver, cloud-hung mountains."[82] Jim comes across as equally adept at recreating the details of cultural and natural spaces. Noticeably absent from book III is the word "My" preceding "Lena Lingard." In this book, Jim's imagination negates his own identity enough to generate descriptions of his subjects with objective details more associated with an omniscient narrator or perhaps what's required of the scholar.

By the end of the first chapter of "Lena Lingard," Jim confesses, "I could never lose myself for long among impersonal things."[83] For me, the operative words in this admission is "for long" because he does display, albeit in fits and starts in his writing, an ability to "lose" himself in what he tries to recreate, as with his work station at school and Cleric's day at Paestum. But this acknowledgment is evidence of how aware he is of his imaginative limitations, and this is crucial to the struggle Ántonia causes him in his efforts to narrate her life story. He goes on to say, "Mental excitement was apt to send me with a rush back to my naked land and the figures scattered upon it. . . . They were so much alive in me that I scarcely stopped to wonder whether they were alive anywhere else, or how."[84] Alive in him is Ántonia. He cannot get her out of his head and emotional grasp. What to do? He brings Lena literally into the narrative and into his room, but this plan is Jim's greatest narrative failure.

Lena becomes a reminder of what a person's presence can do to someone else's response to place and how descriptions of spaces can be so enslaved by a narrator's subjectivity. For Jim, after Lena departs from her sudden visit to his room, "the place seemed much pleasanter than before. Lena had left something warm and friendly in the lamplight." His distance from Ántonia in this book seems to compel Lena closer than ever to him, but she seems even closer to him when she leaves the room. I'd like to make the case that Lena's real presence in the room via Jim's memory pulls him back to the memory of Ántonia he hoped to dim. Lena "brought them [the Bohemian women) all back to [him]," and he is quick to wander into romantic notions of their link to poetry—"If there were no girls like them in the world, there would be no poetry."[85] Jim's mind actually is disturbing here as he confesses confusion about a dream of Lena being "like the memory of an actual experience."[86] Jim seems far removed from being a negatively capable artist at this craft. He seems jolted by his own deliberate removal of Ántonia from his narrative about her. He is far removed, too, from Cather's own ability to avoid "moralistic and explanatory tags"—to "[leave] the reader free to discover the inner meaning of the whole," as Elizabeth Moorhead put it about Cather's writing in her book *These Too Were Here*.[87] Jim has lost the quality of writing that depicts but does not interpret, a skill attributed also to Anton Chekhov. Jim never recovers from what equates to his second loss of Ántonia. The first occurred in real time. The second occurred when, in desperation to reclaim an objective point of view, he removed her in book III. From here on out, the memoir is indeed properly titled *My Ántonia*, with all binary oppositions unleashed from a mind unable to shake a patriarchal view of the world. When Jim says to Lena, after she tells him that Antonia is still with Larry Donovan, "I think I'd better go home and look after Ántonia," he means it.[88] The rest of the book displays his inability to describe Ántonia's life without his protection. The story with the snake and the bed story with Cutter were mere synapses in the mind of a man tragically aware of both his resistance to and attraction to patriarchy. He could narrate like Cather, depicting and not interpreting, but not at the cost of giving up what Ántonia's life could reveal about his. Escape into a delusion is better for Jim than facing the reality of an Ántonia-less life.

In "The Pioneer Woman's Story," a title that signals an attempt to shift the narrative back to Ántonia, it is Ántonia who is now part of Jim's "complete and great" story. When he says to her, "You really are a part of me," the romantic notion of such a statement following his admission to her, "The idea of you is part of my mind; you influence my likes and dislikes, all my tastes, hundreds of times when I don't realize it," severs his credibility as a narrator capable of anything but a romantic view of Ántonia.[89] Frances W. Kaye is right when she says, that upon seeing Ántonia twenty years later in book IV, "Jim describes her grizzled hair and lost teeth only in aesthetic terms, not in terms of her own subjective knowledge of loss."[90] Capable of capturing the "inner meaning of the whole" when it comes to built-in and natural environments, Jim is incapable of narrating a story that reflects a negative capability that can place him objectively in Antonia's shoes.

Book IV's title "Cuzack's Boys" conveys another futile attempt to shift perspective to attain objectivity. In it, Jim negates Ántonia from possession of her own children. And what about the girls? Or Maria, born from Ántonia's relationship with Larry Donovan, one that Jim interprets as leaving Antonia "disgraced"?[91] Being part of "something complete and great" comes with a cost. We will never know Ántonia Shimerda through Jim Burden. Perhaps this is how Willa Cather preserved and protected Annie Pavelka. Jim's *My Ántonia* reveals more about the fictional Jim Burden than it does about the fictional or real Annie Pavelka.

Indeed, *My Ántonia* reveals more about Cather the artist than it does about Jim, Ántonia, or Annie. Merrill Skaggs writes, "characters who most closely resemble Willa Cather are usually males—Jim Burden, Niel Herbert, Godfrey

St. Peter—all of whom she presents in an intermittently negative or critical light."[92] When we experience Jim Burden's struggle to deliver an objective narrative, attention shifts away from Cather the artist. Subsumed into his perspective, she displays her own Keatsian negative capability. She becomes Jim Burden for us to experience how vulnerable we are when we tell stories about others to whose lives we still cling for our own wholeness. As Skaggs observes, the novel is "based in the most elaborate ways on juxtaposed oppositions, particularly on the opposite qualities embodied in Jim and Ántonia."[93] Skaggs situates Cather as the artist here. Cather puts into form Jim's "text that has no form," using "juxtaposed oppositions" to do so. As Miles Orvell states, "all of this [Jim's] artlessness is, of course, part of Cather's great art."[94] By having Jim, who is opposite his subject, narrate, she creates a persona and a voice that help us recognize the complexities that divide us from ourselves and from each other. Jim and Ántonia's opposite qualities, for example, Antonia as "uneducated immigrant," Jim as "a member of the ruling class,"[95] do not attract—instead they create a great divide, one that Jim tries to cross, but his "romantic disposition" and "personal passion [for] the great country," qualities Cather affixes to Jim in the Introduction, make him the unreliable narrator Cather intended. Jim's final visit to Ántonia narrated in "Cuzak's Boys" effectively reveals those intentions.

Books I, II, and III are united by being the three of the five books that begin with the word "I." This, of course, is no coincidence. As I've argued earlier, the first two books contain evidence of Jim's negative capability. The books in which the "I" recedes, III and IV, show Jim's failure to maintain this capability. Book III, however, reveals his own effort to depart from his subject to find it again, but the attempt fails him. What restores it in book V is his ability to reproduce what he did for the friend on the train when she says, "He made me see her again, feel her presence, revived all my old affection for her."[96] At the end of book IV, Jim makes a wish and I think Cather grants it. He wishes he "could be a little boy again, and that [his] way could end there."[97] Cather lets Jim become the narrator that allows readers to see and feel. She lets him take in and let out the world he experienced as a child with Ántonia. At the very end of book IV, he says about Antonia, "I felt rather than saw her smile."[98] When Jim enters book V, his narrative has become one of feeling again—a feeling with the promise of an artist's negative capability. He is poised to—in the description of art in *The Song of the Lark*—"make a sheath, a mould in which to imprison for a moment the shining elusive element which is life itself."[99] Cather's sheath is *My Ántonia*; Jim's becomes "Cuzak's Boys." In the last paragraph of book IV, Jim detaches himself enough to picture himself separate from his narrator self. He writes, "As I went back alone over that familiar road, I almost believed that a boy and a

girl ran along beside me, as our shadows used to do, laughing and whispering to each other in the grass."[100] Jim is able to negate himself to see himself,
hear laughter and whispers, and feel the grass. By the end of the day, which
is the end of this book, Jim crosses the divide separating him from Ántonia.

Book V reads as though the boy and the girl holding hands at the end
of book IV are Jim and Cather. Or rather Jim leads Cather hand in hand to
Ántonia. He does this through a perspective gained by the ripeness of years,
a maturity, and reconciliation with a brokenness that his unfulfilled life has
wrought. Books III and IV, containing the struggle with his narrative self, can
be read as metaphorical exemplifications of his broken life. His recovery after
what may have been the worst that could happen to him leads him back both
literally in the novel and through his memory to Ántonia.

As a temporary visitor to the Cuzak's home, Jim can be detached, unhin-
dered by being on the outside looking in. In fact, his narrative is nourished by
resolve. He can openly admit to Ántonia's children, "I was very much in love
with your mother once, and I know there's nobody like her."[101] He knows
no repercussions will come of such a confession. It is a letting go with the
heart that speaks to being at peace. Cather too, present as the part of Jim that
is Ántonia, may have felt the same way at this point in her life after losing
Isabelle McClung to her marriage with Jan Hambourg. As Woodress recounts
about Cather just prior to her writing *My Ántonia*, "There seems no doubt that
she was accepting Isabelle's marriage and beginning to like Jan."[102] Jim is
accepting of what he sees and perceives in this final book, and his narrative
skills heighten as a result.

Jim shows he can also blend himself into scenes without intruding on what
can be felt upon the page. He even says he feels like one of the children while
walking with them in this scene:

> I walked between the two older boys—straight, well-made fellows, with good
> heads and clear eyes. They talked about their school and the new teacher, told
> me about the crops and the harvest, and how many steers they would feed that
> winter. They were easy and confidential with me, as if I were an old friend of
> the family—and not too old. I felt like a boy in their company, and all manner
> of forgotten interests revived in me. It seemed, after all, so natural to be walking
> along a barbed-wire fence beside the sunset, toward a red pond, and to see my
> shadow moving along at my right, over the close-cropped grass.[103]

Jim vanishes into the group, becoming one of them, negating himself to
encompass the entirety of the scene. In the last sentence of this passage,
man-built structures (barbed wire fence), the natural world (sunset, red pond,
close-cropped grass), and human presence (shadow) all assemble and unite to
paint a picture of all-inclusiveness and coexistence.

This tableau suggests that the novel becomes a defense against the forces that make our world endangered and a resistance to what Cather saw coming in the time she wrote *My Ántonia*, "heaped-up machine made materialism" and "showy extravagance."[104] Without the land, Cather, through Jim and therefore through Ántonia, seems to be saying we will deprive ourselves of a past worth reliving to restore our broken lives. Jim's life is restored at least to the degree that he can write about Ántonia and still move on. I agree with Orvell when he says, "As great as the pull of the past is, however, what Cather compels Jim to recognize is the necessity of moving beyond the past into an acceptance of time and change."[105] The novel begins with change. When Jim hands over the text to the narrator of the Introduction, he adds a title and then changes it with the possessive "*My*." The last sentence of the text, however, speaks of a possession of another sort, "the incommunicable past," that both Jim and Ántonia share. Jim ends his writing with an unmistakable paradox, the past can be written about but in the end it is "incommunicable." But what about all that he just communicated for well over three hundred pages? No matter. The road is all, and it has done a great deal in bringing Jim "together again."

NOTES

1. John Keats, *Keats Poetry and Prose*, ed. Henry Ellershaw (Oxford: Clarendon Press, 1931).

2. James Woodress, *Willa Cather: A Literary Life* (Lincoln: University of Nebraska Press, 1987), 164.

3. Ibid., 196.

4. Ibid., 227.

5. Ibid., 220.

6. Hermione Lee, *Double Lives* (New York: Vintage, 1989), 84.

7. Ibid.

8. Willa Cather, "The Old Cliff-Dweller (Walnut Canyon, Arizona) AD 1400," *Willa Cather Collection*, Drew University Special Collections, Madison, New Jersey.

9. Woodress, *Willa Cather*, 289.

10. Lisa Marie Lucenti, "Willa Cather's *My Ántonia*: Haunting the Houses of Memory," *Twentieth Century Literature* 46, no. 2 (Summer 2000): 194.

11. Ibid.

12. Woodress, *Willa Cather*, 299.

13. Willa Cather, *My Ántonia*, Willa Cather Scholarly Edition, ed. Charles W. Mignon and Kari A. Ronning (Lincoln: University of Nebraska Press, 1994), xi.

14. Ann Fisher-Wirth, "Out of the Mother: Loss in *My Ántonia*," *Cather Studies* 2 (1993): 42.

15. Woodress, *Willa Cather*, 298.

16. Cather, *My Ántonia*, xii.

17. William Barillas, *The Midwestern Pastoral: Place and Landscape in Literature of the Heartland* (Athens, OH: Ohio University Press, 2006), 70.

18. Cather, *My Ántonia*, xii.

19. Lee, *Double Lives*, 92.

20. John J. Murphy, *My Ántonia: The Road Home* (Boston: Twayne, 1989), 7.

21. Willa Cather, *One of Ours* (New York: Random House, 1991), 20.

22. Lee, *Double Lives*, 93.

23. Cather, *My Ántonia*, 58.

24. Lee, *Double Lives*, 94.

25. Cather, *My Ántonia*, 126.

26. Ibid., 31.

27. Ibid., 79.

28. Ibid., 353.

29. Susan J. Rosowski, *The Voyage Perilous: Willa Cather's Romanticism* (Lincoln: University of Nebraska Press, 1986), 75.

30. Lee, *Double Lives*, 1.

31. Rosowski, *Voyage Perilous*, 81.

32. Willa Cather, *O Pioneers!* (1913; Boston: Houghton Mifflin, 1988), 10.

33. Ibid.

34. Willa Cather, *The Song of the Lark* (Boston: Houghton Mifflin, 1915), 135.

35. Ibid., 133.

36. Ibid., 132.

37. Ibid., 133.

38. Ibid.

39. Ibid.

40. Ibid., 190–91.

41. Ibid., 133.

42. Ibid., 205.

43. Willa Cather, *Willa Cather in Person: Interviews, Speeches, and Letters*, ed. Brent L. Bohlke (Lincoln: University of Nebraska Press, 1986), 15.

44. Ibid.

45. Fisher-Wirth, "Out of the Mother," 42.

46. Jan Goggans, "Social (Re)Visioning in the Fields of My Antonia," *Cather Studies* 5 (2003): 170.

47. Cather, *My Ántonia*, 14–15.

48. Murphy, *My Ántonia*, 53.

49. Goggans, "Social (Re)Visioning," 171.

50. Ibid.

51. Cather, *My Ántonia*, 15.

52. Ibid., 18.

53. Ibid., 21.

54. Murphy, *My Ántonia*, 56.

55. Cather, *My Ántonia*, 23.

56. Ibid., 24.

57. Ibid, 25.

58. Ibid., 133.

59. Ibid.

60. Ibid., 135.

61. Rosowski, *Voyage Perilous*, 86.

62. Cather, *My Ántonia*, 312.

63. Vivian Gornick, Introduction to *O Pioneers!* by Willa Cather (New York: Bantam, 1989), x.

64. Ibid., xi.

65. Cather, *My Ántonia*, 18.

66. Barillas, *The Midwestern Pastoral*, 75.

67. Rosowski, *Voyage Perilous*, 91.

68. Goggans, "Social (Re)Visioning," 164.

69. Barillas, *Midwestern Pastoral*, 78.

70. Goggans, "Social (Re)Visioning," 167.

71. Cather, *My Ántonia*, xiii.

72. Blanche H. Gelfant, "The Forgotten Reaping-Hook: Sex in *My Ántonia*," in *Critical Essays on Willa Cather*, ed. John J. Murphy (Boston: G. K. Hall and Co. 1984), 155.

73. Cather, *My Ántonia*, 237.

74. Ibid., 48.

75. Ibid.

76. Ibid.

77. Murphy, *My Ántonia*, 17.

78. Goggans, "Social (Re)Visioning," 164.

79. Cather, *My Ántonia*, 249–50.

80. Ibid., 251

81. Fisher-Wirth, "Out of the Mother," 48

82. Cather, *My Ántonia*, 253.

83. Ibid., 254.

84. Ibid.

85. Ibid., 262.

86. Ibid.

87. Elizabeth Moorhead Vermocken, *These Too Were Here: Louise Homer and Willa Cather* (Pittsburgh: University Press, 1950). In the *Willa Cather Collection*, Drew University Special Collections, Madison, New Jersey, ADAMS 167 23.

88. Cather, *My Ántonia*, 260.

89. Ibid., 312.

90. Frances W. Kaye, *Isolation and Masquerade* (New York: Peter Lang Publishing, 1993), 105.

91. Cather, *My Ántonia*, 305.

92. Merrill Skaggs, *After the World Broke in Two: The Later Novels of Willa Cather* (Charlottesville: University of Virginia Press, 1990), 27.

93. Ibid., 15.

94. Miles Orvell, "Time, Change, and the Burden of Revision," in *New Essays on My Ántonia*, ed. Sharon O'Brien (Cambridge: Cambridge University Press, 1999), 34.

95. Ibid., 35.

96. Cather, *My Ántonia*, xii.

97. Ibid., 313.

98. Ibid., 314.

99. Cather, *The Song of the Lark*, 286.

100. Cather, *My Ántonia*, 314.

101. Ibid., 335.

102. Woodress, *Willa Cather*, 185.

103. Cather, *My Ántonia*, 334.

104. Willa Cather, "Nebraska: The End of the Cycle," *The Nation* 117, no. 3035 (September 5, 1923): 238.

105. Orvell, "Time, Change," 44.

Part V

TRANSITION

Chapter Twelve

A Portrait of a Self-Made Woman

Lena Lingard in My Ántonia

Keiko Arai

The turn of the twentieth century was a time of progress for women. An increasing number of women began to enter the public sphere, and this change was accompanied by the appearance of the so-called New Woman, women who, "rejecting conventional female roles and asserting their right to a career, to a public voice, to visible power, laid claim to the rights and privileges customarily accorded bourgeois men."[1] They went to college, entered professions, and were frequently linked with the Suffrage Movement and the increase in the divorce rate. Some women remained Victorian wives and got involved in social work at the same time, some got divorced, and some, "frequently remain[ing] single," were involved in "establish[ing] networks among women."[2] The change in the position of women was symbolized by the Women's Building at the 1893 Chicago Columbian Exposition, where two murals were displayed—"The Primitive Woman" and "The Modern Woman." While the former by Mary Louise Fairchild MacMonnies-Low illustrates women doing chores traditionally linked with women, such as nursing children and carrying jars, the latter by Mary Cassatt shows female artists and young women picking the fruits of knowledge.

Just as "The Primitive Woman" was placed in contrast to "The Modern Woman" in the Women's Building, in *My Ántonia*, two portraits of women form a stark contrast. Similar to the image of "The Primitive Woman," Ántonia Shimerda is often seen in the kitchen, cooking, nursing, and serving men. Jim's final picture of Ántonia as the earth mother in book V strongly underlines her nature as "The Primitive Woman," as Jim associates her with more ancient roots, universalizing and eternalizing her fertility: "She was a rich mine of life, like the founders of early races."[3] The picture of Ántonia, then, is contrasted with another picture, which illustrates a girl who becomes the "Modern Woman": Lena Lingard. Critics have often contrasted Lena and

Ántonia, explaining that they present different visions for Jim, different attitudes toward rural life, and different values, and often concluding that Lena's
successful life paradoxically serves to celebrate Ántonia's way of life; for
example, Edwin T. Bowden suggests that, despite her material success, Lena
is "a girl of artificial civilization" who "retains her inner isolation to the end,
unwilling to merge it with the isolation of the land to become, by the paradox
lived by Ántonia, 'a part of something entire'"[4]; Robert E. Scholes states that
"Lena and Tiny succeed only in becoming more like the society from which
they had been ostracized, while Ántonia, and other country girls who stay
on the land, ultimately change the structure of society itself"[5]; and Deborah
G. Lambert argues that, though Lena and Tiny "are initially presented favor-
ably" with their independence and unconventionality, "by the end of the
novel, Cather simultaneously praises Ántonia's role as mother and demeans
the value of their independent lives."[6] On the other hand, Marilee Lindemann,
arguing that Lena represents "the dilemma of the woman" who exploits male
discourse but does not have power to change it, states that "where Lena resists Jim's ordering and interpreting, Ántonia aids and abets it" through her
engagement in domestic practices.[7] Lena also tends to be situated in terms of
sensuality and seduction; "Lena, the archetypal Woman, beckons him [Jim]
to full sexuality" while "Ántonia, the eternal Mother, lures him back through
her children, Cuzak's boys, to perennial childhood."[8]

In this chapter, I propose that Lena's character as the New Woman be
reconsidered and investigate how modern womanhood is examined through
her. I will focus on the issue of image making in the novel, discussing how
Lena evades Jim's control and presents a (self) portrait of the New Woman
who was predominantly a construct of image making in the magazine media
and to which Lena seems to aspire. Lena's correspondence to visual culture
is complicated by her resemblance to the Southern Belle in Jim's descriptions
of her and in the way she evokes the Old South for him. Further, the idealized
figuration of Lena contrasts the portrait presented in Jim's wife, Mrs. Burden,
a more radical feminist figure who sets off Lena's New Womanhood as a
product of a less political but nevertheless highly subversive independence.

A SELF-PORTRAIT OF A NEW WOMAN

Although the trope of the Virgin Land figured in cultural symbolism of
America from its inception, the turn-of-the-century cultural imagination saw
a new female figure that was used to modernize the national image and establish norms of race, ethnicity, and gender. The image of the American Girl,
the figure made popular by Charles Dana Gibson's illustrations (figure 12.1),

Figure 12.1. "Mr. Gibson's American Girl" by C. D. Gibson (*Ladies' Home Journal*, February 1903).

was popular in various cultural media—in fine art, magazines, and literature. Artists' images of the American girl more or less revealed their conformity to views of America as well as of the female; such an American Girl as the Gibson Girl—namely the young, tall, rich, white, marriageable, and radiantly beautiful American girl as a debutante, a school girl, or a bride—became the ideal model of the progressive and materialistic society at the turn of the century.[9]

When *My Ántonia* was published, the publisher Houghton Mifflin intended to put a frontispiece that might be similar to the frontispiece in *O Pioneers!*, which was the illustration of Alexandra by Clarence F. Underwood, one of the popular illustrators of the time (figure 12.2).[10] Willa Cather, however, rejected the idea. Instead of adopting a popular type frontispiece, Cather was eager to insert a series of drawings by W. T. Benda, who was known for portraits of ethnic women called "Benda Woman."[11] Also, Cather not only selected the illustrator, but also chose which scenes to draw and even designed layouts of her book.[12] As a result, the tone of the illustrations became

**Figure 12.2.   The frontispiece in the first edition of O Pi-
oneers! The Willa Cather Archive.**

quite different from such a frontispiece as in *O Pioneers!* Cather literally or
visually revises the popular portrait of American Girl; while the frontispiece
of *O Pioneers!* accords with the popular type of the American Girl who looks
proudly at the reader without any background, a series of Benda drawings in
My Ántonia shows each scene more vividly, where characters are situated in
nature without posing.

As suggested in Cather's considerable concern with the illustrations for
the novel, *My Ántonia* is closely related to the question about "the power of
figure-making."[13] In the Introduction, the narrator "I" and Jim share warm
feelings about their childhood memories in a prairie town, especially about
a Bohemian girl Ántonia, and decide to write about her and to "get a picture
of her"[14]; while the narrator cannot accomplish it, Jim succeeds and brings
his "picture" to the narrator. As male illustrators gave their images of girls in
the American Girl illustration, naming the drawings "Gibson Girl" or "Fisher

Girl," Jim succeeds in "get[ting] a picture" of Ántonia, which he titles "My Ántonia."[15] But to what extent is the novel about Ántonia? From under the surface of Jim's narrative about Ántonia emerges another picture that Jim cannot control and that threatens his power of image making.

When first introduced in the novel, Lena is perfectly dressed and creates a "picture" by herself:

> A plump, fair-skinned girl was standing in the doorway. She looked demure and pretty, and made a graceful picture in her blue cashmere dress and little blue hat, with a plaid shawl drawn neatly about her shoulders and a clumsy pocketbook in her hand.[16]

Ántonia and Jim are surprised to see Lena "brushed and smoothed and dressed like a town girl, smiling at [them] with perfect composure."[17] Later, when Lena visits Jim's room in Lincoln, she is dressed so fashionably that Jim at first cannot recognize her:

> She was so quietly conventionalized by city clothes that I might have passed her on the street without seeing her. Her black suit fitted her figure smoothly, and a black lace hat, with pale-blue forget-me-nots, sat demurely on her yellow hair.[18]

Stylishly dressed up and standing with a composed smile, Lena's figure may remind readers of those girls on the magazine covers. In these descriptions of Lena, Jim exclusively focuses on her clothes, minutely depicting what she wears and showing how she looks like a town girl. Looking for new fashion, Lena is "never tired of poring over fashion books" and has "picked up all the conventional expressions she heard at Mrs. Thomas's dressmaking shop."[19] In this sense, Lena seems to be conventionalized—or Americanized—in fashion and speech, trying to be like an American girl in the town.

Lena's seemingly conformist aspect, however, does not necessarily mean that Lena seeks to be a standard American girl. Regarding herself as one of "the Lapp girls,"[20] she rather performs the "American," just as Alexandra chooses to follow the American way to succeed in *O Pioneers!* Moreover, the most essential point that distinguishes Lena from "American" girls in the town is her sexuality. Embodying feminine beauty, Lena's femininity is strongly linked with sexuality, which is suppressed in the gender norm of Jim's childhood. On first meeting her in the prairie, the boy Jim feels that she is "undressed"; then in the famous dream of Jim's, Lena appears before Jim "in a short skirt, with a curved reaping-hook in her hand" and solicits him for a kiss.[21] In Jim's recurrent dream, it is Lena who has agency and Jim who remains passive; Lena says, "*I* can kiss you as much as *I like*,"[22] not "you can kiss me as much as you like." In this dream, where "desire and fear clearly contend with one another,"[23] Jim imagines Lena's potential possession of power and agency that he cannot control. Lena, though not always intentionally, traps men into her net; she is "accused of making Ole Benson lose the little sense he had"[24] when she was a little girl; finds Nick Svendsen chasing her and "rushing [her] pretty hard"[25]; makes Sylvester Lovett crazily love her and have a desperate runaway marriage with a widow; drives Old Colonel Raleigh and the Polish violinist Ordinsky to love her and feel jealous of each other; and fascinates Jim to the extent that his mentor advises him to leave Lena.

Presenting "a figure of alluring and threatening feminine excess,"[26] Jim's portrait of Lena has something in common with a newer type of American Girl in the 1910s, when Jim (and Cather) writes the story. In the 1910s, while the Gibson Girl and the Christy Girl were still popular, a different image of the American Girl prevailed in popular culture, portrayed by such illustrators as Coles Phillips and James Montgomery Flagg (figures 12.3 and 12.4).

Figure 12.3. "Net Results" by Coles Phillips (*Life*, Aug. 24, 1911).

Figure 12.4. "Has This Ever Happened to You?" by James Montgomery Flagg (*Life*, July 11, 1912).

The Phillips Girl and the Flagg Girl were sometimes called a "vamp" type, which showed a new type of playful and sexually alluring girl who became a threat and "a temptation to men that seemed irresistible yet was ultimately destructive."[27] Appearing in popular magazines, the "vamp" type of girl "is dark, she is sexual, she is volatile, she is mobile, and, above all, she lives alone, outside the sphere of home and family."[28] Lena's sexual femininity foreshadows the gender situation in the 1910s, presenting modern femininity or modern female sexuality, which is contrasted with Ántonia's traditional, vulnerable female sexuality.

Jean Schwind suggests that Benda's illustrations in *My Ántonia* play a role as "the novel's visual textual supplements" to Jim's narrative,[29] and Cather's artistic arrangement of Benda's drawings functions in emphasizing the contrast between Ántonia and Lena. Figure 12.5 shows Lena knitting on the prairie, which corresponds to Jim's description of her "out among her cattle, bareheaded and barefooted, scantily dressed in tattered clothing, always knitting as she watched her herd," and especially of her seeming "undressed."[30]

Figure 12.5. Lena knitting on the prairie. The Willa Cather Archive.

Cather's letter to Greenslet shows that "she gloated over this drawing that Lena was fairly bursting out of her clothes."[31] Benda's drawing thus literally plays the role of supplemental interpretation, visualizing what Jim feels about Lena's female and sexual body and at the same time showing the real Lena with a long skirt, not a short one like that found in Jim's recurrent dream. Figure 12.6 shows Ántonia driving a herd in the snow, which accords with what Widow Stevens tells Jim: "After the winter begun she wore a man's long overcoat and boots, and a man's felt hat with a wide brim. . . . One day in December, the snow began to fall. Late in the afternoon I saw Ántonia driving her cattle homeward across the hill."[32] Coming back home after being deserted by Donovan, Ántonia returns to a mannish girl, though she at the same time expects to be a mother. On the one hand, Ántonia is a man/woman; on the other hand, Ántonia's sexuality is safely suppressed by male outfits so

Figure 12.6. Ántonia driving her cattle in the snow. The Willa Cather Archive.

that Ántonia is not so much a man/woman as a man/mother, a trope in which any threatening or vulnerable female sexuality is eliminated.

Schwind juxtaposes these two drawings, arguing that both Ántonia and Lena assert "the 'masculine authority,'" having a cattle whip and knitting needles respectively, which are "iconographic symbols of command, independence, and authority."[33] At the same time, it will be no less important here to pay attention to differences between them. Though both of the two are depicted walking alone in the prairie, their portraits make a vivid contrast, showing summer/winter, knitting needles/a cow whip, whiteness/darkness, and one girl slightly "undressed"/another whose body is tightly covered by a man's clothes. As Schwind suggests, there is some similarity between these two drawings and Jules Adolphe Breton's "The Song of the Lark" (figure 12.7); however, the portrait of Lena resembles Breton's much more than that of Ántonia. In "The Song of the Lark," it is summer and the girl is barefooted with a similar dress as in Lena's portrait. Also, Jim's recurrent dream of

Figure 12.7. "The Song of the Lark" by Jules Adolphe Breton (1884), Wikimedia Commons.

Lena can link her with Breton's girl: "Lena Lingard came across the stubble barefoot, in a short skirt, with a curved reaping-hook in her hand, and she was flushed like the dawn, with a kind of luminous rosiness all about her."[34] A barefoot figure with a curved reaping hook and the image of dawn are similar to Breton's painting, except that the girl in Jim's dream wears a short skirt. Lena can therefore be seen as a sexualized version of Breton's girl—or of Cather's self-made heroines like Thea.

Indeed, while Ántonia shares Alexandra's female masculinity and cross-dressing on the farm, Lena, like Thea, follows "traditionally male patterns" of heroic, entrepreneurial narrative, but with female talents.[35] Lena follows the rags-to-riches story through succeeding at dressmaking and proceeds from the countryside to Black Hawk, then to Lincoln—just as Jim does—and finally goes to San Francisco. While Jim finds Ántonia "battered but not di-minished"[36] after twenty years, Tiny tells Jim in 1908 that Lena is "the only person" she knows "who never gets any older,"[37] just as the narrator "I" in the Introduction describes how Jim "never seems to me to grow older."[38] Both Jim and Lena embody Western dreams. Also, just as Thea, who is criticized in girlhood for her friendship with the Mexicans, is to be admired in the end as one of the "examples of Moonstone enterprise,"[39] Lena, who is seen as "a bad one" in her girlhood, is to be "much respected in Black Hawk."[40] Thus Lena is an alternative heroine in the novel. Creating a tension with Jim's portrait of Ántonia, Lena's success story presents a radical portrait in *My Ántonia*, partially revising Thea's.

Different from Ántonia and even from Cather's previous girls, Lena is fully aware of limitations of women at home and openly rejects the traditional role of wife and mother. While Ántonia adores her father, Lena is always "a good daughter to her mother."[41] In the famous scene where Lena helps her brother choose a Christmas gift for her mother, her brother Chris does not know whether he should buy B for Berthe, his mother's name, or M for Mother, and Lena advises him to buy B, saying, "It will please her for you to think about her name. Nobody ever calls her by it now."[42] Thus Lena resists the idea that marriage gives a woman only a role of "Mother," which is vividly contrasted with Ántonia's being a "natural-born mother."[43] Lena's aversion to traditional female roles is closely linked with her distaste for farm life: "She remembered home as a place where there were always too many children, a cross man, and work piling up around a sick woman."[44] In the town of Black Hawk, the traditional role of a married woman as a mother is broken by Mrs. Gardener, "who r[u]n[s] the business and look[s] after everything."[45] Differ-ent from Lena's mother, who is always called "Mother" and not by her name, Mrs. Gardener's name appears in many places: "'Molly Bawn' was painted in large blue letters on the glossy white side of the hotel bus, and 'Molly' was engraved inside Johnnie's ring and on his watch-case—doubtless on his heart, too."[46] The name emphasizes the individual rather than the societal role.

Loving independence, Lena comes out of the country and proudly tells Jim and Ántonia that she has "a room of my [her] own at Mrs. Thomas's," while Ántonia tells Jim that she would "die of lonesomeness" in a city.[47] Lena insists on her economic independence, and "she wouldn't have a school boy spending his money on her" at the theater.[48] She also declares she does not rely on the men of her family; in the scene of the picnic in "No-Man's Land"[49] at the end of book II, Lena tells the other girls and Jim that she is going to build a house for her mother: "'I tell you what girls,' she sat up with sudden energy; 'I'm going to get my mother out of that old sod house where she's lived so many years. The men will never do it.'"[50] Here is shown a rare example in which

Lena, who is repeatedly described as "easy" and "soft," declares her plan "with sudden energy." After two years, she truly plans to build a house for her mother with her own money; Lena is definitely a self-made woman working to help other women. In fact, fully articulating limitations imposed upon women and openly rejecting conventional gender roles, Lena is a more critical New Woman than Cather's previous girls such as Alexandra and Thea. She stands as a voice of resistance to Jim's nostalgia for Ántonia.

Above all, what makes Lena different from not only Ántonia, but also from other previous immigrant heroines of Cather's is that she remains single. She vows never to marry even though she is involved with heterosexual relationships.[51] Asked by Frances about her relationship with Nick Svendsen, Lena tells her that she does not want to marry because she has "seen a good deal of married life" and she does not "care for it."[52] Later in the novel, Jim says to Lena, "Every handsome girl like you marries, of course," and this is denied by Lena, who insists that she does not "want a husband," who becomes one of the "cranky old fathers" and tries to control his wife.[53] She is much more subversive than her New Womanish sisters in Cather's earlier works; different from Alexandra, who is a mannish girl in male clothes, and from Thea, who is said to be "not the marrying kind,"[54] Lena is almost excessively feminine and marriageable, and she resists the conventional plot.

In the end, Lena settles in San Francisco, having a store in the neighborhood of Tiny's house. In book V, Jim's final reunion with Ántonia and her family in a Nebraska farm is preceded by his meeting "the two women together" in San Francisco—Lena and Tiny, who have a good relationship, supporting each other.[55] Though Lena and Tiny do not live together literally, the idea of sisterhood shown in the end presents quite a powerful alternative to heterosexual marriage—a modern version of the "Boston marriage," which was frequently seen in urban areas around the turn of the century.

Thus from beneath the celebrated portrait of "My Ántonia" drawn by Jim emerges another portrait of a girl who becomes a New Woman, whom Jim cannot control and who serves to relativize Jim's nostalgic and romantic portrait of Ántonia. While Jim gives "a picture" of Ántonia as a goddess figure of the earth mother/the Primitive Woman, Jim cannot "get a picture"[56] of Lena. Lena remains an enigma to Jim, who cannot understand why Lena succeeds ("Lena's success puzzled me"[57]) or why Lena does not want to marry. Lena nevertheless has a powerful presence in Jim's narrative. As Lena in a sense deromanticizes Jim's picture of the pastoral, so she does his romantic idea of the Muse—the female icon. At the beginning of book III, Jim meditates on a phrase in Virgil's *Georgics* about bringing the Muse, who has just immigrated, into the "patria"—"to his father's fields."[58] Jim's association of the immigrant girls in Black Hawk with the Muse in the poetry of Virgil shows his attempt to shape mythically those girls into his version of Columbia. The character who comes to Jim's room, however, is not Ántonia, who stands at the center of his picture of "patria," but Lena. Jim's meditation about the Muse is interrupted by Lena's full body and again by the recurrence of the dream of "Lena coming across the harvest field in her short skirt."[59] Though Jim contains Lena into the image of the Muse at their first reunion, recurrent meetings with her let Lena's physical body burst out of the "image" of the Muse. Lena is "a figure of excess ('too plump,' 'too large') who cannot be contained and therefore must be abandoned,"[60] not only from his life, but also from his narrative. And yet Lena stands at the center of Jim's narrative about his Ántonia; among the five books in his narrative, the very middle book is titled "Lena Lingard"—and it is not "My Lena."

JIM'S GENDER TROUBLES AND A
HIDDEN LINK TO HIS SOUTHERN PAST

Lena's presence at the hidden center of Jim's narrative is more crucial than it seems when we consider how she evokes something other than the "Modern Woman" in the novel. Jim to some extent presents the dilemma and situation of middle-class Anglo-Saxon American men at the turn of the century, when Theodore Roosevelt encouraged them to be a "strenuous man." Michael Gorman, tracing the intertexuality in *My Ántonia* in relation to the Spanish-American War and the following American imperialism, sees "U.S. expansionism" in Jim's narrative and links Jim with "no American more than Theodore Roosevelt, a figure deeply associated with America's territorial expansion at home and abroad."[61] Gorman associates Jim's hostility to the old snake in the story with "rhetoric the American press and politicians voiced of Spain during the Spanish-American War," and states that "Cather shapes Jim's Eurocentric sense of national and cultural identity through his association with Father Kelly and Charley Harling, champions of cultural and martial imperialism."[62] But how much is Jim a Charley Harling or a Theodore Roosevelt?

Jim's masculinity is highly unstable throughout the novel. In the episode of killing a snake, Ántonia admires Jim, saying, "You is just like big mans," but it turns out that this is "a mock adventure."[63] Also, when Jim asks Ántonia for a kiss and tells her that he cares for her most, Ántonia jokingly reacts, calling him "a kid."[64] Called a "kid," Jim is thus made to remain a "boy" by Ántonia, who admires Charlie, cooking and sewing for him. Charlie is two years older than Jim and is "already preparing for Annapolis" when sixteen.[65] Later, Jim gets irritated because Charlie is "already at Annapolis" while he is "still sitting in Black Hawk" and behaving "like the grammar-school children."[66] When Jim comes back from the East in book IV, Charley is "off in his battleship, cruising somewhere on the Caribbean sea."[67] Considering the time span of this novel, it is likely that Charlie participates in the Spanish-American War. Unlike Charlie, Jim cannot get involved in this imperial war as a "strenuous man." Jim is not such a symbol of American imperialism, though he does try and wish to be.

Since the groundbreaking study by Blanche H. Gelfant on Jim's sexual fears, critics have largely recognized Jim's lack of masculinity and his inability to fit the standard of middle-class Anglo-Saxon American man. While he is "a sexual-linguistic gatekeeper, translator, and monitor of female and immigrant language and behavior," he is at the same time attracted to immigrants and likes to be with them rather than with Lincoln—or American—girls, and his "contempt for conventional morality, art, and sexuality" leads to his being called "queer."[68] Hating Mr. Harling, who seems to Jim "autocratic and imperial in his ways,"[69] Jim likes to be with Mrs. Harling and her daughters. Though he curiously notes that "Charley Harling and I had hunted through these woods, fished from the fallen logs,"[70] there is no scene like that in the novel. Jim seems to identify more with girls, enjoying a picnic in the "No-Man's Land,"[71] and is considerably feminized when he is nearly assaulted by Cutter, in place of Ántonia.

As race, ethnicity, and gender are closely intertwined in the novel, Jim's lack of—or deviation from the standard of—American masculinity may be linked with the point that he is a Southern gentleman dislocated in the West. Anne Goodwyn Jones points out the hidden presence of "Dixie" in Jim's narrative in *My Ántonia*, connecting Jim's gender troubles with his Southern connection, which she suggests is shared by Cather:

> *My Ántonia* is . . . a novel that, while it openly embraces Nebraska and Ántonia, keeps a closet date with Virginia and Southern white manhood. The buried text of *My Ántonia* is the story of the burden of Jim's, and Cather's, Southern history, of how to relieve—and how to be broken by—that burden.[72]

Though Jim's Southern memories do not appear on the surface, his traumatic rejection/attraction to his Old World can be traced in the novel; for example, his attachment to Mr. Shimerda, who on first meeting reminds Jim of "the old portraits [he] remembered in Virginia"[73] and who commits suicide from homesickness, which Jim quite sympathetically understands; the appearance of "a country that looked something like Nebraska and something like Virginia" in his dream after listening to Pavel's haunting story about the Old World, the story filled with the black/white contrast[74]; the racist description of Blind d'Arnault, who has "the soft, amiable negro voice, like those [he] remembered from early childhood, with the note of docile subservience in it . . . [and] the happiest face [he] had seen since [he] left Virginia."[75]

As the Southern tradition is inseparably connected with problematic issues of class and race, Jim's portraits of immigrant girls are to a certain extent influenced by the perspective he acquired in his childhood in Virginia. Ántonia is characterized by her brown skin and eyes: "They [Ántonia's eyes] were big and warm and full of light, like the sun shining on brown pools in the wood. Her skin was brown, too, and in her cheeks she had a glow of rich, dark color. Her brown hair was curly and wild-looking."[76] As Michelle Ann Abate aptly suggests, "Ántonia's white European ethnicity often becomes blurred with Southern racial blackness"[77] in the portrait of Ántonia illustrated by Jim. Ántonia works hard on the farm and also works as a servant at the Burdens and the Harlings, cooking, housekeeping, and nursing, and "there was a basic harmony between Ántonia and her mistress."[78] As Jones points out, Wick Cutter's potential rape of Ántonia can be linked with Martin Colbert's of Nancy in *Sapphira and the Slave Girl*.[79] Moreover, the name of Ántonia's baby—Martha—who was born through a kind of "miscegenation" can be linked with the name of Blind d'Arnault's mother, Martha, who gives birth to him probably through miscegenation in the Southern plantation.

Though critics have barely noted it, Jim's Southern connection can be traced also in the portrait of Lena.[80] Frequently going out with her, Jim comes to keep company with the landlord of Lena's lodging house and with a man living there. Her landlord from Kentucky, Old Colonel Raleigh, finds a Southern tone in Lena's voice, though she is Norwegian, and adores her: "He said [Lena's] voice reminded him of Southern voices, and he found as many opportunities of hearing it as possible."[81] Considering that Jim mentions Lena's "soft" and sleepy voice quite often in his narrative, it is likely that he is attracted to Lena with her voice that—maybe unconsciously—reminds him of a Southern drawl. Jim goes to see plays with Lena, one of which is "a war play called 'Shenandoah.'"[82] "Dancing 'Home, Sweet Home,' with Lena was like coming in with the tide,"[83] Jim notes; the dance with Lena is like "the waltz of coming home to something, of inevitable, fated return"[84]—possibly to his suppressed past in the South, or his "patria," of which Lena is the Muse.[85] Neglecting his study, Jim plays not only with Lena but also with the Pole, who has an old tradition of chivalry, and with the old Colonel, who "used to talk to [Jim] about Lena and the 'great beauties' he had known in his youth" in the South.[86] Though Jim's memory of his Old World is suppressed in his narrative, Lena secretly presents a hidden link to it, evoking the Southern Belle.

Vividly contrasted with Ántonia, who has "brown legs and arms," Lena has "a miraculous whiteness" despite always being exposed to the sun in the prairie.[87] In the contrast between Ántonia and Lena can be found Cather's childhood categorization; darkness is linked with tomboyness and whiteness is linked with femininity. In this novel, the Scandinavian whiteness of Lena is linked with whiteness of the Southern Belle, and at the same time Lena's femininity, too sexual and volatile, deconstructs gender expectations for the seductive Southern Belle. It can be possible to see the resemblance between the antebellum Southern image making of the Southern Belle and the turn-of-the-century image making of the American Girl, both using a sexually innocent white girl to symbolize the nation/region, establishing the standard of feminine beauty and racial superiority, and stabilizing the boundary of nation, race, and gender.[88] In *My Ántonia*, the deviation from gender expectations in turn-of-the-century America is linked with the image of the South; while it is impossible for Jim to acquire masculinity, Lena shows overtly abundant and sexual femininity, both subverting the gender norms not only of turn-of-the-century America, but also of the Old South.

CATHER'S IDEA OF MODERN WOMANHOOD

To complicate matters, the Introduction functions in contextualizing Jim's nostalgic, retrospective narrative and in situating his narrative in early twentieth-century America, where men tried to seek—or restore—their masculinity in their imperial enterprise and their romantic myth of the West, while women became more independent and rejected the traditional role of wife and mother. In the Introduction, the narrator "I" presents another New Woman figure, who can be compared with Lena: Mrs. Jim Burden. Mrs. Burden is depicted as embodying the 1910s radical—or political—New Womanhood in New York: "She gave one of her town houses for a Suffrage headquarters, produced one of her own plays at the Princess Theater, was arrested for picketing during a garment-makers' strike, etc."[89] The portrait of Mrs. Burden, who participates in social movements as well as modern art, can be associated with the image of radical New Women in Greenwich Village in New York, where Cather lived when she wrote *My Ántonia*.[90] Greenwich Village was the center of radical movements regarding both social problems and art at the beginning of the twentieth century, called "Bohemia" or "New Bohemia,"[91] where especially from 1912, radical movements became remarkable with, for example, the creation of the Liberal Club and radical women's group Heterodoxy. Though there is no direct reference to Greenwich Village in *My Ántonia*, it will be meaningful to link social situations of the 1910s in Greenwich Village and how the narrator "I" describes Mrs. Burden, whose characteristics have much in common with radical "Bohemian girls" found in Greenwich Village, namely American Bohemia.

Being neither a European Bohemian like Ántonia nor an American Bohemian like Mrs. Burden, Lena seems to reflect Cather's complicated attitude toward the idea of modern womanhood. First, Lena is a fairly subversive New Woman and could be a radical feminist by nature in claiming women's limitations in a domestic space, but she never actively joins radical social movements. In this respect, it is meaningful that Cather makes Lena a dressmaker. In addition to increasing suffrage movements in urban areas, there were a lot of strikes in big cities such as New York and Chicago at the turn of the century. Ladies garment workers founded the International Ladies Garment Workers Union, which had many branches in major cities, and they had two big strikes in 1909 and 1910, which not only working women joined, but also a number of wealthy women supported. In the novel, then, Lena never joins the labor union or strikes, while Mrs. Burden is "arrested for picketing during a garment-makers' strike."[92] Cather does not make Lena work at a garment factory as a factory girl but makes her run a dress shop successfully as a dress designer herself; in this way, Cather keeps Lena away from politics or radical social movements. Lena's success derives from her ability to support women in society with taste rather than subvert societal standards.

Moreover, Lena's commitment to the theater is quite different from that of Mrs. Burden. As the narrator of the Introduction reveals, Mrs. Burden is a playwright, producing her own play at the Princess Theater. This was an actual theater founded in 1913 and was located at West 39th Street in New York City. It was a small Broadway theater and was known to show experimental plays. As the narrator reveals, Mrs. Burden also dabbles in modern art as "the patroness to a group of young poets and painters of advanced ideas and mediocre ability,"[93] and the narrator's ironic comments here may reflect Cather's own sense of irony. While Mrs. Burden's interest in art is rather political, Lena simply enjoys art. In book III, Jim frequently goes to the theater with Lena, and her appreciation of the theater is depicted as emotional and even sentimental. When they go to see "Camille," Jim sees Lena "in tearful contemplation of the ceiling" after the second act, and "through the scene between Marguerite and the elder Duval, Lena we[eps] unceasingly."[94] Jim regards her as superior to other town girls in that she understands and appreciates art: "As I walked about there I congratulated myself that I had not brought some Lincoln girl who would talk during the waits about the Junior dances, or whether the cadets would camp at Plattsmouth."[95] Further, Lena can be compared with Mrs. Burden. The narrator of the Introduction describes Mrs. Burden as "unimpressionable and temperamentally incapable of enthusiasm" while her husband has a "romantic and ardent disposition."[96] Considering that Jim "we[eps] unrestrainedly" until his handkerchief is "wet through" when he sees "Camille,"[97] Cather may partly connect romantic enthusiasm with the sentimental appreciation of art, which is shown as superior to the lack of enthusiasm. Additionally, several plays that Jim goes to see with Lena—including "Rip Van Winkle," "Shenandoah," "Robin Hood," and "Camille"—are all highly appraised by Cather, who was a theater critic. Particularly, Cather's article on "Camille" in *Journal*, written on November 26, 1893, is much reflected in Jim's long, emotional report of the play in book III; in the article, Cather mentions "the most intelligent and cultured audience that has assembled in the Lansing Theatre."[98] Naturally, the reactions of Lena and Jim to the play correspond to Cather's own, and, considering that Cather's reviews frequently commented not only on plays themselves, but also on the audience, it may be reasonable to say that Lena and Jim are shown positively as members of "the most intelligent and cultured audience."

Living as a New Woman and celebrating New Woman personalities, Cather displayed a negative predisposition toward the so-called New Woman novels and distanced herself from the women's movement, which was manifested more forcefully when she wrote *My Ántonia*.[99] The negative portrayal of Mrs. Burden suggests Cather's critique of radical New Womanhood and the "New Bohemia" of Greenwich Village in the first decade of the twentieth century. Implicitly occupying the center of the novel, Lena can be seen as Cather's ideal New Woman, who never fights politically but still manages to effectively overcome women's limitations in a patriarchal society and challenges conventional gender roles. Her portrait is both complex and moderate, attracting Jim as much as Mrs. Burden repels Jim, but ultimately Lena, with her American Girl polish and flirtatious skills, manages an independence all her own.

NOTES

This essay is a largely revised version of a part of my dissertation, "American Girls: Nation and Gender in James, Wharton, and Cather" (University of Maryland, College Park, 2010).

1. Carroll Smith-Rosenberg, *Disorderly Conduct: Visions of Gender in Victorian America* (New York: Oxford University Press, 1985), 176.

2. Ellen Wiley Todd, *The "New Woman" Revised: Painting and Gender Politics on Fourteenth Street* (Berkeley: University of California Press, 1993), xxvii, 2.

3. Willa Cather, *My Ántonia: The Scholarly Edition*, ed. Charles Mignon (Lincoln: University of Nebraska Press, 1997), 342.

4. Edwin T. Bowden, "The Frontier Isolation," in *The Dungeon of the Heart: Human Isolation and the American Novel* (New York: Macmillan, 1961), 46–54, reprinted in *Ántonia*, ed. Harold Bloom (New York: Chelsea House Publishers, 1991), 16.

5. Robert E. Scholes, "Hope and Memory in *My Ántonia*," *Shenandoah* 14, no. 1 (Autumn 1962): 24–29, reprinted in *Ántonia*, ed. Bloom, 20.

6. Deborah G. Lambert, "The Defeat of a Hero: Autonomy and Sexuality in *My Ántonia*," *American Literature* 53, no. 4 (1982): 688.

7. Marilee Lindemann, "'It Ain't My Prairie': Gender, Power, and Narrative in *My Ántonia*," in *New Essays on My Ántonia*, ed. Sharon O'Brien (Cambridge: Cambridge University Press, 1999), 127.

8. Blanche H. Gelfant, "The Forgotten Reaping-Hook: Sex in *My Ántonia*," *American Literature* 43, no. 1 (March 1971): 67.

9. For a study of visual and literary images of the American Girl, see Martha Banta's *Imaging American Women: Idea and Ideals in Cultural History* (New York: Columbia University Press, 1987). For a study of images of American women at the turn of the century and the creation of the American Girl, see David Jeremiah Slater's "The American Girl, Her Life and Times: An Ideal and Its Creators, 1890–1930" (PhD dissertation, University of Minnesota, 2005) and Lois W. Banner's *American Beauty* (New York: Knopf, 1983). Also, recent criticism has developed arguments about Cather's versions of American girls/women from various perspectives. For example, Martha Patterson, in *Beyond the Gibson Girl: Reimagining the American New Woman, 1895–1915* (Urbana: University of Illinois Press, 2005), explores how the WASP icon of the Gibson Girl is revised in several writers' texts in terms of ethnicity, race, and region. She discusses how Cather's heroines, such as Tommy, Alexandra, and Thea, transgress gender normativity. Then, Michelle Ann Abate considers the issues of gender and nation together, exploring the way in which tomboyism had been linked with whiteness and Americanness. She argues that in Cather's culturally pluralist America immigrant heroines' tomboyism helps them present Americanness. See *Tomboys: A Literary and Cultural History* (Philadelphia: Temple University Press, 2008).

10. Underwood published a book of his illustrations in 1912 titled *American Types*, in which he, just as Gibson and Christy had, presents a lot of figures of the "American Girl" as the WASP icon. Cather found his illustration of Alexandra "incongruous" for her novel and asked to have it removed from a new edition in a letter she wrote to Ferris Greenslet, her editor at Houghton Mifflin, on December 28, 1919. See Andrew Jewell and Janis Stout, eds., *The Selected Letters of Willa Cather* (New York: Knopf, 2013), 285.

11. Evelyn I. Funda, "Picturing Their Ántonia(s): Mikoláš Aleš and the Partnership of W. T. Benda and Willa Cather," *Cather Studies* 8 (2010): 363.

12. Janis P. Stout, "The Observant Eye, the Art of Illustration, and Willa Cather's *My Ántonia*," *Cather Studies* 5: *Willa Cather's Ecological Imagination* (Lincoln: University of Nebraska Press, 2003), 132–33. *My Ántonia* has eight drawings, though Cather's original plan was to have twelve drawings, which was not possible because of the limited budget from the publisher. For the whole story about her choice of Benda's drawings, see Jean Schwind, "The Benda Illustrations to *My Ántonia*: Cather's 'Silent' Supplement to Jim Burden's Narrative," *PMLA* 100, no. 1 (1985): 51–67; Funda, "Picturing Their Ántonia(s)."

13. Lindemann, "'It Ain't My Prairie,'" 116.

14. Cather, *My Ántonia*, xii.

15. Ibid., xii, xiii.

16. Ibid., 154–55.

17. Ibid., 155.

18. Ibid., 257.

19. Ibid., 270, 273.

20. Ibid., 235.

21. Ibid., 160, 218.

22. Ibid., 218; emphasis added.

23. Gelfant, "The Forgotten Reaping-Hook," 65.

24. Cather, *My Ántonia*, 160–61.

25. Ibid., 157.

26. Marilee Lindemann, *Willa Cather: Queering America* (New York: Columbia University Press, 1999), 68.

27. Carolyn Kitch, *The Girl on the Magazine Cover: The Origins of Visual Stereotypes in American Mass Media* (Chapel Hill: University of North Carolina Press, 2001), 58.

28. Ibid., 61.

29. Schwind, "The Benda Illustrations," 55.

30. Cather, *My Ántonia*, 159–60, 60.

31. Stout, "The Observant Eye," 141.

32. Cather, *My Ántonia*, 308.

33. Schwind, "The Benda Illustrations," 65, 63.

34. Cather, *My Ántonia*, 218.

35. Susan J. Rosowski, *The Voyage Perilous: Willa Cather's Romanticism* (Lincoln: University of Nebraska Press, 1986), 69.

36. Cather, *My Ántonia*, 321–22.

37. Ibid., 294.

38. Ibid., xi.

39. Willa Cather, *The Song of the Lark* (New York: Vintage Books, 1999), 429.

40. Cather, *My Ántonia*, 305, 290.

41. Ibid., 160.

42. Ibid., 166.

43. Ibid., 310.

44. Ibid., 283.

45. Ibid., 176.

46. Ibid., 185.

47. Ibid., 158, 312.

48. Ibid., 263.

49. Ibid., 226.

50. Ibid., 233.

51. Judith Fetterley, focusing on the issue of Cather's lesbianism, sees Lena as a lesbian: "her sexuality is neither conventionally female nor conventionally male but rather identifies an erotic potential possible only outside the patriarchal, heterosexual territory of rigid definitions and polar oppositions. Characterized by a diffused sen-

suality rooted in a sense of self and neither particularly aggressive nor particularly passive, Lena represents one model of lesbian sexuality." Judith Fetterley, "*My Ántonia*, Jim Burden, and the Dilemma of the Lesbian Writer," in *Lesbian Texts and Contexts: Radical Revisions*, ed. Karla Jay, Joanne Glasgow, and Catherine Stimpson (New York: New York University Press, 1990), 159. Though her essay is convincing overall and Lena's position in the novel is certainly unique, Fetterley's view of Lena as a lesbian is not supported by the evidence because she powerfully belongs to heterosexual order.

52. Cather, *My Ántonia*, 157.

53. Ibid., 282.

54. Cather, *Song*, 94.

55. Cather, *My Ántonia*, 318. Tiny is another New Woman character, who "lead[s] the most adventurous life and to achieve the most solid worldly success." Ibid., 291. Unlike Lena, Tiny follows the male plot of going to the West and making money. In this respect, the title of Book IV, "The Pioneer Woman's Story," does not so much refer to Ántonia as to Tiny. Though achieving material success, Tiny is not depicted positively; in her, "the faculty of becoming interested is worn out." Ibid., 294. Cather's treatment of Tiny suggests her negative attitude toward materialism as well as her deromanticization of the Western myth, which Jim still seeks in the novel.

56. Ibid., xii.

57. Ibid., 270.

58. Ibid., 256.

59. Ibid., 262.

60. Lindemann, "It Ain't My Prairie," 124.

61. Michael Gorman, "Jim Burden and the White Man's Burden: *My Ántonia* and Empire," *Cather Studies* 6 (2006): 50.

62. Ibid., 43, 47.

63. Cather, *My Ántonia*, 45, 48.

64. Ibid., 217.

65. Ibid., 145.

66. Ibid., 210.

67. Ibid., 297.

68. Lindemann, *Willa Cather*, 64, 65.

69. Cather, *My Ántonia*, 153.

70. Ibid., 226.

71. Ibid., 226.

72. Anne Goodwyn Jones, "Displacing Dixie: The Southern Subtext in *My Ántonia*," in *New Essays on My Ántonia*, 107.

73. Cather, *My Ántonia*, 23.

74. Ibid., 59.

75. Ibid., 178. At the hotel, d'Arnault plays "some good old plantation songs," and the men on the floor "gathe[r] round him, as he beg[ins] to play 'My Old Kentucky Home,'" then sing together "one negro melody after another." Ibid., 179. The episode of d'Arnault thus strongly evokes the image of the Southern plantation.

76. Ibid., 22–23.
77. Abate, *Tomboys*, 111.
78. Cather, *My Ántonia*, 174.
79. Jones, "Displacing Dixie," 104.
80. Though Sarah C. Gardam discusses the similarity between Lena Lingard and Lena Grove in William Faulkner's *Light in August*, in relation to their transcendence of their function "as targets for the objectifying male gaze," Gardam does not point out another essential similarity that both are seen as Southern women. Sarah C. Gardam, "Subverting the Male Gaze: Willa Cather's Lena Lingard and William Faulkner's Lena Grove," *Willa Cather Newsletter and Review* 49, no. 2 (2005): 35.
81. Cather, *My Ántonia*, 275.
82. Ibid., 263. The Shenandoah runs through the northern part of Virginia, and the Shenandoah Valley, where Cather's Virginia home stood, was one of the main battlefields of the Civil War.
83. Ibid., 215.
84. Ibid., 215–16.
85. Ibid., 256.
86. Ibid., 280.
87. Ibid., 149, 160.
88. It is interesting to note that in her earlier story, "The Profile" (1907), Cather challenges the icon of the American Girl by making the heroine have a physical deformity. The name of the American Girl, who is a perfect beauty except that she has a scar on her cheek, is Virginia, and her scar embodies a traumatic memory of the portrait painter. The deformity in the American girl in this story implies Cather's ironic reaction to the obsession with physical beauty in the icon of the American Girl, which is linked with the image of the Southern Belle.
89. Cather, *My Ántonia*, x.
90. Cather moved to New York in 1906, living in an apartment in Greenwich Village. For more about radical reform movements found in Greenwich Village between 1912 and 1920, see chapter 7 in Joanna Levin, *Bohemia in America, 1858–1920* (Stanford: Stanford University Press, 2010).
91. Ibid., 339.
92. Cather, *My Ántonia*, x.
93. Ibid., x.
94. Ibid., 267.
95. Ibid., 267.
96. Ibid., x, xi.
97. Ibid., 269.
98. Willa Cather, *The World and the Parish: Willa Cather's Articles and Reviews, 1893–1902*, 2 vols, ed. William M. Curtin (Lincoln: University of Nebraska Press, 1970), 43.
99. In 1894, Cather severely criticized Sarah Grand's *The Heavenly Twins*, a New Woman novel about the woman's rights question. Also, in a book review in the *Leader* on April 8, 1898, she gave a fairly acidic comment on the second volume of the *Woman's Bible* edited under the direction of Elizabeth Cady Stanton. Cather

criticizes "the temerity of these estimable ladies," pointing out their lack of linguistic or theological learning. Cather, *World*, 539. In rejecting Stanton's emphasis on the plight of women, Cather seems to sympathize more with Emma Churchman Hewitt, whose essay Cather as an editor situated next to "Tommy, the Unsentimental" in the *Home Monthly*; in the essay titled "What Relation Does Woman Bear to the Present," Hewitt argues that there had been women who could be categorized as New Women before the phrase as such appeared, and strongly rejects the emphasis on "woman," stating that "the women of to-day who are really 'advanced' have sunk all idea of 'woman's rights.'" Emma Churchman Hewitt, "What Relation Does Woman Bear to the Present?," *Home Monthly* 6 (August 1896): 6. Cather received a number of letters from various women's groups in a short time after the publication of *O Pioneers!* in 1913; and she cried, "Perish all social clubs for women!" Elizabeth Sergeant, *Willa Cather: A Memoir* (Lincoln: University of Nebraska Press, 1963), 117.

Chapter Thirteen

The Gift Economies of *My Ántonia*

Dana Woodcock and Zachary Tavlin

Though a frontier novel engaged with the meta-narrative of Western settlement, Willa Cather's *My Ántonia* is replete with a number of microeconomies of gift exchange and circulation associated in various ways with the overlapping immigrant cultures of the Plains. A complex blend of sociocultural structures in the process of evolving and sedimenting, Cather's Nebraska is the site of a mixed plenitude of closed or partially open communities with their own rules of exchange running up against one another. They all must also content with larger macroeconomic capitalistic logics that threaten to level the contours of immigrant experience. From the presence of Black Hawk's Wick Cutter, a usurer who threatens to bring settler-farmers into the irreversible cycle of debt, to the tenuously sustainable contact zones of Bohemian and Scandinavian homesteading, the fate of Cather's characters is determined in large measure by the particular exchange networks in which they are willing and able to participate.

In this chapter we examine key examples of the anthropological literature of the gift, including the work of Marcel Mauss and Lewis Hyde in the context of Marx's historical analysis of commodification, as a means of tracking the narrative implications in *My Ántonia* of gifting and countergifting and primary and secondary modes of exchange. These modes are further complicated by their situation within a transitional macroeconomy, one positioned between agrarian sensibility and the shadow of industrialization.

The novel underlines this tension between exchange protocols through moments of noncomplementary gift transfer, including the initial gesture by which Ántonia attempts to give Jim a silver ring in return for the loaves of bread and basic English lessons the Burdens have given her. Jim considers the endeavor "reckless and extravagant" and suggests that such a display of gratitude signifies the sort of naiveté that will inevitably "[get] the better of these people" as they attempt to negotiate a free market economy.[1] Yet Ántonia is operating within an oppositional matrix, one that, as Mauss articulates, ensures survival not by exchange or even use value, but through the act itself—the circulation and reciprocation of the gift. Additional moments, including the domestic clash of Mrs. Shimerda's bread offering to the Burdens, the fight between Ambrosch and Jake over the damaged horse collar, the inequality of the cow/sock exchange between Mr. Burden and Mrs. Shimerda, and the extremity of Krajiek's abandonment of Bohemian sensibility in favor of free market exchange, continue to trace the discordance of overlapping communities and, more specifically, their economic codes.

The novel's split consciousness—not only between conflicting immigrant exchange protocols, but also between a broader pastoral sensibility and industrial commercialism—gestures toward the larger crisis of the novel's historical moment, namely the symbolic "closure" of the frontier, which in effect signals the triumph of a homogeneous commercial system. The novel animates such a phenomenon by way of Mr. Shimerda's burial, an attempt to honor the Bohemian tradition of crossroad burial by anticipating the gridding of the land, but which is ultimately thwarted by the same process; the traditional pastoral code of the Shimerdas cannot remain through the expansion of capitalism proper. The fate of gift economies in the logic of the narrative, we propose, mirrors the progress of American expansion through its liminal frontier. By dwelling on the transition, *My Ántonia* marks the crucial loss in communal exchange networks that occurred between the nineteenth and twentieth century.

ON THE GIFT ITSELF

Mauss's 1925 work *The Gift* (*Essai sur le don*) reversed the philosophical-sociological tradition, running from Montesquieu through Durkheim, that approached the study of social phenomena through abstract concepts rather than concrete facts (a general move Mauss shares with Marx). His method was "structuralist" insofar as he examined the totality of relationships among members of a social group, which are always economic, legal, religious, *and* aesthetic. The gift, for Mauss, embodied concretely the entire phenomenon of the social world; indeed, Mauss reversed the common theory of economic evolution, which he claimed "has not gone from barter to sale and from cash to credit" but *began* with the gift.[2] Indeed, looking back from a capitalistic society plagued by labor exploitation and alienation, Mauss mapped a mode of social interaction in which "it is something other than utility which makes

goods circulate" and in which the maintenance of a social bond is more significant than base economic gain.[3]

The central question of Mauss's essay is, "What force is there in the thing
given which compels the recipient to make a return?"[4] The answer to this
question will ground his social theory of the gift. He argues that, in "primitive" societies, a return gift is obligatory because all things possess *hau*, or
the spiritual incarnation of the land, the clan, or simply the owner-donor. If
all things possess *hau*, then in a gift exchange the donor confers upon the
receiver not just an object but "part of one's nature and substance," while to
receive is indeed "to receive part of someone's spiritual essence."[5] On this
spiritual model, the donor retains his hold on the object even as he gives it
away because the *hau* "wants to return to the place of its birth, to its sanctuary
of forest and clan and to its owner." To withhold a return gift is therefore not
only wrong, but also dangerous, and only by making a return can the receiver
(re)gain "authority and power over the original donor, who now becomes
the latest recipient."[6] But Mauss also states that "the recipient has a sort of
proprietary right over everything that belongs to the donor," for ultimately
the *hau* of the owner is the *hau* of the land, a relationship that sets in motion
the gift exchange in the first place; this right "is expressed and conceived as
a sort of spiritual bond" that must be honored (the price of refusal being a
literal declaration of war).[7]

Lewis Hyde's recent study of the gift (*The Gift: Imagination and the Erotic
Life of Property*) builds upon the work of Mauss while also departing from
him in occasionally significant ways. Like Mauss, Hyde contrasts gift economies with modern capital, though his assessment of the former is more ideal-
istic. For Hyde, the act of gifting is not a power play; indeed, contra Mauss,
Hyde elevates the role of receiver in the exchange. The power of the gift, on
this picture, is realized through *gratitude*, and the gift honors the receiver
capable of withstanding the labor of gratitude that involves a complete transformation of the self (one could say that "gratitude" replaces the obligation of
the return gift in Mauss's system). But to understand the significance of gratitude in the first place, one must understand that Hyde's model is not reducible
to a two-party exchange, but is based upon a larger communal circle where
no one individual's claim can dominate the relationship. One of his primary
examples, the *Kula*, requires every member of a wide gifting community to
pass red shell necklaces clockwise and arm shells counterclockwise, so that
one is always in the process of giving and receiving, with the operative principle that a gift "that cannot move loses its gift properties" entirely—it *must*
circulate or else it is not a gift at all.[8]

Gratitude, according to Hyde, is the labor undertaken by the soul to effect
a transformation in the receiver after a gift has been received. Between the

time it is received and the time it is passed along, one suffers gratitude, and it is only when one has been adequately moved or changed by the gift that one can give it away again. Passing the gift along is the final act of gratitude that completes the acceptance of the gift in the first place and finishes this labor, though this labor cannot be performed according to a socially regulated work schedule. Indeed, it is not something that can be imposed from without—like a creditor establishing the terms of repayment—but is instead "dictated by the course of life rather than by society, something that is often urgent but that nevertheless has its own interior rhythm, something more bound up with feeling, more interior, than work."[9] The receiver's transformation is not accomplished until he or she has the power to give the gift on his or her own terms; the end of the labor of gratitude is an accomplished *similarity* with the gift and with the donor.

The major difference between Hyde and Mauss is thus in the logic of the return obligation: they place emphasis on opposite sides of the exchange nexus (privileging receiver and donor, respectively). However, both see the gift as an economic structure entirely opposed to capital, to the way in which it alienates the laborer and turns all gifts into commodities. Section IV of Marx's *Capital, Volume 1* elaborates the attribution of spiritual powers to manufactured objects in a way that nonetheless grounds the process of commodification fully in the material realm of production (rather than in ritual): disordered and pathological consumption, indeed, originates in the process of production under capital. Marx argues that the specific embodiment or materialization of labor power under capital is tangled fundamentally with fetishization—it is only when labor is "alienated" *into* the commodity that the modern fetish arises:

> A commodity is therefore a mysterious thing, simply because in it the social character of men's labour appears to them as an objective character stamped upon the product of that labor, because the relation of the producers to the sum total of their own labour is presented to them as a social relation, existing not between themselves, but between the products of their labour.[10]

When something is produced *purely* for exchange, rather than use (though a minimum of use value is still necessary), it is produced as a commodity, so that by definition production for use by the producer his- or herself does not qualify. In the latter case, there is no alienation, for the laborer is present to the entire process of production. But when we no longer understand, in a rigorous epistemological sense, how the objects we both consume *and* produce are made—for in the case of production the proletarian's labor has been divided and specialized—commodities with exchange value appear without any reference to the social relations that were nonetheless necessary for their appearance (production).

In this case, relations between people (in Marx's famous formula of reification) are substituted by relations between things. As the principle of equivalence in exchange brings "the products of our labour into relation with each other as values," we equate "the different kinds of labour expended upon them."[11] This shift is the result of the way in which the commodity masks, or places under erasure, the very material conditions of its production. Once we cannot legitimately conceptualize labor as an act of existential expression, as a direct and complete product of holistic skill, intellect, or character, a deeply held ontological hierarchy inverts itself (if only at an unconscious or semi-conscious level). Commodification involves reproducibility, so that there is no sign or signature of a person underlying the product or service provided. Metaphorically and materially, the recognizable marks of a craft worker on his or her craft disappear into fetish.

Further, according to Marx, modern economics cannot help but think of the future as a horizon of growth and infinite expansion, while the past is "obliterated." Getting from one state of capital accumulation to another is not a simple symmetrical addition but an irreversible, asymmetric expansion in which the future is brought under the domain of quantity and exchange value. Its horizon is limited by the possibility of commodity realization, the smooth functioning of markets, and the eventual quantification of "futures" certificates in which time itself is assigned a monetary value. This is not the same model of temporality one finds in Hyde, for example, in which the addition of time as a variable in the gift situation adds qualitative nuance, typically benevolent if respected, to the labor of the return gift. Time under capital, however, *banalizes* the social "gift" of the commodity. In a sense there is no real future to speak of, or at least no future of radical alterity, so that the irreducibility of the gift to the workings of the market (which gives the gift its force as a mode of exchange) is eliminated. As Hyde argues, "a fee for service tends to cut off the force of gratitude" in the gift because we cannot really "predict the fruits of our labor," and gratitude requires an *unpaid* debt, the force and feeling of which motivates us to proceed in a gift relationship.[12] But the notion of an unquantifiable future is antithetical to capital, so one could say, perhaps, as a result, that the gift no longer exists under its dominion.

RINGS, COLLARS, AND CAPITALISTS

While it may be tempting to situate the tension between gift exchange protocols and capitalism within a binary model, placing Bohemian and American sensibilities on either side of that model as the competing systems' representatives, neither the novel nor its historical moment can fully substantiate such a reduction. In fact, the text presents its prairie setting as a contact zone for a network of economic and social sensibilities—a pastiche of pastoral, communal, and modified free market logics, the threads of which were likely imported both from the various points of origin of the novel's cast and the standing systems of prairie lifestyle—all of which, for families such as the Burdens, paradoxically compete with and coexist alongside a "purer" capitalism, at least up to a historical point. The relative harmony of this patchwork system seems to emerge as its own frontier sensibility, one that will inevitably fade once this "frontier" no longer deserves the name, but that nonetheless functions in the context of a burgeoning prairie community.

But for families such as the Shimerdas, who must import wholesale more heterogeneous and less capitalistic intuitions, the transition into this frontier economy is fraught with a network of tensions and mistranslations. The animation of this network surfaces quickly within the novel—indeed, even as we meet the Shimerda family—as the Burdens bring "a sack of potatoes and a piece of cured pork from the cellar, . . . some loaves of Saturday's bread, a jar of butter, and several pumpkin pies" to their new Bohemian neighbors, both as a show of hospitality and to minister to the basic needs of the family, which has subsisted on little due to fact that they have "come to live on a wild place where there was no garden or chicken-house, and very little broken land."[13] This gift of sustenance, though an integral part of American community formation, operates independently from any macroeconomic system. Further, at least for the Burdens, reciprocation is not necessarily expected, and even frowned upon given the Shimerdas' economic situation. Yet for the Shimerdas, the provisions represent something greater than simple sustenance or hospitality. Instead, for a Bohemian economic sensibility, these everyday objects serve a function much like Mauss's *hau*—as markers of initiation into the land and the community, and therefore imbued with the spirit of both alliance and of the Burdens themselves. According to this system, the gift begins the Shimerdas' circulation within the community, serving as a contract between them and the other families participating in an extended gifting matrix. Superficially, this idea doesn't seem incompatible with the Burdens' relatively simple hospitality model, which also attempts to integrate the new family into a network. But according to the Maussian model of gift exchange, the stakes are much higher for a family operating within a gift economy, for failure to reciprocate the gift— denying its circulation among the community and an eventual return to its birthplace—is an act of violence that would certainly provoke ostracism from the community *tout court*, without which a family like the Shimerdas likely could not survive the already difficult transition to the American frontier's patchy capitalism. Even Hyde, who would likely put pressure on the link between reciprocation and violence, nonetheless suggests that the act of reciprocation, which ignores schedules of labor and relies on "feeling" and "rhythm" as its motivators, is a vital contribution on the recipient's part to the palimpsestic energy of the *hau* in the larger communal formation. Regardless, the reciprocation of the Burdens' initial gesture is both compulsory and foreordained.

We can perhaps see the family's recognition of these stakes in Mrs. Shimerda's behavior throughout this initial gift exchange. Weeks later, when the Burdens pay the Shimerdas a holiday visit, Mrs. Shimerda is emotional, greeting the Burdens in tears and "pointing to her feet which were tied up in rags, and looking about accusingly at every one."[14] Later, Mr. Burden explains that "they were not beggars in the old country," implying that their old economic system was one they could successfully navigate, in contrast to the new situation to which they have not acclimated (due largely to the fact that, as we will soon discuss, Krajiek has mistranslated the market). Yet despite their poverty, Mrs. Shimerda reciprocates the Burdens' original gesture in the form of a small food gift. Just before Jim mentions this gift, Mrs. Shimerda "[grows] more calm and reasonable," perhaps because she is completing the gift exchange and therefore successfully participating in an economic activity (note that it is also significant that Jim cannot precisely identify the gift, although he does consume it—the gift speaks a language he cannot easily interpret).[15] Importantly, the timing of this reciprocation is determined not by the original giver, but by the original recipient; this principle—or its violation—will later cause friction during the failed gift exchange between Jake and Ambrosch.

While Mrs. Shimerda takes care to complete this exchange according to her own rhythm, we nevertheless see a more immediate return gift in the form of Ántonia's attempt to give Jim a silver ring once he teaches her a few words of English, adding one more "object" to the collection of gifts the Burdens have already bestowed:

> After Ántonia had said the new words over and over, she wanted to give me a little chased silver ring she wore on her middle finger. When she coaxed and insisted, I repulsed her quite sternly. I didn't want her ring, and I felt there was something reckless and extravagant about her wishing to give it away to a boy she had never seen before.[16]

As much as any other in the novel, this moment displays the competition between two largely oppositional codes—one, represented by Jim, that thinks in the (heavily simplified) terms of financial capital, and the other, manifest in Ántonia, that prioritizes the reciprocation of the gift above things like property ownership. The logics of these systems are clear: for the capitalist, the seemingly impetuous release of an asset to a new acquaintance is obviously unwise, especially because the Shimerdas' financial situation is dire and their viable assets few. Moreover, while the use value of Antonia's new vocabulary is high, the exchange values of the ring and the English lesson are disproportionate: according to the free market, even ignoring the sentimental weight it carries, the ring is a "reckless and extravagant" overpayment for a service that is more a connection than a commodity. Apparently for Jim, the consequence for this perceived naiveté is exploitation, or Krajiek "[getting] the better of these people," a point to which we will shortly return.[17]

For Ántonia, this particular act of reciprocity is both appropriate and wise on two levels. Most broadly, the (re)gift of the ring allows her to keep the gift in circulation—to really receive Jim's gesture by returning it to its source, along with the addition of her own spirit and gratitude. Further, the choice of gift itself gestures toward a cornerstone aspect of gift exchange theory—the material object is less important than the labor of gratitude the giver puts into it. Thus the object itself, while not wholly irrelevant, is ultimately a signifier for the intangible rhythms of personal activity, energy, and stress it has "absorbed." The fact that Ántonia's recompense is a ring, an item that has clear emotional and bodily connections, reflects the philosophy behind the gift exchange as much as any object could on its own, while also honoring the axiom that the return object should exceed the face value of the original gift as a means of signifying the additional spirit it now contains. In short, Ántonia's return token, while probably irresponsible within models of exchange *and* use values, would be a solid investment within a gift exchange circuit: the fact that the object is perhaps Antonia's greatest asset, both in terms of sentiment and of monetary value, speaks to the perceived stakes of this project's success—for if she properly executes the gift exchange in addition to the language training she thereby ensures, Ántonia also provides herself with community (as if by unwritten contract). If the gesture fails, the inverse is true, which is a particularly threatening possibility for an immigrant family new to an already difficult frontier landscape. Yet ultimately, this moment's tension, and the conflict of similar moments throughout the text, results from miscommunication or an inability to translate a Bohemian "investment" into the terms of a (modified) capitalistic economic system.

In this sense, perhaps it is especially fitting that this moment of misunderstanding—in which Ántonia attempts to make an investment that Jim cannot read—underpins the Shimerdas' initial attempt to make Ántonia their literal translator, thereby creating a means for them to understand the economic system that they are now required to negotiate. Because the signals this system emits circulate in English, Antonia's lessons from Jim are imperative, thereby loading the attempted gift exchange that follows her first lesson with extra significance—in a way, she is utilizing one economic protocol to help transition into a new one. But in the meantime, the family's transfer from gift economics to prairie capitalism depends upon a different translator, both in a literal and structural sense, as they attempt to negotiate new systems and practices of property ownership without first becoming acquainted with such institutions or even with the language their privileged operators use. This translator, then, is essentially the mediator, interpreter, and guarantor of the family's prosperity and has the ability to (mis)interpret appropriate economic procedure at his own discretion, but at the family's risk. Indeed, the mistranslations of the Shimerdas' translator, Peter Krajiek, prevent the family's acclimation into the new economic climate as a means of ensuring his own success in the same arena:

> The Bohemian family, grandmother told [Jim] as we drove along, had bought the homestead of a fellow-countryman, Peter Krajiek, and had paid him more than it was worth. Their agreement with him was made before they left the old country, through a cousin of his, who was also a relative of Mrs. Shimerda. The Shimerdas were the first Bohemian family to come to this part of the country. Krajiek was their only interpreter, and could tell them anything he chose. They could not speak enough English to ask for advice, or even to make their most pressing wants known.[18]

The central irony of this phenomenon is that Krajiek serves as a representative of capitalistic usury, yet is also the only compatriot and familial tie the Shimerdas have in Nebraska, and thereby likely the only character with the capacity to understand the economic ideology within which the family operates. He essentially relies upon the same dynamic as Ántonia does—using the old protocol as a means to incorporate the new—yet his technique is as exploitative as hers is innocent. The fact that Krajiek is bilingual, both literally and figuratively (in terms of economic savvy), creates a mutual exclusivity between gift exchange and Nebraska capitalism where one needn't necessarily exist, at least not in such an extreme binary form. Had Krajiek not gouged the price of his property and thereby mistranslated the terms of the American Dream, the Shimerdas may have been able to incorporate themselves into the economy with less pain, if only by virtue of having more capital with which they could participate in the free market. Yet because the family reads the market as Krajiek writes it, even their most basic needs are mediated by a discrepant presentation of the economic system, one that forces them to spend the winter in "'that cave of Krajiek's . . . no better than a badger hole; no proper dugout at all,'" and to "'pay twenty dollars for his old cookstove that ain't worth ten'" in order to survive.[19]

Had the family behaved according to free market logic—by treating Krajiek's offers with skepticism or perhaps entertaining other opportunities on the market—their economic decline may have been averted. Yet operating within this logic is impossible, at least at this point, because of the intransigence between the languages of old and (relatively) new systems of exchange, which is crystallized by a more literal language barrier. Further, the trust that the Shimerdas place in Krajiek, while naive according to a cool capitalistic sensibility, is a fundamental underpin of the gift exchange process, which the family apparently assumes Krajiek will operate within, or at least honor. According to this framework, Krajiek would have a responsibility to keep the gift in circulation: to return to the community—in this case the Shimerdas—what the community has given to him, with the addition of his own constructive energy. Because the cost of failing to complete the exchange is so high—an essential banishment from the community and all its "wealth," for lack of a better term—the risk of exploitation on the part of the giver seems low because it would ultimately cost the giver far more than it would the recipient. But as mentioned, this is an assumption on the part of the family—one that takes for granted the viability of terms such as "giver" and "recipient," as well as the belief that Krajiek will uphold this contract in a new arena, or at least use his bilingualism to assimilate the Shimerdas' economic understanding into a new system. Instead Krajiek exploits the contract, as well as his role as translator, using it to rewrite the family's new economic situation as one from which he can profit by exorbitant degrees. And until Ántonia (or another member of the family) can learn to translate things for herself, both literally and economically, Krajiek will continue to present his own version of the market's conditions, asking the family to maintain the implicit faith of gift exchange within a system that can prey on such trust. This misrepresentation creates the conditions for poverty and for excessive violence, which reify on a higher level the novel's initial economic tensions, well after the family begins to acclimatize to frontier capitalism.

This "acclimatization" seems to begin really once the family is forced to adapt to life without their patriarch. Whereas Mr. Shimerda's integration into the free market proved unsuccessful, after his death Ambrosch becomes "more than ever the head of the house."[20] Under this new leadership, the economic balance shifts, and capitalism becomes the family's primary ordering principle, whereas gift exchange is reduced to a subconscious instinct—the family's original sensibility inverts. Nonetheless, this instinct is still present, albeit not in the foreground, as the family strives to participate within the frontier economy, and at times solidifies in the form of tense social moments in which gift exchange sensibilities resurface. One such moment, the fight between Ambrosch and Jake, highlights the discrepancy between these two systems, but does so as the Shimerdas (attempt to) participate in frontier capitalism. The conflict arises as Jake attempts to regain "a horsecollar which Ambrosch had borrowed from him and not returned," then discovers said collar in such a "shameful" condition that it's hardly recognizable.[21] Jake and the Burdens presumably lent the collar to the Shimerdas in the first place to aid in their attempt to live off their land, assisting the family both by the slightly anachronistic means through which they can generate sustenance through agrarianism and also in a more capitalistic sense, which asks the Shimerdas to commodify their goods (as much as is possible) and realize them on the market. Yet this loan is brokered by a different mentality on either side of the creditor-debtor relation: for Jake, this is a gift, but not one that abides by the rules of formal gift exchange. Instead it serves as a means of aiding the Shimerdas as they attempt to establish themselves, and is meant to be temporary (with an expiration date not firmly established, but also not indefinite). In other words, the gesture is one of community building—one that impacts the market only indirectly and with little potential for profit for Jake or the Burdens (though if Ambrosch keeps the collar long enough, it might have the capacity to affect the Burdens' own productivity). Jake's move therefore isn't quite economic in character, but is instead rather neighborly; thus Ambrosch's overuse of the collar seems like a poor repayment (or the abrogation of any possibility of meaningful repayment) for his graciousness.

Yet for Ambrosch, a more originary rule of gift exchange seems to reassert itself and foreclose the system of etiquette by which Jake expects Ambrosh to abide. According to the philosophy of gift protocols, the act of lending the horsecollar is indeed irreducibly economic: it is simply the continuation of the gift circulation between the Burdens and the Shimerdas, which began with Mrs. Burden's original offering that was returned in the form of Mrs. Shimerda's unidentified food gift (see note 1). Thus the horsecollar is not itself an original, self-moving gesture, but the mandatory reciprocation of the *hau*. Moreover, if the rules of the *hau* apply, then the timing of the return gift is up to the receiver, and the object itself is far less important than the energy the recipient imbues in it. The quality of the return gift, in other words, has little to do with the state of the object and everything to do with the condition of the receiver. Presumably, Ambrosch abides by this principle, pouring physical labor into the collar until it reaches the point of breaking—so much so that Jake is uncertain if it's the original object.

According to the assumptions of this system of gift exchange, it is Jake who has infringed on the Shimerdas, or at least on the covenant of the system. As mentioned, one of the key elements within the crucial transformation from recipient to giver is time: the recipient must be allowed to undergo a quasi-spiritual journey and pour him- or herself into the gift before he or she can fully experience gratitude, *then* complete the process by returning the gift to circulation. In short, the original giver cannot place temporal requirements on the return because this compromises the labor of gratitude and the possibility of further circulation. In the case of the horsecollar, Jake has done just that. Moreover, this gratitude—the release of meaningful energy on the part of the recipient—at least according to Hyde's theory of gift exchange, is the end goal of the process, whereas the object is purely symbolic. For the original giver to place materiality above spirituality, then, offends the sensibility of the system.

From a Hydean standpoint, the ostensible disproportion of the violence that ensues after Jake confronts Ambrosch is less than surprising:

> Ambrosch dropped the collar on the ground. "All right," he said coolly, took up his oil-can, and began to climb the mill. Jake caught him by the belt of his trousers and yanked him back. Ambrosch's feet had scarcely touched the ground when he lunged out with a vicious kick at Jake's stomach. . . . This was not the sort of thing country boys did when they played at fisticuffs, and Jake was furious.[22]

Whereas Jake uses minor violence to recompense a slight on his hospitality, for Ambrosch, the stakes are much higher because they jeopardize something far more significant: if Jake has disrupted the proper circulation of the gift, the consequences are akin to banishment from the community as a means of eliminating the threat to that community's socioeconomic circuit. Thus the fact that Ambrosch responds to a simple catch "by the belt" with an extreme and apparently disproportionate measure (a kick to the stomach) corresponds to the severity of the perceived disrespect Jake has shown. Yet the cycle of violence continues, as Jake's sense of frontier etiquette is offended by this seemingly inordinate violence—which is, to be sure, "not the sort of thing country boys did when they played at fisticuffs"—and answers with an aggression that matches Ambrosch's, this time because the offense seems to him all the greater (as one who is assured of the rightness of his position through the naturalization of Nebraskan protocol). In this sense, as in the case of the initial gift exchange between Jim and Ántonia, the problem here is one of translation—the language and semiotics of gift exchange is misinterpreted by that of communal prairie custom, and vice versa.

"MERE SHADINGS IN THE GRASS"

Joseph Urgo, in a play on Frederick Jackson Turner's famous lecture, names the "Cather thesis" the conviction that those "who exerted more direct and more immediate influence [on American consciousness and culture] were those who *did not remain* in the West, but who moved back and forth from one area to another."[23] And indeed, the later chapters of *My Ántonia* consist of much of this sort of movement, including Jim's move back East. But from the perspective of the small community that centers the narrative's beginning, the significant movement that occurs over time is the process of *abstraction*, of the commodification of those small gifting networks that comes to fore-close—as the frontier is everywhere settled—any alternative reconciliation of competing local customs. Mr. Shimerda's death and burial, which augurs a new era for the Bohemian family, foregrounds the macrodevelopment of a capitalistic economy that dissolves local custom when years later, once "the open-grazing days were over . . . when all the fields were under fence, and the roads no longer ran about like wild things, but followed surveyed section-lines," the new roads curve just enough to avoid the grave, swerving from the fulfillment of the Bohemian superstition that one must be buried beneath a crossroad.[24]

Although Ántonia's own family, a reconstituted *oikos*, compose the gentle last tableaux of the novel, there is no doubt that the busy scene at the Cuzaks remains a nostalgic one, with Jim finally scanning the old landscape for signs of the paths he and his friend took when they were children. The world of the American Midwest writ large belongs, we fear, to Wick Cutter and his ilk, or at least the future Wicks who possess slightly healthier sensibilities, who have cleaned up their act and image, if not their ethics. Cutter, a violent usurer more integrated into American culture and more business savvy than Krajiek, was merely one of the "fast set" of Black Hawk businessmen whose advice to the boys of the town was neither the wisdom of frontier know-how nor a proverb from the Old Country, but the commodified maxims of "Poor Richard's Almanack."[25] The soulless (and *care*-less) economic system that he represents and acts for, which draws poor farmers into the unbreakable "mod-ern" cycle of accumulation and debt, also reduces Ántonia (at that point going by "Tony") to a commodity, in her status as a "hired girl" in Black Hawk, an independent contractor who still occupies a paradoxical position neither fully inside nor outside the local economy. Cutter's attempted drunken assault of Antonia—which turns out to be an attack on Jim, who has taken her place in bed—turns his victim into a "battered object," a thing used up not by the labor of gratitude but by the violence of property and possession.[26]

When Jim finds himself walking out over what's left of the "rough pas-tures," searching for the tracks on the old road to the north country that "were mere shadings in the grass," he is tracing the worn marks of the past just like Cather is, through her examination of the gift communities that existed as vanishing mediators —as a disappearing liminal frontier—between two stages in the settling of the American West.[27] The novel's trenchant examination of nostalgia, of childhood innocence before the fall of (sexual) experience and of inspiration and desire before complication and compromise, is on a sociocul-tural register a retrospective reworking of the imperfect material of the gifting community, of the conflict that always-already inheres in the local economy and in the competing interpretations of gifting protocol. The novelist's glance backward is not unlike that of the Maussian sociologist-philosopher, a glance produced by—even as it attempts to break from—the abstractions and alienations of the present.

NOTES

1. Willa Cather, *My Ántonia*, Willa Cather Scholarly Edition, ed. Charles W. Mignon and Kari A. Ronning (Lincoln: University of Nebraska Press, 1994), 26.

2. Marcel Mauss and W. D. Halls, *The Gift: The Form and Reason for Exchange in Archaic Societies* (New York: W. W. Norton, 1990), 35.

3. Ibid., 70.

4. Ibid., 1.

5. Ibid., 10.

6. Ibid., 9–10.

7. Ibid., 11.

8. Lewis Hyde, *The Gift: Imagination and the Erotic Life of Property* (New York: Vintage Books, 1983), 8.

9. Ibid., 51.

10. Karl Marx, Samuel Moore, Edward B. Aveling, Friedrich Engels, and Dona Torr, *Capital: A Critical Analysis of Capitalist Production* (New York: International Publishers, 1947), 42–43.

11. Ibid., 45.

12. Hyde, *The Gift*, 51.

13. Cather, *My Ántonia*, 18.

14. Ibid., 55.

15. Ibid., 58.

16. Ibid., 26.

17. Ibid., 26.

18. Ibid., 19.

19. Ibid., 20.

20. Ibid., 122.

21. Ibid., 123.

22. Ibid., 124.

23. Joseph R. Urgo, "The Cather Thesis: The American Empire of Migration," in *The Cambridge Companion to Willa Cather*, ed. Marilee Lindemann (Cambridge: Cambridge University Press, 2005), 39–40.

24. Cather, *Ántonia*, 114.

25. Ibid., 203.

26. Ibid., 241.

27. Ibid., 358–59.

Bibliography

Abate, Michelle Ann. *Tomboys: A Literary and Cultural History*. Philadelphia: Temple University Press, 2008.

Acocella, Joan. *Willa Cather and the Politics of Criticism*. Lincoln: University of Nebraska Press, 2000.

Adams, R. W. Lewis. *The American Adam: Innocence, Tragedy, and Tradition in the Nineteenth Century*. Chicago: University of Chicago Press, 1955.

Adams, Timothy D. "My Gay Ántonia: The Politics of Willa Cather's Lesbianism." *Journal of Homosexuality* 12, no. 3–4 (1986): 89–98.

Ammons, Elizabeth. "*My Ántonia* and African American Art." In *New Essays on My Ántonia*, edited by Sharon O'Brien, 57–84. Cambridge: Cambridge University Press, 1999.

Anders, John P. *Willa Cather's Sexual Aesthetics and the Male Homosexual Literary Tradition*. Lincoln: University of Nebraska Press, 1999.

Banner, Lois W. *American Beauty*. New York: Knopf, 1983.

Banta, Martha. *Imaging American Women: Idea and Ideals in Cultural History*. New York: Columbia University Press, 1987.

Barillas, William. *The Midwestern Pastoral: Place and Landscape in Literature of the Heartland*. Athens: Ohio University Press, 2006.

Barrie, J. M. *Peter Pan (Peter and Wendy)*. New York: Puffin, 1911.

Bassnett, Susan. *Translation Studies*. Routledge: London, 1991.

Baum, L. Frank. *The Wonderful Wizard of Oz*. Edited by Jack Zipes. New York: Penguin, 1998.

Bederman, Gail. *Manliness & Civilization: A Cultural History of Gender and Race in the United States: 1880–1917*. Chicago: University of Chicago Press, 1995.

Bennett, Mildred R. *The World of Willa Cather*. Lincoln: University of Nebraska Press, 1961.

Bernardini, Caterina. "Religiosa, Provinciale, Modernista: The Early Reception of Willa Cather in Italy." *Cather Newsletter and Review* 59, no. 2 (Fall/Winter 2016): 13–19.

Berg, Van den J. H. *The Changing Nature of Man: Introduction to a Historical Psychology*, 231. New York: Norton, 1983.

Blackford, Holly. *Alice to Algernon: The Evolution of Child Consciousness in the Novel*. Knoxville: University of Tennessee Press, 2018.

———. *The Myth of Persephone in Girls' Fantasy Literature*. New York: Routledge, 2011.

Bloom, Harold. Ántonia. New York: Chelsea House Publishers, 1991.

Bohlke, L. Brent, ed. *Willa Cather in Person: Interviews, Speeches, and Letters*. Lincoln: University of Nebraska Press, 1986.

Bouchal, L. J., to Willa Cather, December 2, 1918. Love Library, University of Nebraska.

Bourne, Randolph S. "Trans-National America." *Atlantic* (July 1916): 86–97.

Brodhead, Richard. *Cultures of Letters: Scenes of Reading and Writing in Nineteenth-Century America*. Chicago: University of Chicago Press, 1993.

Brooks, Peter. *Reading for the Plot: Design and Intention in Narrative*. 1984. Cambridge, MA: Harvard University Press, 1992.

Brown, Bill. *A Sense of Things: The Object Matter of American Literature*. Chicago: University of Chicago Press, 2003.

Brown, E. K. *Willa Cather: A Critical Biography*. New York, Discus, 1980.

Brownell, W. C. Letter from W. C. Brownell to Miss Roseboro. Charles Cather Collection, University of Nebraska–Lincoln Archives and Special Collections.

Bubani, Giorgio. "L'Antonia del Nebraska." *Il Libraio*, August 15, 1947, 3.

Butler, Judith. *Bodies That Matter: On the Discursive Limits of "Sex."* New York: Routledge, 1993.

———. "'Dangerous Crossings': Willa Cather's Masculine Names." In *Bodies that Matter: On the Discursive Limits of "Sex,"* 143–60. New York: Routledge, 1993.

Capote, Truman. *Other Voices, Other Rooms*. 1948. New York: Vintage International, 1994.

———. *Portraits and Observations: The Essays of Truman Capote*. New York: Random House, 2007.

———. "Remembering Willa Cather." *Vanity Fair*, November 16, 2006. http://www.vanityfair.com/news/2006/11/capote-200611.

Carroll, Latrobie. "Willa Sibert Cather." *The Bookman* 53 (May 1921): 212–16.

Cather, Willa. "The Bohemian Girl." 1912. In *Willa Cather's Collected Short Fiction 1892–1912*, edited by Mildred R. Bennett, 3–42. Lincoln: University of Nebraska Press, 1965.

———. *Death Comes for the Archbishop*. 1927. In *Later Novels*, edited by Sharon O'Brien, 273–470. New York: Library of America, 1992.

———. *Death Comes for the Archbishop*. 1927. New York: Vintage, 1990.

———. *Death Comes for the Archbishop: The Scholarly Edition*. 1927. Edited by Charles W. Mignon with Frederick M. Link and Kari A. Ronning. Lincoln: University of Nebraska Press, 1999.

———. "The Enchanted Bluff." *Classic Literature*. Accessed March 6, 2014. http://classiclit.about.com/library/bl-etexts/wcather/bl-wcather-enchant.htm.

———. "Mesa Verde Wonderland Is Easy to Reach." *The Willa Cather Archive*. Edited by Andrew Jewell. Center for Digital Research in the Humanities: University of Nebraska–Lincoln, 2004–2016. Accessed March 7, 2014. http://cather.unl.edu/nf056.html.

———. *La mia Ántonia*. Translated by Gabriele Baldini. Milano: Longanesi, 1947.

———. *La mia Ántonia*. Translated by Jole Jannelli Pinna Pintor. Torino: Einaudi, 1947.

———. *Moia* Ántonia: *roman.* Translated by Aleksandra Kirillovna Savurenok. Leningrad: Khydozhestvennaia literatura, 1979.

———. *Mon amie* Ántonia. Translated by Blaise Allan. Paris: Vent d'Oeust, 1967.

———. *Mon* Ántonia. Translated by Victor Llona. Paris: Payot, 1924.

———. *Mon Ántonia*. Translated by Robert Ruard. Paris: Deuxtemps Tierce, 1993.

———. Моя Антония. Translated by Irina A. Razumovskaya and Svetlana P. Samostrelova-Smirnitskaya. Leningrad: Chudozhestvennaya Literatura, 1979.

———. Моя Антония. Translated by Vasily S. Yanovsky. New York: Chekhov Publishing House, 1952.

———. *Mi Ántonia.* Translated by Gema Moral Bartolomé. Barcelona: Alba Editorial, 2000.

———. *Mi Ántonia*. Translated by Julio Fernández-Yañez Gimeno. Barcelona: Caralt, 1955.

———. *My Ántonia.* Edited by Janet Sharistanian. New York: Oxford University Press, 2006.

———. *My Ántonia*. New York: Signet, 2005.

———. *My Ántonia*. Edited by Sharon O'Brien. New York: Norton, 2015.

———. *My Ántonia*. Edited by Doris Grumbach. 1918. Boston: Houghton Mifflin, 1988.

———. *My Ántonia*. Willa Cather Scholarly Edition. Edited by Charles W. Mignon and Kari A. Ronning. Lincoln: University of Nebraska Press, 1994.

———. "Nebraska: The End of the Cycle." *The Nation*. 117: 3035. September 5, 1923. 236–38.

———. "The Novel Démeublé." 1922. In *Not Under Forty*, 43–51. Lincoln: University of Nebraska Press, 1988.

———. "The Novel Démeublé." 1949. In *Willa Cather on Writing*, 35–43. New York: Knopf, 1968.

———. *O Pioneers!* Boston: Houghton Mifflin, 1988.

———. *O Pioneers!* Lincoln: University of Nebraska Press, 1992.

———. *O Pioneers!* New York: Bantam, 1989.

———. "The Old Cliff-Dweller (Walnut Canyon, Arizona) AD 1400." In the *Willa Cather Collection*, Drew University Special Collections, Madison, New Jersey.

———. "On the Art of Fiction." In *On Writing: Critical Studies on Writing as an Art*, 101–4. New York: Knopf, 1949.

———. *One of Ours*. New York: Random House, 1991.

———. "Paul's Case." 1905. In *Cather: Stories, Poems, & Other Writings*, edited by Sharon O'Brien, 468–88. New York: Library of America, 1992.

——. "Preface." In *The Best Stories of Sarah Orne Jewett* by Jewett. Boston: Houghton Mifflin, 1925.

——. *The Professor's House*. New York: Vintage, 1953.

——. *The Professor's House: The Scholarly Edition*. 1925. Edited by James Woodress, Kari A. Ronning, and Frederick M. Link. Lincoln: University of Nebraska Press, 2002.

——. "The Profile." *McClure's Magazine* 29 (1907): 135–41.

——. *Sapphira and the Slave Girl*. 1940. New York: Vintage, 2010.

——. "The Sculpture's Funeral." 1905. In *Willa Cather's Collected Short Fiction 1892–1912*, edited by Mildred R. Bennett, 3–42. Lincoln: University of Nebraska Press, 1965.

——. *The Selected Letters of Willa Cather*. Edited by Andrew Jewell and Janis P. Stout. New York: Knopf, 2013.

——. *Shadows on the Rock: The Scholarly Edition*. 1931. Edited by Frederick M. Link. Lincoln: University of Nebraska Press, 2005.

——. *The Song of the Lark*. Boston: Houghton Mifflin, 1915.

——. *The Song of the Lark*. 1915. New York: Dover, 2004.

——. *The Song of the Lark*. New York: Vintage Books, 1999.

——. *The Song of the Lark*. In *Early Novels and Stories*, edited by Sharon O'Brien, 291–706. New York: Library of America, 1992.

——. *The Song of the Lark*. *Project Gutenberg*. Produced by Judith Boss, Marvin Peterson, and David Widger. Accessed March 11, 2015. Not paginated.

——. "The Treasure of Far Island." 1902. In *Willa Cather's Collected Short Fiction 1892–1912*, edited by Mildred R. Bennett, 265–82. Lincoln: University of Nebraska Press, 1965.

——. "These United States," 37. *The Nation*. September 5, 1923. 236–38.

——. *Willa Cather in Person: Interviews, Speeches, and Letters*. Edited by L. Brent Bohlke. Lincoln: University of Nebraska Press, 1986.

——. *The World and the Parish: Willa Cather's Articles and Reviews, 1893–1902*, edited by William M. Curtin. Lincoln: University of Nebraska Press, 1970.

——. Cather to Lorna Birtwell, November 27, 1922. Columbia University.

——. Cather to Roscoe Cather, November 6, 1938. In *The Selected Letters of Willa Cather*, edited by Andrew Jewell and Janis P. Stout, 561. New York: Knopf, 2013.

——. Cather to Dorothy Canfield Fisher, April 10, 1921. *The Complete Letters of Willa Cather*. In *The Willa Cather Archive*, edited by Andrew Jewell. Center for Digital Research in the Humanities: University of Nebraska–Lincoln, 2004–2016. Forthcoming, 2018.

——. Cather to Ferris Greenslet, December 28, 1919. Houghton Library, Harvard University.

——. Cather to Greenslet, March 24, 1920. Houghton Library, Harvard University.

——. Cather to Greenslet, December 14, 1920. Houghton Library, Harvard University.

——. Cather to Greenslet, after April 9, 1925. MS Am 1925 (341). Houghton Library, Harvard University.

——. Cather to Greenslet, October 20, 1930. Houghton Library, Harvard University.

———. Cather to Laura Hills, May 1921. *The Complete Letters of Willa Cather.* In *The Willa Cather Archive,* edited by Andrew Jewell. Center for Digital Research in the Humanities: University of Nebraska–Lincoln, 2004–2016. Forthcoming, 2018. originalntlyithe transition they are made of.is madeer the of the trucke starts. There was nothing, but land: Jewell at Unive

———. Cather to Blanche Knopf, September 26, 1929. Alfred A. Knopf, Inc., Archives, Box 689, Folder 1, Harry Ransom Center, University of Texas at Austin.

———. Cather to Roger L. Scaife, October 3, 1918. Houghton Library, Harvard University.

———. Cather to Scaife, February 24, 1920. Houghton Library, Harvard University.

———. Cather to Elizabeth Shepley Sergeant, July 6, 1921. *The Complete Letters of Willa Cather.* In *The Willa Cather Archive,* edited by Andrew Jewell. Center for Digital Research in the Humanities: University of Nebraska–Lincoln, 2004–2016. Forthcoming, 2018.

———. Cather to Yalthah Menuhin Stix, January 23, 1939. In *The Selected Letters of Willa Cather,* edited by Andrew Jewell and Janis P. Stout, 567. New York: Knopf, 2013.originalntlyithe transition they are made of.is madeer the of the trucke starts. There was nothing, but land: Jewell at Unive

Chénetier, March. "Cather's Reputation in France." In *Cather Studies* 8: *Willa Cather: A Writer's Worlds,* edited by John J. Murphy, Françoise Palleau-Papin, and Robert Thacker, 28. Lincoln: University of Nebraska Press, 2010. http://cather.unl.edu/cs008.html.

Chodorow, Nancy. *The Reproduction of Mothering.* Berkeley: University of California Press, 1978.

Clarke, Michael Tavel. "Lessons from the Past: The Cliff Dwellers and New Historicism." *Western American Literature* 42, no. 4 (2008): 395–425.

Cooney, Joy. "A Mediating Presence in Cather's *My Ántonia.*" *The Explicator* 69, no. 3 (2011): 142–45.

Cronon, William. *Nature's Metropolis: Chicago and the Great West.* New York: W. W. Norton, 1991.

Eliot, T. S. "Tradition and the Individual Talent." 1920. In *Quotidiana,* edited by Patrick Madden. Accessed January 23, 2008. http://essays.quotidiana.org/eliot/tradition_and_the_individual.

Facknitz, Mark A. R. "Changing Trains: Metaphors of Transfer in Willa Cather." In *Cather Studies* 9: *Willa Cather and Modern Cultures,* edited by Melissa J. Homestead and Guy Reynolds, 71. Lincoln: University of Nebraska Press, 2011. http://cather.unl.edu/cs009.html.

Fahy, Thomas. *Understanding Truman Capote.* Columbia: University of South Carolina Press, 2014.

Faulkner, William. *Collected Stories of William Faulkner.* New York: Vintage International, 1995.

Fetterley, Judith. "*My Ántonia,* Jim Burden, and the Dilemma of the Lesbian Writer." In *Gender Studies: New Directions in Feminist Criticism,* edited by Judith Spector, 55. Bowling Green, OH: Bowling Green State University, Popular Press, 1986.

————. "*My Ántonia*, Jim Burden, and the Dilemma of the Lesbian Writer." In *Lesbian Texts and Contexts: Radical Revisions*, edited by Karla Jay, Joanne Glasgow, and Catharine R. Stimpson, 145–63. New York: New York University Press, 1990.

Fields, Annie Adams. *Authors and Friends*. Boston: Houghton Mifflin, 1893.

Fields, Annie Adams, and Mark Antony De Wolfe Howe. *Memories of a Hostess: A Chronicle of Eminent Friendships Drawn Chiefly from the Diaries of Mrs. James T Fields*. Boston: Atlantic Monthly Press, 1922.

Fisher-Wirth, Ann. "Out of the Mother: Loss in *My Ántonia*." *Cather Studies* 2 (1993): 41–71.

Foote, Stephanie. *Regional Fictions: Culture and Identity in Nineteenth-Century American Literature*. Madison: University of Wisconsin Press, 2001.

Freud, Sigmund. *The Standard Edition of the Complete Psychological Works of Sigmund Freud*, Vol. 4, Pt. 1: *The Interpretation of Dreams*. 1900. Translated by James Strachey. London: Hogarth Press, 1957.

Fryer, Judith. *Felicitous Space: The Imaginative Structures of Edith Wharton and Willa Cather*. Chapel Hill: University of North Carolina Press, 1986.

Funda, Evelyn I. "Picturing Their Ántonia(s): Mikoláš Aleš and the Partnership of W. T. Benda and Willa Cather." *Cather Studies* 8, no. 1 (2010): 353–78.

Fuss, Diana. *Identification Papers*. New York: Routledge, 1995.

Fussell, Edwin. "Cesare Pavese." In *American Literature: Essays and Opinions*, 43. Berkeley: University of California Press, 1970.

Gardam, Sarah C. "Subverting the Male Gaze: Willa Cather's Lena Lingard and William Faulkner's Lena Grove." *Willa Cather Newsletter & Review* 49, no. 2 (2005): 35.

Garland, Hamlin. *Boy Life on the Prairie*, 166. New York: Frederick Ungar Publishing, 1959.

Gelfant, Blanche H. "The Forgotten Reaping-Hook: Sex in *My Ántonia*." *American Literature* 43, no. 1 (March 1971): 60–82.

————. "The Forgotten Reaping-Hook: Sex in *My Ántonia*." In *Critical Essays on Willa Cather*, edited by John J. Murphy, 147–64. Boston: G. K. Hall and Co., 1984.

Gherovici, Patricia. *Please Select Your Gender: From the Invention of Hysteria to the Democratizing of Transgenderism*. New York: Routledge, 2010.

Glazener, Nancy. *Reading for Realism: The History of a U.S. Literary Institution, 1850–1910*. Durham: Duke University Press, 1997.

Goggans, Jan. "Social (Re)Visioning in the Fields of *My Ántonia*." *Cather Studies* 5 (2003): 153–72.

Goodman, Susan. *Republic of Words: The Atlantic Monthly and Its Writers, 1857–1925*. Hanover, NH: University Press of New England, 2013.

Gorman, Michael. "Jim Burden and the White Man's Burden: *My Ántonia* and Empire." *Cather Studies* 6 (2006): 28–57.

Gornick, Vivian. Introduction. *O Pioneers!*, vii–xv. By Willa Cather. New York: Bantam, 1989.

Greenslet, Ferris. Greenslet to Willa Cather, October 22, 1918. Houghton Mifflin Archive, MS Am 1925 (341), Houghton Library, Harvard University.

———. Ferris Greenslet to Elsie Singmaster, March 25, 1920. Houghton Mifflin Co. Archive, MS Am 1929 (1656). Houghton Library, Harvard University.

———. Greenslet to Cather, May 3, 1919. Houghton Library, Harvard University.

———. Greenslet to Cather, December 17, 1919. Houghton Library, Harvard University.

———. Greenslet to Cather, December 30, 1919. Houghton Library, Harvard University.

———. Greenslet to Cather, March 25, 1920. Houghton Library, Harvard University.

———. Greenslet to Cather, October 25, 1923. Houghton Library, Harvard University.

———. Greenslet to Cather, February 21, 1924. Houghton Library, Harvard University.

———. Greenslet to Cather, January 6, 1926. Houghton Mifflin Archive, MS Am 1925 (341), Houghton Library, Harvard University.

———. Greenslet to Cather, February 17, 1926. Houghton Library, Harvard University.

———. Greenslet to Cather, April 9, 1926. Houghton Library, Harvard University.

———. Greenslet to Cather, May 5, 1926. Houghton Library, Harvard University.

———. Greenslet to Cather, October 23, 1926. Houghton Library, Harvard University.

Gustafson, Neil. "Willa Cather and Hamlin Garland: Parallel Early Lives." *Willa Cather Newsletter and Review* 49, no. 1 (2005): 9.

Hall, G. Stanley. "Boy Life in a Massachusetts Town Thirty Years Ago." In *Proceedings of the American Antiquarian Society*, 1890, 107–28. http://www.americanantiquarian.org/proceedings/44769428.pdf.

Hardwig, Bill. *Upon Provincialism: Southern Literature and National Periodical Culture, 1870–1900.* Charlottesville: University of Virginia Press, 2013.

Harrell, David. "Willa Cather's Mesa Verde Myth." *Cather Studies* 1. In *The Willa Cather Archive*, edited by Andrew Jewell. Center for Digital Research in the Humanities: University of Nebraska–Lincoln, 2004 2016. Accessed March 7, 2014. http://cather.unl.edu/cs001_mesaverde.html.

Harris, Richard C. "Jim Burden, Willa Cather and the Introductions to *My Ántonia.*" *Willa Cather Pioneer Memorial Newsletters* 20, no. 3 (Summer 1986): 33–34.

———. "Willa Cather and Henry Blake Fuller: More Building Blocks for *The Professor's House*." In *Willa Cather and Modern Cultures, Cather Studies* 9, edited by Melissa J. Homestead and Guy J. Reynolds, 114–32. Lincoln: University of Nebraska Press, 2011.

Hegemen, Susan. *Patterns for America: Modernism and the Concept of Culture.* Princeton, NJ: Princeton University Press, 1999.

Helmick, Evelyn. "The Mysteries of Ántonia." *Midwest Quarterly* 17 (1976): 173–85.

Hewitt, Emma Churchman. "What Relation Does Woman Bear to the Present?" *The Home Monthly* 6 (1896): 5–6.

Colestock Hill, Susan. *Heart Language: Elsie Singmaster and Her Pennsylvania German Writings.* University Park: Pennsylvania State University Press, 2009.

Hoffman, Karen A. "Identity Crossings and the Autobiographical Act in Willa Cather's *My Ántonia*." *Arizona Quarterly* 584, no. 2 (2002): 25–50.

Holmes, Catherine D. "Jim Burden's Lost Worlds: Exile in *My Ántonia*." *Twentieth Century Literature* 45, no. 3 (Autumn 1999): 336–46.

Homestead, Melissa. "'Links of Similitude': The Narrator of *The Country of the Pointed Firs* and Author-Reader Relations at the End of the Nineteenth Century." In *Jewett and Her Contemporaries: Reshaping the Canon*, edited by Karen L. Kilcup and Thomas S. Edwards, 76–98. Gainesville: University Press of Florida, 1999.

———. "Willa Cather Editing Sarah Orne Jewett." *American Literary Realism* 49, no. 1 (Fall 2016): 63–89.

Houghton Mifflin. Advertisement. *New York Times Book Review*, August 1, 1926.

———. Advertisement. *New York Times Book Review*, August 8, 1926.

———. Advertisement. *New York Times Book Review*, August 22, 1926.

———. Advertisement. *New York Times Book Review*, December 4, 1926.

———. Record of Book Sales. Houghton Mifflin Co. Records, Houghton Library, Harvard University, MS Am 2030 (33). 1923.

———. Sales. By Cather and Edith Lewis. Financial Records, James R. and Susan J. Rosowski Cather Collection, University of Nebraska–Lincoln Archives and Special Collections, Box 1, Folder 22.

Hyde, Lewis. *The Gift: Imagination and the Erotic Life of Property*. New York: Vintage Books, 1983.

Jacobson, Marcia. *Being a Boy Again: Autobiography and the American Boy Book.* Tuscaloosa: University of Alabama Press, 1994.

James, Henry. "Preface to the New York Edition." In *The Portrait of a Lady.* Second edition, edited by Robert Bamberg, 3–15. New York: Norton, 1995.

Jameson, Fredric. *The Political Unconscious: Narrative as a Socially Symbolic Act.* Ithaca, NY: Cornell University Press, 1982.

Jewell, Andrew, ed. "Bibliography of Translations." In *The Willa Cather Archive*, edited by Andrew Jewell. Center for Digital Research in the Humanities: University of Nebraska–Lincoln, 2004–2016. http://cather.unl.edu/translations.bibl.html.

Jewell, Andrew, and Janis P. Stout, ed. *The Selected Letters of Willa Cather.* New York: Knopf, 2013.

Johanningsmeier, Charles. "Cather's Readers, Traditionalism, and Modern America." *Cather Studies* 10, no. 48 (January 2015): 38–67.

———. "Willa Cather's Tauchnitz Editions and Their Role in Establishing Her European and Worldwide Reputation, 1926–1947." *Resources for American Literary Study*, forthcoming 2017.

Jones, Anne Goodwyn. "Displacing Dixie: The Southern Subtext in *My Ántonia*." In *New Essays on My Ántonia*, edited by Sharon O'Brien, 85–110. Cambridge: Cambridge University Press, 1999.

Kaye, Frances W. *Isolation and Masquerade.* New York: Peter Lang Publishing, 1993.

Keats, John. *Keats Poetry and Prose*. Edited by Henry Ellershaw. Oxford: Clarendon Press, 1931.

Kidd, Kenneth. *Making American Boys: Boyology and the Feral Tale*. Minneapolis: University of Minnesota Press, 2004.

Kitch, Carolyn. *The Girl on the Magazine Cover: The Origins of Visual Stereotypes in American Mass Media.* Chapel Hill: University of North Carolina Press, 2001.

Kolodny, Annette. *The Lay of the Land: Metaphor as Experience and History in American Life and Letters*. Chapel Hill: University of North Carolina Press, 1975.

Knopf, Blanche. Blanche Knopf to Willa Cather, October 5, 1925. Alfred A. Knopf, Inc., Archives, Box 689, Folder 1, Harry Ransom Center, University of Texas at Austin.

Kristeva, Julia. "Women's Time." In *Feminisms: An Anthology of Literary Theory and Criticism*. Second edition, edited by Robyn Warhol-Down and Diane Price Herndl, 860–79. New Brunswick, NJ: Rutgers University Press, 1997.

Lacan, Jaques. *Écrits: The First Complete Edition in English*. Translated by Bruce Fink. New York: Norton, 2006.

———. *The Seminar of Jacques Lacan, Book XI: The Four Fundamental Concepts of Psychoanalysis, 1964–1965*. Translated by Alan Sheridan. New York: Norton, 1981.

Lambert, Deborah G. "The Defeat of a Hero: Autonomy and Sexuality in *My Ántonia*." *American Literature* 53, no. 4 (1982): 676–90.

Lawlor, Mary. *Recalling the Wild: Naturalism and the Closing of the American West*. New Brunswick, NJ: Rutgers University Press, 2000.

Lee, Hermione. *Willa Cather: Double Lives*. New York: Pantheon, 1989.

Leopold, Aldo. *A Sand County Almanac, and Sketches Here and There*. New York: Oxford University Press, 1987.

Levin, Joanna. *Bohemia in America, 1858–1920*. Stanford: Stanford University Press, 2010.

Lewis, Edith. Edith Lewis to Patrick Ferry, February 3, 1954. Patrick Ferry Willa Cather Collection, Colby College, Waterville, Maine.

Lewis, Sinclair. Sinclair Lewis to Willa Cather, January 4, 1945. Newberry Library, Chicago.

Lindemann, Marilee. "'It Ain't My Prairie': Gender, Power, and Narrative in *My Ántonia*." In *New Essays on My Ántonia*, edited by Sharon O'Brien, 111–35. New York: Cambridge University Press, 1999.

———. *Willa Cather: Queering America*. New York: Columbia University Press, 1999.

Lucenti, Lisa Marie. "Willa Cather's *My Ántonia*: Haunting the Houses of Memory." *Twentieth Century Literature* 46, no. 2 (Summer 2000): 193–213.

Lutz, Tom. *Cosmopolitan Vistas: American Regionalism and Literary Value*. Ithaca, NY: Cornell University Press, 2004.

Lyon, Peter. *Success Story: The Life and Times of S. S. McClure*. New York: Scribner, 1963.

MacLeod, Anne Scott. *American Childhood: Essays on Children's Literature of the Nineteenth and Twentieth Centuries*. Athens: University of Georgia Press, 1994.

Macleod, David I. *Building Character in the American Boy: The Boy Scouts, YMCA, and Their Forerunners, 1870–1920*. Madison: University of Wisconsin Press, 1983.

Mandel, Norma H. *Beyond the Garden Gate: The Life of Celia Laighton Thaxter*. Hanover: University Press of New England, 2004.

Martin, Terence. "The Drama of Memory in *My Ántonia*," *PMLA* 84, no. 2 (March 1969): 304–11.

Marx, Karl, Samuel Moore, Edward B. Aveling, Friedrich Engels, and Dona Torr. *Capital: A Critical Analysis of Capitalist Production*. New York: International Publishers, 1947.

Marx, Leo. *The Machine in the Garden: Technology and the Pastoral Ideal in America*. New York: Oxford University Press, 1964.

Maslenikov, Oleg A. "Publications of the Chekhov Publishing House, New York." *The American Slavic and East European Review* 13, no. 2 (April 1954): 252–54.

Mauss, Marcel, and W. D. Halls. *The Gift: The Form and Reason for Exchange in Archaic Societies*. New York: W. W. Norton, 1990.

McCarthy, Cormac. *All the Pretty Horses*. New York: Vintage. 1992.

Meyering, Sheryl. "Fleeting Moments of Beauty: A Literary Analysis of *O Pioneers!* and *My Ántonia*." In *Understanding* O Pioneers! *and* My Ántonia, edited by Sheryl L. Meyering, 1–24. Westport, CT: Greenwood Press, 2002.

Micale, Mark S. *Approaching Hysteria: Disease and Its Interpretations*. Princeton, NJ: Princeton University Press, 1995.

Middleton, Jo Ann. *Willa Cather's Modernism: A Study of Style and Technique*. Rutherford, NJ: Fairleigh Dickinson University Press, 1990.

Millington, Richard H. "Willa Cather and 'The Storyteller': Hostility to the Novel in *My Ántonia*." *American Literature* 66, no. 4 (1994): 689–717.

Moseley, Ann. "The Creative Ecology of Walnut Canyon: From the Sinagua to Thea Kronborg." *Cather Studies* 5 (2003): 216–36.

———. "Historical Essay." In *The Song of the Lark: The Scholarly Edition* by Willa Cather, edited by Karl Ronning, 549–616. Lincoln: University of Nebraska Press, 2012.

Murfree, Mary Noailles. *In the "Stranger People's" Country*. Lincoln: University of Nebraska Press, 2005.

Murphy, John J. *My Ántonia: The Road Home*. Boston: Twayne, 1989.

Nealon, Christopher. "Affect Genealogy: Feeling and Affiliation in Willa Cather." *American Literature* 69, no. 1 (1997): 5–37.

Nuñez, Estuardo. "Semblanza de Victor Llona." *Alpha* 2 (1965): 1–10.

O'Brien, Sharon. *Willa Cather: The Emerging Voice*. New York: Oxford University Press, 1987.

———. *Willa Cather: The Emerging Voice*. Reprint. Cambridge, MA: Harvard University Press, 1997.

———. "Introduction." In *New Essays on My Ántonia*, edited by Sharon O'Brien, 1–30. New York: Cambridge University Press, 1999.

O'Connor, Margaret Ann. *Willa Cather: The Contemporary Reviews*. Cambridge: Cambridge University Press, 2001.

Orvell, Miles. "Time, Change, and the Burden of Revision." In *New Essays on My Ántonia*, edited by Sharon O'Brien, 31–56. Cambridge: Cambridge University Press, 1999.

Palleau-Papin, Françoise. "Slowly originalntlyithe transition they are made of.is madeer the of the trucke starts. There was nothing, but land: Jewell at Unive but Surely: Willa Cather's Reception in France. originalntlyithe transition they are made of.is madeer the of the trucke starts. There was nothing, but land: Jewell at Unive" *Studies in the Novel* 45, no. 3 (Fall 2013): 538–58.

Palmer, Stephanie C. *Together by Accident: American Local Color Literature and the Middle Class.* Lanham, MD: Lexington, 2009.

Parks, Edd Winfield. *Charles Egbert Craddock.* Chapel Hill: University of North Carolina Press, 1941.

Patterson, Martha H. *Beyond the Gibson Girl: Reimagining the American New Woman, 1895–1915.* Urbana: University of Illinois Press, 2005.

Pavese, Cesare. *Lettere 1926–1950.* Torino: Einaudi, 1968.

———. "L'Antologia di Spoon River." *La Cultura* (November 1931). http://cultura .mindpress.it/99/lantologia-di-spoon-river-di-edgar-lee-masters/.

———. "Sherwood Anderson." In *La Cultura* (April 1931).

Piacentino, Edward. "A Study in Contrasts: Impressionistic Perspectives of Ántonia and Lena Lingard in Cather's *My Ántonia.*" *Studies in the Humanities* 12, no. 1 (1985): 39–44.

Porter, David. *On the Divide: The Many Lives of Willa Cather.* Lincoln: University of Nebraska Press, 2010.

"Publishers' Devices: Houghton, Mifflin and Company: Tout Bien ou Rien." *Chumley and Pepys on Books.* Accessed February 6, 2016. http://chumleyandpepys.blog spot.com.

Relph, Edward C. *Place and Placelessness.* London: Pion Limited, 1976.

Reventós, Martínez, and María Dolores. "The Obscure Maternal Double: The Mother/Daughter Relationship Represented In and Out of Matrophobia." *Atlantis* 18 (1996): 286–94.

Reynolds, Guy. *Willa Cather in Context: Progress, Race, Empire.* New York: St. Martin's Press, 1996.

Rich, Adrienne. *Of Woman Born: Motherhood as Experience and Institution.* London: Virago, 1986.

Robertson, Martha. "Messages from the Far-Away: Willa Cather's and Georgia O'Keeffe's Visionary Landscape of the American Southwest." *Language and Culture: Bulletin Institute for Language Education* (2007): 79–98.

Roman, Judith A. *Annie Adams Fields: The Spirit of Charles Street.* Bloomington: Indiana University Press, 1990.

Roof, Judith. *Come As You Are: Sexuality and Narrative.* New York: Columbia University Press, 1996.

Rose, Jacqueline. *The Case of Peter Pan: The Impossibility of Children's Fiction.* Philadelphia: University of Pennsylvania Press, 1984.

Rosowski, Susan J. *Birthing a Nation: Gender, Creativity, and the West in American Literature.* Lincoln: University of Nebraska Press, 1999.

———. "Historical Essay." In *A Lost Lady* by Willa Cather. Lincoln: University of Nebraska Press, 1997.

———. *The Voyage Perilous: Willa Cather's Romanticism.* Lincoln: University of Nebraska Press, 1986.

———. "Willa Cather's Subverted Endings and Gendered Time." In *Cather Studies 5: Willa Cather's Ecological Imagination,* edited by Susan Rosowski, 68–88. Lincoln: University of Nebraska Press, 2003.

Rotundo, E. Anthony. *American Manhood: Transformations in Masculinity from the Revolution of the Modern Era.* New York: Basic Books, 1993.

Satterwhite, Emily. "Reading Craddock, Reading Murfree: Local Color, Authenticity, and Geographies of Reception." *American Literature* 78, no. 1 (2006): 59–88.

Savurënok, Aleksandra K. "Introduction." Моя Антония, translated by Irina A. Razumovskaya and Svetlana P. Samostrelova-Smirnitskaya, 5–22. Leningrad: Chudozhestvennaya Literatura, 1979.

Scaife, Roger L. Scaife to Willa Cather, February 24, 1920. Houghton Library, Harvard University.

Schach, Paul. "Russian Wolves in Folktales and Literature of the Plains: A Question of Origins." *Great Plains Quarterly*, January 4, 1983. Accessed March 1, 2016, from Paper 1708. http://digitalcommons.unl.edu/greatplainsquarterly/1708.

Schama, Simon. *Landscape and Memory.* New York: Vintage Books, 1996.

Schedler, Christoper. "Writing Culture: Willa Cather's Southwest." In *Willa Cather and the American Southwest,* edited by John N. Swift and Joseph R. Urgo, 108–23. Lincoln: University of Nebraska Press, 2002.

Schleiermacher, Friederich. *The Translator's Invisibility.* New York: Routledge, 1995.

Schwind, Jean. "The Benda Illustrations to *My Ántonia*: Cather's 'Silent' Supplement to Jim Burden's Narrative." *PMLA* 100, no. 1 (1985): 51–67.

Sedgwick, Ellery. *The Atlantic Monthly, 1857–1909: Yankee Humanism at High Tide and Ebb.* Amherst: University of Massachusetts Press, 1994.

Sedgwick, Eve Kosofsky. "Across Gender, Across Sexuality: Willa Cather and Others." *South Atlantic Quarterly* 88, no. 1 (1989): 53–72.

———. *Between Men: English Literature and Male Homosocial Desire.* New York: Columbia University Press, 1985.

Sergeant, Elizabeth. *Willa Cather: A Memoir.* Lincoln: University of Nebraska Press, 1963.

Sharistanian, Janet. Introduction to *My Ántonia* by Willa Cather, vii–xxiv. Oxford: Oxford University Press, 2006.

Shields, David, and Matthew Vollmer. *Fakes: An Anthology of Pseudo-Interviews, Faux-Lectures, Quasi-Letters, "Found" Texts, and Other Fraudulent Artifacts.* New York: W. W. Norton, 2012.

Silko, Leslie Marmon. "Landscape, History, and the Pueblo Imagination." *Antaeus* 57 (Autumn 1986): 882–94.

Skaggs, Merrill Maguire. *After the World Broke in Two: The Later Novels of Willa Cather.* Charlottesville: University of Virginia Press, 1990.

Slater, David Jeremiah. "The American Girl, Her Life and Times: An Ideal and Its Creators, 1890–1930." PhD Dissertation, University of Minnesota, 2005.

Smith, Henry Nash. *Virgin Land.* New York: Vintage Books, 1957.

Smith, Lawrence. *Cesare Pavese and America: Life, Love, and Literature.* Amherst: University of Massachusetts Press, 2011.

Smith-Rosenberg, Carroll. *Disorderly Conduct: Visions of Gender in Victorian America.* New York: Oxford University Press, 1985.

Starkey, Penelope Schott. "The Many Mothers of *Peter Pan*: An Explanation and Lamentation." *Research Studies* 42 (1974): 1–10.

Steedman, Carolyn. *Strange Dislocations: Childhood and the Idea of Human Interiority 1780–1930.* Cambridge, MA: Harvard University Press, 1995.

Steinhagen, Carol. "Dangerous Crossings: Historical Dimensions of Landscape in Willa Cather's *My Ántonia, The Professor's House,* and *Death Comes for the Archbishop.*" *Interdisciplinary Studies in Literature and Environment* 6, no. 2 (Summer 1999): 63–82.

Stevens, Wallace, and Holly Stevens. *Letters of Wallace Stevens.* New York: Knopf, 1966.

Stout, Janis P. "Katherine Anne Porter's 'Reflections on Willa Cather': A Duplicitous Homage." *American Literature* 66, no. 4 (1994): 719–35.

———. "The Observant Eye, the Art of Illustration, and Willa Cather's *My Ántonia.*" In *Cather Studies* 5: *Willa Cather's Ecological Imagination,* edited by Susan Rosowski, 128–52. Lincoln: University of Nebraska Press, 2003.

———. "Seeing and Believing: Willa Cather's Realism." *American Literary Realism* 33, no. 2, , Special Issue: Willa Cather (Winter 2001): 168–80.

"Title-Page Devices Used by Houghton, Mifflin and Company." *The Lucile Project.* Accessed February 6, 2016. sdrc.lib.uiowa.edu.

Todd, Ellen Wiley. *The "New Woman" Revised: Painting and Gender Politics on Fourteenth Street.* Berkeley: University of California Press, 1993.

Thacker, Robert A. "'As the result of many solicitations': Ferris Greenslet, Houghton Mifflin, and Cather's Career." *Studies in the Novel* 45, no. 3 (Fall 2013): 369–86.

Thomas, Sue. *Willa Cather.* Savage, MD: Barnes and Noble Books, 1990.

Triplett, Frank. *The Life, Times, and Treacherous Death of Jesse James.* St. Louis: J. H. Chambers and Company, 1882.

Trout, Steven. "Seeing the Rattlesnake in Willa Cather's *My Ántonia.*" *Interdisciplinary Studies in Literature and Environment* 12, no. 1 (Winter 2005): 99–114.

Turner, Frederick Jackson. "The Significance of the Frontier in American History." *American Studies at the University of Virginia,* 2014. http://xroads.virginia.edu/~hyper/turner/chapter1.html.

Urgo, Joseph R. "The Cather Thesis: The American Empire of Migration." In *The Cambridge Companion to Willa Cather,* edited by Marilee Lindemann, 35–50. Cambridge: Cambridge University Press, 2005.

———. *Willa Cather and the Myth of American Migration.* Urbana: University of Illinois Press, 1995.

Vermocken, Elizabeth Moorhead. *These Too Were Here: Louise Homer and Willa Cather* (Pittsburgh University Press, 1950). In the *Willa Cather Collection,* Drew University Special Collections, Madison, New Jersey, ADAMS 167 23.

Walker, Rosanna. "Traces of J. M. Barrie's *Peter Pan* in Willa Cather's *The Professor's House.*" In *J. M. Barrie's Peter Pan In and Out of Time,* edited by Donna R. White and C. Anita Tarr, 127–55. Metuchen, NJ: Scarecrow Press, 2006.

Watkins, Tony. "Cultural Studies, New Historicism and Children's Literature." In *Literature for Children,* edited by Peter Hunt, 173–95. New York: Routledge, 1992.

West, James L., III. *American Authors and the Literary Marketplace since 1900.* Philadelphia: University of Pennsylvania Press, 1988.

Wilhite, Keith. "Unsettled Worlds: Aesthetic Emplacement in Willa Cather's *My Ántonia.*" *Studies in the Novel* 42, no. 3 (Fall 2010): 269–86.

Willa Cather: The Road Is All. American Masters. Produced by Christine Lesiak. PBS Home Video, 2005.

Woodress, James. "Historical Essay." In *My Ántonia: The Scholarly Edition* by Willa Cather, edited by Charles Mignon, 369–402. Lincoln: University of Nebraska Press, 1994.

———. *Willa Cather: A Literary Life*. Lincoln: University of Nebraska Press, 1987.

———. *Willa Cather: Her Life and Art*. Lincoln: University of Nebraska Press, 1975.

Worden, David. "'I Like to Be Like a Man': Female Masculinity in Willa Cather's *O Pioneers!* and *My Antonia*." In *Violence, the Arts, and Willa Cather*, edited by Joseph R. Urgo and Merrill Maguire Skaggs, 273–81. Madison, NJ: Fairleigh Dickinson University Press, 2007.

Worldcat online catalog. OCLC Online Computer Library Center, Inc., 2001–2017. http://www.worldcat.org/.

Zitter, Emmy Stark. "Making Herself Born: Ghost Writing and Willa Cather's Developing Autobiography." *Biography* 19, no. 3 (Summer 1996): 283–301.

Index

About the Contributors

Keiko Arai is associate professor of British and American studies at Musashi University, Tokyo, Japan. She received her doctorate in English from the University of Maryland, College Park. Her articles on Cather, Edith Wharton, Nathaniel Hawthorne, Raymond Carver, and others have appeared in several academic journals and essay collections, including *Style* and the *Nathaniel Hawthorne Review*. Her current work focuses on the image of American girlhood in literature from the mid-nineteenth century to the early twentieth century.

Caterina Bernardini is a postdoctoral research associate in the Department of English at the University of Nebraska-Lincoln, where she teaches and works as an editorial assistant for the Walt Whitman Archive. Her interests include nineteenth-century and early modernist American poetry, reception studies, comparative literature, and translation studies. Her dissertation treated the reception of Walt Whitman's poetry in Italy, as seen within a larger transnational frame. She has published articles in the *Walt Whitman Quarterly Review*, *Willa Cather Newsletter and Review*, and in several collections of essays. As a graduate student, from 2013 to 2017, she worked as an editorial assistant for the *Willa Cather Archive*.

Holly Blackford is professor of English at Rutgers University–Camden, where she teaches and publishes literary criticism on American and children's literature. Her books include *Out of this World: Why Literature Matters to Girls* (Teachers College, Columbia University, 2004), *Mockingbird Passing: Closeted Traditions and Sexual Curiosities in Harper Lee's Novel* (University of Tennessee Press, 2011), *The Myth of Persephone in Girls' Fantasy Literature* (Routledge, 2011), and the edited volume *100 Years of Anne with an "e": The Centennial Study of* Anne of Green Gables (University of Calgary, 2009).

Her forthcoming monograph titled *Alice to Algernon: Child Consciousness in the Novel* (University of Tennessee Press, 2018) demonstrates the influence of early developmental psychology, evolutionary theory, and sexology on "child study" in modern novels.

Jim Cody is a full-time Professor at Brookdale Community College and an adjunct Professor at Fairleigh Dickinson University in New Jersey, where he teaches Composition, Research Writing, World Literature, American Literature, Shakespeare's Plays, and Short Story courses. He completed his doctoral degree at Drew University in Madison, New Jersey where he was awarded the university's Robert Campbell Prize for excelling in the program's literary offerings. He has previously published poetry for the *Paterson Literary Review, Journal of New Jersey Poets*, *Rear View Quarterly*, *White Crow*, *Sojourn*, and *New Jersey English Journal*; and scholarly articles in *Teaching English in the Two-Year College*, *The Journal of Basic Writing*, *California English,* and *Teaching Cather*. His first book of poetry, *Cup-O-Sation and Other Poems* was published in 2010. Most recently, he published an article for an anthology on Bob Dylan's twenty-first century music and film called *Tearing the World Apart* published in 2017. He currently lives in New Jersey with his wife and three children.

Thomas Fahy, a professor of English and director of the American Studies Program at Long Island University, Post, has published fifteen books, including *Understanding Truman Capote, Freak Shows and the Modern Imagination: Constructing the Damaged Body from Willa Cather to Truman Capote, The Philosophy of Horror*, *The Writing Dead: Talking Terror with TV's Top Horror Writers*, and three novels. He is also a classical pianist and performs regularly with the New York Piano Society. He has recently played in concerts at Carnegie Hall, Merkin Concert Hall, and other venues in New York City.

Melissa J. Homestead, professor of English and program faculty in women's and gender studies at the University of Nebraska–Lincoln, specializes in American women's authorship, publishing history, and the novel from the Early Republic through the early twentieth century. She is the author of *American Women Authors and Literary Property, 1822–1869* (2005) and co-editor of *Willa Cather and Modern Cultures* (2011), *Clarence* by Catharine Sedgwick (2011), and *E.D.E.N. Southworth: Recovering a Nineteenth-Century Popular Novelist* (2012). Her essays on Willa Cather have appeared in *Cather Studies, Studies in the Novel, American Literary Realism*, and *Studies in American Fiction,* and her study of Willa Cather's creative partnership with Edith Lewis, a magazine editor and advertising copywriter with whom she shared a home for four decades, is under contract with Oxford University Press. She also serves as associate editor of *The Complete Letters of Willa Cather: A Digital Edition*, the first installment of which will be published in 2018.

Diane Prenatt is professor of English at Marian University, where she teaches American and European literature. She has published essays on Cather's fiction in *Cather Studies* and the *Willa Cather Newsletter and Review*. She is working on a biography of Cather's friend and memoirist, Elizabeth Shepley Sergeant, and recently published an essay on Sergeant's World War I memoir in *Studies in the Humanities*.

Janis P. Stout is Professor Emerita of Texas A&M University. She is the author of a number of books and articles on American and English literature, including *Willa Cather: The Writer and Her World* (2000), *Coming Out of War: Poetry, Culture, and the World Wars* (2005), and *Picturing a Different West: Vision, Illustration, and the Tradition of Cather and Austin* (2007). With Andrew Jewell, she edited *The Collected Letters of Willa Cather*, published by Knopf in 2013.

Monroe Street is a psychoanalytic candidate at the Washington Square Institute in New York, where he studies the work of Freud and Lacan. Beyond the clinical realm, Street's research has explored topics in disability studies, queer theory, and literature. In 2016, Street was commissioned by sound artist Daniel Fishkin and the Pew Foundation to write a psychoanalytic investigation of tinnitus, a condition characterized by painful, psychosomatically triggered ringing in the ears. Street's work has also been featured recently in the arts and culture publications *Deli* and *Monsters & Dust*. Street currently teaches writing, literature, and theory at the City University of New York (CUNY).

Zachary Tavlin is a PhD candidate in the Department of English, as well as the Kollar Fellow in American Literature and Art History and the Richard M. Willner Memorial Scholar at the University of Washington. His research focuses on the intersections between American literature, Continental philosophy, and visual culture. His work has appeared in several academic journals and essay collections, including *The Comparatist, InVisible Culture*, and *Theatre Journal*. Forthcoming publications include articles in *Mississippi Quarterly* and *Wallace Stevens Journal*. He is also the assistant editor at *Modern Language Quarterly*.

Dana Woodcock is a pre-exam doctoral student in the Department of English at the University of Washington, where she teaches multimodal composition in the school's Expository Writing Program. Her specialty is narrative medicine, particularly the intersection of women's mental health care and socio-economic systems in nineteenth- and twentieth-century transatlantic literature and history. She aims to circulate this scholarship within the public square via digital and multimodal humanities.

Martin Woodside earned his doctorate in childhood studies from Rutgers University–Camden, where his research focused on how discourses of boyhood and frontier mythology helped shaped each other and broader ideas of American identity in the second half of the nineteenth century. His work on this subject has been published in *Boyhood Studies* and the *Journal of the History of Childhood and Youth*, while his current book manuscript builds on this research, seeking to expand the relationship between frontier mythos and American childhood into the twentieth century. His broad research interests include children's literature, popular culture, and the cultural history of nineteenth-century America, with emphasis on gender, material culture, and performance studies.

Dr. Sarah L. Young is associate professor of English at Benedictine College, teaching American literature, World War I literature, composition, and linguistics. She has presented research on Willa Cather for the American Literature Association, Literature into Film Conference, the Cather International Seminar, and NEH Seminars focused on the work of Willa Cather. She is a regular contributor to arts journals and newspapers and was a contributing writer to *The Encyclopedia of Stage Plays on Film*. She is also a trained opera singer and regularly performs on both the professional and amateur stage.

Fangyuan Xi is now a lecturer of English at the University of Shanghai for Science and Technology in Shanghai, China. She teaches courses on English literature, comparative literature, and writing in USST. She earned a PhD degree in English literature at Tohoku University, Japan, in 2015. Her studies investigate narrative strategies, ecocriticism, and landscape in Cather's novels.